TEACHER OF TEACHERS

An Autobiography by
AMBROSE L. SUHRIE

This book offers unique information, aid and inspiration to the student of education, to its practitioners — in the public schools, colleges, universities and, particularly, in teacher-education institutions — and to those millions who have children in school or college.

Education, as widespread, as deep, as can possibly be achieved, is one of our primary and most precious democratic goals.

Every phase is known to the author, Ambrose L. Suhrie. At the age of seventeen, he started to teach, in a one-teacher rural school in Pennsylvania, in 1891. At fifty, he was called to New York University to organize the Graduate Department of Teachers-College Education, where he served for eighteen years before he "retired."

Between these two posts, and after, are years of service as teacher, principal, superintendent in public schools, as teacher or executive in seventeen American colleges in ten states, as author, as organizer of professional groups, as editor of a professional journal, as lecturer before educational associations in the United States, Canada, Latin America. Dr. Suhrie feels that he has been much privileged in that he had an opportunity to serve many Negro colleges and college groups.

The full record is more than outstanding — it is amazing. The author never regarded his work merely as a career, never merely as a way of providing for himself and his family. No, his was a "ministry of teaching." The light of this ideal shines on every page.

Ambrose L. Suhrie

TEACHER OF TEACHERS

By Ambrose L. Suhrie

Ph.D., Litt.D., LL.D.

Emeritus Professor of Teachers-College Education

New York University

and

Resident Educational Consultant

Southern Missionary College

RICHARD R. SMITH PUBLISHER, INC.

Rindge, New Hampshire

1955

Published by Richard R. Smith Publisher, Inc.
Topside, West Rindge, N. H.

Library of Congress Catalog Card Number: 55-9050

Set up, printed and bound in the
United States of America by
The Colonial Press Inc.

To my family for love and protection
To my teachers for fellowship in learning
To my students for understanding and appreciation
To my professional associates for inspiration and
    constructive criticism
To my superior officers for wise counsel and generous
    encouragement.

ACKNOWLEDGMENT

is hereby gratefully made to each of the following for wise counsel on the purpose, scope, and organization of this autobiography and for much practical assistance in preparing the manuscript:

Miss Clara Ewalt, Professor of Journalism (retired) and Sponsor College Paper, Cleveland School of Education, Cleveland, Ohio; Dr. Eva B. Dykes, Professor of English, Oakwood College, Huntsville, Alabama; Dr. Harry M. Tippett, Associate Book Editor, *Review and Herald*, Washington, D. C.; Dr. Frank E. Spaulding, Emeritus Professor of Educational Administration, Yale University, New Haven, Connecticut; Dr. Ray C. Maul, Director of Research, National Education Association, Washington, D. C.; my wife, Alice Noggle Judson Suhrie; and to Mrs. Rachel Drachenberg of Buenos Aires, my personal secretary, for her painstaking attention to the infinite details involved in preparing the manuscript of this book.

PREFACE

The time has come when, having completed the happy experience of reliving my whole life in the short compass of a few months and of making a record of my chief professional activities and personal interests, I am expected to set forth my purpose in writing this record.

As I know my own mind and heart, the best reason I can give is that literally scores of mature and thoughtful men and women of my profession—friends of many years—have persistently expressed the conviction that my life story in print would have interest for and be helpful to young teachers and prospective teachers all over America, and that my philosophy of education, as I have lived it and as I have, for many years, taught it in the classroom and interpreted it from the platform, would challenge the imagination of the oncoming generation of school principals and superintendents who want to learn how to make school administration and supervision an increasingly democratic and co-operative enterprise in which officers, teachers, and children may constitute one big, happy, community family.

On a bright January day in 1952 I addressed the Future Teachers of America Club in the Texas Lutheran College at Seguin. The next morning the president of the club greeted me cheerily on the campus and said: "Doctor Suhrie, it surely was a pleasure and privilege to hear the thrilling story of American education by one who was there."

The reception accorded this book will prove whether the convictions of my friends and colleagues are well founded. But I submit that there is at least historical value in a record of sixty-four years spent in educational service, which embraced teaching experience on every level from elementary grades to graduate school, not omitting administrative and consultation service. I am profoundly grateful to God for this privilege.

I was born when the public school systems of the South had scarcely gotten under way. I began teaching in 1891, the year the University of Chicago and Stanford University were opened. I was a high school principal, ready to cast my first vote, the year William Jennings Bryan was first a candidate for the Presidency of the United States. I was already a school superintendent when the Spanish-American War was on. I was a college teacher down in Florida before there were, in all the South, as many as a score of public high schools whose graduates might be admitted to a reputable American college. I was a member of the team of "educational evangelists" which the General Education Board of New York financed in 1908 in its campaign all over the South for the establishment of state systems of public high schools. I was at the head of the municipal teachers college in Cleveland, Ohio, when the whole staff of its great public school system went on the march toward professional goals and standards in public school teaching.

I helped immediately after World War I to "recondition" grade teachers for a complete new city system of junior high schools. I was privileged to organize, shortly thereafter, and to conduct, for a period of eighteen years, one of the first graduate departments for the advanced professional education of normal school and teachers college officers and staff members in a nationally known American university. And I was privileged also to have a little part in the great upsurge of Negro college education which followed World War II. I am still actively "in harness" after sixty-four years of educational service.

At the dawn of my career as a teacher I saw that the paramount problem in public education in our country is to secure for every classroom—for every group of children in public and private schools of every kind—a competent teacher who can create worthy ideals, right attitudes, and permanent life interests; who can help the children and youth of our generation to find worth-while work to do; who knows how to promote co-operation and to develop the team spirit; who as an expert workman himself is able to direct the efforts of others to successful achievement.

It has always seemed strange to me that most men have assumed that money is the measure of wealth, for early in life I came to the conclusion that finding young men and young women of good health, of fine intellectual capacity, of high moral purpose, and preparing them for educational leadership is among the noblest of callings. No amount of gold would be a satisfying equivalent for the joy I have had in playing a part in this enterprise.

This book tells the simple story of a life crowded with human interests, and it emphasizes, in the lines and between the lines, the fact that for me there could have been no substitute for the friendships I have enjoyed across the long span of my years in educational service nor for the precious memories I have accumulated during those happy years.

With all its imperfections, then, and its inadequacies, but with good will, it is sent forth to all who share my belief that the minds of the millions, still in bondage to ignorance, can yet be liberated by the gracious ministry of a true teaching profession at its best.

AMBROSE L. SUHRIE

Collegedale, Tennessee
February 28, 1955

INTRODUCTION

By Herbert D. Welte

President, Teachers College of Connecticut

Former President, American Association of Colleges
for Teacher Education

This is the fascinating life story of a man of good native ability and high purpose who early in his adolescent years dedicated his talents for life to the ministry of teaching. During a professional career of more than three score years he has exemplified the dignity and the power of teaching at its best. In these pages are recorded the hopes and aspirations of a young man who placed service to others above all considerations of wealth or power or fame. Once he had established his educational goal never did he falter in his efforts to achieve it.

The story begins in his boyhood home on a farm in the hills of Pennsylvania. This home was the first and most important school in which he learned the hard facts of life, the trials and tribulations of the early pioneers, and the joys and sorrows of parents and children. Here he learned the meaning of family unity and strength; here he became a willing and experienced participant in the great game of human cooperation. This is the testimony of one with deep religious convictions who appreciated his home as an agency for the building of character.

The accounts of his early efforts to prepare himself for the teaching service against great odds, of his first teaching position in a one-room rural school, and of the obstacles which he encountered along the way are classics in the annals of American education. Surely his success in his first teaching position cannot be attributed to any formal preparation for the task. The teacher education programs as we know them today were non-existent. To what then can his early success be attributed? It must have been to diligent application and to keen insight into the needs and interests of his pupils.

The author's moving description of his varied experiences as teacher, principal, supervisor, college and university professor, administrator of teacher education programs; and of his determined efforts to prepare himself adequately for the task ahead provides us with a comprehensive history of teacher education in this country during the first half of the present century. As his eventful life unfolds he finds himself in positions of leadership and trust in teacher preparation. In this field of specialization he early associated himself with the leaders of his day. As he was influenced by them so he in turn inspired his students and associates the nation over. He was one of the first to appreciate the need of encouraging prospective teachers to participate in planning their own programs of preparation. It was in this area of service that he made his greatest contributions to teacher education in America.

His creative genius was exemplified in his founding of the Eastern-States Association of Professional Schools for Teachers. Each year he brought together administrative officers, faculty members, and students of the teacher-preparing institutions of New England and the East to a great professional meeting in New York City. Students were encouraged to discuss ways and means of organizing on a democratic basis in their own institutions—a new idea to many. They were invited to share in the formulation of institutional policies and programs which affected their welfare. Faculty members and administrative officers were urged to assist these students in accomplishing such purposes.

The author served as the first president of the association

and he continued in this capacity for seven years. For eighteen years he was its guiding spirit. It was only fitting that a bound volume of letter tributes from his friends and associates was presented to him at a public banquet in New York City on March 27, 1942. This *Book of Remembrance* served officially to recognize his leadership in the great democratic movement embodied in the organization which he founded and directed for so many years.

Few men in American education today are as widely known among the leaders of teacher education as is this notable educator. He holds the unique distinction of having visited all of the state and municipal teacher-preparing institutions of all kinds in each of the forty-eight states; also hundreds of church-related and private colleges. He is America's Mr. Chips, a natural leader, a wise counsellor, the friend of all teachers and all children everywhere.

This book will have appeal for prospective teachers, teachers in service, principals, administrators of school systems, and staff members in the colleges and universities of the nation. It will also appeal to parents, citizens and friends of education who are genuinely interested in the preparation of teachers and in the improvement of teaching. It is an effective defense of the professional integrity of those who serve in the classrooms all over the United States. It will have special appeal for all who want to know what the intangible rewards and personal satisfactions of the deeply dedicated teacher can be and are in the evening time of life.

What a great privilege it has been to know this great American educator as a counsellor and personal friend! What a challenge he has here issued to all who dare enter the noblest of all professions, teaching!

CONTENTS

istrative Problems. Supreme Opportunity. Problems, Personal and Domestic. Western Reserve University Goes into Partnership with Cleveland Public School System. Consultant Survey. Administrative Policies and Practices. Distinctive Emphases in Instructional Program. Off-Campus Professional Services. Farewell to Cleveland. Tribute to a Great Public School Superintendent.

TEACHER OF TEACHERS

1

EARLY YEARS

It is said that one's success and happiness in life are conditioned, or perhaps even determined, by his choice of grandparents. It is equally important that he choose with care and discretion the place in which he is to be born and the community in which he is to spend his childhood and his adolescent years.

One's biological inheritance, so the scientists tell us, determines the potentialities he brings into life and these scientists are equally sure that his social environment determines in large measure, what he will do with his inheritance.

My grandparents chose my birthplace for me; my parents chose the physical and social setting in which I was to spend my childhood and adolescent years. They were wise parents. They knew I'd like, as all normal children do, to live in the open country, to work in the soil, to experience the joy of seedtime and harvest, to hear the cock call up the sun, to see the lambs at play in the springtime, to hear cows moo for their meals, horses neigh in their stalls, birds sing in the forests at dawn, and crickets chirp in the dark.

My parents knew that education is harder to provide for than mere schooling, that, rightly conceived, it includes the spiritual, the ethical, and the emotional as well as the intellectual; that ideals are caught, not taught, and that they are our silent mentors, on guard every day and every hour; that conscience, which "doth make cowards of us all," also helps to make us prophets and patriots and saints; and, finally, that true education is not a thing to be superimposed by authority, but must be acquired by self-imposed effort and willing co-operation, by useful work as well as by study and reflection, and that it results from nature as well as from nurture. They knew that co-operation means that we must so conduct ourselves that others may be able to live happily and work comfortably and effectively with us; they knew that all true education is self-education and that while grades may be *given* and degrees *conferred*, education must be *earned*.

Birthplace in the Hills

When Daniel Webster had concluded the presentation of his arguments to the Supreme Court of the United States in the famous Dartmouth College case, he paused for a moment to lay some legal documents on the table; then, turning and facing the court again, he added: "Dartmouth College, sirs, is a small college; *but there are those who love her.*"

New Baltimore, my birthplace in the hills, is a small town; *but there are those who love it.* And I proudly proclaim myself to be one of the "chiefest" of these.

The village, at "the forks of the crick," only five miles down the valley from where the roaring traffic of the Pennsylvania Turnpike issues from the east end of the Allegheny Mountain Tunnel, numbers today scarcely two hundred souls after more than a century and a quarter of toil and turmoil and struggle.

In my boyhood days, while acquiring the rudiments of an education, I learned little of the early history of my home town, even though my great-grandparents were its first settlers and first home owners. Since leaving the community more than sixty years ago, when I was but nineteen years of age, I have returned to the scene of my birth only six times at irregular intervals and for very brief visits. The clearest memory I have of any of these visits is of the occasion, now more than fifty years ago, when my three stalwart brothers and I gathered there, from the east and the west and the north and the south, to bear the remains of our beloved father to their final resting place in the country churchyard hard by "the little brown church in the vale." I did not receive any word of my mother's last illness and death, some four years later, until after her burial had taken place. All of the members of my own family moved away not long after her passing, except my eldest brother who continued to occupy the old homestead until his death, several years ago, at eighty-two.

I have been a diligent student all my life of the history of my country. I have had a special interest in stories of pioneers and of their early settlements in the wilderness; and so I never cease to be disappointed, not to say amazed, at how little one can learn from the local residents of any average American community concerning its early history or its famous men and women.

Let me illustrate: Some twenty years ago I was driving up the Shenandoah Valley with my daughter and some friends. As we came into the outskirts of the little city of Staunton, Virginia, I suddenly remembered that this was the birthplace of Thomas Woodrow Wilson and, that at the time of his birth, his distinguished father was resident pastor of the local Presbyterian church. I pulled up to the curb three different times to ask as many different elderly men carrying market baskets, and therefore local residents, where I might find "the Manse" in which President Wilson first saw the light of day. Each of them insisted, the last of them vehemently, that there was no such place in town; and all of them questioned the correctness of my statement that the President had been born at Staunton. Finally, I remembered that Mary Baldwin College had purchased "the Manse" a few years before and was holding it in trust against the day when some patriotic society might convert it into another one of our many shrines of American democracy. So I drove up on the hill to where the college campus commands a view of the beautiful valley;

and there I saw, with my own eyes, on a little house below the road the authentic name plate: *Birthplace of Woodrow Wilson*.

Except from the members of my own family (and chiefly from my youngest sister, Mary Fisher, of Bedford, Pennsylvania), I have been able to learn little, on any of my visits or by correspondence, about significant events or important persons of New Baltimore and its countryside. The pastor of the village church, Reverend Adrian Lichteig, generously furnished me with the dates of births, marriages, and deaths of my own ancestors and other relatives, and a little pamphlet giving the history of New Baltimore and of the Church of St. John the Baptist.

Daniel Boone, the explorer, was once asked whether during his long travels he had ever been actually lost. It seems that he indicated both surprise and annoyance that such a thing could ever have happened to him, and answered curtly with an emphatic "No, certainly not!" Then, so the story goes, his countenance relaxed a bit; and he added with a smile: "But I must admit that, on several occasions, I was *slightly bewildered*."

The scrappy and incomplete records that exist of the early explorations of the great wilderness areas of southwestern Pennsylvania, 'way back in colonial times, indicate clearly that the explorers who first invaded these heavily wooded mountains, these narrow valleys and silent coves, fertile with the leaf mold and vegetable deposits of centuries, must have been, on many occasions, something more than "slightly bewildered."

It is clear, however, that when Colonel George Washington with his Virginia Volunteers by-passed this area on his way to Fort Pitt, at the confluence of the Allegheny and the Monongahela rivers, to relieve General Braddock and his band of British Regulars, a road had already been laid through Cumberland to the new West. Doubtless, for a full generation, hunters and trappers had been covering wide areas of mountain terrain north of this road in Pennsylvania and south of it in Maryland and West Virginia. But the site of New Baltimore at the west end of the fertile tract known as Harmon's Bottom and extending from Bedford westward to the Allegheny Mountains seems to have attracted little attention from the land agents and land speculators until at least a decade after our new Federal Government began to function in 1789. Even though these fertile meadow lands were more accessible to the hordes of immigrants landing in Baltimore and Philadelphia than the new settlements around old Fort Pitt one hundred miles farther west, homesteading, it seems, did not begin in earnest on the Raystown Branch of the blue Juniata until the first decade of the nineteenth century or possibly even later.

It was not until Michael Riddlemoser, immigrant resident of Baltimore, had assured the building of the first church in the upper valley, the Church of St. John the Baptist, that families became interested in moving in. It was he, too, who built the first stone house in the upper valley and within the present limits of the borough of New Baltimore and not far from the church. His adopted daughter, Anna Black, and her husband, Anthony Luken, were the first occupants of this house and the first permanent residents of the community. There is a rumor abroad that within that pretty little solidly built stone house this pair of sturdy pioneers entered into a conspiracy to become my first American ancestors.

By 1788, sections of Glade Pike (now route 30), skirting the new community six miles to the south, were in use. It served as a connecting link between Bedford and the big cities in the East, on the one hand; and Little Washington, Pennsylvania, and Chillicothe, the new capital of Ohio, in the West, on the other hand. By 1817, the Pittsburgh Pike (now route 31), skirting the new community seven miles to the north, was completed. It served as a connecting link between

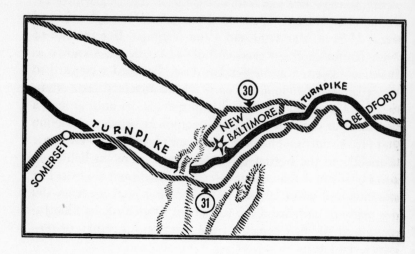

the East and the rapidly growing city of Pittsburgh. These two highways served as the main arteries of heavy traffic between the "Old East" and the "New West" until they were superseded by the Baltimore and Ohio Railroad and the Pennsylvania Central Railroad many years later. Almost continuous lines of covered wagons, with herds of cattle and flocks of sheep and turkeys interspersed streamed over these highways daily on their way to the markets. The Mosersburg Community, as it first was called (later New Baltimore), lying almost midway between these traffic lanes, found a ready sale for the produce of its farms, its orchards, and its gardens.

For decades, the young people of the New Baltimore community, on reaching manhood or womanhood, found their way out over one or the other of these two main thoroughfares to easy employment and better commercial opportunities in other places; and the community, notwithstanding its very high birth rate, seemed doomed to stagnation when suddenly in the early eighties, a new hope was aroused by the rumor that unheard-of prosperity was "just around the corner." William H. Vanderbilt, the chief stockholder of the New York Central Railroad Company, was about to begin building a new Southern Pennsylvania Railroad on a low-grade level paralleling the great Pennsylvania Central Line. It would pass through New Baltimore and would have nine tunnels through the mountain ranges between Harrisburg and Pittsburgh. The longest of these, the Allegheny Mountain Tunnel, one and a quarter miles in length, would be five miles up the valley. Its location, just above the heaviest grades on the line, would make the broad valley below New Baltimore the natural location for engine repair shops and possibly, in due time, for engine- and freight-car building enterprises. The outlook was bright. The exodus of young people from the community would surely cease, and its older sons and daughters who had moved away would surely return in numbers.

And the rumor, in part, came true.

Exhaustive surveys had been made, a final location agreed upon, and contracts with construction companies signed by the fall of 1883. Contractor McFadden of New York City had moved the heaviest grading machinery known in those days to both ends of the proposed Allegheny Mountain Tunnel, five miles west of the almost forgotten village and only three miles west of my father's farm. New Baltimore quickly became a boom town. Hundreds of immigrant workmen, principally from Ireland, Italy, and Hungary, moved to sites at both ends of the tunnel. They were single men or married men who had left their families in faraway places. They lived in rude mud-covered huts and bought their provisions from merchants in the village and from farmers in the countryside. They did their own cooking. They were heavy consumers of hard "licker" and parted freely with their money when "under the influence." Over week ends their drunken brawls and their reckless use of firearms brought terror to the once quiet and peaceful countryside.

The grading of the roadbed and the work of boring the nine tunnels was progressing satisfactorily, and the local community, for the first time in its history, was enjoying real prosperity, a veritable boom.

After two years of tunnel boring and the grading of approaches, suddenly, like a bolt from the clear sky, word reached New Baltimore and the countryside that the completion of the promised railroad was to be abandoned. It seems that J. Pierpont Morgan, the Wall Street banker, was disturbed by the cut-throat competition of the New York Central Railroad Line and the Pennyslvania Central Line and feared that, if long continued, it would send railroad stocks a-tumbling, and thus precipitate another financial panic. So he called William H. Vanderbilt and Andrew Carnegie to his office for a conference with the officers and principal owners of stock of the Pennsylvania Central Railroad Company. The outcome was speedily announced all over the countryside that the Pennsylvania Central Railroad Company had bought off all Vanderbilt competition in this area and that the Southern Pennsylvania Railroad tunnel boring and its nearly completed roadbed building were to be abandoned at once. Within twenty-four hours the grading machinery at both ends of the Allegheny Mountain Tunnel and on the roadbed, down the valley to and below New Baltimore, had been lifted and was on its way out.

The oldest residents of New Baltimore still remember September 12, 1885, as Black Saturday.

The Southern Pennsylvania Railroad, the proposed Vanderbilt Line, had completely abandoned its charter and its partly completed roadbed.

After half a century, the "cut-outs" and the "fill-ins" all along this abandoned roadbed were covered again with good-sized voluntary native trees, blending in with the once "logged-over" adjacent mountain terrain. The deer, the wild turkey, and the fox were again in their old haunts. The rhododendron and the mountain laurel, the dogwood and the flame azalea and the serviceberry covered the hills with their glory in the springtime; the bees hummed drowsily over the clover-fields and the buckwheat patches in the summertime; and the squirrels and the wild hogs picked up the acorns and the hick-ory nuts in the woodland leaves of autumn. Here and there one might also see, in the fall of the year, the frost on the pump-kin and the fodder in the shock on the hillside farms as he gazed over the all but deserted countryside up along the woodland trails. There was indeed "quiet on the Potomac" and there was "peace on the Western Front," but it was the quiet of the cemetery and the peace of the tomb. *The town of New Baltimore was dead,* and its young men and young women had already learned to repeat with deep resignation their favored passage from Dante's *Divine Comedy:* "All hope abandon, ye who enter here." The community's fondest hope had been blasted.

A generation later, in the depths of the Great Depression, came the resurrection of another hope.

In 1937, the Pennsylvania legislature granted a charter to the Pennsylvania Turnpike Commission and authorized this corporation to function for the state in the financing, con-struction, and operation of a four-lane, high-speed traffic boulevard on the abandoned roadbed of the once hoped-for Southern Pennsylvania Railroad.

Within two years, this new Pennsylvania Turnpike was completed. As its roaring traffic now flows endlessly through the valley, it leaves the village on one side of its enclosed right-of-way and the Church of St. John the Baptist on the other side. A wide over-pass spans the boulevard and again unites the church and its people; but no resident of the village can get into the traffic of this superhighway without driving

down the bottom road twenty miles east to Bedford or up over the Glade Pike twenty miles west to Somerset. The new four-lane boulevard has brought no substantial commercial advantage to the village.

Shortly after the project had been completed, an old resident of the community, standing on the over-pass from the village in the valley to the church on the hill and watching the cars go by, was heard to wail plaintively: "Now all that New Baltimore and its hilly surroundings can do is to raise broilers for the Cumberland market, girls for the Pittsburgh domestic service, and boys to work in the steel mills of Johnstown and the coal mines of Windber."

When I left my childhood home at age nineteen in the fall of 1893, never to return again as a resident, I took inventory of the number of my brothers, sisters, and first cousins, almost all of whom were still living in the community. The grand total was eighty-six. More than half of them were younger than I. A substantial fraction of this total must have died between the fall of 1893, when the count was complete, and the fall of 1953 when I made my most recent visit to the community. On this visit, I found but one of all the survivors (and there were at least twenty of them) still residing in the community. This one had recently had the misfortune to lose both of his lower limbs. This handicap, I hasten to explain, was not the reason for his failure to join the exodus.

George Ade, the Hoosier author and humorist, once remarked, a bit facetiously of course: "I come from Indiana. Indiana is a good state to come from and the smarter you are the quicker you come."

By 1890, New Baltimore had few attractions to hold its young people who belonged to the class which John G. Holland once described as "crowned with power and cursed with poverty." Let me remind the Spartan two hundred who still live in the village, that in the second paragraph of this section I literally shouted my love for my old home town; and now let me add, with emphasis, that my love for it has not been decreased one iota by the misfortunes which it has suffered through the years since I cast my lot elsewhere.

Two of my pioneering great-grandparents founded the town; each of my four sturdy grandparents made a significant contribution to the early history of the community; my parents were among the most respected and enterprising citizens of the valley. All of these are buried in the little country churchyard on the hill above the village.

As long as I live, I shall cherish the memory of my childhood and adolescent days on the farm. It was here that I was awakened from my childhood slumbers at the break of dawn by the hallelujah chorus of birds in the forest. It was here that I first experienced the joy of seedtime and harvest. It was here that I learned, in the springtime of life, to enjoy hard work and to sing in the fields like a lark at the break of day. It was here that I followed the farm horse through the rows of tall corn in the blazing heat of a July day sun. It was here that I drove the cows in from the frostbitten meadows in the autumn mornings. It was here that I developed the power of digesting a hearty meal and the habit of calling for seconds. It was here, too, that, on a thousand occasions, after working hard all day in field or forest, I was lulled into sweet slumber at nightfall by the babbling of the brook in the nearby glen.

My profound thanks go out today to all the good friends and neighbors in the village and out in the countryside who encouraged and helped me in childhood and youth when the going was not always easy.

May God in His infinite mercy grant to my birthplace in the hills some new and inspiring hope.

American Forebears

Many of the wise men of my generation have insisted that no human being, in this enlightened age, may reasonably expect to achieve either success or happiness unless he has chosen his grandparents with care and discretion. Success and happiness, it has always seemed to me, are both desirable objectives in a well-planned life; and so, I had, from the beginning, a deep concern about the choice of my grandparents. But there were, as my reader may well imagine, some very real difficulties. It is obvious that I could not be present in person when these choices had to be made 'way back in the days of the Napoleonic wars at the turn of the nineteenth century. Then, too, I naturally hesitated about delegating so important a matter to even the wisest men in that crude and unscientific age. What was I to do? I surely was puzzled. If the choice should be too long delayed, I might not have any grandparents at all and that would have been fatal; for, since the dawn of history, no baby has ever come to this earth, "trailing clouds of glory" or otherwise, unless he has had four grandparents chosen more than a full generation in advance with ample time to arrange all details.

While I tarried somewhere, 'way out yonder in space "on the shivering brink of uncertainty" as to how I might choose me a couple of pairs of acceptable grandparents, lo, "time was marching on!" And, just when the matter was about to go by default—"in the fullness of time"—a kind Providence, without any help whatsoever from anyone and without even consulting me, made the final and irrevocable choice for me, just as He has made it for countless millions of other human beings adown the long centuries since time began. And may His name be praised "world without end" for the goodly inheritance He gave to my parents and, through them, to me and to each of my thirteen brothers and sisters.

Diligent and long-continued search of the records of my forebears of three generations, on this side of the waters, has given me the unshakable conviction that their contemporaries, who must have known them intimately in the close-knit community life of the frontier, universally regarded them as *good people*—as men and women who were biologically sound, intellectually alert, morally clean, ethically upright and dependable, socially acceptable, and spiritually God-fearing and reverent.

I never had the pleasure of knowing my great-grandparents, Anthony and Anna Luken, first settlers of the New Baltimore community. With three of my grandparents I had a very delightful and intimately personal acquaintance through all my childhood and early adolescent years. I have golden memories of numerous visits with each of them by the fireside during long winter evenings, out in the field and woodland in the springtime and autumn, in the flower gardens and fruit orchards in summertime, and, on occasion, on the snow-covered uplands on the bleakest of winter days. Their interests were active, their health was excellent, their spirits were resilient, and their outlook on life was optimistic almost to the end. My clearest memories of them are of the days when they were on the last stretches of their long sojourn on the sunset trail of life. These are precious memories. Long reflection on them has convinced me that, in spite of the physical and other infirmities of old age, the men and women who have lived the good life are likely to reveal most clearly whatever of divinity is in them just before the shadows fall—in the last glow of life's setting sun.

I once asked the distinguished president of a great American university, at the time of his retirement, how I might account for his physical vigor and vitality, his intellectual alertness and acuity, his emotional stability and poise, his resiliency of spirit, and his optimistic outlook on life in our war-torn, confused, and troubled world. "First of all," said he, "I attribute nearly all of my blessings in life to a godly ancestry." Then he gave half a dozen other reasons. All of them seemed trivial to me as compared with the first one. This one, "a godly ancestry" is inclusive and to me profoundly significant and impressive. What a marvelous heritage is such an ancestry! It is better than houses and lands and bank accounts. Rust doth not corrupt it, nor can thieves break through and steal it. Early in life, I was somehow made conscious that I was heir to the goodly heritage of a godly ancestry, all of whose members stood for something good in the community in which they lived. This consciousness gave me a certain assurance that I too, might be able, in due time, to achieve, to do, and to be. I have long been convinced that such an assurance in childhood is an important factor of both success and happiness in later life. This thesis will be more fully developed as the story of my professional lifework unfolds itself.

Here seems to be the place to begin to set forth in broad outline the record of "my folk" and of the dates, places, and circumstances related thereto.

My people all came of German stock. One of them, my paternal grandfather, came from a Swiss canton where German is the language in use. All the others came from somewhere in Germany. Tradition has it that one came from the middle Rhine country, one from the hill country of Bavaria, over against the Alps, and one from Alsace-Lorraine. The record of the European background of most of my forebears is so altogether scrappy and inadequate as to arouse the suspicion that perhaps some of them were fugitives from justice; but their record here in America completely discredits any such assumption.

The first of my ancestors to arrive on this side of the Atlantic was Anna Black. She was an orphan and, in all probability, no more than ten years of age when she landed in Baltimore, Maryland, with a company of German immigrants. This was about the time when General Washington was first inaugurated as President of the United States. The group of immigrants to which she belonged was met at the wharf by a well-to-do German resident of Baltimore who, so tradition has it, was personally known to many of the newcomers. He was a successful businessman, interested in the sale of lands and the development of a new settlement in the wilderness of Southwestern Pennyslvania, thirty miles above Cumberland, Maryland. His name was Michael Riddlemoser. He quickly formed an attachment for little Anna Black and shortly thereafter adopted her as his daughter. She lived with him and his family until the time of her marriage, at the age of twenty, to a young Baltimorean named Anthony Luken, who had come from Germany a few years earlier.

By about 1820, Mr. Riddlemoser had completed the erection of the first stone house in the pioneer settlement called Mosersburg (later to be named New Baltimore). This house was built at the western edge of Harmon's Bottom, a goodly stretch of choice farm land. It is still a landmark in the historic community, thirty miles north of the Mason and Dixon Line and halfway between Somerset and Bedford, Pennsylvania. The Luken family was its first occupants. They moved into it about 1820. Here, in the wilderness, were born to

Anthony Luken and Anna Black Luken, his wife, the last three of their ten children, the other seven having been born in Baltimore, Maryland, before they took up residence in the new settlement. The first two of their offspring were boys, the last eight were girls. Of these, Mary was the oldest. She was twenty when her mother died at the birth of her youngest sister, her father having died three months earlier. The untimely death of both parents meant that the eldest daughter, Mary Luken, had to take over at once the care of the new-born babe and that, with her older brothers, she must somehow hold the family together and provide a living for its ten members.

In 1836, when "Old Hickory" was still in the White House in Washington this sturdy young woman, my future grandmother, Mary Luken, at the age of twenty-two, was married in New Baltimore to Peter Topper, who was about the same age. Born in Germany, he was brought to Baltimore by his parents when he was a small child. His family resided for a year or two in that city and then moved to their permanent home in New Baltimore. This young couple continued to provide a home for the Luken girls until each was able to shift for herself; and, in due time, eight children were born to this pair, Peter and Mary Topper, my maternal grandparents. Of these my mother Mary, was the third and oldest daughter. This in brief is the history of where and how I came by my maternal great-grandparents, my maternal grandparents, and my mother.

My paternal grandparents were both born on the other side of the waters in Central Europe. My father's father, John Mathias Suhrie, must have first seen the light of day in a rural home in one of the German-speaking cantons of Switzerland. In my boyhood, I often heard him wax eloquent over the glories of the Swiss Alps and the countryside east of the city of Berne. He seemed to be familiar with the characteristic features of that historic capital. His German family Bible records his birth in 1803. His wife's maiden name was Katherine Understall. Her family Bible records her birth in 1805. There is a record, too, of their marriage in 1834, which must have taken place before their arrival in America. Just where or when they met and where they were married are not known. It is possible that on his way from Switzerland to America, Grandfather Suhrie tarried for a time with friends or relatives in Alsace-Lorraine and that he there met and married his bride.

When they arrived in Baltimore, Maryland, in 1834, they were accompanied by his bachelor brother George, with whom he established a partnership for a period of years in the operation of a flour mill at Hays Mills, between the village of Berlin and Myersdale, Pennsylvania, and about ten miles from New Baltimore. My father Francis, and his older sister Sophia, were born in Hays Mills before their parents moved with their growing family to their permanent home some three miles west of New Baltimore, where Grandfather Suhrie secured title to a six hundred forty-acre tract of mountain woodlands on the eastern slope of the Alleghenies. On this site, he carved out for himself a woodland estate and built a log cabin thereon in which to rear his family. In due time, each of his three sturdy sons, Francis, my father, Elias, and Cornelius, did likewise. The original Suhrie tract is located around the headwaters of the Raystown branch of the blue Juniata. Its center is about two miles downstream from the eastern entrance to the Allegheny Mountain Tunnel on the famous Pennsylvania Turnpike that runs from Harrisburg to Pittsburgh. This turnpike divides the original six hundred forty-acre Suhrie tract of mountain land as it does the village of New Baltimore some three miles farther downstream.

My father, Francis Suhrie, born at Hays Mills, Somerset County, Pennsylvania, on October 10, 1836, and my mother, Mary Theresa Topper, born at New Baltimore, Somerset

County, Pennsylvania, on November 17, 1839, were married in New Baltimore on April 29, 1860.

For a year before this marriage, my father devoted much time to the strenuous labor of clearing off a few acres of heavily timbered woodlands on the upstream allotment of one hundred sixty-five acres which his father had assigned to him from the original six hundred forty-acre Suhrie tract. During the winter months preceding the marriage, he cut and "framed" more than fourscore heavy white oak logs for the cabin in which he and his plucky mate were to rear a family of fourteen children. He was ready for the house-raising ahead of schedule.

On a certain day early in April, his father and his brothers and his fiancee's father and big brothers, with plenty of reinforcements from the village and countryside, assembled on the premises for the country-wide "frolic" of a frontier "cabin-raising." Theirs was the task of lifting into their places all of the heavy timber which Father had "fitly framed," through many months of arduous toil. Before sundown every timber was in its place and, except for the split-shingled roof and the broad-board floor which Father later completed alone, the new cabin was finished. For extra good measure, the stone foundation had been laid for the new "spring house" over the bubbling fountain that welled up from under a stratum of rock spanning the nearby glen.

Needless to say, the women-folk from the countryside had a frolic all their own that day in preparing and serving the loaves and fish, with many very special "trimmings" peculiar to the noonday "feed" or "barbecue" on such an occasion in a pioneer Pennsylvania community.

A year later a hillside barn was raised on the premises. This enterprise, too, was made a community "frolic."

These buildings are now (1955) owned by a Pittsburgh hunting club. Both rest as solid and secure on their rock foundations as when they were built almost a century ago, and both still stand all but perfectly plumb and erect half a century after their builders have fallen asleep.

> In the elder days of Art
>   Builders wrought with greatest care
> Each minute and unseen part,
>   For the gods see everywhere.

Now I have accounted for both of my maternal great-grandparents, for all four of my grandparents, and for my father and mother; and I have finally placed all of them in the geographical setting in which they lived to the end of their days.

In a subsequent section I shall give a very brief personal characterization of each of the three grandparents with whom I was acquainted and of my parents as I knew them in their respective home settings.

Childhood Life on the Farm

There were two things distinctly characteristic of my childhood home life on the farm: First, my home was an educational institution. Second, my family life was a completely co-operative enterprise.

I was once asked to describe, for a large audience of teachers, the best school I had ever known or attended. I had no hesitation in making the choice and so I responded gladly. It was my home life on the farm. I attended this "school" continuously from my earliest infancy until I was nineteen years of age and ready to leave the parental roof.

I never have been quite sure who was the principal of this home-school. Sometimes I thought Father was; sometimes I knew Mother was; sometimes I was. And sometimes, the youngest baby in the cradle was, by her very helplessness, the most effective teacher of us all. We all gladly did what we could for her comfort and happiness; for we knew instinctively that she, better than anyone else, could teach us sympathy and love and the understanding of human need.

I cannot remember the time when I was not regarded by my father, by my mother, and by all my brothers and sisters as absolutely indispensable to the welfare and happiness of all the other members of our household. I never doubted for a moment in my childhood that I really belonged, that I had stock in the company, and that I might expect to draw dividends. I knew I was useful. How did I know? Well, my father, my mother, my big brothers, and my sisters had often told me so and had told each other so in my presence. They built up my confidence; they bolstered up my wavering courage, they shared with me their joy in my accomplishments and in my growing usefulness; they strengthened my every effort to participate in doing the work that had to be done to keep things going. I cannot remember the time when I was too young to drop the grains of corn, at somewhat regular intervals, in the freshly opened furrows. And I cannot remember when my good father failed to speak a word of approval or to give me his hearty commendation when I had done my best to be useful. Oh, the joy of those precious moments and the golden memories I have of them even while I write these lines!

My best "school" was our family at work and my family life at its best was our school in session. Everybody was willing to teach everybody else whatever he knew or could do, and nobody was willing to be ignorant of what others knew or to be unable to do what others could do. When I was big enough to pick up the potatoes from the freshly opened furrows and place them in the basket, Father or big brother looked his approval of my industry and then lifted the basket to the wagon. Each of us children instinctively knew the work best suited to his strength; no one failed to do what he could to support the leader of any enterprise undertaken in the interest of the family welfare or the family economy; and there was always complete co-operation.

All of us children instinctively knew that the farm, the farm equipment, and the farm animals belonged to Father and that the house and all its furnishings and equipment belonged to Mother. So Father planned with us boys how best to get the farm work done on time in the proper season; and mother planned with her girls how to get the cooking, baking, scrubbing, cleaning, dusting, washing, ironing, bed making, knitting and sewing done in the best possible way and on time.

When Father, who was a country squire or justice of the peace, found it necessary, as he often did, to go to the county seat more than twenty miles away, he called his boys together the evening before to plan the day's farm operations in his absence. If a "worm fence" foundation was to be laid or postholes to be dug and posts set therein, we all willingly agreed that Vincent, our eldest brother, should be in charge, and that the rest of us should help him as best we could and as he might desire or direct. If there were sheep to be sheared, my next older brother John, was in charge and we all helped him. If there was fruit tree trimming or grafting to be done, both my older brothers willingly agreed without argument that I was the best qualified by training, experience, and interest, to direct the enterprise. So they set the ladder, carried away the cut-off limbs, furnished me the graft settings and grafting wax, and, in general, acted as my assistants. Each one of us instinctively felt that his talents were being engaged to the best advantage of the whole enterprise.

When Father came home in the evening, no matter how tired he might be, he somehow mustered the strength and took the time to acquaint himself with what had been accomplished in his absence; and he had a perfectly uncanny way of sensing the spirit in which the day's work had been done. When all of us children were seated with Father and Mother for the evening meal, we were served something more than bread. After the blessing was said, Father first dispensed his well-thought-out approvals of the group and the individual accomplishments of his boys, and Mother dispensed her approval of the achievements of her girls. Commendation, when merited, was generous; and when no commendation could justly be given, Father's silence (or Mother's) was so eloquent that it could be heard without being spoken.

Both Father and Mother were companions of their children in the work that had to be done. All of us—parents and children—were by turns teachers and learners. All of us children had been taught to yield graciously to the discipline of the group, and even Father and Mother sought group approval in all important matters. One day Father, who was a high and mighty justice of the peace, became, so it seemed to us children, a little "cocky." We all were in the habit of giving him full credit for keeping peace not only in the family but, generally speaking, in the countryside as well; but we were a bit divided as to whether the verdict of his court in a certain community squabble was well calculated to give us peace in the valley.

It was agreed among all of us that his verdict should be reviewed by the higher court of public opinion in the Suhrie family. We discussed the matter, therefore, at length and over a period of days. I was finally appointed to inform the "high court" of our conclusion and to administer to Father the effective discipline of a minority or dissenting opinion. I did so. Then I took him by the hand and led him into his own courtroom, the family living room, where all court secrets were covered by a roll-top desk. Above this desk hung his framed commission as justice of the peace. It had been duly signed by the governor of Pennsylvania and sealed with the seal of the commonwealth—ribbons and all. Father was proud to see his name carefully lettered on this important official document. I pointed to the text of a certain passage in the center of it which said that he might continue to be justice of the peace "so long as he shall behave himself well." I solemnly warned him that unless he should at once reform and improve the quality of his judicial decisions, he was surely running the risk of our reporting him, in the name of the family, to the governor. He openly repented, and the quality of his judicial opinions thereafter, in the judgment of the family, greatly improved. Our diplomatic use of a kind of informal "referendum" had made it wholly unnecessary to employ the "recall" technique in effecting the reforms we desired.

Father was firm, but never authoritarian, in outlook or in practice. He believed in the inalienable right of appeal and encouraged his wife and children to exercise this right. Mother was less intellectual than he was, but she had more heart power and he knew it. Because they respected and loved each other, we all respected and loved them. They must have believed in Henry Drummond's theory that children are given to parents to teach them love and devotion; for it was clear that they knew instinctively that no child is likely to stand out long against the wishes of either parent unless he finds them divided. If he finds them in good-willed agreement, he is likely to fall in line quickly with their united counsel or their united demand.

The first law establishing free schools in Pennsylvania was passed in 1834, two years before Father was born. At least twenty-five years had passed before such schools were established in the remote hill sections of the Commonwealth; so Father was not a schooled man. He had, however, learned to read in his childhood in a three-months'-subscription school. Mother likewise had learned to read in a subscription school. Father read widely all his life. Mother's household duties seemed to make it impossible that she should do so.

Having made clear the pattern and spirit of our home life as a co-operatively managed educational institution, I may now proceed to list the educational projects in which we as a group engaged in childhood and early adolescent days in our home and out on the farm.

Spring and summer and fall and winter, each in turn brought its special assignments of farm work to be done. Early in the spring the sugar maple trees had to be tapped, the sap gathered and boiled down into sirup; and then, on special occasions, there were "stirrings off," that is, the water in the sirup was completely evaporated and the concentrated residue converted into maple cakes to be wrapped in paper and stored for future taffy-pulling adventures.

About the same time of the year Father and his older sons, with ax and mattock (or grub hoe), would clear off the underbrush of a five- or ten-acre piece of woodland. This tract had to be converted during the summer into a "new ground" and sowed in winter wheat in September.

In May or early June we planted corn, oats, and potatoes, and a little later, sowed buckwheat. At this season, we also felled the chestnut-oak trees on our prospective "new ground," spudded off the tanbark from their trunks and larger limbs and stacked it to dry. This was to be our "money crop." A little later, between seasons of corn cultivation, we dragged this bark down on sleds to the valley and then hauled it on wagons fourteen miles to the nearest tannery, at Mann's Choice, where we sold it for $3.50 per ton.

Then, in turn, came haymaking, oats cutting, wheat and rye harvesting, grain threshing, and brush burning. Soon thereafter, came buckwheat cutting and flailing, corn shocking, cider making, fall plowing, grain seeding of winter wheat and rye acreage, and finally cornhusking and fall butchering. Throughout the winter, farm work consisted chiefly of woodcutting and attending to the feeding, watering, currying, and bedding down of farm animals. Each one of us boys was early given a definite assignment to care for horses, cattle, sheep, hogs, or poultry, and to keep the woodshed stored with dry fuel. When we were all large enough to perform difficult tasks, the assignments were rotated so that each one should, in due time, know how to take care, in a responsible way, of all farm animals and poultry.

During the winter, when we were in school, this work had to be done in the mornings and evenings. This meant that we all had to get up before the break of day in the season of shortest days. We often used the kerosene lantern in the morning to find our way to the feed bins and to the animal stalls, and to "dung out" the stables and lay down the bedding in the evening. Generally, the milking could be done after daylight in the morning and before dark in the afternoon. In the shorter days of December, January, and February, we had to hurry our way through the barn work in order to get to school, two miles down the valley, on time. And in the afternoon we could not afford to lose any time in getting home to our evening chores.

On Saturdays, during the winter months when snow was on the ground, we helped Father to deliver large lumber logs on drag sleds to the sawmill two and a half miles down the valley.

Educators, so called, have done a great deal of quibbling in recent years over such terminologies as *education* and *training*. A few of the wise ones have concluded that education is for men and training is for animals. Mother had clarified her thinking better than that. She knew that education, particularly in the domestic arts, consists chiefly of training and of training that is exacting and long continued. So her girls were *trained* under her personal supervision in cooking, bread and cake baking, canning, fruit preservation, knitting and mending stockings, the making of rag rugs, house scrubbing, cleaning, sweeping, dusting, bedmaking, apple-butter boiling; food preparation for harvest hands, threshing squads, and barn-raising frolics; vegetable gardening, flower raising, and the preparation and serving of meals to large family parties.

Whatever Mother was not, she was a good neighbor. She trained her girls so well in all domestic matters that any one of them over sixteen was prepared to take over the running of the household of any neighbor woman at the time of "confinement." There were times when all of my older sisters were on such duty for short periods in the springtime and when I was, for a corresponding period, my mother's best domestic helper—learning to bake bread, put out a wash, or help in ironing the men's shirts.

Mother in her girlhood had learned square dancing and liked it. She had attended many church and community picnics in the pioneer community in which she lived; but because she knew the associations were not morally wholesome or personally refining, her girls were encouraged to get along somehow without this accomplishment. Her viewpoint was duly reinforced by the motto: "Evil communications corrupt good manners."

Here is a little incident that is worthy of a place in the records. My older brothers, Vincent (aged 18) and John (aged 13), and I (aged 11), had been engaged for several days with the neighbors up and down our valley in working out road taxes. The men formed one crew, which we boys called the "leaners-on-the-shovel-handles" crew. The adolescent boys formed another crew, which the men called "the workers." The men were credited with a dollar a day; the boys with forty cents a day. At the end of three days in intimate association with the big boys from up the valley who had been off to the cities of Pittsburgh and Johnstown I knew many things I should have been better for never having learned.

One of the things they had impressed on the minds of my brothers and me was that we couldn't hope to be recognized as men till we had learned to smoke. So we agreed among ourselves that we'd save our money till we could afford to pay for "some good smokes." Three months later we had the price—a nickel—and I was sent to town to get a Pittsburgh stogie. It was at least a foot long, made of heavy black tobacco, and wide open at both ends.

On a Sunday afternoon after a big dinner of stewed chicken we boys went out behind the spring house to light up: I cut the stogie into three pieces of equal length, each piece wide open at both ends. We took our "light" from the same match. Each pulled hard lest the other should get the advantage. In less time than it takes to tell this sad tale we fell in three different directions—all "mortally wounded." Just before I "passed out" I saw Mother coming toward the springhouse loaded with the left-over dairy products from the noon meal. She was walking on the storm clouds. A few moments later when we all "came out of it," Mother was standing by my side, a "Red Cross nurse" ready to minister to the dead and dying. She had texts for a dozen sermons; but she was too wise to preach on any one of them. She saw with her own eyes that Old Mother Nature was teaching us an impressive lesson about the effects of narcotics, and she saw, too, that we were in a mood to learn fast. After we had "recovered," not one of us ever referred to this unhappy incident again and not one of us has ever taken another puff. We were all completely satisfied with the experiment. If Father had known about this episode, he would probably have attempted to reinforce Old Mother Nature by giving each of us a good paddling, but that was really not necessary. I am not one of those morons who is willing to walk a mile to prove that he has ceased to be a free man and has finally become a camel.

I, as an individual, had certain personal interests or hobbies which my brothers generally did not share. I broke the colts to ride and was twice impaled on the garden fence. I liked to help Father in half-soling and mending shoes and, in due time, learned to make, and did make, several pairs of shoes for myself and my younger brother. The shaving horse in Father's carpenter shop was adjustable; and, while yet a half-grown boy, I learned to make ax handles on it and got my first cash by selling these to Uncle John's store and to the hucksters who came to our valley periodically to gather up eggs, poultry, and berries for the market.

I also had developed a sale for many handmade market baskets; but my real hobby was fine fruit trees, expert trimming, grafting, and budding. At the age of twelve, I had completely reconditioned our family orchard. Early in his married life, my father had planted an apple orchard of such varieties as his pioneer community afforded. Most of these varieties were native to the hills. They had good root beds, sturdy trunks, and ample limb spreads. The virgin soil was free from insect pests and the trees bore the best possible samples of all the scrub varieties. Each spring, I set a part of each treetop in grafts of some select variety in suitable distribution to take care of the seasonal needs—some Early Harvest, an excellent early summer eating apple; some Maiden Blush, an unexcelled late summer sauce apple; some Northern Spys, a superb late fall eating apple; and some Rhode Island Greenings, a hard, long-keeping, winter apple suitable for eating or cooking. One fall, Father found, fourteen miles down the valley, a new variety of choice eating apple. Most of its specimens weighed twenty ounces each. He was able, on a special trip early in the spring, to procure for me a single twig from the parent tree. I set the grafts from it on a young tree whose roots reached down into the nearby stream bed. All our neighbors, in due time, sampled its fruits and some of them asked for more than one twig for grafting. Fifty years later, I procured some twigs from the parent tree, which I first grafted, to set on some scrub stock I found on a little acreage I had bought in Laurel Park in western North Carolina.

In three seasons the whole orchard had been replaced without any cutting of an old tree or planting of a new one. I also set out several new and improved varieties of pears, plums, peaches, and cherries.

How sweet and everlasting is my memory of the encouragement my father always gave me on these "creative" activities! He loved to see evidences that his boys were growing in the ability and disposition to think out plans and procedures for themselves. What a companion he was! I never was as far as thirty miles from home until after I began teaching at the age of seventeen, but while I was yet a small boy, Father took me on many short trips to nearby towns, to Berlin (ten miles away), to Buena Vista (seven miles away), to White Horse up on the Glade Pike (five miles away), and to Mann's Choice, the nearest railroad siding (fourteen miles away).

My first long bark-hauling trip was taken when I was only six years old. If Father had not strapped me securely to old Bill's saddle, I should surely have fallen to the ground and been run over. I had gotten up so early for this trip that I had fallen asleep in the saddle before we were three miles on our journey; but, arriving at our destination, I was amply rewarded for I became, for the first time in my young life, my father's guest at a dinner in a hotel. He ordered soup for each of us from a list of three varieties. When the waitress called off about a dozen varieties of meat from venison to roast turkey, Father was content with the choice of two for himself and one for me. That did not seem entirely fair although my helping of stewed chicken surely was ample. When the waitress came to call off a list of at least six or eight different kinds of pie, I beat Father to the gun by announcing my decision promptly and with gusto: "Yes, please." I shall never forget the look of consternation on my Father's face nor the unconcealed joy the girl had in the prospect of satisfying my dearest wish. She "had a heart." She must have known the classical definition of a boy as "an organized appetite with a skin drawn over it." Furthermore, she knew that in a Pennsylvania Dutch hostelry, the supply of pie never runs out; so off to the kitchen she went. Father was a bit concerned about her delay in returning. When she reappeared on the scene she brought him an ample serving of apple pie, and she brought me a half circle of pie in the form of a mosaic of six varieties "fitly framed together." She was not the victim of any conventional notions of how to cut pie. She was evidently a disciple of the old French chef who always justified his over-generous helpings of pie by assuring his guests that no one knew better than he that "all really good apple pie should always be cut at an angle of three hundred sixty degrees." When Father got his first glimpse of the bill which the waitress had given the clerk at the desk he looked a bit disconcerted for a moment as if seventy-five cents must surely represent a twenty-five cent's overcharge for my extra five pieces of pie. In our family circle, I never heard the end of that story; and, needless to say, I never again gave just the same kind of answer to a waitress when she called off a list of desserts.

Despite all the hard work we had to do, our family was given to much merriment, and we had the necessary actors and stage carpenters to put on a good show at almost any time and on short notice. The Gilbreaths had no monopoly in this matter though we were a full generation ahead of them.

Now a word about the size of our family. All of my uncles and aunts except one, had families, and most of them large families, six or eight or ten children each. My father and mother had a baker's dozen plus one for good measure.

"Were they rabbits?" some sophisticated uplifter asks.

No, they were healthy, happy, much loved, suitably and

comfortably clothed, promising children whose parents were faithful to their trust in training them to be useful, upright, liberty-loving American citizens.

"But," someone will ask, "Were these youngsters properly spaced?"

Yes, perfectly.

The next question, "Why wasn't the number kept within 'proper limits'?"

I don't know except that we wanted all the children we had. Father and Mother and all of us children did. The more children we had, the happier we were. It would have been different if Father and Mother had not desired any one of us or if every one of us had developed the bright notion that no one should have been invited except himself. I wouldn't wish to overwork the theory that babies are cheaper by the dozen. I don't believe they are, but what I am concerned about is that all babies that come into the world should come because their parents want them and have the interest and the resources—physical, mental, moral, spiritual, and sentimental—to give them a fair start in life. If parents don't want babies or have nothing to bring them up on but money, and too little of that, it isn't fair to bring them into life.

Where do babies come from? Well, any normal child five or six years old who has lived on a farm knows nearly all there is to know about that. He already has too much sense to listen to old Aunt Susan's stork theories. He already knows enough real science to put her to shame when she attempts to substitute prudery for purity. We never had any storks around our place. We just had babies. Father and Mother knew where they came from and the approximate date when each should arrive. Our big sisters and brothers knew, too, about when we might expect the next one; and Mother or one of the big sisters always told us in good time, as in all well-regulated families they are likely to do—so that none of us was too much surprised. We always made a feast on the coming of a new baby. We had satisfactory shelter and plenty of good food; and so we had a the-more-the-merrier philosophy.

I can never forget the coming of brother Norbert when I was five or of sister Martha when I was seven—just big enough to be admitted to an open secret. We all lined up in the order of age to go in to see the new baby. When I got my first look at that pretty little black-haired, black-eyed babe, I fairly shouted for joy, "My sister!" Why there could never be another so utterly charming and delightful as she, and so it was with all her successors to the end of the line. There is no space to tell of the family fellowship we all enjoyed with each other and with our parents always. In the gathering twilight of the years no one of my treasured memories could be more precious or abiding.

How about the family economy? Well, we lived, in those faraway days, in a somewhat self-contained and self-sufficient economy. Exchange of goods was no longer on a barter basis, but our village store was a kind of banking institution in which Father built up the family credit account by taking to the store, as he could and when he could, any materials or produce from the farm in excess of the needs of his family for such materials or produce. These materials and produce included lumber, grain, potatoes, hams, poultry, fruit, wool, and the like. These items when delivered to the store were credited at their assumed value on my father's "Pass Book." Likewise, items which our family secured from the store were entered on the opposite page of the same book. At any time in the year, the merchant, my uncle, or my father could strike a balance and see from the book who owed whom and how much. This interchange of goods and services sometimes went on for a year without an official balancing of accounts. Everybody fully trusted the honesty and integrity of Uncle John, the merchant, and, generally speaking, he had no occasion to distrust the honesty and integrity of the people who traded at his store.

There were certain goods we had to secure at the "exchange," or store, each year. Father and Mother in council with their older children would make a reliable list of these needs: so many pounds of sugar, so many gallons of blackstrap molasses, so many pairs of shoes, so many suits and dresses (it wasn't many, for Mother did most of the sewing for both her boys and her girls, so many yards of cloth for suits, so many yards of dress goods, so many skeins of knitting yarn, so many hoes, rakes, grain cradles, mowing scythes, plowshares, etc.

There were some goods and materials which had to be paid for in cash because they couldn't be secured at our local store, such as horse rakes, mowing machines, and the like. Also there were school taxes, state and county taxes, and church dues which had to be paid in cash. We secured the money to pay these cash items by selling tanbark in Mann's Choice fourteen miles away, and by selling colts, horses, beef cattle, and sheep. The road taxes were "worked out" annually on the public highways.

It generally took careful planning and sometimes skillful maneuvering to keep accounts in balance. I can't remember a time when I was too young to understand these matters as Father explained them periodically to his household or family. I have never ceased to be grateful to him for making crystal clear to me early in life that there are few forms of dependence which can so quickly and so subtly rob us of some one or more of our basic freedoms as to be in debt. I can think of nothing more tragic in our modern family or state economy than the nonchalance with which parents actually train their children by example how to enslave themselves by recklessly running into debt for things they would be better off without.

Father's citizenship still merits my highest admiration. He always voted at every primary as well as at the local, county, state, and national elections; and he was remarkably well informed concerning issues and candidates. He despised the grafters and their political legerdemain. Certain men in public life, such as Senator Matthew Stanley Quay, and Donald Cameron, he regarded as traitors to everything which the fathers of our country had fought for and some of them had died for. He was always willing to carry almost any burden to insure honest elections and to make it possible for everybody who wanted to vote to get to the polls. When he was given an assignment as road supervisor he was careful to see that no one on his payroll should spend time leaning on his shovel handle. He considered it his duty to see to it that the township should get full value in road improvements for all the credit which was allowed on tax bills.

Grandfather Suhrie was a bit taciturn and seemed to enjoy life most when he was alone with his animals, his trees, his fruits, his vines, and his garden vegetables and flowers on the two-acre plot of choice land which he had retained as his own and which was located so close to the Suhrie school that he must have at times regretted donating a school site so close to his home. On school days, almost all of his grandchildren were wont to call on Grandma Suhrie to sample, at noontime, some one of her numerous varieties of tasty European breads or cookies. On Sundays when we went to church, or more particularly when we had errands to town on weekdays, we were almost sure to call on Grandmother Topper whose cookies and fruit butters were far famed. She had the reputation of being the best neighbor in all the valley, and when she was old she traveled miles afoot each week to call on "the fatherless and widows in their affliction" and to help any of her neighbors in distress. I have very pleasant memories of my grandparents and especially of Grandmother Topper who was just about the dearest old lady I have ever known in all my life.

None of my grandparents dominated our family life in any way. Grandfather Topper had died at the age of fifty-

one and only my older sister had known him; but Grandmother Topper, his widow, and Grandmother Suhrie were
well known to all of us children. They rarely came to our
home although our Suhrie grandparents lived less than two
miles down the valley, and Grandmother Topper no more
than three miles away in the village. The home of each of
them was a rendezvous for all her numerous grandchildren.
Our Suhrie grandparents had about thirty-five grandchildren,
and Grandmother Topper had more than fifty.

Before I left home my eldest brother had gone to work on
a stock farm in Greensburg, Pennsylvania. Three of my older
sisters were away teaching or attending school. John, my next
older brother, had gone to the lumber woods in Alabama.
Our family, before Father's death, had been scattered in half a
dozen states. Norbert, my younger brother, was a railroad
man and made an annual visit to each of my brothers and
sisters and to me. This, more than any other one thing, kept
the family bond intact. He continued to go the rounds until
his death at seventy-three. By that time, all his older brothers
and sisters except two had passed on. Brother John, only two
years older than I, was the only member of our family to acquire an estate. John had married twice but left no children.
He died at fifty-two. He left a comfortable house for his
widow and placed his estate in trust to provide income for her
maintenance so long as she should live. On her death, by the
provisions of his will, his estate was divided among the surviving brothers and sisters, providing for each of the eight
survivors a sum sufficient to procure a comfortable modern
dwelling house. I gladly acknowledge my obligation to him
not only for providing the roof that is now over my head but,
more particularly, for lending me small sums of money to
make it possible for me to begin my schooling and for the
voluntary cancellation of a part of this obligation.

I am now (1955) the oldest surviving member of our large
family; only three younger sisters are still living. To one of

them, Martha, I owe a debt of gratitude I shall never be able to repay. She cared for my younger daughter, Ruth, through her first three years when the child's mother was ill and unable to do so. My other two surviving sisters, Margaret and Mary, also challenge my admiration as wives, mothers, and good neighbors.

My youngest sister, Mary, had six stalwart sons in the American Army during the Second World War, and Margaret and Norbert each had two sons in that historic conflict.

Four of my sisters, one of my brothers, and I have taught a total of one hundred sixty-nine years, mostly in the elementary school grades.

It does not seem necessary that I summarize here the influence of my childhood home and family life upon my character development inasmuch as Professor Frank E. Spaulding has, in a recent book, so admirably set forth the frame of reference he had built up by the age of fifteen largely as a result of the education he had acquired from his home life on the farm and his intimate daily association with his parents, his brother and his uncle. My home life experience out on the farm was so much like his in most essential respects that I can accept his statement of the outcomes in character development as an adequate summarization of my own. Furthermore, he has stated these outcomes so concisely that I could not hope to do it as well. It follows:

> My fifteenth year found me the possessor of a substantial, comprehensive, and clearly defined frame of reference . . . It was a working frame of reference that found expression in my thinking and activities . . .
>
> As items in this frame of reference I shall record those which seem to me the most important ideals, objectives, values, ambitions, principles of conduct, attitudes, and habits, without attempting to avoid overlapping. As already stated, each item was a part of an integrated and, as I believe, a generally harmonious whole.

a) The ideal of personal independence, based on economic independence, not for the time being, but for life; this for the sake of personal freedom in thought and action.

b) The ambition to achieve and maintain my ideal of independence through my own efforts.

c) The ideal and the habit of thrift, including not merely financial savings, but economy in the use of materials, time, and effort.

d) Self-reliance in thought and action.

e) The habit of expecting nothing as a gift, but of depending on my own efforts for the satisfaction of my desires.

f) The habit of discriminating and weighing values, giving precedence to permanent or long-range values.

g) The habit of making independent choices of procedure, long-range as well as immediate, on the basis of a comparison of values.

h) The habit of careful planning and selecting of suitable means for the achievement of any desired result.

i) Recognition of the importance of adequate knowledge and appreciation of the facts and conditions involved in carrying out any plan of procedure.

j) The sense and acceptance of personal responsibility; also the imputing of responsibility to others.

k) A concept of efficient co-operation: in any job involving the participation of several, each one doing that part for which he is best fitted, and taking full responsibility therefor.

l) The habit of willing obedience to anyone to whom it is felt that obedience is due, and to the extent that it is due.

m) Instinctive resistance to any command to do—or to refrain from doing—anything ordered by anyone lacking the right to give the order; resistance doubly strong whenever moral principles or values are involved.

n) A keen sense of right and wrong; of honesty; of justice and fairness, in all matters involving the interests of others.

o) The expectation, rather than fear, of punishment in some form—possibly only the punishment of disapproval —for the violation of accepted principles of right conduct.

p) Respect for sincerely observed, conventional forms of religion.

q) Belief in the religion of right conduct. Lack of definite beliefs, due to lack of knowledge on which to base belief, respecting matters beyond the range of human experience.

r) A feeling of self-confidence, not baseless nor exaggerated, but the product of successful experience.*

There Were Tragedies, Too

In the previous section I made it clear that my childhood on the farm was a happy one, that our family life was surcharged with co-operation and good will, and that my adult life has been full of happy memories of childhood days.

But there were tragedies too. The memories of some of these are very poignant. Our home was, generally speaking, a very happy one, but dark shadows sometimes descended without warning upon it. One of the earliest remembrances I have is of an occasion when my second oldest sister Lucy, came down over the snow-covered hill above our farm home leading old Bill, our trusty farm horse. He was hitched to a drag sled on which my father lay bleeding and moaning piteously. Only Mother, my oldest sister Agnes, the three youngest babies, and I were at home at the time. Agnes and Lucy carried Father's limp body to a bed in a first-floor room near to the main entrance. Then Agnes mounted old Bill and hurried off in search of our beloved family doctor at his office in town three miles away.

The story of what had happened is this: Father had been alone cutting a big tree that stood at the edge of the forest just above the last cleared wheat field. When this tree finally

---

* *One School Administrator's Philosophy:* Its Development. Frank E. Spaulding. New York, 1952, Exposition Press.

broke from its moorings, it fairly leaped out into the open space. Its falling released a broken limb that had long found lodgment in one of its branches. Father was aware of the presence of this unattached limb but was unable to make retreat quickly enough to escape its impact. It struck him a heavy blow on the back of the neck and above the right shoulder. Sister Lucy, who was in sight and on her way to him with a message from Mother, saw the accident happen. She knew Mother was ill, and so, with rare presence of mind, she ran down to the barn, hitched the horse to an old drag sled, and hurried again to Father's side at the scene of the accident where he lay bleeding and unconscious. Alone she placed his body on the sled and proceeded with it down the hill to our home half a mile away.

The doctor soon arrived and found on examination that Father's injuries were very serious. He lingered for weeks without giving any clear indication that he might ultimately recover. A day after the accident, Mother gave birth to her tenth child. It was stillborn.

After three long months Father was up and about again and ready to make his first trip to town to be greeted by many happy neighbors and friends at the Easter service in the village church. He was one of the two best-known men in the valley, and I verily believe he was the best loved of all. I shall never forget how happy we all were on that day when he was ready again to don his best Sunday-go-meetin' black suit, which had been freshly pressed, and his shoes, which had been given an extra shine. We all knew from the beginning that Father just had to live and he knew it too; when his physical injuries were healed and the mental anxiety that we all felt for many weeks was over, all of us thanked God in our hearts, as never before in our lives, that he had not died as the doctor and all of us had expected he would.

I had my troubles too: first, a serious accident, then a minor tragedy, and finally two major accidents. At the age of nine

I began to break our two-year-old colts to the bridle bit and to carry a jockey. I was the jockey. I soon learned that the colt was sometimes more skillful in disciplining me than I was in disciplining him. On occasion, one of these fine young steppers could "spill" his cargo so quickly and so skillfully that the rider did not know what had happened to him until he found himself suspended by his trouser belt on the sharp tops of the palings of the garden fence. On one of these occasions I was pretty seriously hurt and was put to bed for about two or three months. My spine, in the lumbar region, had evidently been injured and my kidneys badly bruised. I lost the greater part of a year's schooling. When spring came and the school term was over, I gradually recovered. The spring and summer work on the farm seemed to bring my injured organs into normal functioning again. I don't think I suffered any permanent injury, but for weeks both the doctor and my parents seemed to have as much anxiety as I had pain and distress.

At the age of ten, the removal of the two back molars on my upper jaw was long past due. A traveling dentist visited our valley once every three months. His next visit was not due for two months. The pain I was suffering was excruciating and had been acute for several days. It was at the height of the harvest season, and I was needed as a water-carrier. Finally, I got up my courage and went alone afoot a distance of ten miles over the mountain trails and the Glade Pike to the village of Berlin.

I presented myself at the door of a two-story dwelling house on the main street where there was a sign hanging out over the sidewalk reading: "Doctor So and So." I asked for the doctor. The lady who greeted me invited me upstairs into a large room where I met a bleary-eyed, nervous man whose appearance frightened me. He said gruffly, "Sit down." I did, with a bang, and in less time than it takes to tell it he had yanked out two upper teeth one on each side; they were new molars in perfect condition which I could least afford to spare. It happened so quickly that I had no time to protest; and, when finally I told him that the teeth which were making the trouble were still there, he turned around and said: "I didn't want to pull them. They'll break into pieces. You better see the dentist down-stairs. The charge is one dollar." I was so frightened that I gave him a dollar and hurried downstairs. The dentist there gave me a very kindly reception and seated me gently in his dental chair. When he looked into my mouth he said, "Why, what has happened?" I told him. He was mad enough to tackle a wild cat, but he calmed himself and proceeded to take out the aching teeth. I gave him the only dollar I had left; and, after listening to the kindly advice he gave me, I started on the long trail home in great pain though in greater distress over losing two perfectly good permanent teeth.

The next week Father read in the county newspaper that the man who had drawn the sound teeth had, a few days before, committed suicide by shooting himself.

It may interest the reader to know that more than thirty years later I was told by one of America's top-ranking orthodontists that the removal of those two sound teeth at the time it was done accounted for the contraction of the upper jaw and the corresponding protrusion of the lower one resulting in the impairment of my mouth drainage and constituting a menace to my general health. Consequently, I paid him, in due time, $600 for "rehanging" my lower jaw so as to retrieve an abnormal undershot lower mandible and consequent deformity in the facial profile.

At the age of eleven, I was big enough to be very helpful to Father and my big brothers in "peeling" the tanbark from the chestnut-oak trees on the tract we were clearing for the fall's sowing of wheat.

About eleven o'clock on a hot morning early in June, my eldest brother was felling a tree of intermediate size, about ten inches in diameter. It stood on a steep embankment. Not realizing how brash it was when the sap was up, he took but a few chips out on the under side and began prematurely to make the chips fly on the upper side. The result was that the trunk of the tree "split up" leaving a snag on the lower side at least ten feet high and casting the falling trunk sidewise from the top of this snag. The butt of the tree caught me ten or fifteen feet away from the stump before I could make a retreat through the briers. At the critical moment Father appeared on the scene to take charge of the tragic situation. My left leg had sustained a compound fracture of the tibia and fibula just above the ankle. I was pinned down; the trunk of the tree was too heavy to be lifted off. Father and my eldest brother Vincent, sawed off a ten-foot length and rolled it away while brother John bathed my brow and gave me such poor comfort as he could. The bones of my foreleg had been crushed through the flesh into the woodland loam and were black with leaf mold. The foot seemed about to drop off.

My limp body was placed on a six-foot piece of bark and covered with green boughs to shield me from the blazing June day sun. The journey down over the three-quarter mile trail to my cabin home was, for me, a veritable *via dolorosa*. At last the long journey was ended, and I fell off into unconsciousness while Father and Mother straightened out my bruised body and badly mangled limb. Before they washed up the wound, major bleeding had ceased. My brothers had, in the meantime, gone off in haste to town to find our faithful country doctor.

The remainder of the story I am loath to relate. This man had for more than a quarter of a century been the trustworthy and capable guardian of the health of our family. He had taken care of us with unusual fidelity and devotion. In all our childhood epidemics and all our family accidents he had cared for us and had given his best services to my dear mother at the birth of each one of her fourteen children. He was the idol of our family and of the whole community. He had an unhappy home. He and his wife differed fundamentally over the matter of how Martin Luther should be classified. Was he a heretic or a reformer, a sinner or a saint? One said he was a heretic and a sinner. The other contended that he was a reformer and a saint. When the argument got too heated or was too long drawn out, the good doctor who knew the soothing effects of a certain soporific that had, for many years, been freely dispensed at the country tavern, hitched up his old bay mare to his black buggy, took out his fishing tackle, went to the tavern to stock up with "licker" and then headed out of town and up Breast Works Run to the ancient "breastworks" which had been built during the French and Indian War. At the right place in the cool shades of the valley and not far from the stream bed was the stem of a fallen tree. It was well padded on the upper side with leaves and leaf mold. There the good doctor was able, for the time being, to forget all about his fishing tackle and his skill as a fisherman and to set-tle down by the fallen tree for the quiet slumber he had been denied the night before. He knew he had what it takes; and he proceeded to close, for at least a few transient hours, the haunting argument of the night before.

My brothers had found the trail up the valley and had sighted the horse and buggy. The doctor, however, was not to be found. In the middle of the afternoon one of my brothers reported at home after at least fifteen miles of foot travel. Father in the meantime had considered sending him to Berlin, ten miles over the mountain, but he knew no doctor there and was by this time getting increasingly concerned lest some calamity had befallen our family doctor up in the Breast Works Run; he sent brother back so that both brothers might go over the whole terrain again in search of the doctor. When they had reexplored every part of the woodland tract, they finally came upon the good doctor, where they might least have expected to find him, at a considerable distance from his horse and buggy and not far from the stream bed where it was assumed he would be found fishing. He was in deep slumber. They woke him up, took him to his buggy, and drove him to our home.

In the meantime, I had somehow gotten along without benefit of tourniquet or blood transfusion and was still alive. During that endless afternoon my mother and my sisters often sought in vain for any clear evidence that my pulse was still ticking.

When my brothers finally arrived late in the evening accompanied by the long-looked-for family doctor, mother uncovered my mangled leg that he might see it. He took a quick glance and, realizing that he was in no condition to help, staggered into the next room and poured out his grief at his utter helplessness when he was most needed. Knowing him as we all did, I am sure he pitied me "as a father pitieth his children." I am sure he grieved with my father and mother (and with my two remaining sisters who had not been completely knocked out by the strain of the long vigil) as fully as he grieved for me. In a little while he was at his post of duty. I can still hear him say to my Father, "That foot will have to come off."

Father was silent for a moment; then he spoke in clear but calm and determined tones, "No, doctor. He is young, he has good blood, and he will outgrow this terrible accident."

The doctor insisted, but to no avail, for Father, though not a physician nor a scientist, was a man of faith and determination.

Then the doctor said: "But, Francis, the boy will surely die if I don't."

Father was unmoved; his final response was: "Doctor, I would rather follow this boy to the churchyard than to have him go around all his life a cripple."

I overheard this conversation and was for the first time made to realize that my life was hanging in the balance. I wondered for a brief moment if even my dear father was not deserting me. The strain was too great. I went off in a swoon from which I did not awake until I felt the firm grasp of my father's arms and hands around my trembling body and saw the physician bringing the exposed bones into position inside the lacerated flesh. Then I passed out again.

Father was a man of faith, and that helped me mightily even when I was but dimly conscious. He had often told me of the love of God for his children. In my utter helplessness I spent every waking moment in promising my Maker and myself that if He would heal my deep wounds, I would give my life and all my strength to doing whatever I should believe to be His will. My surrender was as complete as my father's faith was unfailing.

Father was as all but completely unschooled as was Abraham Lincoln, but in the crises of life he had a cool head and a completely trusting heart. His faith was the only hope I had of being made whole again. I have wondered a thousand times since—yes, ten thousand times—whether the most profound scientist of our times—or of all the centuries—could have expressed the assurance he had in his mind and heart any better than he did: "He is young, he has good blood, and he will outgrow it."

The family was soon going its rounds of daily duty. After days of sodden sleep I again had a purpose to live and a consuming purpose to be well again and to walk. Throughout the hot summer months all the members of my family vied with each other in doing for me the things that would make me understand, if that were necessary, that my restoration to health and my happiness were each one's deepest concern.

Father and my big brothers were busy day after day with the farm work. Mother and her girls were busy with a multitude of household duties. All had time to bring me the cup of cold water, the glass of apple juice or lemonade, samples of the first fresh fruit, flowers from the garden, and always a word of good cheer. The youngest of my sisters was less than two years old. The two oldest were gone, but of all the faithful ones who were at home and who, it would seem, were almost willing to quarrel over who should have the privilege of giving me some gracious manifestation of their love, one stands out above all others in my precious memory of those trying days. It was Bernard, my youngest brother, only three and a half years old. When all others were out in the field or in the garden or on some errand to town or to a neighbor's home, Bernard was in my room and by my bedside, and much of the time, with his warm little hand in mine. I love the memory of that precious child for what he was far above anything he could ever have said to me or done for me. He still is to me the most perfect example of personal devotion—pure and undefiled—that I have ever known or could ever imagine, and these memories are all the more vivid as I recall with them his sudden taking off in the late fall of the same year.

I came home from school one afternoon—Wednesday it was—and found him the happiest of all children I had ever seen. He showed me a new pair of jumpers which Mother had just completed for him. He put them on to show me how pretty they were. They were bright red, which is always, with me, a very appropriate color for children of his age. Then I took him in my arms and reminded him of my tender love for the sweet companion of my long summer days when, for hours at a time, we were alone together and when he slept on my pillow every afternoon.

I noticed he seemed tired. I put him to bed. It wasn't long until I noticed that his countenance was flushed. He wanted no supper. During the night he was restless and feverish. Mother gave him some croup sirup the next morning, which was Thanksgiving day. At noon he ate but a few spoonfuls of soup with some difficulty. My two older brothers were in bed with colds; so it fell to my lot to get out old Bill and trot him off to town at his best speed to get the doctor. Since Bernard was loath to have me leave him, I hurried home, the doctor following me no more than a quarter of a mile behind.

On my arrival at home, I went quickly into the bedroom where Bernard was anxiously waiting for my return. He desired to rest in my arms. I had scarcely lifted him from his bed and covered him carefully with a large woolen blanket before the death struggle began. A few minutes before the doctor arrived his face was black, and he ceased to breathe. The dread plague of diphtheria had done its deadly work.

I cannot recount the unhappy events of that sad day without remembering vividly what happened many years later down in Georgia when my own lovely daughter, at about the same age, would have had her life snuffed out in a brief moment of struggle but for Dr. William H. Park's discovery of diphtheria antitoxin. When, many years later, I saw him in the fullness of his years stand up at a New York university commencement to receive the honorary degree of Doctor of Public Health, I could not restrain the tears of pure joy that such a man as he had come upon the scene to bless a waiting world.

Little Bernard, the best loved of all our family, was buried the day after his death in the little hillside churchyard down in the village when the snow drifts were piled high.

It was Father's custom to lead his flock morning and evening in family prayer by the fireside. That evening we all knelt for prayer. Father was unable to utter a single word. Finally we rose one by one and went off sobbing to our several rooms. Bernard, the bright, fair-haired, blue-eyed, happy boy, the most promising and best loved of all our family, had been laid to rest.

Three score years and ten have passed since that sad November Thanksgiving day. I have helped to lay away the remains of scores of my dear friends and sometimes their little ones, but never has my grief been so poignant as on that faraway November day; and I can never cease to wonder what it might have done for the glory of our family name if this precious life could have been spared to reach its zenith.

Three years after the tragic accidents recorded above and after the loss of my little brother I had another accident that was very serious. On a certain day early in August the storm clouds were threatening to drench our shocks of wheat, which after a long season of intensely hot weather were bone dry and ready for the threshing machine. Father and my older brothers worked feverishly all day to beat the threatening showers and to get the grain into the barn. I drove the horse rake and gathered up the gleanings—the stalks of ripened grain that had fallen out of the grain cradle when the harvesters were laying down the swathes to be raked up and bound into sheaves. We had all gone without supper in order to complete the ingathering of grain before the long overdue showers should drench the landscape and possibly set the grains of wheat to sprouting in the shocks. Finally the last sheaf of wheat was on the wagon, and the last lot of grain had been driven in on the barn floor.

Would there be time also to gather in the winnowed rows of ripened gleanings? We all hoped so. The oldest wagon we had on the place with the largest bark rack we had on the farm was taken out into the field by a three-horse team and quickly piled with the rakings I had winnowed down the middle of the field during an afternoon of hard work. I was lifted to the top of the load to anchor the last dozen forkfuls of grain ere they should fall off the top-heavy bark rack. Near the end of the windrow and above a steep embankment I was working feverishly at the top of the load to take care of the forkfuls of grain that were being handed up with quickened tempo.

Suddenly the horses sprang into the air, made a sharp turn to the right, and upset the load of grain just above the steep and stony embankment. It seemed that they had been thrown into a panic by the frightening sound of a rattlesnake under their feet. When the wagon was suddenly upset at the top of the embankment, I realized I might be thrown thirty feet from the top of the load down over the declivity. Instinctively I held on to the largest possible armful of tangled grain, which I hoped would serve as a cushion to my fall. I reached ground after a few anxious moments during which I wasn't sure whether I should be buried under an avalanche of grain or be thrown violently on the rocks.

The shock of the impact upon the rough terrain was not so severe as I had expected. When I climbed up again to the top of the embankment, I knew I had been seriously bruised on the right hip, leg, and knee and that I had sustained a compound fracture of my left arm just above the wrist. I was able with a little help to reach home just before a torrent of rain fell. The family doctor was summoned and arrived promptly, ready to give me the best possible service. The fractured bones were put into place and fastened securely between two wooden splints. Because of my very uncomfortable bruise I was propped up in a big parlor chair and slept there—or tried to sleep—during the next several nights.

On the third night, I was so utterly uncomfortable that in my sleep I made my way up to my bed in the attic and fell into a stupor there until morning. When I woke up it was soon found that I had displaced the splints on my arm and that my broken bones were sorely in need of resetting. I was taken to town and without delay the physician reset the bones; but the damage was done. The resetting was not completely successful, and the ulna and radius bones have, as a result, never failed to impinge upon each other when I rotate my hand to the left; and so I suffer much discomfort even to this day.

My arm was kept in a sling for several months and it was several years before I ceased to "favor" it in the performance of the ordinary work of the farm. If Father had not been wise enough to insist that I use my left hand as much as the right one, I am sure there would have been serious atrophy of muscles and loss of normal function.

This accident was important because, in no inconsiderable

degree, it affected the choice of my lifework. Up to this time, I fully expected to be a farmer. The physical handicap which resulted, for a time, from this accident, in part incapacitated me for farm work and forced me to consider seriously for a time whether I should ever be able comfortably to perform the duties of a farmer. In the fall of that year, not having yet fully recovered from my accident, I went to school early and without a full array of the books needed. This circumstance prompted my new teacher to take an active interest in me, and it doubtless was a determining factor in his employing me as janitor for the year. My service there brought me into intimate and very personal relationship with him whom I came, in due time, greatly to admire and love. These circumstances combined to predispose my mind toward teaching. I have found such complete happiness in this calling that I am by no means sure that the accident above related did not in the end turn out to be a great blessing.

Suhrie Rural School in the Eighties

The common school, "free to all and good enough for all," is a grassroots American institution. It began to come upon the scene in New England and the East generally in the days of Jacksonian democracy in the early 1830's. Pennsylvania's law establishing a public school system (the Thaddeus Stephens Act) was approved in 1834, just two years before my father was born. It required many years to get school districts organized and schools established, especially in the remote and mountainous areas of the state, in the backwoods sections, and up in the mountain coves. In my father's boyhood days, schools in such areas had not yet come into existence; and when they did come, they were very rudimentary and primitive in character.

No public school is known to have been organized in New Baltimore until about the opening of the Civil War; and the Suhrie School, two miles up the Raystown Branch of the

Juniata, was not opened until shortly after the close of that conflict, when my eldest sister was about ready to enter the chart class. This school was located at the extreme lower, or eastern, end of my Grandfather Suhrie's farm on a tract of two acres which he had donated for the purpose to the Board of School Directors of Allegheny Township, Somerset County, Pennsylvania. The school building erected thereon about 1866 or 1867 was a very plain rectangular frame structure, about thirty-five feet long and twenty-five feet wide, without vestibule, cloak rooms, or storage closets. It was one of those far-famed "little red school" houses which, in most instances, had never been painted any color.

There were two plausible reasons which the board of school directors gave for officially designating it "the Suhrie School." These were as follows: first, the land (or shall we say the swamp) on which the building was erected had been donated by John Mathias Suhrie, my grandfather; and, second, most of the lumber and the labor involved in its erection had been donated by Francis Suhrie, my father, and his brothers, Elias and Cornelius. A third reason might later have been equally valid, namely, that in due time, the three Suhrie families contributed more than half of the children enrolled in the school.

The Suhrie school was located at the "forks of the crick" on meadow land that was swampy during the fall, winter, and spring seasons when the building was actually in use. The premises were not properly drained for a quarter of a century after the building had been erected. All the elementary school children from the area once served by this Suhrie school are now transported by motorbus on hard-surfaced roads to a consolidated school near Berlin, Pennsylvania.

The Suhrie School had no playgrounds, as such, but there was ample space on unfenced pastures adjacent to its premises for games of town ball at recess time and at noon intermissions. And the woodlands, the stream beds, the rock caves, and many mountain trails within striking distance of the school afforded ample facilities for "excursions" in great variety during playtime. Such excursions were sometimes unduly prolonged or extended by the pupils themselves with the perfectly plausible excuse, "We didn't hear the school bell."

All furniture in use in the school was carpenter made, of white pine or sapwood-hemlock boards grooved and joined. The school desks were of uniform height and width. Nearly all of them were fairly adjusted to the comfort of the older pupils but generally maladjusted to the comfort and hygienic requirements of the younger ones. Most beginners sat with their hips at least four inches away from the back wall of the seats they occupied and with feet dangling at least six inches above the floor. These school desks, made of soft wood, actually invited "the jack-knife carved initials" and every boy responded heartily to the invitation and promptly made his contribution to the history and lore of the place just as soon as he had learned the initials of his own name.

The teaching equipment of the school consisted for many years of a reading chart devoted chiefly to the display of the alphabet in capitals and lower-case letters and a few such inspiring literary classics as: "The fat cat caught the rat," "The black cat sat on the mat," and the like. When I was about ten years of age, on a bright fall day, a school board member brought to our school *A New Map of Pennsylvania*. It was about ten feet long and five feet high with names of counties and important cities printed in bold-face type large enough to be read from almost any part of the room. By the time I was twelve years old, an unabridged dictionary was added. The little folk used the "reading chart" almost continuously, and the upper-class students used the map every day, especially in their geography and history studies; but nobody seemed to make any real use of the dictionary. That was before the day when every good teacher has a concern to make all her pupils at every age level word conscious. One boy facetiously remarked that if we should ever get a school organ, we could use the dictionary, as his folk at home did, to build up the organ bench to the right height for his little sister when she played the organ.

The school was well located. Four valleys converged on its neighborhood—two of these at the school and the other two at a point a quarter of a mile below it. Sometimes, in the early years of its history, and at the height of the winter season, as many as sixty pupils were enrolled, ranging from five to twenty-three or twenty-four years of age. In the early fall, when the big boys and girls were husking corn making cider, gathering winter apples, boiling apple butter, and butchering, the attendance was low and consisted chiefly, or wholly, of those in the first, second, and third reader classes. In the spring, likewise, the attendance was low and consisted exclusively, or almost exclusively, of the little ones. The parents decided who might attend and when; no law had yet been enacted to prescribe who must attend school and how long each must attend each year.

The funds to support the operating costs of the school were supplied by an annual tax levy. The rate of the millage tax on houses, farms, and woodlands was determined by the needs of the school district on a vote of the members of the school board. The district "supported" thirteen one-teacher public schools located generally about four miles apart. There were some children in the township, or school district, who had to travel as much as three miles, and a very few as much as four, over rough mountain trails and unimproved country roads to reach the nearest school, but the great majority could get to their several schools in little, if any, more than two miles.

The school board of the township consisted of six members serving for three years each. They were elected on staggered terms, two at each succeeding spring election. Generally speaking, these were the most enlightened, enterprising, and public-spirited men of the township. The township by common consent was divided into six districts with no legal, but nevertheless well-understood, boundaries. Each board member was assigned to represent one of these districts as its spokesman for the one or two schools located therein. He looked after repairs, replacements, fuel supply, painting, and other "temporalities." His voice generally, though not always, prevailed in the selection of the teacher for his school or schools.

The teachers in the Suhrie school, during the period of my enrollment therein from age seven to seventeen, when I became its teacher, were nine in number. Only one served a second term and his two terms were not consecutive. None of my teachers was a Suhrie. I was the first Suhrie to go on the public school payroll of the township as a teacher. But three of my teachers were my mother's brothers, namely: Frank, Ambrose, and Joseph Topper; and three of them were my mother's first cousins, namely: Frank Gillespie and the Luken sisters, Janet and Irene, granddaughters of the first settlers of New Baltimore. The other three were "outlanders." One was from the township west of us, one from the township south of us, and one from over the line in Bedford County.

All of these teachers except one, a young man, lived in their own homes or boarded with patrons in the immediate vicinity of the school. This young man rode horseback from a point five miles away. All of them were well known and highly respected in the community. No one of them was a dullard. Each of them seems to me to have fully improved such educational opportunities as he had had. No one of the entire number had been schooled beyond the sixth-reader class of a rural one-teacher school except for an occasional six-weeks' term or two in some one or other of the county normal schools or college preparatory academies. Most of them had studied such texts as David Page's or Emerson E.

White's *School Management* in preparation for the county superintendent's examination for the teacher's license. Few, if any, had taken any specific training for teaching any one or more of the so-called common branches. All of them knew these common branches reasonably well, some of them, very well.

My teachers were, for the most part, personable individuals, about the most attractive young or early middle-aged people in the community. Some of them—the Luken girls, Frank Gillespie, and Allen Hillegas were very charming people. A third of them were married and had children of their own. All of them were "chuck full" of good intentions and the spirit of service. I cherish the memory of every one of them. I deeply revere the memory of four of them, namely: Frank Gillespie, for his charming manners, his affability, his bubbling good humor, and, above all else, for his never-failing patience in teaching me to read; Miss Janet Luken, for her brilliancy of mind, and for the perpetual challenge she gave me, every day and every hour, to "beat today your own best record of yesterday"; Mr. Richard Brandt, for continually contesting with my big brother for the "privilege" of carrying me piggy-back over the snow drifts in the winter time; and Mr. Allen Hillegas for definitely encouraging me to prepare for teaching and helping me to plan intelligently to that end. I remember each one of my teachers as a friend and would enjoy his or her companionship today if living, but, alas, they are all dead.

Free textbooks were not provided in Pennsylvania until the year when I began to teach—in the fall of 1891. My father's problem in providing books for all of his children, when as many as seven or eight of them were in school at one time, was not an easy one to solve. Books were not cheap; they cost real money, and had to be paid for in cash. When a new book was bought, it was with the definite expectation that it would serve, in turn, a half dozen of us children, sometimes two or three of them concurrently, and that it would never be outmoded before it was completely worn out. This policy in vogue also in other families made it almost impossible ever to get a change of texts. Our family's textbooks, which were at any given time in acceptable condition, were usually in short supply. I well remember how, on one occasion, I solved the problem "all on my own." When I was fourteen years of age, I had the *grain* wagon accident referred to in a previous section. It occurred early in August. I was, for some months thereafter, unable to perform any useful farm work. This made it possible and desirable, for the first time in years, for me to enter school at the opening of the term in middle October.

The teacher, a very charming young fellow, eighteen years of age, from over the mountain, came to the school on horseback the first day of the term an hour before the time of opening and saw me limping up to the porch with my left arm and hand in a sling and with a crutch under my right armpit and held in my right hand. He gave me a friendly salutation, dismounted, threw the reins of his horse over the hitching post, unlocked the door, invited me in, asked my name, and invited me to a seat near his desk. Then our conversation began. He said his father knew Squire Suhrie, my father. He said he was counting on the Squire and me to help him. He said he had taught only one term near his home and that he desired to continue to live at home and to ride horseback to school daily. Then he told me he wanted to find some bright young fellow, twelve or above, who could sweep the school room every afternoon, dust it early the next morning, and, on cold days, have a roaring fire in the stove by eight-thirty in the morning; also to shovel the snow off the porch and walks when necessary. He asked if I had any such person in mind. Without any hesitation or a moment's delay I replied with a question: "How would I do?"

"Well," said he, "you seem to be, at least for the present,

a bit out of commission. I just don't see how you could hold a broom and swing it comfortably."

"Let me show you!" said I.

Casting aside my crutch, which I no longer needed except on the long walk to and from home, I stood firmly on my sound leg, the left one, placed the knob or end of the broom handle under my left armpit, and, with the right hand firmly grasping the broom handle, swept a square yard of floor space before his popping eyes. The demonstration seemed convincing, but he delayed the decision to inquire:

"How could you split kindling and carry in coal?"

"My brother John," said I, "will split the kindling and fill the coal-bin for me every week."

The young teacher relaxed and made a complete surrender, and was I happy! The pay was to be five cents a day, one dollar a month for five months. I had never before in my life seen so much money in prospect. I could have shouted for joy. Then he examined the textbooks I had brought. Some of them were remnants. I remember that the arithmetic had lost something more than its "Aliquot Parts," that the last page, still intact, was headed "Partial Payments." That topic seemed to me to be a very important one for if I were to buy any new books, it would surely have to be on the basis of partial payments, that is to say, on the installment plan.

The teacher concluded his inspection with the following statement: "Obviously, Ambrose, you'll need a complete text in arithmetic, for you have properly mastered the part you still have and will now want to work on the part that is missing. I have a text in arithmetic, almost new, which I can let you have on loan or, if you prefer, you can pay for it by one month's service in sweeping, dusting, and making the morning fires." I told him I preferred the latter arrangement. He gave me the book at once.

Then I told him that I was in need of a geography, that I had completely outgrown, long ago, my primary geography text, and that the aged copy of the advanced geography which had served all my older brothers and sisters had, like the one-horse shay, completely collapsed while in use by my next older brother the previous year. The teacher, growing more generous every minute as he observed my joy in the prospect of having an arithmetic all my own, promptly decided to provide me, on the same terms as on the arithmetic, a geography that was almost new and that, by its appearance, must have cost him at least $2.50.

This meant that for two months of faithful performance those two virtually new books would become my very own. The conference ended amicably, and when I went home that afternoon I could have shouted for pure joy. Before I closed my eyes that night, I had read that geography book through from cover to cover. I did not find the arithmetic such good reading. So I decided to master its contents "on the installment plan."

When two months had passed I held the unencumbered title to both books. They had been provided for me on faith and I had redeemed my obligation; better still, the teacher had, on many occasions, commended me for "the completely satisfactory character" of my service. When three more months had passed and my beloved teacher had said good-by to us and had gone on his way back over the hills to be heard from no more except in an occasional letter to me, I had three silver dollars piled one upon another in the corner of a bureau drawer. This round tower reminded me of the Leaning Tower of Pisa and seemed almost as tall. Each one of these dollars played an important part in helping me to prepare myself to take his place as teacher of that school three years later.

Good discipline was considered, in my childhood days, the earmark of a good school; quiet and order were rigidly enforced, at any and all costs, in our school. The teacher got attention by tapping a desk bell or sounding a gavel. Response was expected to be instantaneous and complete, and it generally was. Dismissals and movements to and from class in the front of the room were quiet and orderly. The call of the school bell in the morning, after the noon intermission, and after each mid-session recess was instantly obeyed. The most hotly contested town ball game could end very suddenly without the batter's even attempting to strike the ball that had started on its way but had not actually arrived before the first "tinkle, tinkle, tinkle" of the school bell was heard. Dismissals for recess, for noon intermission, and for the close of the day were also on time. All of the twenty-to-thirty-class periods came in quick succession and on time.

As I think back upon my experience of those days, three things stand out in sharp contrast between classwork at school and homework on the farm. First, schoolwork always began on some artificial time signal and was rarely finished when the ending came suddenly by bell tap or otherwise. At home on the farm, one project followed another without reference to the clock; and, unless for a very good reason, a project once begun was not abandoned until completed. Even when the dinner bell rang, the plowman drove to the end of the row nearest to the barn, unhitched his horse and stabled him and fed him before getting ready for dinner. Second, at school we were reproved, and sometimes punished, for helping each other with our lessons; at home we were commended, and sometimes publicly rewarded, for voluntarily helping one another on any project. Third, at school the teacher's approval was considered sufficient without the approval of our school fellows; at home we sought for and felt we needed the approval of the whole family in all matters of consequence affecting the happiness of all.

"There shall be no cruel or unjust punishment," says our United States Constitution. Most of our teachers conscientiously obeyed this precept. Seldom was there any corporal punishment; and, generally speaking, no pupil was punished unless and until, on private examination, he had confessed his guilt. There were exceptions. The only time I was given a whipping it was done in direct violation of this principle. It happened in this way: A group of the larger boys, with their baseball bats, went up into a neighbor's meadow pasture to have some sport "battering into smithereens" some dried cakes of cow manure. As they swept down over the green grass, a few small boys unwittingly became their camp followers. I was one of these. One cake of manure landed in the sap pail attached to a sugar maple tree. The owner's hired hand was near enough to see what had happened and to note that I was nearer than anyone else to the scene of action. He so reported to the teacher, my Uncle Joe. In doing so he must have made it appear that I was loaded with "guilt by association."

When the school session was called, Uncle Joe invited me to come out of my seat and stand before the whole body of students. I did so, not knowing what for. Without a word of explanation he laid on the old hickory. I "hollered" as if I were really being hurt. That was my most effective technique for gaining mercy. The punishment was not severe. I think the teacher must have realized that there was some doubt about my guilt, for he had never before punished me corporally for any offense whatsoever. When the punishment was over he quickly shifted gear and was more friendly to me than usual, showing that he was at least willing to be forgiven if he had punished me unjustly or too severely. I didn't report the incident at home; for, though Father was a "just judge," within the domestic circle and in the community at large, he *never* criticized the verdict of that judge (the teacher) who presided over the much more important jurisdiction; namely, the community school.

From a book entitled *The History of the Rod* which I found on the shelves at the University of Pennsylvania li-

brary when I was a graduate fellow there more than forty-
five years ago, I gained the impression that ordinarily punishments in the schools of our colonial days were often both
capricious and unjust and that corporal punishments were
more often than not brutally severe. And from other and
more recent publications I have gained the impression that
even in our own public schools prior to 1880, corporal punishment was an almost daily affair and often very rigorous.
In my day, which of course was after 1880, I saw few whip-
pings; none of them were really extreme. It is true that one
of our men teachers did inform us on the opening day of the
term that he was well stocked up with properly seasoned
hickory sticks ready for use without a moment's notice and
that he would not hesitate to use them "on the slightest prov-
ocation." One slender little lady teacher, it would seem just
to be contrary, informed us on the opening day that she had
no hickory sticks, that she didn't intend to get any, and that
she was sure none were needed in our school because she
was convinced we all wanted to do right. Then she added,
for good measure, "You all know that I want to be the
friend of every one of you." And she kept faith with her
word. She won our confidence and our love from the start,
and she had our united and loyal support to the end of her
term.

Our teachers differed greatly in their notion of what the
younger students should do during periods when they were
not in class. Some seemed to think the best thing a second- or
third- or fourth-reader pupil might do in the period before
he was able to enter upon such content studies as history and
geography would be to listen to the upper classes reciting.
It would, so these teachers said, help the lower class children
to learn to study; it would improve their vocabularies; and
it would give them better standards of performance generally. Other teachers insisted that any student not in class
should "tend to his own knittin'." They held that going

to school was for "learnin'" and not for "listenin'" and "thinkin'."

The story is told of a teacher of that day who, while engaged with a class in the front of the room and "teaching away with a vengeance," suddenly looked up and saw, down there in the middle of the classroom, a ten-year-old boy, sitting on his belt line and slipping down toward his collar button, his knee up on the desk and his eyes sweeping the wide horizons 'way beyond the classroom, dreaming great dreams, getting ready to discover the law of Einstein before Einstein should get around to it. It troubled her weary soul to see anyone looking so supremely happy and contented in her classroom. So she broke in upon his peace with: "Johnny, what are you doing?"

He couldn't just remember. He had been caught off guard, taken short as it were. So he blurted out the best answer he could think of: "I guess, Mam, I was just a thinkin'."

Then she gave him not a twelve-pound look, but a thirteen-ton look and snapped back: "Well, Johnny, I'd have you understand that this is a school and I'd have you know, too, that *a school is a place to learn but not to think.*"

On one occasion, we did get into an open conflict with our teacher over the matter of a Christmas present for each "scholar." Almost all our teachers announced, well in advance, that they would distribute some sticks of candy to each pupil on the Friday before Christmas. However, one of them, who was a married man with heavy family obligations, made it known, well in advance, that he would not be bound by this well-established custom. So the older students agreed among themselves that, on a certain Friday in middle December after the four o'clock dismissal, the group acting in concert would lock the door and close and bar the shutters of the six windows and do it "all in the twinkling of an eye."

The plan was carried out without a flaw, and it did help the teacher to change his mind. At first, the surprise threw his temper out of gear and he said a few things which he must have regretted afterwards, but he did surrender before there were any casualties. No teacher ever tried again to change the custom although some students claimed, that, by actual count, the number of sticks of candy decreased from year to year theraefter and that the quality of the candy deteriorated.

There is one episode of my boyhood school days that I am not particularly proud of, but, since it is a part of the authentic record and may not be omitted except at the expense of completeness, it is here recorded with some colorful details. It occurred on a cold and snowy Friday afternoon in middle January. Our schoolroom had been, since the Christmas holidays, badly in need of its mid-term scrubbing and general cleanup. The matter, it seemed, just could not be longer postponed; and so, in spite of the inclemency of the weather, all of us, teacher and students, immediately after the noon intermission went to our several posts of duty after first carrying all books, maps, and charts across the road to Grandmother Suhrie's storeroom and after committing the younger children to her care and protection for the afternoon. The regular assignments were as follows: the big boys were to be our "hewers of wood and drawers of water." It was their duty to keep the schoolroom well heated, to bail out plenty of water from a hole we had made in the ice covering on the lower end of the skating pond near the "crick," and to deliver it as needed. The big girls were to wipe the cobwebs from the ceiling, wash down the wood-paneled walls, scrub the floor, sand off all ink stains from the schooldesks, scour the seats, and give the interior of the room a general cleanup. The younger boys were to pulverize rock sand and prepare a kind of cleanser from it for use in scouring the desks and floor. The younger girls were to keep the water drenchings floating toward (and through) the door and then, to chase them off the porch before they should freeze.

Out at the woodshed I was pulverizing rock sand. Sam McVicker, a bosom friend of mine and two years older than I, came upon the scene and, out of the clear blue, made an ugly remark about my little red-headed girl friend. I hauled off and knocked him sprawling on the floor. He got just what he had asked for and so did not too much resent it. He knew instinctively that mine was an act of chivalry. Just then two of the larger boys came along on their way to the pond. Each one volunteered at once to be a sponsor, one for Sam and one for me. They said we ought to go out on the further ice pond behind the bushes where the teacher could not see us and "have it out," and settle the question once and for all as to which one of us henceforth should be considered "the better man." I thought I was and Sam knew he was; so we went. The big fellows were not really interested in the outcome of the contest, but they did want to see a lively spirited cockfight. In just a little while the cockpit on the ice pond, like a magnet, drew all the big boys. They left their pails over at the hole in the ice and found their way to the more secluded place behind the thick clump of tall bushes. Some of the little boys joined them. As soon as the water supply ran low, one of the big girls went over to the pond to summon the boys to supply the need. She located their water pails and reported to the teacher that "they must have gone off on a fox hunt or something." Then several of the big girls took over the matter of supplying water for the scrubbing and cleanup. The little boys who had not found the cockpit provided a never-ending supply of finely pulverized scouring sand.

In the meantime there was an uninterrupted performance at the ringside. My big brother was absent from school that day helping Father with the hauling of the lumber logs to the sawmill; my next older brother was down with a severe cold. No one of the big boys seemed to understand the "perilous times" that had befallen me. Sam pounded away with his hard fists on my cheek bones, nose, forehead, and chin. He had completely softened up my face before the ringing of the dismissal bell that scattered the boys from the cockpit without a decision. Everyone knew the score long before I was ready to "throw in the sponge." The big boys didn't want to meet the teacher, and so they quickly scattered out over the mountain trails in all directions for their homes. I had a splitting headache long before the adjournment of the fight. I had pounded away on Sam's breastplate while he had literally destroyed the contour of my face. A neighbor boy "whence all but him had fled" accompanied me to my home where I fell bleeding at the door. My mother helped me in and put me to bed.

Father was late in coming home that evening and spent the next day, from before daylight until after dark, on his logging enterprise. At the breakfast table on Sunday morning, he missed me and inquired where I was. Mother told him I was in bed and "not very well." She was right. I wasn't. Father came up to see me and, after making his own observations, decided that, though I did present a somewhat unusual appearance with shining bumps all over my face, I was well enough to go to church with the family. I did go but in a spirit of deep humiliation. Everybody stared at me as if I were the white elephant at the circus. After church I went home. I went to bed again and stayed until Wednesday morning.

It was zero weather on Monday and Tuesday and small children did not venture out. When Wednesday morning came, I was anxious to see Sam. I liked him and I knew he liked me. I didn't want the cockfight to cancel our friendship and I knew he didn't either. So within two minutes after we arrived at school Sam and I were sitting in the same double-seated desk near the stove with his left knee over my right knee and my right arm over his shoulder, "thick as peas in a pod." We didn't explore each other's wounds nor even refer to the battle of a few days before or to its outcome. Neither one was "the better man"; we were buddies, and buddies never care too much about championship records.

The incident was soon forgotten but not by me; the surgical attention which I should have had immediately after I left the fight was long delayed; and, when it came, it was on the installment plan. Over a period of thirty years thereafter, I was still going for expensive surgical relief by specialists of distinction in three different American cities. The incident was important to me long after my little red-headed sweetheart had married a handsomer man and long after the promoters of an afternoon of spirited entertainment had scattered to the ends of the continent.

The county superintendent of schools in those days was an important factor in the success of the school. He had little authority conferred upon him by law; but, if he was "a man of parts," that is, a man of real personal worth, he would be sure to exert considerable influence upon board members, patrons, teachers, and pupils. He was elected for a term of three years by a convention of the school board members of the sixty-three boroughs and townships of the county. He aimed to (and was expected to) make one visit each year to each of the two hundred and sixty classrooms in the county. Since the term, in some districts, was only five months, it was necessary for him to use the fall season in visiting about three classrooms each day in the remote mountainous and rural sections of the county. Then, during the severe winter weather, he usually visited four or five classrooms per day, chiefly in boroughs. He traveled in a one-horse buggy or sleigh at his own expense. Often he was the guest of teachers, patrons, or board members and frequently attended and addressed community meetings of school patrons in the evenings.

We had two different county superintendents of schools in

my time. The first one was an old man, older than his years. He wore a severe and unhappy countenance. One of our boys, who lacked reverence, said of him: "Looks as if his dyspepsia has finally gotten north of his neck. Every time he opens his mouth he says something that is sure to give you the blues. I wish he would quit comin'." That is about the way we all felt.

I well remember that one cold, damp, disagreeable morning in December when our stove in the center of the room was giving off much smoke but little or no heat, he appeared upon the scene. We all were awed (or was it scared) into silence. I was nearest to him and, therefore, least at ease. He put his cold, clammy hand on my fevered brow and said, in that nasal, or shall I say sepulchral, tone of his: "My boy, these are the happiest days of your life." I didn't believe it, for I had burned a good deal of Standard kerosene the previous night on a problem in cube root and I had gotten everything right except the answer. His remark was ill-timed, to say the least. In due time he did "quit comin'."

His successor was a very bright looking, kindly man, under forty years of ago, and in the very prime of life. He always made a cheery address full of inspiration and encouragement. We always anticipated his coming with much delight and never failed to regret his leaving. Always, when he wrote a letter to the teacher, he sent his greetings to us; and the evidence was convincing that he actually remembered us and the woodland setting of our school. After he had heard of my accident and had learned that I desired to become a teacher, he always had a special word of encouragement for me. Some years later, he gave me my first license to teach and I used to remark that it was a "pure gift." Between the lines of this document, if not in them, were written "faith" and "hope," and doubtless he showed more "charity" for my shortcomings than I was at the time aware of or able fully to appreciate.

In the early days of my teaching he gave me counsel of infinite value. He followed my career with interest always and was my friend to the time of his death at ninety-five, some ten years ago. He always rejoiced with me over every success and grieved over my sorrows and misfortunes. This J. M. Berkey, later in life the beloved associate school superintendent of the city of Pittsburgh, was a good, great man who will live forever in the inner chambers of my heart. On his retirement, I journeyed from New York to Pittsburgh to participate in the public tribute which the school officers and the special workers in his own department had arranged. I brought him many special gifts from the men of the mountains whom he had, "in the long ago," befriended. I personally presented a special red-letter edition of the New Testament with the following inscription:

Mr. J. M. Berkey, Educator of Many and Friend to All, To you who have been my best boyhood counselor and my steadfast friend through all the years since then, this old, old Book is presented as a token of gratitude and affection on your retirement from office after fifty years of distinguished service in the public schools of the Commonwealth of Pennsylvania.

You have fought a good fight to establish and to maintain the integrity of the public profession of teaching; you have kept faith with the children of your time; and to multitudes of adults of every race and nationality you have graciously ministered in the spirit of the Great Teacher.

May the sunset time of your well-spent life be full of contentment and peace. Affectionately, Ambrose L. Suhrie.

The little isolated Suhrie school of three score and ten years ago had a life and a spirit peculiarly its very own. It cannot, therefore, be passed up as just another forgotten incident in the great panorama of American pioneer struggles to create a school system for all the children of all the people. Its rusty old school bell rang out its requiem a score of years ago, but this school is not dead. It lives in the minds and hearts of all those to whom it ministered in the now dimming shadows of the long ago. It is like Daniel Webster's: "Massachusetts, there she stands!" But where?

This little school, recently converted into a two-story frame dwelling house, stands about three hundred yards north of the Pennsylvania Turnpike at a point one and a half miles west of New Baltimore and marks a place where the grass-roots of American democracy sank deep into the everlasting hills in the last quarter of the nineteenth century. No San Jacinto monument, "two feet taller than the Washington monument," has been erected there; but, if I should ever get to be as rich in money as that place is rich in memories, I'll build a tower three feet taller than the Washington obelisk in the National Capital to mark the place where I was privileged to attend school, where I began the ministry of teaching in the long ago, and where I first made a full and complete dedication of every talent God had given me to the education of the children and youth of America.

What Was Taught and Why and How

The curriculum (kerr-i-ku'-lem, as Uncle Frank used to call it) was primarily a figment of the imagination. It didn't actually exist, certainly not on paper until about the time I began to teach. The county superintendent of schools then issued a "course of study" in pamphlet form, listing topics in the several school subjects, suggesting sequence of treatment, and gradation of difficulty.

In my day, the textbook adopted by the school board constituted, for all practical purposes, the school's program of study. Other books, while not positively *verboten*, were not actually available. There was no library, and there were no supplementary reference books. It was years later that some bright boy first made the distinction clear between *basic* and *supplementary* reading material. Said he: "In the mornin', we can only read *readin'*; but in the afternoon we are allowed to read *real books*." No university professor had yet discovered that teaching children to read by the ABC method is the least effective of all possible ways of helping them to acquire either speed or comprehension in reading. The very first exercise which I heard the teacher call for on my first day in school was, "Now the ABC class!" On any number of occasions during the same day, and every other day for weeks, the ABC class was called to the chart.

I am perfectly sure that my teacher did not know the meaning of "reading readiness," the difference between "intrinsic" and "extrinsic" interest, or the relation of interest to effort. So, "day after day in every way," the exercise grew duller and duller. Weeks after I might have been reading, I was still repeating "A" after the teacher had said "A"; "B" after the teacher had said "B"; until I actually hated to hear him call "Chart class next!" By the end of five months in school, I had covered the first reader once by stumbling through it a word at a time.

There were no primers or pre-primers in those days. At the end of her first year in school a generation later, my daughter had read, actually read and enjoyed, at least one hundred books, some of them at the fourth-grade level. At the time of her first year in school I was a young university professor and knew all the basic and all the supplementary readers on the market. I had the assistance of a librarian, trained in children's literature, in selecting books for the child and could supply—and did supply—her any good good for which she was ready. I think the difference between my accomplishment in reading at the end of the first year, and her accomplishment at a corresponding point in her first year, was not primarily a matter of the superiority of her I. Q. over mine, but rather a matter of the superiority of the subject matter she had to read, of the motivation she had been given, and of the methods used in teaching her to read. My teachers understood, I suppose, about as well as teachers do nowadays, that reading is a fundamental skill, basic to achievement in any and every subject in the curriculum. Notwithstanding the monotonous word-by-word, distinctly rote character of my reading in the lower reading classes, by the time I entered the sixth-reader class, I was considered a good oral reader.

The reading texts we used were those of the Swinton Series, and they had a wealth of good material in them. I think no one realized how slow my silent reading was or knew that the limitation of available reading material and consequent lack of practice was, in my case, the principal cause. We never used the word "grade." The reading class in which one was enrolled was considered as indicating the degree of his advancement in school generally. When one reached the sixth-reader class, he was as high as he could go in that or any other subject; and all subsequent attendance in the elementary school simply meant repetition and review of material already gone over.

There was much good literature, including both prose and poetry, in each of our readers above the second one in the series, and I learned much of this by heart, that is to say, primarily from choice rather than by assignment or requirement. All reading in the class period was oral. Sometimes a half dozen or more students read, in turn, the same passage from the same selection in an effort primarily to improve on the oral interpretation of thought and emotion. Much emphasis was placed upon enunciation, pronunciation, inflection, and accent. I "learned by heart" and, at the Friday afternoon programs, presented many a fifteen-minute passage from some one of the orations of Daniel Webster, or some other well-known orator and patriot, and likewise many short poems by one or the other of our New England writers of that day, as well as passages from Shakespeare or from the Proverbs of Solomon.

There has been in recent years, a good deal of discussion as to whether the moral of a story should be made obvious and be specifically dwelt upon; that is, explained. In my school

days it was taken for granted that the chief reason for including a particular story or literary selection was that it might
be used effectively to teach a moral lesson. In many of the
selections, the moral of the story was explicitly pointed out
at its conclusion and was made so obvious that there could be
no doubt of its intent.

A good example comes to my mind. It was a third reader
selection. It showed a boy sitting on the top of a high rail
fence at the top of a hill commanding a view of a country road
for a considerable distance each way. Down over the hill, at
some distance below the road, was a man with a sack in one
hand and a spade in the other. It was obvious from the look of
guilt on his countenance that he was about to steal a bagful
of potatoes, and that he had placed his boy on the "watch
tower" to give him notice if the owner should come in sight.
The following conversation took place:

Father to his son on the hill:

"Son, is anyone coming down the road?"

"No, father."

"Is anyone coming up the road?"

"No, father."

At this point just as the father was about to put his spade
into the ground to get some potatoes, the son took up the
dialogue again; "But Father, there is one place which you did
not bid me look."

"Where is that, my son?"

"Up in heaven, where God is."

The next picture showed the father coming up the hill with
an empty potato sack in one hand and the spade in the other.
It was pointed out in the text that the son wanted his father
to listen to the voice of conscience and that the father had
finally done so. That may not be good modern pedagogy; but
I must confess the story and the pictures made a powerful
impression on my mind. I suppose that if I were getting my
moral training today, as many children do, from the "fun-

nies," the boy on the fence would be armed with a pistol to shoot the owner of the potato patch for coming down the road at the wrong time.

Spelling was taught more as a "mental discipline" than as a practical subject. The specific habits we develop in oral spelling (which are voco-motor habits) have little relation to the specific habits we develop when we write or type the same words. These habits are hand-motor habits. The emphasis now is on learning, while in the elementary school grades, to write or type a limited list of about four thousand words and not necessarily the difficult ones; certainly not unfamiliar ones. The emphasis in my day in the Suhrie school was upon oral spelling of the hard ones in all the spelling books.

By the time I reached the sixth-reader class I was sure to encounter in the periodic spelling bees that were held in the school or community, if not in the regular spelling class period, such words as *eleemosynary, caoutchouc, imperturbable,* or some other polysyllabic "knock-out" word which none of us ever had occasion to use in any of our school essays or examinations, or in our personal correspondence.

The then prevailing practice, in selecting spelling words, was as consistent with the then accepted reason for teaching spelling as the best of our current spelling lists is consistent with our professed purpose today in teaching spelling. In my school days spelling was taught "to develop the mind," and, of course, the harder the word the more development was thought to be possible. In our day the "faculty psychology theory" has been completely abandoned, and we teach spelling for the very practical purpose of preparing students to hand-write and type-write the words they will need in practicing the art of communication. It seems to be now generally believed that children do not spell as well as they used to. That prevailing notion is certainly in error if the test is on words commonly used in writing or typewriting. The spelling bees did provide excellent entertainment and much effective drill on the infinite number of ways in which a really hard word can be misspelled. The story is told of a twelve-year-old boy, who after having seen both sides spelled down three times on the same word, addressed the teacher with this encouraging announcement: "Teacher, teacher, I know another way to misspell that word." He had somehow gotten the notion that the quest was for a variety of spelling patterns rather than for the one correct spelling pattern for each word.

Grammar, too, was taught as a "mental discipline" rather than as a practical or applied subject. Diagraming and parsing may have served—nay they did serve—a very useful purpose in exhibiting the skeletal structure of difficult sentences and the correct forms of words; but, unless the teacher helps the student to apply the principles of sentence structure and proper word forms to the correction of the awkward sentences and incorrect word forms heard daily in the classroom and outside of it, pupils will get no assistance in avoiding constructions; such as: "He don't know nothing," or "Everyone of us have their own faults."

Writing was taught as an art often with more emphasis on flourishes and "ink slinging," than on legibility. The student copybook did, however, attempt to inculcate certain moral principles, ethical precepts, and standards, by providing for the copying of a whole page full of a maxim found in Ben Franklin's *Poor Richard's Almanac* or *Solomon's Book of Proverbs*.

The standard textbooks in arithmetic were Brooks' *New Mental Arithmetic* and his *New Written Arithmetic*. These texts were widely used in my day and had been ever since they were *new*, at least a quarter of a century earlier. Each was so written as to provide the necessary helps to the student of appropriate advancement so that he should not need to lean on the teacher for assistance. Problems were arranged in groups or by types and a type solution was given for the first one in each group or series. The teacher's function was to check not only for the correct answer, but for departures from the orderly and correct procedures indicated in the solution of examples given. To take a short cut to the correct answer or to depart from the "correct" procedure in arriving at it was frowned upon, if not positively *verboten*. Arithmetic, too, was taught as a "mental discipline" for "the training of the mathematical faculties of the mind."

I still recall vividly how I struggled to get the correct answer on the length of a fish when only the length of its head had been given in fractional relation to the length of the body and the length of the tail. It never occurred to any of us that we should examine the whole fish to see whether the location of the "line fence" between its head and its body or between its body and its tail could, in actual practice, be satisfactorily located. This is not surprising; for our assignment in the text was to "work" examples in the abstract; not to "solve" problems in the concrete, problems actually occurring in life and in our own experience and needing to be solved.

Two outstanding practical benefits I can now clearly recognize from the study of arithmetic on this ancient pattern in my boyhood days. First, in the solution of the "oral" or "mental" arithmetic problems, the "conditions of the problem" called for a clear statement; and, even though we were expected to state these conditions in the language of the author of the textbook, this did require us to concentrate on language which was exact and precise and to make our statement of conditions unequivocal. Such exercises must have had some definite value in teaching us "to say what you mean." In both "mental" and "written" arithmetic problems of great difficulty, there was always a challenge.

I can remember burning the "midnight Standard oil" on many occasions in the fixed determination to get the correct answer if it should take me to the "crack of dawn" to do so. I can remember a particular occasion, too, when a number of the big boys, young men, famous as fox hunters, were "crabbing" about a certain problem which the teacher had assigned. Its language was tricky, "foxy" they said. I knew I could get the answer, and so I confidently challenged the whole group of them. "Watch me nail the pelt of that old fox to the barn door before daylight and without the help of any of you!" And I did. A few such victories over the big boys gave me some much needed confidence and prepared me to compete with a whole class of sixty-five girls in the normal school some years later and to come off "more than conqueror" over all of them in a few notable contests.

Generally speaking, competition in our school was all but completely restricted to games of town ball and to Friday afternoon spelling bees and rarely added any zest to our ordinary classwork.

History was taught as a rote subject and students were encouraged, though not required, to commit the text to memory and to recite it *verbatim*. Most of the more industrious students did so. The text was written in fairly good English. It was at least grammatically correct, and committing it doubtless added something to our knowledge of words and tended to make habitual the use of correct sentence structures. The content of the book surely did not justify any such effort. If we had spent an equal amount of time in learning by heart an equal number of pages of great literature, prose or poetry, we should surely have had far greater rewards for our pains. There was never any disposition on the part of any of our teachers to question any of the statements in the history text. Our teacher probably did not know, nor did we know, that the same author had written two versions of the conflict over slavery in the United States, one for the public schools of the North and the other for the public school children of the South. The former was called *The Civil War*, the latter *The War Between the States*. These were published in two different editions of the same textbook which, except for the two chapters just referred to, were identical. That reminds me of the candidate for a certain teaching position who, when asked by the school committeeman, whether he believed the earth to be round or flat, replied that he was prepared to teach it either way as the board might wish. No wonder that the children of that generation were so prone to believe anything they found in print. "Why of course it is true," said one of them, "for I saw it in the county newspaper."

It was the custom of the times to emphasize "place" geography. This was a favorite subject of mine. I early learned to read maps and found them fascinating. While still enrolled in the primary geography class and in my fifth and sixth years at school, I learned to name and locate the capital and the largest city in each of the states and territories and the county seat and principal city in each of the sixty-seven counties of Pennsylvania. We were made to believe that it was important; and for me, it still seems important, for in the course of a lifetime I have had to travel in each one of our forty-eight states to fill lecture engagements and to each one of the counties in my native state on some educational mission. "Place geography" might have been a good deal over-emphasized in my boyhood days. I am sure that it is under-emphasized now, for example: I fell into conversation a few years ago up in the Great Lakes Region with a young high school graduate, about a farm which he had recently purchased near his home town. I asked him whether the soil was fertile. The answer was an emphatic "No." I said jokingly, "Why don't you come down to Tennessee where I live and where all the land is fertile?"

Said he in reply: "Do you know I have thought of that, either Tennessee or Montana. They are close together, aren't they?" I assured him that "except for a little alleyway about fifteen hundred miles wide" between them, these two states all but literally touch elbows.

Geography in the main was taught as a factual study. There was little place in the text or in class for the study of cause and effect or for the study of what is now called "Human Geography." The teacher assigned a certain number of pages on certain topics and then subsequently heard the student recite his lesson thereon.

Physiology, Hygiene, and the Effects of Narcotics by J. Norman Steele, who also wrote textbooks in history and other subjects, was a standard text in Pennsylvania public schools; its content was almost uniformly required in all American common schools in the latter part of the nineteenth century. The W.C.T.U. had secured legislation in most states making such a course mandatory. The text we had was ultra-technical, paid no attention to Herbert Spencer's question, "What knowledge is of most worth?", and required much memory work on "facts," some of which we now know cannot be scientifically demonstrated to be facts. The moral purpose of the course was commendable and the results, so far as I am able to determine, were probably altogether praiseworthy. I learned that alcohol is a narcotic, and I somehow got the notion clear that whiskey does not lose its alcoholic content by being served at a cocktail party. I learned, too, that tobacco is a narcotic; and I still think that when I was taught that "A cigarette is a coffin nail," I was not nearly so badly misled as millions of our school children are now by the widely advertised statement that "There isn't a cough in a carload."

No music, vocal or instrumental, was taught. I do not remember that even our patriotic songs were ever sung. There were no musical instruments on which an accompaniment could have been played even if anyone had desired to teach these songs.

Art, too, received no attention either in the form of classroom decoration or class instruction. Our school rooms were as bleak as Greenland's icy mountains and as bare as the old Bald Knob that overshadowed our valley at sunset. I well remember that at about the age of ten I had, as I think all normal youngsters at some time have, "the divine impulse to draw." I took down my ancient slate, got out my slate pencil, and, strictly on my own and without any instruction whatever, began to draw what, to me, seemed the most interesting thing in sight. Just then that thing suddenly came as close to me as a brother, confiscated my creation of great intricate worth, and sternly said, "You may stay in after school." I had not asked for the privilege but decided it would be wise to accept the teacher's invitation. What he did to me in the woodshed is really nobody's business but my own. Suffice is to say, however, that, as a result of this historic "conference," more physical than mental or spiritual in its import, I lost, for all time, the "divine impulse to draw."

Our program of studies, as will be seen, was a poverty-stricken one. It included only the purely traditional subjects. Each textbook was thorough in only the most restricted sense of the term. There was endless repetition and reiteration which, in due time, seemed to the best students to be "stale, flat, and unprofitable," and only the students of great industry and persistence were likely to continue long in a program that had so little of intrinsic interest in it. The result was that most students lost most, if not all, of their childhood curiosity to know about things by or before the age of puberty. Undoubtedly, the reason for the remarkable holding power of the public elementary and secondary school in recent years is to be found in the wide range of subject matter offered, the more universal appeal to interests that are intrinsic, and the improved teaching procedures which have accompanied the broadening of the education and professional training of our school teachers.

2

TWIG BENDING

THESE ARE elemental truths: first, that the wisdom one exercises in choosing his lifework and second, that the zeal with which he applies himself in preparing for it are among the most determining factors of his success and happiness in life. How important, then, that each person's choice of calling be wisely made and made early enough that he may be able adequately to prepare for achievement in it. And how largely his enjoyment of his daily occupation is dependent first, upon the adequacy of his preparation to meet its responsibilities and second, upon the completeness of his dedication to it as a service or ministry.

My life work was chosen at the early age of fourteen. My dedication to it from that day forward was complete and unqualified by any rival interest. For years, I was without any intelligent or effective guidance concerning the best steps to be taken in making real professional preparation for what I conceived to be my best field of service and satisfaction; namely, elementary school teaching.

All the county superintendents under whose jurisdiction I taught except the first one (Mr. Berkey, referred to in a previous section), were relatively uneducated persons, politically minded. Now-a-days we'd call them "educasters." As a result, I was without professional guidance or practical assistance during my early twenties.

The problem of financing my living expenses, to say nothing of advancing my scholastic and professional equipment for effective service in my chosen calling, was a baffling one. Salaries were paid for only two-thirds of the calendar year, at best. My first "token" salary was $20 per month for five months, or $100 per school year. The second year, I received a "merit differential" of $1, making $21 per month, or $105 for the school year. This was not even then a "subsistence" wage for an unmarried teacher, unless he were living with his parents, as I did during my first two years of teaching.

Crashing the Gates to a Professional Career

Ever since the day when Allen Hillegas gave me a contract to serve as his school janitor, I had it on my mind to become his successor as soon as I should become old enough to get a license to teach. I had only three years to go and knew that my "shortages" were many. I was well aware that my immediate problems were two in number, namely: I must lose no opportunity in term-time or during school-vacation periods in improving my scholarship in the subjects in which I should, in due time, have to pass a formal examination; and, second, I should have to gather up enough actual cash (say $35.00 or $40.00) to bear my expenses in a final review term in a summer normal school in nearby Berlin or Myersdale.

I went to work on these problems, concurrently. I was something more than diligent in the study of my class assignments. I sought perfection, and, to that end, I was willing to burn, and did burn, "the midnight oil." I concerned myself, not only with the preparation of assignments but sought to get hold of exercise books which should present more difficult problems than those in my textbooks, and, too, I borrowed from many teachers of my acquaintance, such reference books on teaching as David Page's *School Management* and E. E. White's *School Management*. I found these books fascinating, especially the latter. It gave me some insight into the art of motivation and the relation between interest and effort. I also read with pure delight William Hawley Smith's *Evolution of Dodd*, the story of the success of Amy Kelly, a country school teacher, in redeeming the neglected and consequently wayward son of a circuit-riding-itinerant preacher.

I had no real companions in study. It was clear that no one else, among the older students of my immediate acquaintance, was under the compelling drive of a serious life purpose. When John C. Calhoun was a seventeen-year-old boy at Yale University, he was urged by his school companions on a certain Saturday afternoon to go out with them to play ball. He declined the invitation on the grounds that he must study the Constitution of the United States.

Said one of them: "You will not need that to pass your examinations."

"I know that," said he, "but I will need it when I get to the United States Senate."

He was already under the spell of a compelling life-career motive. At the age of fourteen, I came powerfully under the urge of a very real motive for concentration in study and for continuing application.

Three years before I could present myself for examination by the county superintendent of schools at the age of seventeen, I acquired reliable estimates of what it would cost me to attend a six-weeks'-final-coaching term in the Myersdale Academy, fifteen miles away. I found the items of cost to be about as follows: Tuition, $6.00; board, room and laundry, $15.00; books and stationery, $4.00; miscellaneous, $2.00. Then I'd need a complete outfitting of better clothes than I had ever worn.

I already had in my "ginger-jar" savings account in the bureau drawer the $3.00 I had been paid in cash for janitorial services. Baby brother, Bernard, who had died three years before had been the fair-haired idol of all the railroad workers who thronged the valley. He had assembled in his "ginger-jar" savings account $20.50 from contributions made by the visitors who came to our door to buy eggs, garden produce, and the like. After his death, Father and Mother divided the legacy which Bernard had left, and I was allotted $2.00. During two summers I was able to pick and sell to the hucksters about sixty quarts of blueberries and blackberries at six cents a quart. These sales netted me $3.60. In Father's carpentry shop, there was a "shaving-horse" on which I carved out each winter, a dozen ax handles which I was able to sell at Uncle John's store for ten cents apiece. This added $2.40 to my "on hand." It was clear that I should have to secure a good ingathering of mountain ginseng root each summer to make up the additional funds needed. My next older brother, John, was deeply interested in my plans and volunteered to help me to make a "stake" from ginseng on rainy days when ordinary farm work had to be abandoned. So, in the course of two summers, the total proceeds of our find amounted to $30.00

When the time came for me to go off to the Myersdale Academy, fifteen miles away, on July 15, we had on hand a little over $40.00. It was necessary for me to get a new outfitting of clothing. I had a good, almost new, pressed, flat-top, narrow brimmed, Sunday straw hat and new Sunday shoes, but I needed a new suit, a change of linen, and underwear, stockings, necktie, and a celluloid "washable" collar. On Friday before the opening of the term in the Myersdale Academy in the summer of 1891, I went to town in the buggy, accompanied by my mother, to get myself outfitted. Uncle John was at the counter that morning. He had had his start in life as a schoolteacher. He remembered that I had had two serious accidents in recent years. Mother was his favorite sister; so he was in a mood to be generous and to give me "a break." He had a slightly shelf-worn suit priced $7.50, which fitted me perfectly. He said I might have it for $3.75, half price. Other items, he gave us at a bargain. The last item in the list was the necktie; Uncle John said it would be nice to have a change of neckties. That was enough to bring tears to Mother's eyes as she knew that I had never had one necktie before. We thanked him and gave each other a half-dozen nudges and glances of supreme satisfaction and delight as he rapped up our purchases in some back numbers of *The Somerset Democrat* in reserve on his shelves. I was interested to note when the package was complete that on the top side was printed in large letters "Johnstown Flood" and a full report on that well-known tragedy of two years before.

My purchases had amounted to a little more than $6.00. It was clear that if I could keep my expenses at the Myersdale Academy within the estimates previously made I should come back with a little surplus.

When Mother and I arrived at home the girls had a good dinner ready. At the table Mother and I kept from any discussion of our trip to town and its mission. While we were all seated in the family circle, a pouring rain fell and we rejoiced that our hay crop and our wheat were in the barn. After dinner Father and I went out to the porch to watch the torrents of rain fall on Uncle Cornelius' field full of wheat shocks. Our shocks were all under roof and we were happy. A glance at the swollen creek down in the valley told us that the good earth must be soaked and that fall plowing could begin ahead of schedule.

I broke the news to Father that I wanted to go to Myersdale for six weeks to get ready for the teachers' examination. He looked both surprised and worried, surprised that I had kept my secret so successfully and worried about the demands he thought my going would make on his small reserve of savings. His first response was, "But Ambrose, where do you think I will get the money?" I relieved his mind at once by telling him about my "cash on hand." It was obvious that he thought this could not be. I excused myself for a moment and then returned from a hasty errand to the ginger jar. We counted out the hard cash. It was over "thirty pieces of silver." I remembered the items of cost and assured him that this money was sufficient to cover it.

"But," said he, "you can't go to the summer normal school without a complete outfitting of new clothes."

I then told him what Mother and I had accomplished on our trip to town that morning. I stepped into the living room and brought out a package and opened it up in his presence. By that time Mother and brother John appeared on the scene and confirmed my statement that these items had all been paid for. Father just could not say 'no' to my request for a leave of absence from the farm for six weeks at the time when I was least needed. Early the next morning, I was off on a trek over the mountains to Myersdale, fifteen miles away. I carried my books and change of clothing in a package and wore most of my purchases of the day before on my back. When I arrived at the home of Dr. Meese, the principal of the summer normal school, it was 11:30 A.M. He invited me to stay for dinner. I told him that Mother, fearing that I might not find a boarding place before noon, had packed me a substantial lunch which I had in my bundle. He accompanied me to the home of Mrs. Kinsey, who agreed to take me and to give me board, room, and clean laundry once a week, for a period of six weeks, for the total sum of $15.00; that is, for $2.50 per week, providing that I was willing to room with her grandson, Joseph Blake. So I settled down, ate my lunch, and had a short nap. Before Joseph came in I made up my mind that I was going to like him. I soon learned that his father had died some years before, that his mother had worked hard to give her children a start in life, that he loved her and his sister dearly and was determined not to disappoint them. He was "in hot pursuit" of a license to teach. So we began to drill each other without delay and with much mutual profit on irregular verbs, hard words in spelling, and tricky problems in arithmetic.

On Sunday we went to church together. Dr. Meese called on us in the afternoon and assured us that he thought we would "make the grade" by August 28.

On Monday morning we went together to the principal's office, which was in the pastor's study of an abandoned Methodist church, down by the railroad, where the review session of six weeks was to be held. Each of us had the $6.00 in exact change to pay his tuition bill.

The school had three teachers, Dr. Meese, the Principal, a Mr. Bender, who later became a college president in Kansas, and a Miss Amy Roop, the daughter of a widely-known local pastor.

The summer program was geared to review and drill, in class during school hours and in informal groups outside of class during the late afternoon and evening. Joseph and I worked into the late hours of the night six days each week, also early in the morning hours, long before breakfast. All the teachers were superb drill masters during the six weeks of refresher courses, formal and informal! Or shall I say six weeks of unremitting toil? Grammar was my hardest subject. My Suhrie grandparents, who were fairly well educated in German, had for some unexplainable reason, chosen to learn their English from the Pennsylvania Dutch; and the curse for their sin had been visited on the first and second generations of their offspring. Dr. Meese soon advised me to get coaching lessons in grammar from a certain Mr. Adolph A. Strang, who had taught several terms and was in the review class to "brush up" for a certificate renewal examination. I acted on Dr. Meese's advice. Mr. Strang proved to be a most effective and faithful drillmaster. He gave me three solid hours each Saturday afternoon for six weeks at fifty cents a session, $3.00 total. I had the money in my budget to pay for this much-needed help.

The examination day came, Thursday, August 28. It was a day of strain for all of us. Mr. Berkey, the County Superintendent of Schools, was a very kindly and considerate man and quickly set us all at ease. All his questions in each of nine subjects were printed. The reading test was the only one administered orally. This test was in progress throughout the day and within the hearing of all who were taking the written examinations. Some of the inapropos answers which we could not help hearing afforded considerable amusement and some relief from the prevailing tension. One of these incidents is especially clear in my memory. After hearing the candidate read an assigned passage from some familiar English classic and after questioning him thereon, the examiner plied him with other questions, especially designed to reveal the range and scope of his "volunteer" reading in books and magazines that were not necessarily on the required list. He asked one tall, lanky mountaineer: "Have you ever read *Looking Backward?*" The candidate, for a moment, looked as worried as though he were being persecuted for his faith and then answered confidently: "No, but I think I could." He quite obviously did not know that *Looking Backward* by Edward Bellamy was a best seller and was listed in the reading course or that the superintendent was trying to ascertain whether he enjoyed reading books of this type. Some of the class were quite involuntarily giving much attention to the examination in reading, thinking they might get some clue of value when their several turns should come. All of them seemed to have heard the answer quoted above, and it surely afforded much merriment and relaxation.

All the examinations in reading, spelling, grammar, penmanship, geography, history, arithmetic, physiology, school management, and theory and practice of teaching had been completed by three o'clock P.M. The Superintendent of Schools and Dr. Meese retired to the latter's home where he was a guest to grade the examination papers. By three o'clock the next day they were through, and the little green "Teachers' certificates" for every candidate who had passed the test satisfactorily had been signed. By previous arrangement with Dr. Meese, I had waited under a shade tree on his lawn since the noon hour. My certificate, therefore, was the first to be delivered. Promptly at three o'clock, he came to the window of an upstairs room and called me by name in a tone that was packed with confidence and good cheer. As soon as he had my attention, and it wasn't hard to get it, he set afloat on the breeze my long-awaited certificate. I had believed, all through the waking hours of the night before, that I had done pretty well on the tests. As soon as the document reached me, I saw that it had the Superintendent's signature on it "at the southeast corner." That made it valid as a teacher's license. In the absence of his signature it would have served only as a report of the extent of the candidate's failure. I searched for the grade in each of the ten subjects. The scale of scores ranged from one to two, the former a perfect score, the latter a near-complete failure. My scores ranged from one to one and a half, with a median of one and an average of one and a fourth. I called back my thanks and a hearty good-by to Dr. Meese.

I had packed my bundle of books and clothing at the noon hour, and now I was off alone on a fifteen-mile trek for my home in Allegheny township. I wasn't tired; I was joyous and resilient; I had gotten over the first hurdle. About ten miles out on the trail, I sat on a log by the bubbling spring that started a new mountain stream and ate the evening lunch which Mrs. Kinsey had graciously prepared for me. Just after dark, I reached the east end of the Allegheny mountain tunnel. I stopped and shouted my joy into its deep caverns. The echoes seemed to be a bit too "spooky" for comfort. I hurried down the trail to the head of our valley. It was so dark I had to trust my memory of the location of the curves and culverts or lie down in the forest and wait until morning. Suddenly, I heard a voice calling in the valley. That was reassuring. When I reached the foot of the long incline in the mountain road and was only two miles up the valley from my home, a voice rang out in the dark. It was as clear as a silver bell: "Ambrose, has du das gemacht?" ("Did you make the grade, have you passed?")

It was the voice of Jacob Wambaugh, the father of seventeen children and the patriarch of the valley. He had passed our home down the valley hundreds of times in my boyhood days without even a salutation; now he suddenly "came alive." His own children had been a grave disappointment to him; so his interest had, at least for the moment, focused itself on the fortunes of "Squire Suhrie's son," as he had, in recent months, been calling me. I sat down with him in the dark on a rock by the side of the road, near his cabin home, and we talked at some length. It was clear that he earnestly desired to see me succeed in life. When we parted, he volunteered to speak to the two school directors whom he knew and to ask each one of them to give me appointment as a teacher. I hurried with dangerous haste down the valley to my home. I knew by heart the ups and downs and curves of the mountain road. I saw the light in the kitchen from afar and knew that Mother was waiting with supper for me. Father and the younger brothers and sisters had gone to bed, the older ones had not yet returned from the village. I sat down with my mother to tell her in detail of my successes. She was very happy. I told her of my plans for the morrow. I ate half of the apple pie she had baked especially for me, and then I retired without waiting for the folks to return from town.

Saturday morning! I had to be up early and off on a long and very important journey. I was at breakfast ahead of schedule when Father came in to give me his greetings. I showed him my teacher's certificate. He acted like a doubting Thomas. He raised the question: "Do you really think, Ambrose, that this certificate is valid?"

Even though I knew he was speaking in jest, it half annoyed me, and I replied a bit impiously, "Father, can't you read?

Can't you see that the Superintendent's name is signed to it?"

I quickly persuaded him to let me have the new buggy and the three-year-old bay mare I had "broken to harness" a few months before. I was doubtful of the wisdom of talking out my plans too much in detail with him. I was sure that he would have some doubts of the wisdom of my asking for assignment to the Suhrie school, and I was in doubt, to say the least, whether he would be enthusiastic about my applying in person to the President of the Board of School Directors, his ancient political enemy, Charlie Dorn, Chairman of the Republican Primary Committee of the township. So I merely said that I had assurance of the two local directors down in the valley (both Democrats) that they would vote to give me an appointment, and I told him that I wanted to call on each of the remaining four Republican members in person at their homes. This meant a hard day's drive on rough mountain roads. I told him that the board would meet to make the appointments by middle September, two weeks hence; so he gave his consent to my going, and I was off before sunrise for Mount Zion and the other end of Allegheny township.

Mr. Dorn, the President of the Board, was my first point of attack. He greeted me very pleasantly. He knew something about me. He asked me how well the superintendent knew me and how long. I gave him a full and explicit answer. Then he asked me if I liked Mr. Berkey, the Superintendent. My answer: "Very much. My father does too. When Mr. Berkey was running for office a few years ago, Father told all the Democratic members of the board in our end of the township, that he hoped they would vote for him even though he was a Republican. Father told them he didn't think that party politics should play any part in the choice of a school teacher, a school principal, or a school superintendent."

Mr. Dorn said with enthusiasm, "Good for your father!"

I was sure that my speech had been not only diplomatic

but effective. He then asked me about my age and, with a twinkle in his eye, how many years I had taught.

To the first question, I answered frankly: "Only seventeen." But I assured him, "I'll quickly outgrow my youth if you will give me a chance to teach."

To the second question, I simply said: "You seem to think it important that I should have some experience. I don't have any, and I will not have any next year either unless you men let me start teaching this fall."

Then he asked me whether I thought the patrons of the Suhrie school would be pleased if I were appointed to be the teacher in their school. I told him confidently that I *knew* they would, that all of them had said so to me personally and some of them many times during the past year. Then I thanked him for his courtesy, but did not ask for a commitment. He assured me he was glad that I had called on him and then drew a sketch of the roads that I should have to travel and gave the location of the homes of the other three board members I planned to call on. I visited all of them and was well received. I asked no one for a commitment either to vote me an appointment or to assign me to the Suhrie school. These requests I included in a carefully prepared letter which I sent to the secretary of the board with a copy to the chairman. In that letter I promised to be present when the board should meet so that they might interview me in person if they desired to do so.

When the day of the meeting came, they did call in a number of the applicants for interviews, but they did not call me. While the candidates waited quietly at the tavern the board completed appointments to all the thirteen schools in the township and gave me what I had asked for. Just before the board adjourned, all candidates were invited in for a parting word and a handshake. The president said that if we needed any equipment or repairs we should write to the secretary at once. I managed to be the last to leave the room, and, just before taking my departure, I asked the president if I might make a request. He granted me permission. I proceeded: "The Suhrie school has never been repainted since the fall it was built. If the board will supply the paint, I'll put it on in good shape before the opening of the term. It was so voted *vive voce.*

The secretary estimated that eight gallons of white paint would be sufficient. He supplied me four two-gallon cans of paint from the board's depository, and I carried it home with me in the buggy. The next day, Uncle John volunteered to donate enough additional paint that I might give the dark, smoked-up interior of the school two good coats. These I applied on the side walls before the opening of the term, and on the ceiling after the opening.

The whole community, parents, pupils and local board members applauded the transformation. It was very evident that the new school term scheduled to open on Columbus Day, 1891, a few days after the reconditioning of the dingy old school building, would open under the most favorable auspices. I was very happy and impatient for the day to come when I might begin my career as a teacher.

Half-Teacher in Rural School

Said President Frank Thomas, of Fresno, California, a bit facetiously, of course: "California has a teacher and a half for every rural school but unfortunately it often happens that the half teacher gets the school."

I am not sure that the Suhrie school in Allegheny Township, Somerset County, Pennsylvania, fared any better than that in the fall of 1891, when I was its teacher. And yet, I must confess that I honestly believe that with all my limitations—and they were many—I was probably as well prepared to give the service that was expected of me then as most beginning teachers of today are prepared to give the service that is expected of them now. My schooling was very limited. My education, in contrast to my schooling, was broader, more fundamental, and more distinctly practical. In book learning, I had no versatility. The range of my knowledge was limited; in class instruction I was didactic, formalistic, and "thorough" in only the most restricted sense. But *I was surcharged with good intentions*. I had drive, energy, zeal for service. I was determined to make a success of my career as a teacher. I was *dedicated* to the service of the childhood and youth of our valley and I had big dreams for the future.

The year 1891 was a great year in American history. That was the year in which the University of Chicago swung open its doors under the leadership of William Rainey Harper, who was a great "opener-up" of new vistas in American education. That was the year in which Leland Stanford Junior University at Palo Alto, California, swung its doors open under the leadership of the great David Starr Jordan, scholar and university builder par excellence. That was the year when the School of Pedagogy of New York University, now its School of Education, the largest professional school for teachers in the world today, opened its doors under the leadership of Dr. Albert Shaw, public school superintendent of vision and power. That was the year when Dr. Paul Hanus, educational trail blazer, left his eyrie in the Rocky Mountains and came down to the campus of Harvard University to experiment with courses in education for school superintendents, school supervisors, school principals, and school teachers, long before the University was willing to allow credit for such courses; and to lay the foundations for a graduate school of education long before that conversative seat of learning was aware of her need of such a professional school. And that was the year I began teaching, just three hundred ninety-nine years after Columbus discovered America and just two years before the great Columbian exposition on the Midway in Chicago.

Far be it from me to seek a place in the American Hall of fame alongside the great men whose names and achievements have just been listed. But is it not possible that any one of ten thousand little one-teacher rural schools scattered all over America might have that year made some unique contribution to the glory of the American birthright? Did not Woodrow Wilson, in one of the greatest of his orations at the dedication of the Greek Temple that encases the log-cabin birthplace of Abraham Lincoln down in Hodgenville, Kentucky, proclaim to all the world: "It is the genius of American democracy to look for her leadership in unexpected places and to find it there."

The great day of the opening had come, Columbus Day, 1891: I was up early and splitting kindling wood for the kitchen stove. I would make a cup of coffee and then be off early to school. Suddenly, I remembered that in the afternoon I'd be teaching a lesson on narcotics. I remembered, too, that the text said coffee is a narcotic. I took the kindling in and built the fire in the kitchen stove but told Mother not to make any coffee for me. She looked concerned: "Why, Ambrose, aren't you well?"

"Yes, fine," was the answer.

"Then why don't you want coffee?" she inquired.

"Because it's a narcotic," said I. "I'm going to teach my class this afternoon that coffee is a narcotic and that no one should use narcotics."

"Oh," said Mother, "then you're going to give up coffee because you're a school teacher."

"Exactly," said I. "I can't consistently advise my children against its use while I continue to use it." So coffee went off my menu and has remained off.

On that never-to-be-forgotten morning, there appeared

at the Suhrie school only thirteen "hillbilly" boys and girls ranging from the chart class (there were no grades in those ancient days) to the fourth-reader class. The older boys and girls were at home husking corn, flailing out buckwheat, making sausages and apple cider, and canning fruit.

Even the little school children noticed that:

The school was freshly painted, outside and inside.

The broken desks had been repaired.

The cast-iron coal pit in the heating stove that had, for years, been "spewing ashes on the floor" had been replaced.

The stovepipe had been cleaned of its elbow deposits of soot.

There were a few pictures on the wall, advertisements to be sure, but relieved of their business connotations and appropriately framed.

There was a magazine rack full of samples of the best current magazines.

The process of draining the swampy playground had been begun.

Cinder paths had been made to the coal bin, to the source of water supply, and to the places we now call "rest rooms."

The program of classes, recesses, and intermissions had been worked out in detail, and by nine o'clock the school was in full operation, every part of its mechanism functioning smoothly.

When the fall work on the farm had been completed, somewhat ahead of schedule this year and the big boys and girls entered, almost all of them on the same Monday morning before the middle of November, they rejoiced with me in the improved appearance of the place. I invited the big boys to help dig the deep drainage ditches that were necessary to "dry up" the space available for town ball and other group games. They helped me for an hour each morning before school opened to build the culverts at appropriate places over the ditches, to plant posts around the playground as notice to the farmers up both valleys not to park their saw logs on the school premises in the winter season to await the pleasure and convenience of the operator of the sawmill a quarter of a mile downstream. We also built a bulkhead at the curve of the Raystown Branch to direct its flood waters away from the school grounds. And, finally, on a Saturday morning, six stout farm boys came to the school grounds; and, "when nobody was looking," moved the school privies from their moorings at the center of the school lot to a less conspicuous place on the periphery thereof. Then, in the springtime, we planted in front of each entrance thereto a proper screening of trees and shrubs.

My elder brother, John, was the chief engineer directing these operations. He had obviously determined that I should succeed in my first teaching assignment, and he left nothing undone to help me make a good impression on the community and especially on the boys of his age who were older than I and whose enrollment in school was considered in the community as a distinct indication that they were accepting my leadership in matters academic.

There was nothing unusual in the program of the school or in its operation; but we did make an attempt, with the help of the older boys and girls, to interest the whole community in the development of civic pride not only in the outer appearance of their school but also in the appearance of their homes, their fences, their barns, and their gardens. To this end, we organized and conducted each week a Friday afternoon literary program and a Friday evening debating society to both of which patrons were invited to come and, on occasion, to participate.

Late in the fall the school had a week's vacation. While the older boys were out hunting for wild turkeys and deer, I attended the county teachers institute. This institute had its distinct uses in that day. It has now long since been discontinued. Sixty or seventy years ago it was the one standardizing and professionalizing agency among teachers of any given county. In our county of Somerset there were but one college graduate and only two normal school graduates among the staff of two hundred sixty public-school teachers. All the others were provisional certificate holders; they were, for the most part, eighth-grade graduates. Most of the county teaching staff had had less than three years of teaching experience.

On a cold and snowy day late in November, I walked twenty-seven miles to the county seat, Somerset, to spend a week at the county teachers institute. I had prepared myself to meet my financial obligations. On Saturday, the day before, I had taken my enrollment record book, about twenty inches long, sixteen inches wide, and an inch thick, to the secretary of the board, seven miles away, to get his approval on it and to get the treasurer's voucher for my first month's salary of $20. This voucher I was able to "cash in" at Uncle John's store three miles down the valley. I had traveled twenty miles to get my first month's salary.

In Somerset I found "board and lodging" at the home of one of Mother's girlhood friends. The rate was fifty cents per day. I stayed from Sunday evening to Friday afternoon —just five days. The charge was, therefore, $2.50. Early on Monday morning, I went to the best clothing store in town and bought a new suit for $6.50. Stripes were woven into the cloth; and these stripes seemed to run, as one teacher described them, from the northwest corner of my left shoulder to the southeast corner of my right hip. The edges of the coat were bound in black tape. When I donned this new suit and a new necktie I was a well-dressed man.

Just before noon I went on my way to the county courthouse to register for the teachers institute and to pay my enrollment fee of $3, which was my contribution to the honoraria and the traveling expenses of the distinguished lecturers who should appear before the institute and townspeople at each evening lecture hour.

My memory fails to recall any other single week in my whole life that was so full of true inspiration and genuine uplift. How profoundly impressive was the singing of the great hymns of the Christian Church under the leadership of a certain Dr. Leslie of Chicago, the Scripture readings by Dr. Nathan C. Schaffer, State Superintendent of Public Instruction, the prayers offered by Dr. Martin G. Brunbaugh, President of Juniata College, later school superintendent in Philadelphia and still later governor of Pennsylvania! The addresses were given by these gentlemen and the soul-awakening evening lectures by Dr. Russell H. Conwell, the great (Acres of Diamonds) Philadelphia preacher; Du Chaillu, the African explorer; Dr. A. A. Willits, the preacher-humorist of Louisville, Kentucky; and General John B. Gordon, soldier-statesman of Georgia. Mr. Berkey, our county superintendent of schools, was a genius in program building and was somehow able to command the best lyceum talent in America. The men he brought to us made the program of the whole week a never-to-be-forgotten feast of good things.

Dr. Conwell was scheduled to appear at 8:00 P.M. on Monday. His train was caught in a snowdrift near Rockwood; and his audience waited patiently, and with expectancy, until his arrival at ten o'clock. He came to the platform without supper. After a brief introduction, he began: "I am sorry to be late. I am grateful to all of you for awaiting my arrival. I wanted to meet this appointment, principally because I need the honorarium which it will bring me. I have ninety-three young men in college and theological seminary this year for whose expenses I am primarily responsible. Your patience has given you a share in this important enterprise."

Then he launched forth into his great message. He told us the story of Al Hafed who set out from his home to find treasure in foreign lands and returned, in old age, empty-handed to find that the young men he had left behind had discovered "acres of diamonds" in the immediate vicinity of the palace he had deserted. He held us all spellbound for an hour and three quarters with a message I can never forget.

The week sped on to its close. Each day our group of teachers was more closely bound together by the common bond of altruistic service. We were led to appreciate teaching as a privilege, and we were pleased to hear it frequently referred to by our speakers, most of whom were truly dedicated men, as a great "ministry." Every day we had a new sense of Christian fellowship as we sang together and prayed together and listened together to the great educator-evangelists who were our instructors and lecturers. When Friday noon came and Mr. Berkey had completed a farewell address, he asked us to sing together: "God Be With You Till We Meet Again." We did so with spirit; and when the gavel dropped on this great gathering, there wasn't a dry eye in the house.

The final hymn had been a devout prayer in which all had joined with the fervor of an old-time revival. The impact of the whole week's association with young men and women who shared with me, in some measure, a sense of dedication to the historic ministry of teaching as a life-calling, served to confirm me in my dedication and to stabilize my plans for the future. What rewarding memories I should always have of the wisdom I had gained from the great men whom we had heard at their best and on themes that were inspiring and challenging in the highest degree!

I was soon on my way afoot out on the Glade Pike to Rocksbury and White Horse on a twenty-two-mile journey to my home in the hills. The winter winds whistled through the telegraph wires by the roadside as I increased the tempo of my march over the countryside. Every moment was filled with reflection on the great messages I had listened to and on the personality, charm, and power of the great messengers I had heard. Throughout the year I passed on to my students the words of wisdom I had heard and did what I could to impress my children with the ideal of service as I had been impressed by this ideal.

I still think the county teachers institute, as conducted by Superintendent Berkey in my home county of Somerset, in my young manhood days, was a heaven-ordained institution. With better and more numerous educational institutions and advantages for the preparation and re-education of teachers in our day, we no longer need its service, but in its day there was no substitute for it.

Shortly after the Christmas holiday, Superintendent Berkey paid a visit to the Suhrie school. We had had an open winter. The ground was dry. The temperature ranged a little above zero. Many of the children were late to school that morning. Before presenting himself at the door of the school, our visitor made a full survey of the improvements that had been made on the school premises during the fall season. When he entered the door, he was obviously pleased. After "thawing himself out" in front of the roaring fire in the heating stove, he announced that he could stay for only an hour and that he would like to hear the first- and second-reader classes. He seemed pleased with the performance of these classes. Then I invited him to speak to the school. He responded with much praise for all of us on the improved appearance of the premises, on swamp drainage, on new cinder walks, and on the bright and attractive exterior and interior of the school building. When he found it necessary to end his all-too-short visit, we felt that we had had a distinct lift in morale and that our horizons had been widened.

What a godsend a kindly and inspiring school man can be if he has made of himself an arch encourager of teachers and of children! Mr. Berkey always aimed to be a ray of sunshine in every classroom he visited.

The five-months' school term moved on toward its close.

Winter months had come and gone. Most of the big boys and girls had taken up their spring work on the farm before the closing day. On March 28, I was on my way to enter the State Normal School at California, Pennsylvania, down on the Monongahela River, fifty miles upstream from Pittsburgh. I was warmly greeted by Dr. Noss, the principal, and by his gracious wife, who was a teacher in the school, and also by Dr. Meese of Myersdale, who had joined the staff but recently.

I had saved almost every dollar paid me during the last four months of my first term's teaching. Tuition at the normal school was free; board and room were $3.50 a week for fourteen weeks, a total of less than fifty dollars. Laundry was an extra. I was not financially embarrassed at any time during the term, for I had saved my money and always had a small reserve of funds.

The school was operating a two-year curriculum. My classification was in the third preparatory class. That meant that I had two promotions to secure before I could be regularly admitted to the normal school proper. Within two weeks I was moved up one step, and two weeks later I was moved up another step. This did not mean that my achievements had been outstanding. It probably meant that my first classification had been too low. After the second promotion, I had ten weeks in which to complete the first preparatory step. This I was able to do. At the end of the year, therefore, I was ready for, and was promoted to, the junior class in the state normal school as distinct from its preparatory department. On the basis of this promotion certificate, Superintendent Berkey gave me a one-year extension of my teacher's license of the previous year.

I returned home just when I was most needed for the wheat harvest. I lost no time in reapplying for the Suhrie school. I was assured by Mr. Dorn, the president, and Mr. Tipton, the secretary, that I should be unanimously re-elected for a second term, though to do so would be breaking a pretty well-established precedent.

The county superintendent had sprung a problem upon the board. He had given each of the thirteen teachers in our township a rating on the merit of his or her performance as a teacher during the previous year; and it so happened that I was the only one recommended for a merit differential in salary. The superintendent did not recommend a differential of any particular amount, but he evidently felt I should have at least a "token" increase in recognition of distinctive service. There was some resentment on the part of the other teachers, one of them my uncle, who had heard about it. When the board met, all teacher candidates were on hand. The secretary read the superintendent's letter to the board. The board was not much impressed with the desirability of introducing such a precedent-making innovation. After three hours of debate, it was found that the four Republican members of the board were opposed to it and that the two Democratic members were for it.

Finally the minority view became the majority view by the presentation of this argument: Said the Democrats: "This recommendation comes from the county superintendent of schools, a Republican, re-elected the last time by the votes of many Democrats who were unwilling to make a partisan issue of the election of the superintendent of all our teachers and all our children. We Democrats voted with you and for him. Now it would seem the least you can do is to vote to accept his recommendation."

The Republicans conceded the point in good spirit but insisted that one dollar per month differential was enough. It was so ordered and I got a raise from $100 to $105 per year, and was I happy!

My second year at the Suhrie school was less eventful than the first. The major reforms which the teacher's limited vision could conceive had been accomplished during the previous year. It remained only for me to improve my classroom teaching.

The debating society, which in reality was a community improvement society, was moved to New Baltimore, where we could count on more active participation and a larger audience of "gallery gods." Dr. Reidt, our family physician, took an active interest in this organization, and that helped mightily to give our public forum standing in the whole community.

The county teachers institute was, for me, the big professional event of the year as it had been in the previous year. Mr. Berkey had, as usual, planned the program with finesse. His speakers were of high caliber. Dr. Byron W. King's Scripture readings from the Psalms of David and the Proverbs of Solomon made us all wonder whether we had ever before heard the Scriptures read. His readings from Shakespeare made the Avon poet truly "come alive."

Dr. Henry Houck, Deputy State School Superintendent, was one of our instructors throughout the week. He was a unique type of man. Like Will Rogers, he could give everybody a good wholesome laugh while presenting some serious topic. For example: He wanted us to know that, professionally speaking, our academic qualifications were almost at the zero point and yet he did not want to discourage us; so he told us a story (with a moral) in his own inimitable Pennsylvania Dutch dialect to indicate that we were on the way up but had not yet arrived. Here is the story:

"Ven I vas coundy superintenden of schules in Lebanon Coundy, I vent oud von day wisitin schules in de coundry. A young girl came to me unt sait: 'Mr. Houck, my mudder vants you to come oud unt stay overnight mit us.'

"I said, 'I'll do id. Dat vill be cheaber dan going to a hotel. Ven de schule was oud I vent mit her. I helbed de boys to split de vood unt to tend to de sheeps unt den ve vent into de haus for subber. After de subber I vent oud into de kitchen unt helbed de missus to vash de dishes. Unt den ve all vent into de parlor unt I tole dem everyting I knew. Unt den ve retired early.'

"De nexd mornin' at de breakfas table de mudder sait: 'Mr. Houck, Chennie made dat subber lasd nide unt she made dat gravy.' 'No,' sait I, 'Chennie is chest a leedle girl; she couldn'd make dat subber.' 'Yes,' sait her mudder, 'Chennie made dat gravy. She is comin to de coundy courthaus in Chune to take de teacher's examination unt, Mr. Houck, you vant to remember Chennie. Sure enough, ven I god to de coundy courd haus, dere vas Chennie big as lif, ready to take de examination. De first examination I gave vas in spellin. Unt vud you believe id; ev she hadn' wridden de vord 'spellin' at de beginnin', she vould have missed only twenty-five vords, but ven she rode dat vord she got twenty-six oud of de twenty-five wrong. No, dat paber vas nod so very gud. I looked at it unt sait to myself: 'Does she pass or does she fail in spellin?' Den I looked at id again unt I could see dat she meant vell, but I vasn't sure she vould pass till, all at vonce, I remembered de gray. Oh de gravy! Unt she passed in spellin."

"De nexd examination vas in aridmetic unt, vould you believe id, she god everyting ride except de answer; unt I could see dat she meant vell unt dat she knew de rule, too, but, really, dat paber vas not so very gud. I looked ad id again unt I asked myself very seriously, 'Does she pass or does she not pass?' I vas not sure til suddenly I remembered de gravy. Oh de gravy! Unt she passed in aridmetic."

He rang the changes on all the other subjects and "Chennie" finally passed and got her teacher's certificate—a license to teach.

He was conveying to us the lesson that county superintendents are human and subject to political pressure just as other public officials are and that, maybe, many of us were teachers because our mothers or our sisters or our friends had reached the superintendent on a gravy boat.

The second institute I attended was less inspirational than the first one had been, but it opened up for me many more avenues to professional advancement. The first one defined the objectives of the journey and inspired the members to go; the second, gave us a more definite charting of the course.

Superintendent Berkey organized the county into a dozen local teachers institute districts, set up a schedule of dates and meeting places for each district, and supplied a list of twenty or thirty topics suitable for discussion. These included topics of public concern to laymen and topics of professional interest to teachers in the improvement of their services.

In our school district where the term was five months— twenty weeks—there were fifteen Saturdays on which I could find appointments to local teachers institutes within fifteen miles of my home. I was able to be present at meetings on all these dates except one, when I was snowbound. The morning sessions were usually spent in hearing four or five ten- or fifteen-minute presentations on topics from the super-intendent's list and the open discussion of these topics. I presented eight topics during the year. Much practical bene-fit came to me from these presentations and discussions. Usu-ally from fifteen or twenty to thirty or forty teachers were in attendance, and the discussions were generally lively and sometimes heated.

At noon, the visiting teachers from outside the local dis-trict were dined at the homes of farmers or villagers in the community.

The afternoon was given over to impromptu speaking. We drew our topics out of a hat. They were very miscellaneous in character. A speaker might draw for his topic "Free Trade," "Free Silver," or almost any topic of public interest. Some-times there was a surprise topic. The teacher who drew the topic "Musk" as his subject for a discourse began by telling us he did not know the meaning of the word; and then for fifteen minutes he held us spellbound with his speculations as to what it might mean. When we went home and looked it up in the dictionary, we found he had not come within gunshot in any one of his guesses; but we had had some entertainment and we were learning the art of exposition and also to speak up in public without quaking in the knees.

I held myself in readiness to speak, on every occasion when an opportunity came, on the glories of the Pennsylvania State Normal School at California which I had attended during the previous spring term down in the Monongahela River Valley, two counties west. The results were most gratifying; for when I left in late March to enter for the second spring term, I took with me from Somerset County, twenty-one new recruits to our student body. The previous spring, there had been but three students in the school from the whole of Somerset County. When my second term on the campus in the spring of '93 opened, Dr. Noss introduced me and my group in chapel and ever afterwards referred to us as the "folk from Mr. Suhrie's section of Somerset County." This group was a conspicuous entity in the life of the normal school, and my place in the student body was secure.

When my second term closed in the Suhrie school, I did not announce my plans. I had arranged to leave immediately and did leave for my second spring term at the State Normal School. I knew I could finance that term, for I had saved $75 of my salary of $105. I planned, if I could arrange finances, to go on in the fall for my senior year. I hurriedly said good-by to the children I loved and never returned again to be their teacher.

Telescoping Normal School Program by Private Study

In my first spring term ('92) in the California, Pennsylvania, State Normal School, I cleared off all preparatory work and gained admission, in good and regular standing, to the junior class.

The work of the junior year could be done in those days by a year's residence work or by a spring term in residence, plus the successful passing of examinations in a list of about ten required subjects. This examination was administered by the state normal school board of examiners. For practical reasons, I chose to clear off the Junior requirements by a spring term in residence plus the examinations. In anticipation of these examinations I had worked out, in my own private study while teaching my second term, during the year 1892-1893, every exercise in Sensenig's *Practical Algebra*, and had done much supplementary reading in literature, history, geography, physiology and hygiene, drawing, Latin, and methods of teaching.

I returned to the normal school for the fourteen weeks' spring term of 1893.

At the first meeting of the Philomathean Literary and Debating Society, I presented the names of thirty-two candidates for membership. Almost all the young people in my Somerset County delegation were included. I was regular in my attendance at the meetings of the Society and steadfast in my loyalty to it. I profited greatly by participation in its weekly programs.

Class work on the campus was interesting but uneventful. It was much interrupted by an epidemic outbreak of the mumps, which, for weeks, kept forty or fifty students in the infirmary or in their own rooms in the dormitory. About fifty of them were so depleted in strength after the ordeal that they had to withdraw before the conclusion of the term and without taking the state board examinations. There were a score or more of withdrawals by runaways headed for the World's Fair in Chicago.

The state board of examiners consisting of two state normal school principals (our own being one of them), a represent-

ative of the office of the state superintendent of public instruction, and a county and a city school superintendent
came to our campus about the twentieth of June and remained until all examinations had been completed, about
four days later. The program was a strenuous one for the examiners and for us. The examinations, as it seems to me now,
were both "catchy" and perfunctory. Dr. Henry Houck,
Deputy Pennsylvania State Superintendent of Public Instruction, conducted, *in group,* the examination in vocal music. He
stood on a chair at the front of a large room and asked the
class of eighty to join him in singing what he said was his
favorite classic, *So Say Ve All of Uz.* He pretended to listen
like a choral director for discords. When we had completed
the first stanza, he said we had done well but that there were
about a half dozen he could not pass—no, not yet. He looked
both puzzled and worried; he had us all guessing. Finally, he
said he thought it best to give us all another trial before announcing the names of the half dozen whose singing had so
seriously disappointed him. So we all literally roared on the
second stanza (which, by the way, was the same as the first
stanza). His countenance lighted up and he announced
with joy and enthusiasm: "Now you have *all* passed." It must
have been a relief to him not to have to name and identify the
six who had "failed" on the first attempt, for it was clear to
most of us that he couldn't name or identify any one of us.
Music was not generally being taught in the schools of that
day and he knew it and so he "tempered the wind to the shorn
lamb" and made the examination in this subject an occasion
to give us at least a short period of relaxation.

After the full list of state board examinations was completed and the record of my scores was placed in the registrar's office, I was granted an official certificate of promotion to the senior class.

On commencement day, it was announced that Principal

and Mrs. Theodore B. Noss and Dr. and Mrs. Edwin W. Chubb had been granted a year's leave of absence for study in Jena and other German universities and that Dr. Charles L. Ehrenfeld, a professor of philosophy and religion in Wittenberg College, Springfield, Ohio, and a former principal of our state normal school would serve as acting principal in Dr. Noss' absence during the academic year of 1893-1894, which was to be my senior year.

In September, I was back on the campus of the state normal school. After the June commencement was over, I had a reserve of $20 from my previous year's salary. During the summer, I had been able to earn a new outfitting of clothing. Brother John, who was making three times as much money per month, in addition to his board and keep, for twelve months of the year in the lumber woods as I had made in any one of my five months of employment as teacher during the previous winter, had volunteered to stake money on my expenses during my senior year. The total outlay, as I estimated it, would be no more than two hundred dollars, for tuition at that time was free. But there were two extras I had not anticipated. I had a very throaty speaking voice and no proper breath control, and so I was strongly advised by the teacher of speech, a graduate of Emerson College of Oratory in Boston, to take twenty private lessons in speech at one dollar each. This I did. Also, to represent my literary society properly on the contest program just before commencement, I needed a new suit and a pair of new shoes. My brother volunteered to supply the funds for these two extra items, not anticipated at the beginning of the year. So by graduation time, I was in debt two hundred and fifty dollars with no suitable appointment in sight.

We all liked Principal Ehrenfeld and his gracious wife, but we did greatly miss Mrs. Noss and Mrs. Chubb. They had been my best teachers during the two previous spring terms.

At Thanksgiving vacation time, I was invited to be the guest of Principal and Mrs. Ehrenfeld in their apartment. That was a very happy and enriching experience.

On my way home for Christmas vacation, I visited the county teachers institute at Somerset. That, too, was a profitable and happy experience as was the week of fellowship in the family circle at home. On my return to school, early in January, I found there had been an outbreak of smallpox in California and that we were all required to be vaccinated on the very first day of the winter quarter.

Several routine features of our program during the year were inspiring. These included Dr. Ehrenfeld's Sunday evening discourses and the lyceum course, which brought to our campus a half dozen very notable lecturers and several musical and literary artists. The Friday morning chapel hours, at each of which we had one, and sometimes two, senior orations, commanded the interest of all, not only of the seniors, but also of the under-classmen as well.

The program of studies we had would now be considered greatly overweighted with courses in special and general methods. Methodology had become our standard diet. It was, as one young man explained it, "amazing that any one of us ever got out of that school without becoming a Methodist." For young people of our meager scholastic and cultural backgrounds who had no actual pressing need for the innumerable methods and devices which we were required to assimilate, all this seemed to me a terrible waste of time and energy.

In general, the instructional program of the school was a great disappointment to me. The strongest members of our faculty were on leave. Some of the teachers were inexperienced, not to say inefficient. There seemed to be no money available to provide for the ordinary comforts of our students. Sanitation on the campus was worse than disgraceful. The state normal schools of Pennsylvania were at that time quasi- or semi-public institutions. They were known as non-profit institutions, but, in actual fact, the owners of stock in any one of these corporations was in a position to bring pressure upon the administration for the appointment of friends, almost without reference to their capabilities or their specific training for particular assignments on the staff. The state made no appropriations for capital outlays or for the cost of operation and maintenance. It did reimburse the corporation in such sums as would cover the cost of the free tuition scholarships granted to all individual enrollees. It was not until after the adoption of the new school code in 1913 that the Pennsylvania state normal schools became bona fide state-owned, state-controlled, and state-operated public institutions.

I had a benefactor and friend in the person of Miss Esther MacPherson, who had spent the precious year in travel and study in Europe, who knew good literature and good art, and who was genuinely interested in helping other students and me within the immediate circle of her influence to acquire some of the social graces and such other evidences of culture as might serve us well when we should become teachers and leaders of children and youth.

Early in the fall, I was selected to represent my literary society, the Philomathean, in the spring oratorical contest. This responsibility determined, in a fundamental way, many points of emphasis in my extra-curricular reading and study throughout the year. Dr. Ehrenfeld gave me good guidance in my reading. I found myself deeply interested in the addresses of George William Curtis, the civic reformer. This reading led me to the conclusion that our country was cursed by party bossism and subservient members of Congress and state legislatures; so I chose for my subject "The Higher Partisanship," a very abstract subject for a boy of twenty. It was almost as bad as "Cancer in Liberty's Bosom." I secured much good guidance from Professor Meese of our

English Department in the preparation of the text of my formal oration and was well rehearsed on its delivery by Professor Aiken, our speech teacher. I won this contest and our society won nine of the ten points allotted to the contest as follows: to debate, four; to oration, three; to essay, two; to recitation, one.

My opponent had a marvelously pleasing voice, and knowing I was up against stiff competition, I was more than fearful I might lose the contest. When our society carried the day, there was high celebration for a good part of the night. Our debater was too heavy to be easily carried on the shoulders of the merrymakers, and so the chief public honors in the celebration fell upon me. This did much to build me up in confidence.

The next day was commencement. I confidently expected to be approached by one of the many visiting superintendents of schools from down the river and offered a job as school principal. The debater who had lost the contest the night before had a call at $100 a month for ten months. The day passed without my getting the nod.

On commencement morning, with all of the sixty-three members of my class on the platform, the principal came to the lectern and announced that the board of trustees had just had a meeting and had instructed him to expel Mr. "X," the most attractive and one of the most accomplished members of the on-coming senior class, and Miss "Y" of the same class, surely the most charming and most promising girl on the campus. He didn't state the offense. We knew that it could not have been murder, for we had seen both of these students at large on the campus that very morning. Then with our curiosity at high pitch, the commencement proper opened with prayer. After the address had been delivered and the diplomas had been conferred, the word leaked out that Mr. "X" and Miss "Y" had been buggy riding the night before and had not arrived in their respective dormitories until after eight o'clock. I never have ceased to mourn over the loss from the teaching profession of these two promising young people.

I left the campus promptly after noon luncheon on commencement day never to meet again with any one of my classmates for many years thereafter. The first reunion I had with any considerable number of them was held thirty years later, when I was the commencement speaker. I was at this time at the head of the Cleveland School of Education and was shortly thereafter to go to New York University to organize a new department of teachers-college education. About forty-five of my sixty-three classmates were present at the reunion banquet.

On the fiftieth anniversary of our graduation and after my retirement from New York University, I was again the commencement speaker. Twenty-one of my classmates were present, twenty-one were absent, and twenty-one were reported deceased. On that occasion it was my privilege to present to the college authorities on behalf of my class a portrait of our beloved Mrs. Noss who was present at the age of eighty-seven to make a response. She seemed as sprightly as ever. I can still hear her say: "It's nice to live to a ripe old age. It gives one time to see how the laws of God work out in His universe. The boys who used to steal out of the dormitories fifty years ago to get liquor, while Mr. Bair, Mr. Brown, Mr. Kunkleman, Mr. Tipton, and Mr. Suhrie were in their rooms engaged intensively in studying, are not here today to rejoice in this happy occasion. They have long since fallen asleep."

Mrs. Noss and her daughter, Mary, head professor of modern languages in Ohio University at Athens, entertained me at their hotel in Florida several years later. Mrs. Noss exerted a salutary influence on my life to the end of her days.

After my graduation from the state normal school in June, 1894, I headed up to Phillipsburg in Center county to be with my brother John while hunting for a position as teacher for the next year. On my way, I made a trip through the coal-mining areas of Westmoreland county but with no success in securing an appointment. I lived during the summer with my brother in Phillipsburg and made trips out from there every week through Center, Clearfield, and Blair counties in search of a vacancy. I spent hours each day trying to find some clue to a suitable opening. The mines were closed, everybody was in distress, and I naturally took on some of the depression and gloom.

Something happened on one of my excursions job-hunting that added to the gloom. I was candidate for the principalship of an elementary school in a beautiful county town in central Pennsylvania. I had struck up a very promising friendship with the president of the board, who was the local postmaster and the editor of a county weekly paper. He was a man of great personal charm and wide influence in the community. He dropped his work to drive me around town and to introduce me to the other members of the board. I thought I had made a conquest and was assured in my own mind that I'd get the job. After filing my application, I thanked my host for his great courtesy and went on my way. The board was to meet that night. I unwittingly concluded my letter of application with the mis-written subscription: "Yours greatfully." A day or two later, I received a letter from the secretary returning my application and testimonials, and notifying me that another man had been chosen. Significantly there was written on the margin of my application in red ink in the editor's bold handwriting, "Can't spell." I had often asked myself the question: "Is spelling really important?" After that experience, I was no longer in doubt. I was sure it is. It had cost me about $30 a month throughout that year for the misspelling of a single word. I tried to comfort myself with the thought that I had often spelled the word *eleemosynary* at the spelling bees when nobody else could do so, but that recollection didn't help me to pay my board bills.

Early in September, I found a place as teacher of the seventh and eighth grades in the Osceola Mills, Clearfield county, schools. The salary was only $45 per month for a term of eight months, but it promised a living. In no position to be "choosey," I accepted the place.

Teacher and Social Worker in Mining Town

Less than a week after my appointment as teacher of the seventh and eighth grades in the public schools of Osceola Mills, Clearfield county, Pennsylvania, and three days before the opening of the term, I turned up in town in search of a boarding place. I called at the home of the principal for advice. He ended my quest promptly by introducing me to his wife, a very gracious and matronly woman who, in a dozen ways, reminded me of my mother.

She began about as follows: "Mr. Suhrie, my husband and I decided a few days ago that if you cared to live under our roof, we would try to make life pleasant for you here. We know you'll have a school that is hard to handle, and we want to insure your success by giving you as good a home as possible. We consulted our maid too. She is willing to take on the extra work of washing and ironing your personal linen. We have a vacant room we thought you might like. You can receive your friends in our parlor. We thought $25 a month might be about right."

I assured her that I would be delighted to move in.

Then she said, "Now wait; you haven't seen your room yet, and you haven't met our Pennsylvania Dutch cook."

She showed me a well-ventilated room with a good bed, a rocker, a desk, and a good light. The room, she explained, would have to be heated by a coal stove which had not yet been set up. Just then, the cook appeared upon the scene to ask whether I liked my shirts starched or "soft." I was puzzled, for I thought she ought to know that every gentleman and scholar always wore starched linen, the only allowable exception being a "washable" celluloid collar. But in the confusion I answered, "Either or both." Everybody had a good laugh and I felt quite at home.

"When may I come?" I inquired.

Said the madam: "Aren't you here now? Why not stay?"

I had my suitcase and a handbag full of books out in the vestibule. These constituted about all of my earthly belongings; so I stayed.

Within twenty minutes the supper bell rang. The food was ample and always well cooked, palatable, and served piping hot. The cook took special pride in the flavor of her deep-dish apple pie. One day this genial and hefty woman, of let us say fifty, came to the dining room near the close of the dinner meal to exhibit one of her best specimens of pie—un-cut—and to ask what size piece each of us desired. Papa Vaughan said, "Sixty degrees." Mother Vaughan said, "Forty degrees." (She was, so she said, trying to reduce.) Then it was my turn. I gave the cook a "yum-yum" look in appreciation of the quality of her pie and assured her that I would trust her judgment and that I was not trying to reduce. I weighed one hundred thirty-five pounds at the time and was six feet two. I did, however, add that I had deep-set convictions as to just how apple pie of such superb quality should be cut. Then I sank off into deep silence until all had coaxed me for a moment; then I gave them my conclusions: "All apple pie of such quality should always be cut at an obtuse angle."

There was a roar from all sides of the table, and from that day forward the pie cuts served were in inverse ratio to the weight (or assumed weight) of the host, the hostess, and myself. The master of the house always received a cut of intermediate size—much larger than the madam's and much smaller than mine. Meal time was always a happy time—free exchange of pleasantries, stories in wide variety, good food, and good fellowship always.

The hostess always controlled the conversation at the table. Her husband, she feared, might offend me by his violent disapproval of the official acts of President Cleveland, and so she steered him away from topics that had political implications. I often brought him back to the political arena by asking him some such question as this: "Mr. Vaughan, how do you think the good people in our country tolerate the public treasury raiding of Matthew Stanley Quay and his political henchmen?" This made him realize that perhaps I wasn't so much in need of coaching in my political thinking as I was in need of a forthright answer to a serious question of public morals.

The master of the house at the second or third meal told me that, as principal of the school, he felt he ought to warn me that I would have a few—not many—very notorious characters in my eighth grade. He began to name them. I raised the point that maybe it would be just as well for him to let me find out by their behavior the first few days whether there were any I couldn't trust.

On the Saturday before the opening of school I had my schedule of classes posted and all the free textbooks mended and ready for distribution.

Opening day came—Monday, September 15. I placed a beautiful bouquet, which our maid had provided for me from her kitchen garden, on my desk at the front of the room. I greeted each individual student, associated his or her name on my alphabetical roll of expected students, and made such notes thereon as would enable me to call the student by name from the beginning. By noon, I could identify each of my twenty-eight enrollees, also name the missing ones—expected, but not present. I found all my students very pleasant and seemingly anxious to please me and to make friends with each other. Class organization was easy. The classwork was based upon assignments in textbooks, for we had no school library; and the textbooks were on hand. The classwork of the year was, as I think of it now, a bit routine but never really dull. There were fine voluntary participation and willing response.

I was, early in the term, invited to the homes of many of my students, for I had inquired about parents and about little brothers and sisters. I was welcomed everywhere I went. I found that the lovely young people in my classes came, for the most part, from homes in which there was dire poverty. I soon found myself involved in relief work. I went quietly to the secretary of the board, a prominent merchant in the town, and begged a pair of shoes for one of my girls. She never knew where they came from nor how. They were sent to her home at night. Mr. Hirsch, the merchant (and secretary of the school board), and I kept our secret in seven languages. We had an accomplice in the girl's own mother who made us the "never, never" promise before we delivered the shoes. In due time I became a good school pastor and the head of a social welfare society of my own.

It was a very severe winter and there was much unemployment. Some of the homes of the miners were much in need of coal. I persuaded the president of the board to have coal delivered to the homes of a few of my students in dire need of it.

About the close of the first week, the principal of the school asked me one day whether I had found out yet who were going to be my trouble-makers. I told him I was very glad to be able to say that, to date, no one had assumed the role of a trouble-maker nor given any intimation of his desire to be one.

"Well," said he, "if I could see your roll, I could tell you at once whether they have arrived."

I answered by saying, "Mr. Vaughan, I have made up my mind that no one of my boys is going to be a trouble-maker this year just because he was last year. I am not planning to challenge anyone's worst; I mean to challenge his best. From what I have heard from some of my students I think you are referring to Fred—He is in school and has been for some time, and I distinctly like him. It is true he is a very nervous cigarette smoker and a loafer, but he is not in the least unpleasant or defiant. He hasn't learned to work, and I don't think he really cares much for books, but he certainly is in no ordinary sense objectionable to me or to his classmates. He comes from a good family and has good breeding. Perhaps if I can hold his good will until I can win his parents, we may later be able to induce him to do some useful work."

We did not succeed in making him a student. Every one of his classmates was doing about his best and Fred, in due time, got lonesome and dropped out. There was left in the school no trace of the "gang" that had made life so miserable for my predecessor and for the principal the previous year.

I made one major mistake during the year which almost cost me my hold upon my boys and girls. I yielded to the request of my pastor to teach a Sunday School class of early adolescent boys including many who were in my day-school classes. I had no preparation for this assignment. I did not know my Bible. I had not been a serious Bible student, nor had I had opportunities really to acquaint myself fundamentally with the scope and meaning of the Good Book. My experience in teaching this class, or trying to teach it, enabled me to discover, earlier in life than most college men do, just why so few American youth go voluntarily and regularly to Sunday School. I came to the conclusion that it's because the rank and file of Sunday School teachers do not have anything like as good preparation, either in content or method, for the teaching they attempt to do as public school teachers in the secular school, have for teaching the subjects in their day-school program. The viewpoint I gained from this experience prompted me years later, after I had made up in some measure for my deficiencies, to help set up some agencies for the improvement of the quality of Sunday School teaching and Sunday School teaching materials.

During an exceedingly cold spell in January when we saw the temperature go down to −49°, when the school was adjourned because our steampipes were frozen, when the streets and lanes were piled mountain-high with snowdrifts, the town enjoyed a very unusual intellectual feast. The pastor of the local Presbyterian church on the hill was a public-spirited man recently from England who, in his earlier years in Birmingham, had interested himself in the conduct of public forums. He was able to persuade a boyhood friend of his, then pastor of a big Methodist church in Yonkers, New York, to spend three days as his guest in Osceola Mills and to speak to the town's intelligentsia. His name, not then widely known, was S. Parkes Cadman. He gave three evening lectures at the church to packed audiences. One of these was on "Life in London," another on "Working in the Coal Mines of England and Wales," and a third on "Abraham Lincoln." I was present, sitting on the front row, every evening. It was easy to see that here was a man, the like of whom we should not soon see again in our little town, a man who would be heard from in the councils of the nations. Surely I had never in my life heard such eloquence and rarely have I since. What an impact he made upon my mind and heart! I listened to him as to a prophet. I did not hear him again until two score years had passed, but I treasured the memory of his wisdom and his eloquence.

Forty years later we were speakers, he and I, on the same program of the New York State Teachers Association and were guests together at a luncheon. I reminded him of his visit to the little coal town in Pennsylvania when he was yet a newcomer in America. To my amazement, he recalled vividly all the principal happenings of that week. He seemed tremendously grateful for what I told him of the impact his lectures had made upon me as a young school teacher. A little while later I saw and heard Elmer Ellsworth Brown, Chancellor of New York University, confer upon this notable "radio preacher" the University's highest public recognition —a doctorate *honoris causa*—in the presence of thirty thousand of his fellow American citizens.

During December, January, and February I conducted a subscription night school for adult miners who had recently come from Scotland and Ireland. I had the satisfaction of making some very good friends among the newcomers to America. Some of them had children in my class in day school. My total enrollment was about twenty-five. I charged each of them $1 per month for two one-hour periods of instruction each week. A few discontinued after the first or second meeting. The total amount of the tuitions paid was $60. We met in the I.O.O.F. hall which was heated and rent free. This venture, therefore, provided me a much-needed wardrobe—suits, shoes, hat, shirts, underwear, stockings, and neckties.

Long before the end of the school year approached, I had many evidences from the principal and members of the board of education, as well as from my students and their parents that my continuance in the school was desired. The president and the secretary of the board were both local merchants. Each invited me to a position as clerk in his store for the summer months. It was obvious that each of them desired to help me earn my maintenance during the vacation period when I should draw no salary from the public treasury. I declined their invitations for two reasons. First, I had made a partial commitment to a chart-and-map concern to serve as its agent in Clearfield and Elk counties during the summer vacation period; and, then too, I feared that if I accepted either of these invitations, it would bind me to return for the next year. I was hoping, of course, for promotion in salary and sphere of influence. The principal urged me to return, and I promised him that I would let him know before August 1, if by that time I had decided not to return.

When the school term was ended, I launched out on a campaign to sell school maps and charts. The outlook was not promising, but in the course of my travels I learned of a number of vacant school principalships. The one that appealed to me most was the principalship of the high school at Emporium, Cameron county in Pennsylvania's newest county up in the area of primeval forests. I accepted the call on July 1. Shortly thereafter, I returned to Osceola Mills in the course of my canvass of district-school boards. When it became known that I would not return, my former classes got up a farewell party and presented me with some gifts. I was downright ashamed to accept anything from these dear young people who must have made unusual sacrifices in my behalf.

I left town, after eight months of very hard work, without debt and without having been able to accumulate a penny to pay on my indebtedness to my brother. I was unhappy about that and determined to make a stake as a salesman. During the previous year while I was at the normal school and while he was making me several loans, he was prosperous in the insurance business; but in these hard times he had been too generous in carrying the premiums for families out of work, and so, early in the spring of 1895, he was broke. By May, he was in the lumber woods making good money again, and I was relieved of my principal worry.

During the year when I was at Emporium, I planned a trip home at the Christmas vacation time which would take me through Osceola Mills. I wanted to see my boys and girls. It so happened that over at Du Bois, en route to Osceola Mills, I went to a restaurant for lunch and that for the next hour on the train I was desperately ill.

When I arrived at Osceola Mills, most of my students were

there at the train to meet me. The big boys had the unpleasant experience of taking a very sick man off the train to the hotel. When I arrived at the hotel, I was scarcely conscious. The hotel keeper reprimanded the boys for bringing a drunken man into his hostelry. Resenting his attitude, they said, "We know this man, and we know that he never touches a drop of intoxicating liquor."

Just then my friend, Dr. Henderson, who was a member of the school board and had been my personal physician, arrived on the scene. He gave me a very warm greeting and assured the hotel manager that he had completely misjudged the nature of my illness. The hotel keeper immediately gave me a good room. The doctor gave me good care; and one of my former students, who was a bell boy at the hotel, brought me, with obvious personal satisfaction, three good meals a day as soon as I was ready again to partake of food. Later in the week, my former students came to me in numbers for a visit in the parlor. I had to abandon my journey home altogether and go back, as soon as I was able to do so, to my work in Emporium. I would not have believed it possible on January 1, 1896, when I last saw my former students of Osceola Mills, that fifty-eight years should pass before I would be free to make a return visit to that lovely town. When I did return, accompanied by my wife, in October, 1953, I found no one of the community whom I had known while a resident in town. One of my night-school students living in a suburb sent me greetings through his daughter, the school nurse; and another former student who had read of my anticipated visit sent me, from Clearfield a letter of greetings and good will on this visit to her old home town.

I was privileged to speak in the new consolidated high school up on the hill where the little elementary school in which I once taught had been located. I was introduced in the high school auditorium as an old timer. I did what I could to discredit the indictment. The young people gave me a glorious response, and I shall long remember them and their gracious principal, Miss Verna Gack, and her associates.

Of all my students in that place, the one I remembered best was May Mallon. She wrote me shortly after that from the arm of her wheel chair in Clearfield, Pennsylvania, and gave me later, at my request, in a second letter, the full story of her eventful life as a trained nurse; a Red Cross worker, first in American cities and then among the allied armies in six countries of Western Europe during World War I; the organizer of a school for the training of nurses in the city of Paris in which she served as director for a period of years; and finally, a worker at the Red Cross headquarters in Washington for eighteen years. Her career beautifully exemplified the spirit of service which characterized "my boys" and "my girls" when we were "comrades in arms" 'way back in the middle of the "gay nineties."

How happy I should be to have a reunion now with the most loyal group of youngsters I was privileged to serve in the springtime of my career as a teacher!

3

BOARD MEMBERS,
TEACHERS AND PARENTS

WHEN I accepted the principalship of a high school, with an enrollment of two hundred, in a lumber town up in the wilderness of northern Pennsylvania at age twenty-one, my chief and about my only equipment for the undertaking were good intentions and the habit of industry.

I had no adequate basic education, either academic or professional, and no training in supervision or administration. The motive that had prompted me to accept the call was that I could not live, away from home, on a grade-teacher's salary. I had to have an administrator's salary or leave the "profession."

Education was, in those days, "the noblest of professions" in theory and "the sorriest of trades" in actual practice. In one county in which I had taught, there were two hundred sixty teachers and principals. Of these only one, a principal, was a college graduate, and only two, both principals, were two-year normal-school graduates. All the other two hundred fifty-seven teachers (and principals too) were, at best, little more than eighth-grade graduates and were chiefly the products of the one-teacher rural school. By the age of twenty, I was a normal-school graduate with a life certificate, and so I had good "professional" standing in what was then in reality a laymen's calling.

But I liked the work. I had achieved a maturity that was beyond my years. I had initiative, industry, and drive. I was able to win co-operation in the school and to hold the confidence of fellow teachers, parents, and citizens of the community; so I continued in administration and supervision for seven years before I got a real awakening to the fact that I needed to prepare myself far more adequately if I were ever to achieve professional leadership in education. I had spent the last six of the years which followed my graduation from a state normal school, in a county in which the school leadership had been political not professional. The schools of the United States were calling loudly for professional leadership, and my experience had awakened me to the need for a widened horizon in academic and professional education.

High School Principal in Wilderness County Seat

I had met School Superintendent Harry F. Stauffer early in June, 1895, and distinctly liked him. We exchanged a few letters during the summer, and, on his advice, I arranged to get room and board at the Commercial Hotel in the heart of the town of Emporium. I arrived in town on Thursday preceding the opening so as to be on hand for the first meeting of the faculty on Friday morning. This meeting proved to be a very inspiring one. I met all of the teachers, eighteen in number; they were very fine personalities "hand-picked," as Mr. Stauffer used to say. I was the youngest—just half past twenty-one. When I was introduced to the group, all of them women, I saw at once that they had already sized me up as a minor, in need of a guardian; and one of them, the assistant principal, made it clear to me at the close of the meeting that she had had plenty of experience and would assume the task at once.

Over the week end, I heard so much vile profanity, saw so much sodden drunkenness, and witnessed so many fist fights and brawls in the hotel and on its premises that I quickly made up my mind I could not long remain at the Commercial.

The opening date of the school term, Monday, corresponded to the date for the beginning of the quarterly session of the county court. This fact accounted in part for the crowding at the hotel. At noon, I found it impossible to get near the dining room, much less into it. There was no restaurant in reach except those connected with one or other of the twenty-one saloons of the town. Since I did not care to get my lunch in any one of these places, I went back to my afternoon teaching assignments without a noon meal. Two days later, I found a very satisfactory place in which to room and another good place to board in a private home.

The new high-school building, completed the year before, was designed, though of course unintentionally, to be a man-killer. It had a central study hall with seating capacity for two hundred and fifty students at individual stationary desks. It had a large, high platform in front of the hall and two wing classrooms, each designed to seat about twenty-five students in pews that had no arm rests or writing extensions.

The principal was expected to supervise the study hall, or auditorium, to conduct a class in the front part of it at each recitation hour during the day, and to discipline the bad boys who at any given period attended classes in the wing rooms in which the two lady-assistant teachers conducted their instructional programs. The assistant principal was a charming woman in appearance, but she had a genius for winning the complete dislike of all her students the very first day. The other lady was a much younger and a very attractive woman, a graduate of the Leland Stanford Junior University at Palo Alto, California. She was a very active young woman who won the hearts of all her students the very first day.

After the few days of adjustment were over we, all of the high school teachers, found ourselves dining at the same home—a beautiful residence, high on the hill overlooking the town and occupied by its most prominent merchant with his charming wife and red-headed family. The women teachers had their living quarters under the same roof while I roomed at a nearby private home on the hill. We had excellent meals and accommodations at very reasonable rates. Sitting down three times a day at the same table might have compromised our professional relationships had we not agreed in advance that no table conversation among the seven teachers present should ever include ordinary shop talk. Such conversation was strictly *verboten*. Fortunately, we had at the same table a very bright and sparkling conversationalist who claimed some distinction as a novelist. She could talk California history even before the turn of the century just as effectively as the very best paid agent for California climate you have ever heard in the East in recent years. When she got started on the folklore of the Indians in California or on the Spanish missions out there, she ran on something like Tennyson's *Brook*.

One day, when she was off on a lecture tour, our gracious hostess invited each of us to tell a short story. In those days, Professor William James, of Harvard, was about the only educator who could "hit the headlines" with any frequency. I relished the opportunity to tell the latest story about this very popular college professor. It seems that one of his dearest friends of early manhood days, who had been an instructor for a few years at Harvard, had gone to China for thirty years during which time he had never been home on furlough. On his return to the Harvard campus, the elite got up a banquet for him and asked Professor James to preside as toastmaster and introduce the guest of honor for a short address. He did so as only a James—William or Henry—could have done. He "said it with flowers," chiefly orchids.

Two and a half hours later when the address had been completed someone asked the toastmaster: "Is your friend well?"

"No," said James, "can't you see that he is suffering from the most terrible of all diseases?"

"What," said the auditor, "is that dread disease?"

Professor James, so the story goes, fairly shouted: "The most terrible of all diseases is the malady of total recall."

After I had finished that story, one of the young women at the table said: "Mr. Suhrie, I dare you to repeat that story at this table when the novelist comes home." I didn't take the dare for, after all, she was a very gracious lady. So we continued indefinitely to suffer from her "malady of total recall."

My first job at the school, obviously, was to come to know my students personally, that is, as individuals and by name. Before I came, the superintendent had posted the full combined list of all the boys and girls whose enrollment he expected. He had arranged their names in alphabetical order and indicated after each name, the class to which the student belonged. When we opened the first session, he was present with me on the platform and introduced me to the students— about one hundred ninety-six. They were already seated in the places assigned by him. He gave me a very pleasant introduction, and then he tarried a moment to advise me to get all names in mind as soon as possible. A good part of each period, he thought, after assignments had been made, should be devoted to study. This would give me an opportunity to learn the names of individuals and to associate them with faces. I acted upon his suggestion and daily, even hourly, throughout the week I reviewed the list. On Thursday afternoon, during a period in which I had no teaching assignment, he and I sat on the rostrum at my desk; and he tested me by random samples, at least fifty of them, to find out whether I knew all the students he had designated by row and number. He repeatedly told the other teachers around town that, in less than a week, I had learned to know all the high-school youngsters by name. I am not sure that was quite true, but the report didn't hurt my reputation as the new high-school principal in this little lumbering town of two thousand people.

Many of the students were not very diligent in the pursuit of learning. They were typical American youngsters, only a small fraction of whom, in that day, were either bookish or eager to know. To gain and hold the interest of all was, of course, impossible for even a skilled and experienced teacher, and I was not. Out in the community at large there was a good deal of rowdyism and much drinking among young men. While now and then one of our boys came to school quite obviously "under the influence," there was generally a respectful attitude toward me and especially toward Mr. Satuffer whose office was on the first floor of our high-school building.

The organization and instruction which he sanctioned was, of course, a bit formalistic and routine rather than creative. The strain of my work was great, and long before the end of the school year I was looking peaked and pallid. I had no little trouble living within my income of $55 per month. The term was to have been eight months; but when the board found out that its "funds on hand" would carry the teachers' payroll only seven months, they voted an extra month of unemployment to the teachers and closed our high school at the end of seven months. This caused me much personal worry and distress; for, although I had contracted to go on the road in three counties as an agent for school supplies, I knew that not many commissions would come in before July 1. Mr. Douglas, our delightful home proprietor, volunteered to provide me with room and board while in town and to await payments until commissions should come in.

Commencement day came. There was much enthusiasm among parents and class members and both in public and in private the wish was expressed that I return in the fall. I was officially invited by Superintendent Stauffer to make plans

to that end. He gave me the complete order for school supplies for all the schools of the district. This was worth more
to me than a month's salary.

I had heard and read so much during the year about the
new Leland Stanford Junior University of Palo Alto, California, that it was granting free tuition to acceptable young
men and young women, that its teachers were hand-picked
and heaven-sent, "angels and ministers of grace," that an industrious young man could earn his expenses by two hours
a day at chores, that President David Starr Jordan was a
kindly father to all his family, etc., that I decided to "cast
the die." I thanked Mr. Stauffer for holding my place open
for so long and told him I had determined to go to Stanford University. Suiting the action to the word, I went to the
depot and bought a one-way ticket to San Francisco on a
tourist train. The price of the ticket was $56.

For the next few days, I wrote letters to all the school
board secretaries in Elk, Cameron, and Clinton counties in an
effort to round up my orders for school supplies. The response was good. Orders were coming in nicely, when one
day I received a telegram from the secretary of the board of
school directors of Jones Township at Wilcox in Elk county
offering me the supervising principalship of the twenty-four
schools of the township at a salary nearly twice as much per
month as I had been getting—and for nine months. He added
that he had recently had a conference with Superintendent
Stauffer, of Emporium, and that it had made him and the
whole board anxious to have me accept his offer at once. It
seemed best, under the circumstances, that I defer my plans
for going to California. So I redeemed my railroad ticket at
once.

Before the time came to go to Wilcox, I was able to clear
up all obligations in town, but not to make any payments on
my indebtedness to my brother. He was very kind and repeatedly reminded me that as an ax-man in the woods and a

lumber-piler at the sawmill he was making three times as much per month for the whole year as I had made per month for seven months in teaching. He understood perfectly well that I was not intentionally postponing the fulfillment of my obligation. He reminded me that he was only twenty miles away and that I might call on him freely if I needed any further help. In one of his letters he expressed a very real truth: "Every teacher who really attends to his job needs a patron if he is unwilling to starve or to go in rags." That statement was, alas, almost literally true in those days.

When the time came to go to Wilcox not more than fifty miles up the Erie Branch of the P.R.R., I was sorry to leave my friends among the young people of Emporium. I had had, too, an unusually happy relationship with a group of superb young, middle aged, and elderly ministers in the town. But, most difficult of all was the separation from Mr. Stauffer, my big chief during one of the happiest years of my life up to that time. He was honest and true, fair and just, and always my friend. He later became a distinguished school man in New Jersey and for years, from time to time, as we met in the state or national conventions sought to induce me to join him in the work of that state. When I finally moved East in the fall of 1924 to take up my work at New York University, he helped me to find a suitable dwelling house in Montclair and was one of my fans to the end of his days. How much this good man taught me all along the way about human relationships! He used to say that the school principal's best asset for the successful administration and disciplining of his school is the good will of its patrons, teachers, and pupils.

He liked to tell the story (and did so often) of the early American missionary who went to Tokyo, Japan, for one of the mission boards. The first time this man went through a certain street in Tokyo the Nipponese men, women, and children, disappeared from the streets, went inside, and bolted the doors. He went home and told his wife how the people of that country had all given him the cold shoulder. He felt utterly helpless. Said she, "You wait. I'll give you what you need."

So she set herself to baking sweet cookies. The next day he went up the same street with a basketful of cookies on his arm. Again everybody retreated before him. He was wondering how he was going to win them. While he stood quietly in the middle of the street gazing at the little buildings, he soon saw here and there a pair of slant eyes appearing in unexpected places around the corners.

Then a good idea came to him. Said he: "I'll shoot each pair of slant eyes that I see with a cookie." He did, and when the basket was empty he went home to report. His wife had another basketful of cookies for his next visit down the street. To his surprise the street was full of people the next time he appeared, and they all wanted to talk with him in person and at close range. He had been accepted as a missionary. Cookies had opened the Nipponese homes and hearts more successfully than Admiral Perry's guns had opened Nipponese ports.

Mr. Stauffer was a dedicated man. He put the best he had into the service of the children and youth in every school system in which he ever served, and he won and held the respect and unquestioned loyalty of his teaching staff. He was alert and growing in mind and heart to the end of his days. He greatly impressed me by his faithfulness to his public trust. He was a good and great community father and a friend to everyone who ever needed his help.

Six years after I left Emporium, I was able to visit the place with some frequency to court a fair maiden who had been in my classes. Our marriage had to be postponed for four years till after the death of her invalid mother. Ten years after I resigned the principalship, I returned to claim the hand and heart of my bride. Her people had moved away shortly before. I have since then visited the place but twice prior to the month of October, 1953. This recent visit was an altogether delightful experience. The principal of the high school, Dr. O'Malley, and his gracious wife were the host and the hostess of Mrs. Suhrie and me for a day of pure delight. I addressed the high school in the morning, teachers and students, and I was a guest at the Rotary luncheon and spoke to that group, also. We inspected the new two-million-dollar high school building in the course of construction. We were driven up each of the beautiful valleys which converge upon Emporium as I knew it sixty years ago. We saw the great industries in this delightful and rapidly growing city, the hundreds of beautiful modern homes and not a few new churches and public buildings, and finally, I had a delightful reunion with four of my best students of sixty years ago. They made it clear that much of the remarkable advance that has taken place in that interesting commercial and cultural center in northern Pennsylvania was the result of the leadership, industry, and fine citizenship qualities of many young men and young women who were students of mine in their high-school days back in 1895 to 1896. But alas, most of them have passed on!

School Master in Tannery Town

In the fall of 1896, when William B. McKinley defeated William Jennings Bryan for the presidency of the United States, Jones Township, Elk county, Pennsylvania, had twenty-four schools and forty-five teachers; and I was the new district superintendent of schools.

I was on the job early in September helping the secretary of the board to distribute textbooks, to make allocations of school supplies, and to deliver furniture. In actual practice I was not free, after the opening day of the school, to go the rounds of all the schools in the discharge of any supervisory functions or services. My duties as teacher of the two highest grades in the school kept me on the campus of the local high school in Wilcox, the principal village in the township.

My title of district superintendent of schools was, therefore, somewhat of a misnomer. I was in reality, a teaching principal in a local school in one end of my school district or township.

I had a very pleasant home at the one and only hotel in town. It was a quiet, well-managed hostelry. The food was good and the service was excellent.

The population of the village of Wilcox was not more than one thousand. There were four teachers in the local school below the high-school level. They were well trained, experienced, competent, successful, and loyal to the core. It was a privilege to work with them.

The only industrial establishments of the town were a very large tannery and a wood-alcohol plant. The managers, who were Americans, were intelligent, cultured, high-type businessmen. All employees were new immigrants, chiefly Swedes. They were, for the most part, heavy-liquor-drinking ruffians wholly unlike the highly educated, refined and cultured Swedes I have since come to know. Almost all children in school above twelve were Americans. Few of the Swedish children were allowed by their parents to go to school after that age.

It was impossible to get any response from the Swedish group when a call was issued for a parents' meeting. The majority of the parents could not speak any English and, by the same token, English was a foreign language to their children. The school accomplishments of most children in all grades were, therefore, substandard. The young people in the high school, in most instances, came from American homes and were excellent students. In this group, limited in number, I had some of the most alert students I have ever known in an American public high school, and it was a real privilege to teach them.

Only one incident involving any difficulty in discipline stands out in my memory. There was a fifteen-year-old boy named Oscar in the ninth grade. He was never mean-spirited or defiant but always a bit surly. One day, he was seated at the end of a half-circle row of desks and was disturbing the attention of others near him. I asked him to take another seat which I designated. No response. I repeated the request. No response. I swung into action. My authority was being challenged not by any overt act, but by disobedience; so I placed my hands under his armpits and lifted him so quickly that the school desk which he held on to like grim death was instantly detached from the floor. He held on to the desk, and I held on to him while desk and boy moved on at a quickening pace toward the door. Oscar weighed as much as I did and, with the cast-iron desk, twice as much; but I was in a mood to make light work of the job. When we arrived at the door which opened into the corridor, I dropped my cargo, and we parted company. I told him he might return as soon as he had made up his mind to obey orders from his chief. He beat it for home while I took the desk back to its place. I apologized for losing my temper. The youngsters in the class seemed willing to overlook my lapse and all were pleased that no one had been injured in the scuffle. I explained that I was sorry to lay hands on anyone but that I could not afford to be disobeyed when I had made a reasonable request. They gave me a look of approval, though I have no doubt they were sorry, as I was, for Oscar. They knew his background as I did not. His father, it seems, was the most notorious ruffian in town. He weighed nearly three hundred pounds. He drank much hard liquor. He swore like a trooper. When he drove his big tannery truck through town, he brandished his big black horse whip and threatened everybody. He terrorized all children and many adults too.

When noon came two of the girls in Oscar's class, delightful teen-age American youngsters, came to me and, in bated breath, warned me that Oscar's father, whom I had seen but had never met, was the terror of the town and that I might expect a visit from him as soon as the news of what had happened should reach him.

I went down to the hotel for lunch; then I came back early to the school; so did the two teen-age girls. We went into my office which commanded a view of the entrance to the school. The girls were at the front window watching for the appearance of Oscar's father. There he was! The big dray horses were standing in front of the entrance, and the giant driver was striding up the boardwalk brandishing his big black horse whip. The girls begged me to make a quick exit by the back window; instead I went down the front stairway to meet him at the entrance. He had already reached the porch landing and was ready to come into the corridor of the building. I extended my hand, giving him a friendly greeting.

Said I: "You are Oscar's father and I am his teacher. I am surely glad to meet you. I have long wanted to know you. I have heard about you, and know you are one of the most influential citizens of our town. Where is Oscar? I want him to come back, and you know I will welcome him if he is willing to obey me and to co-operate. I know you wouldn't let him disobey you."

"You bet I wouldn't. I would lick the blitzen out of him if he tried."

"Well," said I, "he tried once with me, and in all probability he won't try again."

"You bet he'll do what you tell him at school or I'll lick blitzen out of him at home. Just let me know. I'm on your side always." He folded up his whip and walked back to his truck. Then he suddenly turned his team around and drove off toward his home near the tannery.

About twenty minutes later Oscar turned up, anxious to make his peace. I took him aside and had a private chat with him. He said he would behave well so that I could give a good word to his father. He always kept the peace thereafter. We all went to work again in a good spirit.

At the close of the day I quietly asked Oscar to remain and help me fasten the desk again to the floor. He seemed happy to do so. I requested him to go to the store and get eight new screws, and I gave him the money to pay for them. He returned in a few minutes with the screws. He said he had told the merchant what had happened and that the merchant wouldn't take any money because "it wasn't the principal's fault."

Then Oscar said to him: "You're right, it wasn't the principal's fault; it was mine."

The merchant said he wouldn't take any money from either because he was glad Oscar was willing to help mend the damage and had learned to obey the principal.

Oscar and I reset the desk and fastened it securely to the floor. We got on well thereafter; and when I had gone on my way into another community, Oscar wrote me several times telling me he was not going back to school any more because I was no longer the principal.

For some reason I never felt very proud of my performance in Wilcox. I had almost no previous experience or training to prepare me for the duties of a principal in a community of that character. I got on well with the children in my upper classes, but as a supervisor of "the grades" I knew I was not able to offer much help to either the teachers or the children. The teachers were not broadly educated or professionally trained, but they were competent and successful notwithstanding their limitations. They knew their work well. They had no sociological background for making a correct diagnosis of the language and other difficulties peculiar to this group of recently arrived working-class immigrants, unfamiliar with our American culture patterns. I was not able to help them.

When the end of the year came, we had a very successful commencement. Dr. Lincoln Hulley, of Bucknell University, was the speaker. The class president presented me with two sets of expensively bound books: the complete works of Alfred Lord Tennyson and the complete works of Washington Irving.

I had been toying with the idea of going on to Leland Stanford Junior University and told the secretary of the board of my continuing interest in that way of getting on. I had not said positively that I should not be willing to return, but filed no formal application. The members of the board didn't expect that I would; and inasmuch as they were interested in placing a man of wider experience over the whole school system of the district or township, they proceeded early in June to elect my successor.

I went on with my school-supply agency and made good commissions during the following summer. Early in July, I was in Saint Marys, Pennsylvania, staying at the Franklin Hotel whose proprietor was the president of the school board. He inquired about my plans for the next year.

"Why," said he, "wouldn't you be just the right man to become our supervising principal or superintendent here in Saint Marys?"

"Do you think I could be elected?" asked I.

"There is one thing that stands in your way as I see it. You're a single man," said he.

Said I, "But that is not to be, with my consent, my permanent status."

So when the board met, he took me with him and, in introducing me, said that he was going to vote for me.

As I had expected, one member of the board inquired: "Mr. Suhrie, are you married?"

Quick as a flash I answered, "No, but willing." I had not intended to deceive anyone, but I found out after the election was over that he interpreted my answer as indicating that there was a young lady just around the corner waiting for my election to a principalship somewhere. Nothing could have been further from my intent than to mislead or deceive him or the board.

I was unanimously invited to become the supervising principal or superintendent of public schools at Saint Marys at a salary better than I had ever received, and I abandoned again, this time quite reluctantly, my plans to go to Stanford University in Palo Alto, California. There were circumstances at my home, down in Somerset County, that made me feel it would be unwise for me to go so far away from home when my father might need me.

When I first visited the campus of Stanford University with its very beautiful college chapel in the summer of 1922, I felt just as I imagine a man might feel when standing for the first time beside the grave of the mother whom he had never known. I still feel as though, spiritually speaking, I am an alumnus of that great university.

My sales of school supplies netted me a good income during the summer and I was getting out of my economic doldrums and able to make some significant payments on my indebtedness to my brother.

My fondest memory of Wilcox is of the two charming little teen-age girls who warned me to "flee from the wrath to come" when they saw the big, burly, Swedish teamster striding up the front walk brandishing his black horse whip.

Supervising Principal in Brewery Town

Saint Marys, in 1897, had perhaps five thousand souls chiefly of Bavarian descent. This city is situated at the center of a good farming area. In my day it had several breweries, a big saw mill, and the beginnings of a carbon industry. It is now known as the capital of the world's carbon industry and is a very prosperous growing town of twelve thousand.

When I went to Saint Marys, the community was almost solidly Roman Catholic; and the public school, though patronized by many Catholics, enrolled perhaps less than one-third of the school children of the community. The public school itself had been staffed by Roman Catholic nuns for many years prior to 1895, when the Pennsylvania State Legislature enacted the so-called "Garb Bill" prohibiting persons from teaching in the public schools while wearing a religious garb or other insignia of a religious body. This bill removed the nuns from the public-school payroll. There naturally was some contention over the matter in the community. When I arrived on the scene two years later, Catholic crucifixes and other insignia of Catholicism were still on the walls of the classrooms in the public-school buildings. Fortunately for me, the attorney for the board of education had advised that these would have to be removed, and it was done.

But there was friction in the community. The public-school board was charged by law with authority and responsibility for enforcing attendance of all children within certain age limits at some school, not necessarily a public school. The board found it exceedingly difficult to get full co-operation from all the nonpublic-school principals in reporting enrollments and absences. Notwithstanding, the board's secretary was required by law to certify under oath, periodically, that the compulsory attendance law was being satisfactorily enforced, it was difficult for him to get the full co-operation of the nonpublic schools of the city. The school district was in danger of having its state appropriations cut off if the reports on enrollment and attendance were not satisfactory. The board, therefore, had some concern about the matter and finally voted to make me its legal agent in enforcing satisfactory attendance at all the schools of the city—public, parochial, and private.

I was very unwise in accepting this assignment, for I knew in advance that I would not get the co-operation that nowadays would be given without question from all schools in any enlightened community. I disliked this special assignment heartily and persuaded the board, as soon as I could do so, to relieve me of this burden and to delegate its authority to enforce the law to the janitor in our school system. He was a man well suited for the assignment; he knew the whole town thoroughly and almost everybody in it and he had time to perform this duty. My recommendation was finally adopted; but not till after I had made some enemies in the performance of the assignment the board had given me.

The majority of the children in this characteristically German community were allowed, and many of them encouraged by their parents, to leave school at the age of twelve, or soon thereafter, and to go to work. Building up a high school was, under these circumstances, all but impossible. Only the mill men, chiefly from New England and other newcomers—plus a few such stalwart local citizens as M. C. Butsch, J. A. Hanhauser, F. A. Jacobs and Thomas Ernst—actively supported the idea of maintaining a good public high school. The school in the meantime was understaffed and I had to serve as a teaching principal, giving half my time to teaching the highest two grades in the school. In those days, there was no careful gradation. If there had been grades as we now understand that term, the two upper classes might properly have been called ninth and tenth grades.

Everything went on smoothly in our schools from the beginning of my administration. Enrollments increased by transfer into the public school, and attendance was increasingly regular from year to year. At the end of the first year, I was re-elected at an increased salary, and at the end of the second year I was re-employed for a three-year term at an advance in salary. The holding power of the school had greatly increased. We were getting a good sized group who wanted to complete a program of twelve years' schooling and be ready for admission to some reputable college. By the time I had concluded a five-year tenure, we had more than a score of excellent quality twelfth-year graduates, some of them admitted to such institutions as Pennsylvania State College, Yale, and Cornell.

The high schools sponsored a lyceum course and brought to town some notable concert talent as well as some outstanding lecturers, and, year after year, made some money for the school library.

Our school was popular in the best sense of the term and attracted an increasing number of transfers from the non-public schools. It was always difficult to place such students satisfactorily in our system inasmuch as many of them not only spoke German in their own homes but had had most of their elementary schooling in that language. We were sometimes accused of deliberately giving transfer students a lower classification than was their due. The constant transfer into our school of students who were retarded in English, and the temporary transfer of Catholic children out of our school at about the age of twelve to receive religious training for their first communion, was the cause of much dissatisfaction among our teachers and among parents who had good New England standards in mind and hoped to see things settle down to a stabilized pattern of orderly promotion from year to year.

In the spring of 1898, at the close of my first term in Saint Marys, our country was being governed by slogans as it has been in many other crises before and since. The slogan then most popular was "Remember the Maine!" War was in the air. President McKinley knew that Spain was ready to grant, with the least possible delay, the chief demands our country had made for reforms in Cuba. He also knew that a short victorious war would be popular; so he recommended that Congress declare war on Spain. Action was taken promptly and the call was issued for volunteers. Superintendent Bauer, of the schools of adjoining Benzinger Township, and I proceeded in due time, to organize a company of volunteers. We were elected officers of the company. We sent a telegram to President McKinley and another to Secretary of War, Russell

A. Alger, informing them that our company was ready to be mustered in. The Queen Regent of Spain and her Prime Minister evidently heard that the "Yanks" were coming and immediately got goose flesh. At any rate, the next day the war was over. Some folks have been so ungenerous as to suggest that these events were coincidental, but I still insist that there was a cause and effect relationship between what Mr. Bauer and I did and the abject surrender of Spain the next day. It has always seemed to me that a military hero's true greatness is best manifested by his ability to frighten the enemy into surrender thus avoiding bloodshed.

Late in January of 1902, at the end of which year my three-year contract was to expire, my father died very suddenly. I settled his estate in accordance with his wish. After the funeral, I returned to Saint Marys bringing my younger sister, Martha, with me. Mother, having moved into the village, could easily spare her. She had never been away from home, and I wanted her to have at least a few months of change in a pleasant environment. She was well received by the young people of the community and was very happy.

A month later, I received an invitation to join the faculty of the State Normal School at Slippery Rock, Pennsylvania, and shortly after that a similar one to join the staff of the State Normal School at Lock Haven, Pennsylvania. I thought it might be the right time to sever my connection with the Saint Marys school system at the close of my three-year contract. The board, two of whose six members would be replaced, could not legally reorganize until early in June. The president and the secretary insisted that I should not consider severing my connection with the school system and suggested that a meeting of the entire incumbent membership of the board, plus the two newly elected members be held to discuss what the entire membership—the hold-over members and the incoming members—might think best to do. Such a meeting was held early in March. After full discussion of the interests of the school system, the six members of the new board soon to be organized voted unanimously to offer me a new contract for three years. The two retiring members expressed their hearty approval. The six members who, in due time should constitute the board solemnly pledged themselves to each other and to me that if I'd accept, I should be legally and unanimously re-elected at a satisfactory salary which we had agreed upon and that this would be the first order of business when the new board should be legally organized early in June.

So I declined both calls to the state normal school service, arranged for an apartment rental, bought household furniture, and settled down in April to keeping house with my sister as my homemaker.

We had a very delightful commencement season with the largest class the school had ever had and with Dr. Lincoln Hulley, of Bucknell University, as the speaker. He urged me strongly to ask the board to release me so that I might finish my college work. He offered me a scholarship at Bucknell. After commencement we had a senior-class picnic; and then my sister, Martha, went back home to visit with Mother while I attended King's School of Dramatic Arts in Pittsburgh.

While in Pittsburgh, I heard the disquieting rumor that the board was going to repudiate its agreement. Just why no one seemed to know. I arranged to return to Saint Marys and did return to town a few days before the June meeting of the board. I found that a considerable number of my friends had heard the same rumor. I went to see all the holdover and all the new members of the board soon to be reorganized. None of them seemed to know anything about such a rumor nor any reason for any board member's repudiating his agreement of several months before. I remained in town until the meeting should be held.

The president and the secretary, both of whom had long

been members of the board, invited me to be present at the opening of the reorganization meeting. I was present. After the new members were sworn in, the president asked me if I had anything to say before the board should proceed to business. I placed my formal report on the year's work in the hands of the secretary and then told the board of the rumor I had heard. I said I knew no reason why any member should not keep his agreement in good faith, but added that if there were any charges of any kind against me, I thought I had a right to hear them and to make answer before the entire board without delay. There was deep silence and then the president said: "Obviously there are none."

I withdrew so that the election might proceed in my absence. The president and the secretary, both hold-over members, were the only two who voted for me. The president demanded an explanation. He got none. Then another man's name was presented and received the votes of the other four members—a majority. He was legally elected. Later in the evening the secretary telephoned me and told me what had happened. In a few minutes, one of my friends, an Italian boy, called to see me. I repeated to him what the secretary had told me over the telephone. The boy was excited and angered. He asked me whether the men who voted to repudiate their agreement had told me that they were going to do so and why. When I gave him the answer, "No," he flushed with rage and said: "When my grandfather from Italy was struck by a rattlesnake without notice, he kept shouting 'til he dropped dead, 'Son-a-de-gun-a-de-why-did-he-not-a-de-ring-a-de-bell.' "

The next day a storm of protest arose among the community's youngsters. When evening came several hundred parents and adolescents came to my home to give me a serenade and an expression of their confidence and good will. I was called upon to address them and did so in part as follows:

"I appreciate this expression of good will from my students

and their parents and from my neighbors of long standing. I notice that my neighbors who are accustomed to forthrightness and fair dealing and who have supported our public-school program are here and are willing to stand up and be counted. I notice, too, that the politicians are conspicuous by their absence.

"When I go on my way, as I shall in a little while, I'll be able, thank God, to take my self respect with me. I am glad to believe that I may take your good will and your good wishes also. May God bless the public schools of this city and multiply their friends and active supporters. Good night and good-by."

From that point on, the board members who had broken faith—two hold-over members and two new members—were put heavily on the defensive by the best citizens of the town.

One of the new members replied, "Well, surely you must know that Mr. Suhrie can get a new job more easily than I can."

Another, a hold-over member, said: "If you know me at all, you know I never willingly disregard the advice of my pastor."

The other two were able, in spite of tremendous pressure, to keep their secret as to why they had repudiated their agreement.

It soon became clear to all good citizens that my chief offenses were as follows:

First, I had firmly resisted the attempt of the elderly head of a neighboring nonpublic school when he came into my school to inflict punishment upon one of my school boys for an alleged offense that had not previously been called to my attention nor ever been proved.

Second, I had publicly rebuked a saloonkeeper for selling beer to an orphan boy of ten who was daily delivering a can of it from the saloon to his grandmother, an elderly sot, with whom this little street waif was living. I well remember how this saloonkeeper had warned me that he "wasn't taking orders from any pedagogue who didn't know enough to mind his own business" and had said, "I'll get even with you when the time comes."

I was too young in experience and, thank God, too independent to care what the Tammany-Hall-type of county political ring might decree as my punishment for defying its authority. One of its leaders was serving as Congressman and another as associate judge of the county court. The latter had full authority to grant liquor licenses in the county. He was the chief owner of a big brewery and was in the habit of granting licenses to the faithful who patronized his business. There was, of course, no politics in his judicial acts. He was the community's first-ranking citizen and political boss.

A much discredited local political hack was generally believed to have executed the *coup* for the county political bosses. When confronted with the rumor, he denied it. And that reminded me of a story I once heard of Abraham Lincoln. He was fifty-two years of age and was soon to go to the White House. He was reputed to be a man of great wisdom; and so one of his neighbors, in a little farewell visit they had, said to him:

"Abe, what have you learned from the practice of law for twenty-five years here in central Illinois?"

"I've learned," said he in reply, *"that there is no man living who has good enough memory to be a successful liar!"*

This local political hack's memory was notoriously untrustworthy.

In those days there was no such thing as tenure in the public-school service. The newly elected superintendent didn't violate any professional code of ethics in seeking an election to a vacancy that did not exist for there was no such code. To be sure we had the Golden Rule then as now but politically minded schoolmen doubtless believed then, as some do now, that that Rule was intended for the Hittites, the Hivites, and the Jebusites. At any rate, Professor George Gailey Chambers, of the University of Pennsylvania, had not yet begun to arouse the teachers of the state to the fact that they needed *a teachers' code of professional ethics*, not primarily to serve their own interests, but to protect the public interest.

I was invited by the secretary of the board to buy his weekly paper, to take over its editorship, and to open fire at once on the political gang. I was smart enough to know that my prestige was with the children of the community and their mothers and fathers and that I had no significant hold on the gang-ruled men voters of the county. Furthermore, I had no interest in a career as a small-town editor. I had dedicated myself years before to the ministry of teaching.

So I went on my way again to the summer session of the School of Dramatic Arts in Pittsburgh and to a wider field of opportunity. I had been, as my best friends in town expressed it, "kicked upstairs."

Across the span of more than half a century, I have kept in touch with "my boys" and "my girls" of this community. They have played a significant part in making Saint Marys the splendid community it is today. The few who survive are my friends still.

I cannot remember when I have spent a happier day, in half a century, than on October 7, 1953, when Mrs. Suhrie and I were the guests of Superintendent H. M. Ryan of the Saint Marys Public Schools; Honorable D. J. Driscoll, one of my predecessors in that office, who has served as United States District Attorney, member of Congress, and chairman of the Pennsylvania Public Utilities Commission; W. G. Bauer who, at the turn of the century, was the principal of the Benzinger Township schools and is now the city's leading business man; and Frank D. Lambert, a member of the class of 1902, now retired General Manager of the Shawmut Mining Company. All of these gentlemen are citizens of high standing and all are my friends.

4

APPRENTICESHIP IN
COLLEGE TEACHING

MY "UNHORSING" from the public-school service by influences that were political gave me an impulse to prepare for another type of educational service that was more appealing.

My first college teaching at the lower levels of salary, rank, and sphere of influence was in two different regional areas of our country having radically different types of collegiate patterns and standards. This helped me to rid myself of provincial attitudes and biases. Fortunately, I was able to secure employment, in turn, in institutions of the academic, the vocational, and the professional type. This tended to free me from adherence to any one of the cults in higher education of that day and to give me a wider range of educational interests and a broader tolerance.

Though I was not actually drifting, the accident of circumstances, as it now seems to me, was, in considerable measure, determining the direction of my interest and giving me a wider range of experience in preparation for a career in college- and university-teaching and administration.

By the time I had completed my doctoral studies, my personal acquaintance with many university and college officers and professors of distinction in a wide geographical area gave me an opportunity to choose without difficulty the locale of my service and the institution having the most dynamic leadership and the most democratic spirit. I was concerned to choose my superior officers with great care and was fortunate in the highest degree in the choices I made.

Some one has written a book in support of the thesis that life begins at forty. When I arrived at forty, I felt that I had had an apprenticeship in the field of higher education that had prepared me to accept the call to a service that would be increasingly national in scope. The call came at forty-one and I accepted it. I had developed during this apprenticeship a very wide national acquaintance among American educators in public school systems and in colleges and universities. This was, in due time, to be a very real educational asset to me.

Dramatic Arts in Pittsburgh

In a previous section, I listed some of the great events in the educational history of the United States which were crowded into the year 1891 when I began teaching. Now I must list some of the outstanding events of our educational history which were crowded into the year 1902, when I took leave for a time of the public-school service a bit discouraged, not to say disheartened, by the treachery of a few unscrupulous men.

The year 1902, looms large on the pages of the history of education in the United States.

It was in that year that Andrew Carnegie gave five million dollars for the endowment of the Carnegie Foundation for the Advancement of Teaching.

It was in that year that John D. Rockefeller gave five million dollars to a sanitary commission to clean up malaria and hookworms in the South and fifty-five million dollars to the General Education Board of New York for the promotion of education in the United States.

It was in that year also that President D. B. Dabney and Professor P. P. Claxton of the University of Tennessee opened the Summer School of the South at Knoxville, enlisting the services of scores of the ablest men in America and nearly two thousand of the most enlightened public-school teachers, principals, and superintendents of the South in the most comprehensive effort at regional planning of education that has yet taken place anywhere in the United States in all its history.

Well do I remember the summer of 1902. Comprehensive long-term planning of education was in the air. I caught the spirit of it. Never before had I seen so clearly the inadequacies of my own preparation for genuine professional service in American education.

When Saul of Tarsus was unhorsed on his way to Damascus, he saw a great light; and he cried out, "Lord, what wilt Thou have me to do?" The answer came clear and, in due time, sent him on his way to the ends of the known world on great missionary enterprises.

When I was politically "unhorsed" in Elk county, I was more than disillusioned. I was almost "stricken blind." I was deeply wounded in spirit, but my career in education was not permanently cut off. I saw a new light, but the way was not immediately made clear. My friends gave me conflicting counsel.

One thing was certain. I must spare no effort in getting on with my studies somewhere. I was well aware that if I should ever have an authentic message in American education, I'd need to be an effective speaker or I could not gain a hold on my potential audience.

Professor Lincoln Hulley, who had powerfully influenced my thinking during the previous five years, counseled me to come to Bucknell to finish my undergraduate work and get on my way into a good graduate school such as the University of Chicago. By three previous summer sessions in the King's School of Dramatic Arts in Pittsburgh I had gained standing in its senior class and could support myself by administrative service as the president's assistant while completing its diploma program within a year. So I was off in a few days for the summer session of the School of Dramatic Arts which was held in the mountain town of Curwensville, Pennsylvania. When fall came, I had taken up my residence in President King's home and had my apartment on the third floor of his fine residence on Heron Hill, overlooking the smoky city. He was away much of the time on long lecture trips, and I was not only his administrative assistant to carry out assignments in his absence, but I was the unofficial guardian of his family. I had never before spent so happy or so fruitful a year in systematic study. I received a kind of practical training in coaching Shakespearean plays and in supervising and directing in their public presentation that greatly increased my vocabulary, my versatility in public speaking, and my ease before audiences. I worked up a number of full evening programs of lecture-recitals from Shakespeare, Tennyson, Browning, and other poets. I was prepared to accept appointments before teachers institutes and Chautauquas.

Ben Greet, the English Shakespearean interpreter, was in Pittsburgh that winter with his full cast in the Fifth Avenue Theater. I so thoroughly appreciated his method for making Shakespeare "come alive" to adolescents and got on such intimate terms with him personally during his stay in the city, that when I visited him in Regent Park in London thirty years later, Sir Ben made me his personal guest at his outdoor presentation of *A Mid-summer Night's Dream*.

During the year in Pittsburgh, I had the privilege of holding membership in the extension course of a notable University of Chicago Professor of Biblical Literature, Dr. Richard G. Moulton, the translator of the *Modern Readers' Bible*. He gave thirty weekly lectures on Hebrew poetry—the *Book of Job*, the *Psalms*, *Proverbs*, and *Ecclesiastes*—in our Carnegie Hall to a class of about three hundred of the city's intelligentsia. His inspiring interpretation of Hebrew poetry together with President Byron W. King's dramatic vocal interpretation of the Book of Job, "the greatest poetical drama ever written in any language," and his impressive devotional presentation of such Psalms as the 23rd, the 91st, and the 107th has made it a bit painful to me ever since to hear the listless and routine presentation of these biblical classics by the average preacher in his regular church services.

Also, I was privileged to hear Dr. Edward Howard Griggs of the Bureau of American University Extension give several series of his classical lectures on *Heroes of History*.

At the theater, I heard during the year, many of the great players of the day, such as Richard Mansfield in his Shakespearean roles and Joseph Jefferson, the inimitable, in the play *Rip Van Winkle*, his own theatrical creation.

I heard public lectures on a great variety of themes by university scholars from at home and abroad as well as powerful sermons by notable local and visiting preachers.

When spring came, I represented the president of the School of Dramatic Arts in arranging with the Board of Education of Corry, Pennsylvania, for the conduct of our summer session in the high school of that city and got out the announcements for it and for the Finley Lake, New York, Chautauqua of which President King was the official manager. At the conclusion of the Chautauqua season of 1903, Dr. and Mrs. King and their family made me their guest on a two-weeks' vacation fishing and swimming trip to Orelia, Ontario.

I had completed my diploma requirements in Dr. King's School of Dramatic Arts and was ready for the next step. I was by this time painfully aware of the inadequacies of my language foundations and had made up my mind I needed nothing so much as a broader foundation in the humanities and in the sciences. I knew I could somehow gratify this desire in some good college of liberal arts, but where? The fall term opened in most American colleges while I was on the much needed vacation up in Canada. While there I had much pleasant and profitable conference with Mr. B. R. MacHatton, a minister whom I had known in Pittsburgh and who also was a guest with the King family. He strongly recommended Wooster College, Wooster, Ohio, his alma mater, as the place where I could get an eclectic program that would set me on my way to college graduation "in good and regular standing." The die was cast. I would go to Wooster. I would sell my stock in the Saint Marys Telephone Company and be on my way with the least possible delay. I returned to Pittsburgh. It took me a little while to arrange my affairs and get off to Wooster. When my train pulled out of Pittsburgh I read in the morning papers about the Wright brothers' first flight at Kitty Hawk, North Carolina, the previous day.

Odds and Ends with Dean Compton at Wooster

I arrived at Wooster College in time for luncheon at one of the men's boarding halls. I found, to my surprise, that the manager of this hall was a college sophomore thirty years of age, who had been a successful businessman but was now preparing himself to become a schoolman. I found a half dozen other men who had started all over at twenty-eight or thirty years of age and who, likewise, were getting ready to teach. I was to be less exceptional than I had thought.

I soon found a suitable rooming place near the college at which a half dozen very congenial men were quartered. I found rates for room, board, laundry, and tuition very reasonable.

Early in the afternoon, I went to the Dean's office by appointment. Dean Compton was a *person*, quiet, dignified, thoughtful, courteous, and understanding. The Compton boys, Karl, Arthur, and Wilson, all of them destined to become presidents at the same time of great institutions of higher learning, were youngsters and were, so I was told, the chief concern of their mother since the college boys and college girls were the chief concern of the father. Father Compton was Dean of the College and Professor of Philosophy and Psychology. He looked the philosopher when I came to grips with him on my program of studies. He was so courteous, and kind, and deferential, that I wasn't even shocked when he drew a line through almost all the credits I presented on my transcript from the California, Pennsylvania, State Normal School, and from the King's School of Dramatic Arts in Pittsburgh. "These, after all," he said, "are not liberal arts colleges." So he assigned me to academic courses in Latin in each of which he assured me I should have really competent, indeed inspiring instructors. I never batted an eye. I had been for years *in* authority; now I was *under* authority. He also assigned me to freshman biology. My studies ranged from middle academy to junior class in college. I was picking up odds and ends.

I dug in. I gave about all my time to my studies and almost none of it to the social affairs of the campus. I was engaged and would have by this time been married had not my fiancée been sorely needed at home to earn a part of the family's support and to help care for her invalid mother outside of working hours.

I had some excellent companions in study. I aimed to find as a companion in each of the courses I took a student who, like myself, was willing to do not only what the professor expected or required, but, if possible, a great deal more; a person who would "trip me up" on the inadequacies of any preparation on any given assignment and who would inspire me to "consult the references." I had no difficulty in finding such persons and they were a group of very congenial fellows. As a result, my grades were uniformly good and, in most subjects, superior. It soon became apparent to my classmates and to my teachers that my studies over in Pennsylvania, even though not *credited*, must have been *creditably* done. Dean Compton, on several occasions, told me with unconcealed satisfaction that my teachers in Latin, science, and government had spoken of my work as showing considerable maturity. The mature men who were my companions in and out of class preparation were appreciative of my industry and of the schedules I often set up for them before breakfast.

The cultural atmosphere of Wooster was excellent. The daily chapel hour was not a routine or perfunctory performance. There were many interesting and not a few inspiring talks given. The musical performances of the year were many and excellent. The lyceum numbers included musical artists, dramatic readers, and lecturers of distinction covering a wide range of interest. I vividly recall the lecture given by W. E. B. DuBois, the Negro sociologist, who placed before us, in bold relief, the outstanding problems in race relations of the South, some of which are now well on their way to solution.

Wooster was a center for the training of prospective missionaries in the Presbyterian Church. At the Sunday morning services, the congregation heard great missionary leaders back from the ends of the earth. Collectively, their discourses of a year constituted a well-organized course in world geography, world politics, and world religions.

After the first year's work at Wooster, I spent the summer with my brother out on the farm plowing corn, and cradling buckwheat to keep myself physically fit. During the vacation period I read two years of Latin and passed examinations successfully on each—Sallust, Ovid, Tacitus, and some of Cicero's orations; also on a course in Medieval History.

During the second year, I had the most enjoyable courses I have ever had in college or graduate school any time or anywhere. And, strange as it may seem, it was in Latin, the subject I had literally despised in the normal school. Professor Notestein, a thorough scholar in languages and philology, taught us *De Amicitia* and *De Senectute*. I am not sure even now whether the word studies he gave us out of these classics or the philosophy of life which he read into or out of the lines of these two superb classics was the more valuable. I cannot escape the conviction that they were both invaluable. My program of studies during this second year at Wooster College included many subjects of my own choosing. I was trying to get courses that would make up for the outstanding deficiencies in my previous college work and to avoid taking any course that would be a repetition of those previously taken but not accepted for credit. I was sure, for instance, that in the field of English literature, especially dramatic literature, I had had a much more adequate training than Wooster College afforded. In my last year, I had two courses—*Comparative Government* and *International Law*—which have proved invaluable. The basic texts were one by President Woodrow Wilson, of Princeton University, called *The State* and the other by Professor Lawrence, of Yale University, entitled *International Law*.

I spent my Christmas and Easter vacations coaching college boys from a number of different colleges for state, regional and national oratorical contests. I was well paid for these services.

On one of my spring vacations, I heard President Woodrow Wilson, of Princeton University, make a notable address to a capacity audience in Carnegie Hall, Pittsburgh. When I went back to my government class in Wooster in which class we were using his *The State* as a basic text, I announced that he would, in due time, take over the White House. I was sure of it, but most of my classmates were equally sure I was neither a prophet nor the son of a prophet. I little dreamed that eight years later I should have the pleasure of being personally present to see him nominated in the Baltimore Convention of 1912.

Before the end of the year I had made up my mind to enroll elsewhere in some institution that could piece together my credits and within the year grant me a Bachelor's degree. I knew Dean Compton had done me no intentional injustice in drawing a line through most of my credits from the California, Pennsylvania, State Normal School and the School of Dramatic Arts in Pittsburgh. He was administering a high-class institution with a somewhat inflexible academic pattern. Dr. Lincoln Hulley, the new President of Stetson University in Florida, which was affiliated with the University of Chicago from which he held the Ph. D. degree, assured me that, in view of my maturity, my experience, and the cultural and professional value of the courses and training I had in good institutions without recognized academic college status, I should be entitled to a reappraisal of my academic record by some institution which had the Eliot idea of electives and the Harper idea of equivalents. He invited me to make plans to come to Stetson in the fall, principally to teach public speaking and possibly to administer the Normal Department of the institution. He promised to study my transcript from the California, Pennsylvania, State Normal School, the School of Dramatic Arts in Pittsburgh, with whose work in both instances he was entirely familiar, together with my transcript from Wooster College and to get a rating for me in terms of Stetson's requirements for the Ph. B. degree. In the meantime, acting on his advice, I spent the summer of 1905 in the summer session of the King's School of Dramatic Arts at Swissvale, Pennsylvania, and in completing two reading courses for credit at Wooster College. I took my examination in these subjects under the proctorship of Superintendent Harry F. Stauffer, of Millville, New Jersey, on my way South and had my credits entered on my Wooster transcript to Stetson.

While at Wooster College, I formed a lifelong friendship with Harry N. Irwin, of the class of 1905, whom, a dozen years later, I appointed as my immediate associate in the administration of the Cleveland School of Education. He became my successor, in due time, in that institution. When we were together at Wooster he served as my tutor in Greek, and I in turn coached him in public speaking.

I found it exceedingly difficult to part company with a half dozen choice friends who had been my intimate companions in daily study. They were brilliant cross questioners on the text of our more difficult assignments. They were all preparing for professional careers. Most of them were some years older than their classmates. They were industrious and were actuated by the desire to achieve distinction in their several fields of interest and service. Collectively, they did more for me during the two years I was in college than my professors did. One of them begged me to go with him to the Divinity School at Princeton. He offered to pay my way through. He thought that in due time I'd have a call to the gospel ministry. I told him I had already had a call to the ministry of teaching and that I had long ago dedicated myself unreservedly to this service.

Lure of the Old South

Early in September, 1905, I sailed on the Clyde Liner, the Comanche, from New York to Jacksonville; then I went by rail up the St. John's River to De Land, the seat of John B. Stetson University, arriving at 2:30 A.M.

After breakfast, I started out to explore the little town of fifteen hundred before reporting at the president's office. On the way up Woodland Avenue I dropped into a haberdashery. When I introduced myself to the proprietor, he invited me to pick out for myself, a new Stetson hat, which he said was always provided by Mr. John B. Stetson of Philadelphia, the president of our university board, for every new member of the faculty. When I had donned this expensive snow-white felt with black band and had started up street,

I heard a boy across the street shout to his friend: "That new 'perfesser' sure is well dressed from the neck up."

On my arrival in President Hulley's office he told me that he and the Dean, who was also the holder of a Doctor of Philosophy degree from the University of Chicago, had gone over my transcript from the three institutions in which I had studied and found that, with a little substitution in the restricted electives category, I could meet the requirements for the Ph. B. degree at Stetson. This was gratifying. He and the Dean assigned me a service program that included the teaching of public speaking and the administration of the Normal School Department.

Stetson, in 1905, had fewer than one hundred college students and about two hundred and fifty academy students. The public-school system of the state was very rudimentary. The General Education Board of New York is authority for the statement that when it began its operations in the South in 1902, just three years before my going to Stetson, there were not half a dozen public high schools south of the Potomac and Ohio Rivers in which a young man or a young woman could make satisfactory preparation for admission, either by examination or on credentials, to a reputable American college. Florida, in 1905, had no public high schools that could meet such standards. Stetson had a strong faculty. Under the terms of its affiliation with the University of Chicago, its curriculum and its faculty had to be approved by the authorities of that institution.

My classes were few and enrollments were small. During the fall and winter quarters, I spent much of my time in coaching plays for public presentation. During the previous year, Mrs. Otis Skinner was in charge of this work. I had high standards to meet, and we came through with what seemed to be acceptable public performances.

In anticipation of the spring quarter I built up a program

of review courses for Florida public-school teachers who were seeking certificate renewals. I conducted some of these courses. Our enrollment was three times what it had been in any previous year.

I had been at Stetson no more than a month when President Hulley assigned me an office next to his own suite of offices on the ground floor of the administration building and made me his administrative assistant. I was soon taking on heavy correspondence of a promotional nature, writing articles for the Jacksonville and Tampa papers, making public addresses at teachers institutes all over the peninsula, and serving, in general, as a public-relations officer. At the Christmas vacation period, I was asked to substitute for the president on the program of the State Teachers' Association at Miami, a new Florida East Coast railroad terminal of fifteen hundred souls down near the end of the peninsula. President Sledd, of the University of Florida (not yet removed from Lake City to Gainesville), President Murphree, of the State College for Women at Tallahassee, and Superintendent Gilbert, of Rochester, New York, were on the same program.

Before the close of the year, I had completed plans to spend the summer quarter, or at least its first term, in the University of Chicago. Stetson had conferred the Ph. B. degree upon me. This would now be regarded as a somewhat irregular performance inasmuch as I had not been a student in residence. My actual performance as an instructor and as assistant to the President during the year, had given the officers and faculty a satisfactory impression of my academic standing. There was no effective accreditation association in the South in those days. Each institution set its own standards for the granting of its baccalaurate degrees. My experience at Stetson in getting my normal school (and other) credits finally straightened out closely parallelled that of Glenn Frank at Northwestern, many years later.

President Hulley had had considerable correspondence with Dean Nathaniel Butler at the University of Chicago, and my acceptance in good and regular standing for graduate courses in Education there was approved by him. I enrolled in two courses with him and in one course with Professor Wilber Jackman; the former had been president of Colby College in Maine and the latter was fresh from some years of service in Colonel Parker's Cook County Normal School. He was considered a radical in education. His class was made up principally of middle-aged school superintendents from all parts of the country. I was probably the youngest man in the class. The discussion was very lively every day. It was not a lecture course. The professor laid down propositions for discussion and there was never any lack of response. There was fine fellowship in this group. Some of my classmates later rose to distinction on the national scene, and many of them have been my lifelong friends.

The educational atmosphere of the University of Chicago was most inspiring. Florida had only about a half dozen enrollees in attendance during that summer quarter, all of them Stetson graduates seeking the University of Chicago degree by an additional quarter of resident study. Georgia had for years sent delegations of three hundred who came through from Atlanta on a special under the direction of M. M. Parks, later my prexy at Milledgeville. Texas had a delegation of three hundred and fifty who came in on a special train from Dallas. The whole South was well represented. President Harper, of the university, who had died early that spring (1906), had had big plans for the development of affiliated regional centers of university extension in the South. John D. Rockefeller was ready to finance these ventures. President Harper's untimely death resulted in many modifications of the plans he had been making for the expansion of the University's service in the South.

While in Chicago, I heard many of its great preachers,

Gunsaulus, Jenkin Lloyd-Jones, Bishop Quayle and others; and I heard in public lectures in Leon Mandel Hall a number of the University's best-known men with whom I did not have classwork, notably George H. Vincent, later president of the University of Minnesota, Albion W. Small, the editor of the *Journal of Sociology* and James Angell, later the president of Yale University. At the close of the first six-weeks' term, I withdrew to meet some lecture engagements I had made at chautauquas in Illinois, Indiana, and Ohio. In filling these engagements I became acquainted with President King, of Oberlin; Sam Jones, of Georgia; Russell Conwell, of Philadelphia; and William Jennings Bryan, of Lincoln.

By August 15, my engagements had been met, and I was in the East to claim my bride who had been a student in my classes ten years earlier in the Emporium high school and then a teacher in the public schools in that area. (She taught Joe McNarney, the future U.S. General, to read.) We went for our honeymoon to the Findley Lake Chautauqua in Western New York and then on sight-seeing tours in Philadelphia and New York. We sailed from the latter city by Clyde Liner for Jacksonville, Florida, in the company of President Hulley and family, of Stetson. Our boat left one of the wharfs on the North River at sundown on Saturday. Dr. Hulley was scheduled to conduct religious services on Sunday morning at eleven o'clock on the boat. We had scarcely cleared port when a violent equinoctial storm broke along the Atlantic coast. Our captain put out to sea. There were no religious services on that boat on Sunday. All the passengers including the honeymooners were *mal de mer*. On the evening of the second day, when the stewardess came to the bridal berth to offer such comfort as might be possible, she found the bride alone and unconsolable.

Said the stewardess: "Why, I thought you had a husband. Where is he?"

The bride replied disconsolately: "I had, but the last I saw of him twenty-four hours ago, he was lying helpless on the deck. I suppose he has long since been washed overboard. Boo hoo!"

The bridegroom turned up, in due time, and was not even accused of desertion when he returned and claimed his own just before the vessel put in to port at Charleston on Tuesday afternoon. Incidentally, I have always advised newly-weds not to take passage on any ship sailing the south Atlantic coast in September.

We sailed up the St. John's River to Beresford and, a few minutes after leaving the boat, arrived in the beautiful little town of De Land and went at once to a furnished apartment at the home of the superintendent of grounds on the university campus.

At the Christmas vacation season of that year, Mrs. Suhrie and I attended the state teachers association's annual meeting at St. Augustine and were present at a reception Mr. Henry Flagler and his bride gave at the Ponce de Leon Hotel in that historic city. Professor Edwin E. Sparks, of the University of Chicago, and Professor P. P. Claxton, of the Summer School of the South at Knoxville, Tennessee, were the chief speakers.

Our first year together at Stetson was a very happy one. I was a member of the Vesper Committee. At 4:00 P.M. on each Sunday Professor Morse, of the music department directed a college chorus and President Hulley preached a powerful twenty-minute sermon. Sometimes on a good mid-winter day when the town was crowded with tourists, a line two blocks in length patiently awaited the opening of the college chapel doors. Seats were always at a premium. This Sunday vesper service was one of the distinctive features of college life at Stetson for almost thirty years during the administration of President Hulley. Visitors from the North early insisted that a collection be taken and the proceeds devoted to any purpose the president might designate. In due

time, this accumulated fund was used to purchase the "Eloise
Chimes," named for Mrs. Eloise M. Hulley, the beloved wife
of the president. These chimes were placed at a central point
on the campus atop a beautiful campanile erected by Dr.
Hulley at his own expense, a little before his death in 1934.

During the academic year of 1906-1907, President Hulley
was preparing me to take complete charge under his long-
range supervision during the following and subsequent summer vacations while he should be absent giving lectures
before Bible institutes, chautauquas, and universities in the
North. This proved to be a very rich experience for me during the summers of 1907, 1908, and 1909. I traveled to all
parts of the state meeting appointments in churches and addressing summer teachers institutes. I wrote daily newsletters
for the principal papers of the state. I supervised assignments
to rooms in residence halls. I reported weekly on the progress
being made in the erection of our new Carnegie Library
building on the campus and on repairs being made.

The president expressed himself frequently as much pleased
with the promotional letters I had been writing to prospective
students and their parents in all parts of the North. He was
surprised, on his return at the end of the first summer in
which I had been in charge, to find that the secretary of the
board of trustees expressed pronounced dissatisfaction with
my work. He was outspokenly critical and I could not help
knowing about it. The president told me not to worry and
said that he'd take care of the matter in due time. The secretary was a local real estate man. At an early meeting of the
executive committee of the board, he stated his grievance. I
had sent a carbon copy of each of my letters written to prospective students and their parents to his office so that he
might know the housing needs of persons desiring to move
to De Land. That, he said, was good and he appreciated it;
but I had not stopped there. I had sent a second carbon copy
of each letter to another real estate man in town who was

the secretary's chief rival in business. That was bad. No one, it seems, thought the secretary had any occasion to be really offended or annoyed at what I had done, and no one was quite willing to tell him so frankly. Finally the president asked a local minister of good standing, who was present on invitation, if he would not be willing to umpire the difference. He took hold immediately and with relish. Said he: "Whether this man, Suhrie, be a sinner I know not, but I do know that he has worked like the very devil all summer for this university." He assured the group that his reference was primarily to my zeal and not to my method. The meeting broke up in a hearty laugh, and the secretary's zeal for the service of prospective newcomers seemed thereafter to have greatly increased.

During that summer an incident occurred that might have changed the course of my life had I not been deeply committed to a career in teaching. On a bright June day the head of the most active real estate company in central Florida came to my office for an interview. After a few preliminary remarks he began: "Mr. Suhrie, I don't know what your salary is, but I have made up my mind I can afford to offer you four times what you are getting to join me in selling real estate." He was surprised when I declined the offer. He thought he had made it wholly impossible that I should do so. He argued the matter: "I'll make you a millionaire!"

"I'll be a millionaire in due time," said I. "I am sure of that, but I don't want to be a millionaire in money only. I want to be a millionaire in fine friendships and, when I get old, in precious memories!"

He thought I was crazy and argued the point so strongly that I knew he was. In the course of the years, he did become a millionaire in money and died a very unhappy man. I have never regretted my decision.

"Four times your present salary!" It wasn't even a temptation.

Our Shakespearean presentations during the first three years seemed to have made an excellent impression. Our Stetson cast put on the play of *Damon and Pythias* in Orlando in the spring of 1908 before the state convention of Knights of Pythias. Invitations came to reproduce the play in Jacksonville, Tampa, Key West, and Pensacola. When I requested an assistant in dramatic arts work so that I might give some courses in education in the fall and winter quarter as well as in the spring quarter, I was authorized in the summer of 1908 to call Professor Irving C. Stover, of Susquehanna University, in Pennsylvania. He accepted. He had been well trained at King's School of Dramatic Arts in Pittsburgh and took hold at once with vigor. I had already planned to bring the Chicago Art Institute Players down for a week's engagement at the height of the winter season. This we were able to do in 1910. Together, Professor Stover and I, with the help of these players, were able to offer the people of De Land an opportunity to hear in one season ten Shakespearean plays well given.

After 1908, I gradually shifted my service over into the field of education.

When Professor Stover had completed thirty years of service at Stetson (1938), he published a pamphlet giving the casts of all the Shakespearean plays presented in that institution since the day I opened up the list in 1905. It is an impressive list, and I venture the opinion that no other collegiate institution of comparable size during that same period provided its students, its faculty, and its community a richer and more varied program of Shakespearean offerings. A Stover Memorial Theatre was, in due time, erected on the campus of Stetson University.

While at Stetson, I took a very active interest in the work of the state teachers association and succeeded in the winter of 1908 and 1909 in securing the meeting for the next year in De Land. I was made chairman of the local entertainment committee and raised fifteen hundred dollars from local merchants to decorate the town suitably for the occasion. At that meeting, Dr. Lincoln Hulley was elected president of the association by acclamation.

I made an extended schedule for the Stetson Glee Club which took the Club to all the principal towns in the state.

In the summer of 1908, I purchased a building lot from President Hulley for $125; and, on plans and specifications made by my colleague, Professor Colton of the manual arts department, I proceeded to build a seven-room frame house of carefully selected, high-quality lumber furnished by a member of our university board. The total investment for the house and lot was $2,000. I have been told that this house, with the addition of a bedroom over the kitchen, a new roof, and a fresh painting, was sold thirty years later for $10,000.

Three years after I came to Stetson, the General Education Board of New York launched its campaign to promote the establishment of public high schools in all parts of the South. I was chosen to serve on a team that visited towns of three thousand or over to put on a symposium program, the purpose of which was to enlist the interest of citizens in this new movement.

In these meetings, I was usually the first speaker on the program probably because I was about the youngest member of the team. Usually, the most prominent citizen of the community, a local judge or ex-Confederate soldier, was introduced to close the argument before the audience. Too often this man's speech threw cold water on our hopes by saying something like this: "If the public schools will teach our children to read—and this can usually be done in about three years—they have done very well. They will have discharged their full responsibility; for, if a child has the stuff of success in him, he ought to be able to make his own way, and at his own expense, from there on." I noticed, however, that in many towns the young people, in spite of such counsel from their elders, became ardent supporters of the new movement; and high schools soon began to multiply in Florida at a rapid rate.

During these years the Summer School of the South under the able and aggressive leadership of Professor P. P. Claxton was exerting a powerful influence in stimulating progress in public education and in giving direction to its course. In 1910, the old Peabody Board voted to appropriate from the residue of its principal fund a good sum of money to build a new education building on the campus of each of the Southern state universities.

In the spring of the same year, I was ready to go forward with my long contemplated graduate study. I was elected to a Harrison Fellowship in Education at the University of Pennsylvania and granted a leave of absence. Though there were many friends who encouraged me to believe that I could be elected state superintendent of schools at the expiration of the then current term if I should remain in the state, I had no real interest in serving in that office because I knew full well that I was not prepared academically or professionally to discharge its duties.

President Hulley granted me a leave of absence and urged me to plan to return to Stetson on completion of my studies in Philadelphia.

I sold my house for $2,400 cash. This enabled me to cancel a mortgage of $2,000 on it and to bank the other $400 for use in meeting my expenses at the University of Pennsylvania. The Harrison Fellowship would pay tuition and books and provide a payment of $500 in eight installments. I spent the summer in Philadelphia drumming up enrollments for the Frye Business College.

When the time came for the opening of the fall term at the university, I had enough money in the bank to insure comfortable living for the year. I reveled in the thought that I should be free for more intensive study than I had ever before undertaken. I was surely not happy at the thought of severing my connection, even temporarily, with Stetson University. President Hulley had been up to then, and continued to be until the time of his death a quarter of a century later, one of the best friends God has ever given me.

While at Stetson I formed intimate friendships with a number of young men students of the University who have played very important and significant parts in the remarkable development of Florida in the years since then. Among them I may mention:

Doyle E. Carlton, an able, industrious, and affable young man from Wauchula, Florida. I never have known a college boy in any college in which I have taught who was able so completely to win and to hold the confidence, respect, and admiration of all the members of the faculty and student body as he. He became, in due time, the state's most notable governor of his generation. Mrs. Suhrie and I have recently been guests at his home in Tampa.

Then there was "Uncle Dan" Blocker who had been a lay preacher in the Baptist church in Florida for some years, was a freshman in Stetson the year I arrived on the campus, and was dean of men at about my age. He commanded the respect of the boys as fully as any faculty member, completed his college program on time and with honors, went to the University of Chicago for three years of graduate work in the divinity school, became president of Shorter College, and then finally served a long term as head professor of sociology in William and Mary College and pastor of the Baptist church in Williamsburg. He was a good friend always.

Frank W. Wideman, another Stetson student of distinction, was Solicitor General of the United States during the Roosevelt regime in Washington until he presented the N. R. A. case to the Supreme Court and lost it. Then the President's disappointment was so great that Frank thought it best to resign. My most intimate recollections of him as a college boy are associated with occasions when I coached him on his contest orations on the temperance issue. First, he won the Florida state contest; then the Southern regional contest; and finally, he came to Philadelphia to be coached for the national contest in Atlantic City which he also won. Frank was a winner until he attempted to defend the N. R. A. and then, thank God, he was a loser. But maybe he didn't lose after all for there is a wise saying among defenders of American liberty that when the Government is defendant in a case before the Supreme Court and loses both the people and the Government win, because in the last analysis they are one.

My fondest memories of Stetson center around President and Mrs. Hulley and their interesting family of one son and three daughters. Dr. Hulley was a great inspiration to me from the day I met him in Wilcox, Pennsylvania, in the spring of 1897 to the day of his death in Florida in January 1934. He was a scholar, a thinker, a powerful preacher and always a devoted friend. Mrs. Suhrie and I named our only son, Lincoln, for him, and our eldest daughter, Eloise, for his wife. The Hulleys often visited us in the North, in West Chester, Philadelphia, Cleveland, where he taught for me one summer, and in New York. Year after year Dr. and Mrs. Hulley came to New York at the Christmas Holiday season for a week of theatre going. Always they came to see us or had us as their guests at a dinner party at the Astor Hotel.

On their last visit, they invited my daughters, Eloise and Ruth, and me for dinner; then took us out for an evening of entertainment. I sat between them while Dr. Hulley renewed his acquaintance with Eloise on his right and Mrs. Hulley got acquainted with Ruth on her left. On our way back to the hotel, Dr. Hulley engaged me in private conversation. I shall never forget what he said: "Dr. Suhrie, your daughter, Eloise, has a brilliant mind and high ideals of duty and service. She should be able to go a long way in life if she can maintain her health. She is so charming." We said good-by to them at the hotel. The next morning they started South and the next evening Eloise started West. Two weeks later his death came suddenly in Florida and within two months hers came suddenly in Missouri. The memory of our last visit together will never die.

Graduate Fellow at University of Pennsylvania

When I entered the University of Pennsylvania, in the fall of 1910, to begin my graduate work on a Harrison Fellowship in Education, my chief adviser was Professor Albert Duncan Yocum, the head of the Department of Education. I told him I desired to make plans for at least two years of continuous study. He advised me to seek wide counsel from all promising sources in the departments in which I desired to study, namely: education, history, sociology, and social economics. For several days, I interviewed professors in these several departments. I had had my mind set on taking a course with a certain widely known authority in American history. I was quietly advised by Professor Yocum to visit one of this man's classes in the undergraduate college before enrolling in any one of his graduate courses. I did so; I found that he had a class of sixty-five, that he was able to hold the attention of only about five per cent of them, and that in the back of his classroom a number of his boys were playing cards unmolested and unnoticed. For what seemed to me to be good reasons, I decided not to enroll in any of his courses. By that time, I was cautious and deliberate in making my final decisions. I enrolled in eight different courses—two in education, two in history, two in sociology, and two in social economics. Every professor I had was a scholar, an interesting lecturer, if not always a good teacher, and every one inspired me. The courses I most enjoyed during the first term were one with Professor Yocum in institutes of education, one with Professor Edwin P. Cheyney on the British Empire, and one in sociology with Professor

James P. Lichtenberger. I studied also with Dean Ames in a course in American constitutional history and with Professor Simon Pattern on the development of economic thought.

The enrollment in the graduate school numbered about three hundred, most of them part-time students engaged in public-school service. There were about thirty Harrison Fellows distributed in all departments of the graduate school. These men received the special attention of all graduate professors. I found I might ask for a conference of some length on reasonable notice with any of my professors. These conferences, I still think, provided me most of what was of real worth to me in my graduate-school experience. I had never before known such fellowship in learning. I quickly acquired the art of rapid and discriminating reading. I had full access to the three hundred and ninety-thousand volumes in the Henry C. Lee Library and did a lot of very fruitful reading in many fields. The range of my interests widened. I was amazed at the number of titles one might find on the shelves on almost any topic in which he was interested.

I was encouraged to write many papers not required of the members of my class in general. I well remember the first of these. It was prepared for Professor Cheyney. When he returned it, there were many marginal questions and some notations which seemed to me might fairly be considered as commendatory. But, when I saw the grade of "D" written at the close of the twenty-fifth page of my paper, my heart sank; my humiliation was complete. I was sure I could never face the men at Stetson and Wooster who had recommended me for a Fellowship. When I went to Professor Cheyney for a conference on the reading I had done in preparation for writing this paper, he gave me an unusually cordial reception and said he liked my paper. I was more confused than ever. I had already gained such a profound respect for him as a scholar, a teacher, and a man that I couldn't bring myself to a critical attitude toward him, no matter how much my pride was in agony at the moment. But finally, I mustered up courage to say in as kind a tone as possible,

"But, Professor, if you liked my paper, why did you mark it 'D'?"

"Oh!" said he, with a flush of embarrassment, "I should have explained that 'D' means distinguished."

The tension was off. I was ready to show my grade to anyone interested, even to my wife and to my major professor, who greatly esteemed Professor Cheyney, having once been a student in his classes. Nor did I have to be persuaded to tell President Hulley by early letter; and, when I met Provost Harrison who had endowed my Fellowship, I was not too modest to let him know that I was off to a good start as judged by the rating which Professor Cheyney had given my work.

Early in my stay, I was impressed by the number of lecturers, distinguished for scholarship and/or public service at home or abroad, who were brought to the university for special convocations; and the number of men of real distinction from at home and from abroad who occupied the pulpit at the Sunday morning service hour in the Houston Hall chapel; and also, by the number of small group or departmental meetings of Fellows and other graduate students of maturity who were entertained at some professor's home in order to provide for personal conference with some distinguished visiting scholar. Under one or other of such auspices, we were privileged to hear Count Albert Apponyi, Prime Minister of Austria-Hungary; Governor Charles E. Hughes of New York; President Van Hise of the University of Wisconsin; President Nicholas Murray Butler; President Woodrow Wilson, of Princeton University; School Superintendent Martin G. Brumbaugh, of Philadelphia; judges of our state and federal courts; municipal research officers from Philadelphia and New York; social workers of distinction, such as Margaret Wilson, of Philadelphia and Judge Lindsey, of Denver.

Late in the fall of my first year, the Harrison Fellows took the initiative in organizing a University of Pennsylvania Graduate Club. I was elected president and at the end of the year was re-elected. This office gave me many rare privileges; among them, the privilege of a seat on the dais at banquets arranged in compliment to visiting speakers on such occasions as Founders' Day. The holding of this important office also gave me a superb opportunity to demonstrate my capacity for attracting top-notch guest speakers for the monthly meetings of our Graduate School Club, and greatly enlarged my opportunity to get acquainted with officers of high rank in our university, and with men and women of academic distinction and persons of high repute in public life who came to our campus.

The contact which I remember with most pleasure and satisfaction was with President E. A. Alderman, of the University of Virginia, who, some years later was chosen to deliver the tribute address on Woodrow Wilson before a joint session of Congress. As ranking student officer, I was seated on his right at the banquet table on Washington's birthday when he delivered the Founders' Day address and received the honorary degree of Doctor of Laws. He urged me to return to the South for my life work.

By the middle of my first year on the campus, Dr. Yocum, my major professor who was also director of the university summer session, invited me to teach two courses in the 1911 summer session. This gave me standing among regular university faculty members, and greatly multiplied my opportunities for fruitful conference and association with leading professors in many departments in which I was not a student.

I was offered a reappointment to my Fellowship for the second year and promptly accepted it, at the same time, notifying President Hulley in Florida that I should not return to Stetson in the fall of 1911. He assured me he was glad to continue my status for another year as "on leave." In June, 1911, I received an A.M. degree in education.

After the close of the summer session, I secured lecture engagements of one week in each of three county, or city teachers institutes in Ohio and Pennsylvania. I was well paid for these services as also for single-day lecture engagements in city institutes in Pennsylvania and New Jersey during the next year. The honoraria received, which were substantial, greatly helped me to finance my family during my second year of graduate study.

I reached a point in my graduate studies during the second year of my Fellowship, when Professor Yocum was reasonably sure I could finish my thesis and complete requirements for the Doctor of Philosophy degree, in June 1912. He was ready to offer me an appointment for the next summer school and also an appointment as Assistant Professor of Elementary Education and Director of the Practice Teaching Department of the University. The outlook was very bright. I was profoundly appreciative of the call to professional service Dr. Yocum had given me as his Harrison Fellow in Education and looked forward with great pleasure to the privilege of working with him in the future. I requested President Hulley to accept my resignation at Stetson.

I received the Ph. D. degree at the June commencement, of 1912, on the approval of my thesis entitled *The Inductive Determination of Educational Method*. My committee consisted of Professor Yocum (education), Professor Singer (philosophy), and Dean Ames (American constitutional history).

I spent the summer term teaching at the university and the last two weeks in August, I lectured in county teachers institutes in Ohio.

About the first of July, my plans were temporarily wrecked

by the announcement which Professor Yocum relayed to me from the provost's (president's) office, that at a meeting of the board, held that day, no appropriation was made to cover the salaries of the last six assistant professors whose appointments he had authorized early in the spring. Professor Yocum expressed himself as much embarrassed, not only because of the disappointment it might bring to me, but because my courses for the following year had already been announced.

I went immediately to New York for a conference with Dr. Bruce R. Payne, the recently appointed president of the new George Peabody College for Teachers in Nashville. I had been advised he might have a suitable opening for me. He told me, however, that no classes would be conducted at Peabody until the summer of 1914, two years later. He expressed positive interest in my coming to Peabody in due time and then advised me to write to the presidents of three newly created state normal schools in the South—one at Hattiesburg, Mississippi; one at East Radford, Virginia; and one at Fredericksburg, Virginia. I made application by letter to the president of each. Candidates with the Ph. D. degree, in education, were at a premium in the South in those days, and so I was invited to be the first dean in each of these new institutions. Two of the presidents came to Philadelphia in person to extend the call and press for an early acceptance.

In the meantime, I was invited by President Parks of the Georgia State Normal and Industrial College at Milledgeville, on his own initiative, to meet him at the Democratic National Convention in Baltimore. I thought it best to postpone acceptance of any of the invitations in hand until I had had an interview with him.

When I arrived in Baltimore, the convention was about to reach its climax. William Jennings Bryan was holding out against Tammany Hall's candidate, Champ Clark of Missouri.

The star of Governor Wilson of New Jersey was in the ascendancy. President Parks and I decided to put off any serious conference on the matter I had come to discuss with him until after Governor Wilson's nomination. He and I were both for the governor, and we thought it important to settle this matter of his nomination first. We were both sure we could not talk education while the nomination was pending; when that had been completed, we could drop politics and concentrate on our problem. Dr. Parks had an alternate's ticket from the Georgia delegation and President Hulley, who was a delegate from Florida, provided me with a ticket. I saw Wilson nominated; and when President Parks and I met soon thereafter, we were both happy and ready for conference on the Georgia opening.

Dr. Parks offered me the headship of his department of education at a salary and with a rank below that offered by any one of the three other institutions which had invited me, and I accepted for reasons that seemed good to me. Early in my professional career, I had made up my mind that rank and salary are relatively unimportant as compared with sphere of influence and the reputation, character, and standing of one's big boss. I had chosen the type of service most congenial to me and, more important still, a leader who impressed me most favorably. I never had occasion to regret that decision.

I left the university with sincere and heartfelt regret. Much as I loved the South which had always received me warmly, I was reluctant to give up the thought that Pennsylvania was to be the scene of my life work; and, too, I had a respect that almost amounted to reverence for Professor Yocum with whom I had thought for some months my lot was to be cast, perhaps permanently.

My little girl, then three years old, who had been born in Atlanta during a temporary sojourn of her parents in that city, relieved the strain by piping up: "Oh, Daddy, am I going to be born again in Georgia?" The answer was an emphatic, "Yes."

Deep Again in Dixie

Milledgeville, the site of the new capital of the empire state of the South, was laid out in 1804 on the rolling cotton fields of central Georgia on the right bank of the Oconee River. The landscape architect was the eminent Frenchman, L'Enfant, who had just completed his designs for our national capital on the banks of the Potomac. All the streets of this new city were to have wide tree lawns, and all except two of them were to be one hundred feet from curb to curb. These two streets were named Washington and Jefferson and were to be one hundred and twenty feet from curb to curb, with a twenty-foot shrubbery bed separating the two traffic lanes. These two streets were to meet in the State Capital building. In due time, all streets of the city were to be lined on either side with stately elms (dogwoods, and crepe myrtles had not yet come). The state capitol was to have ample, well-kept grounds with leading churches on their periphery, a city park, a state cemetery, and a site for the state penitentiary— now the campus of the Georgia State College for Women.

The city was also to furnish a beautiful site on the hill for the first governor's mansion which was superseded thirty years later, in 1838, by a better one. It was here that General Lafayette was received by a grateful people when he visited America and made his triumphant procession from state capital to state capital in the summer of 1824, fifty years after his first landing on American soil. It was in this capitol that the great battle of secession was fought out between Senators Robert Tooms, who favored it, and Alexander Stevens, who opposed it. It was here that General William T. Sherman had his headquarters for a time, while his army was on its fateful march to the sea, in the spring of 1864. After the fall of the Confederacy, the capitol was kidnapped and taken to Atlanta by the carpetbaggers who were, for a time, in control of the state government of Georgia. Milledgeville was something of a ghost town for many years thereafter.

When I first saw this historic city late in the summer of 1912, there were no sidewalks, streets were unpaved, the red clay dust was so fine and so deep in the middle of each traffic lane that it flowed like water about the tires and spokes of the cotton-carrying wains as they were driven through the streets. Houses were unpainted. The once beautiful city wore a very forsaken look. Income was low. Cotton was selling for twelve cents a pound and citizens were depressed, not to say despondent. I was sure that President Parks who knew his state's history well had been describing Milledgeville as it had been, not as it then was, when he waxed eloquent during our conference in Baltimore, two months earlier, over the glories of the old college town. I, too, was depressed by the general aspect of things until I first met with the faculty in the spacious parlor of the old governor's mansion, the home of the president and his family.

There were sixty bright-faced, nicely dressed, intelligent, and happy people in the faculty group, none of them much above forty years of age and many of them under thirty. They had come chiefly from the best colleges and universities all over the north. The president appointed me secretary of the faculty, and I had, thereafter, much to do with making up the agendas for our monthly (sometimes fortnightly) faculty meetings.

I had left Mrs. Suhrie and our little daughter in Philadelphia for medical care, pending the time when I should find a suitable place in which to live in Milledgeville. Finally, after two months of waiting, a new house was ready to receive us. When I brought my wife and the little one to the campus on a certain Monday early in November (Monday was the day when classes did not meet), they were given a truly "royal" reception. Seven hundred girls closed in on them at the center of the spacious college campus, each one hoping to have the first opportunity to shower her pent-up family affections on our three-year-old Eloise. To the day of her death at twenty-four, she always remembered the Georgia girls as the complete fulfillment of her dearest dreams of young womanhood at its springtime best.

The college was not yet a degree-granting institution. It had an enrollment of about seven hundred of Georgia's choicest young women who had been admitted on a quota basis, from all of her one hundred and fifty-two counties. In a half century of college teaching, I have not seen any other group of undergraduate college students that would compare favorably in either natural ability or personal charm with this group of young women.

The curriculum of the college placed its emphasis not on any Bryn Mawr or Wellesley pattern, but on the practical needs of young women who were planning to be wives, mothers, and teachers. The whole program of studies was highly motivated by intensely practical considerations.

My classes were large, my hours of teaching excessive; but students were earnest, co-operative, and, above all else, courteous and thoroughly appreciative. Classrooms, dining halls, and dormitories were crowded, but every student seemed to think it a real privilege to be in college and a special privilege to be in this particular college. If any student's conduct was even temporarily called in question, she needed only to be reminded that in her home county were other splendid young women on the waiting list and eager to have her place in the college. I have never yet seen manifested anywhere else such genuine gratitude for the privilege of going to college.

The women of the old state capital, famous for their gracious hospitality and for their personal charm, never, in the course of one hundred years of Georgia history, showed up to better advantage than on the occasion, November 18, 1913, when they served a Georgia products dinner to a group of the city's most distinguished citizens. The scene was the rotunda of the old governor's mansion, now the home of the president of the college. To this public function Dr. Vittum, professor of English in the college, Mrs. Suhrie and I were invited as special Yankee guests. The toastmaster was the Honorable James Sibley, childhood playmate of Woodrow Wilson. Such a flow of wit and wisdom, such clever repartee, such gracious sociability I have rarely witnessed in a long life of banqueting. The old mansion, it would seem, was chuck full of history, and the voices of the dead were never more vocal and articulate than in its banquet hall on this particular occasion.

Sanitation in Milledgeville was not good. Within a week after my arrival, I had acquired malaria. I struggled through the first year in a substandard condition of health. When spring came, I found it necessary to spend six weeks in the Clifton Springs, New York, Hospital and Sanitarium in order to recondition myself for my teaching in the summer school of the University of Pennsylvania.

Early in May, 1913, I went down to Rollins College, Winter Park, Florida, to give the commencement address. At the conclusion of the exercises, I was the guest of President and Mrs. Blackman at their home on Virginia Lake. The President informed me that the board had authorized him to extend to me an invitation to become vice-president of the college for two years until he should be ready to retire and to assure me that I should then be elected as his successor. I was full of malaria and thought it only fair to all concerned that I should decline. Three months later, President Blackman came on to Philadelphia to visit me in the summer school at the university and again to urge me to accept the call. He assured me that the board desired, as he did, that, two years later, I should become his successor. Again I declined. It is an interesting fact that I was a member of the lyceum committee at Stetson University that gave Mr. Hamilton Holt his first lecture engagement in Florida on the same tour on which he first visited Rollins College, which, in later years, he advertised to the ends of the earth.

In February of 1914, I attended for the first time, two notable national educational meetings in Richmond, Virginia, namely: The Department of Superintendence of the N. E. A. and the National Council of Normal School Presidents. This trip, taken at my own expense, opened the way for me to begin an acquaintance with our national leadership in education. I had previously attended two sessions of the midsummer meetings of the N. E. A. These seemed like carnivals. But the symposium and the open forum discussions I heard in Richmond awakened me to the professional significance of the more restricted and highly professional character of the mid-winter meetings. From that year on I was a regular attendant at the annual meetings of the two associations above mentioned, the latter becoming, in due time, the American Association of Teachers Colleges. On its programs, I appeared as a speaker almost annually for a period of years while in the Cleveland School of Education and later while in New York University.

By the end of my second year at Milledgeville, I was in excellent health again. Mrs. Suhrie's health was not good and she desired to return north. About that time, a call came from Governor Hunt of Arizona to come out to Phoenix for an interview concerning the vacant presidency of the Arizona State University at Tucson. Mrs. Suhrie's condition made it seem wise to decline this bid. A friend and former student in Arizona repeatedly assured me that if I'd come on for the interview, I should surely have the call; but I went off to the University of Pennsylvania for the summer fully expecting to return to Milledgeville in the fall. I thoroughly enjoyed my work there, greatly appreciated my neighbors and friends outside of the college circles as well, and I dearly loved the South; however, when I got to Philadelphia and took into account what seemed to be the best interests of my family, I decided to ask President Parks for a release so that I might accept the headship of the Department of Education at the State Normal School in West Chester, Pennsylvania, some thirty miles out of Philadelphia. The salary was very inadequate, but the call to lecture at substantial honoraria would be insistent, for I was again well established in my native state. President Parks offered me every possible inducement to remain and he knew I wanted to do so; but when I gave him my reasons for asking for a release, he graciously accepted them and voluntarily wrote a very strong endorsement of my record in Milledgeville to President Philips of the State Normal School at West Chester.

None of my friends in Milledgeville or in West Chester could possibly understand how sorry I was to leave the old southern state capital in the heart of the ante bellum South where I had been supremely happy for two years. President Parks frequently invited me to come down from Pennsylvania, and later from Ohio, to lecture in the summer school at Milledgeville. I was never free to do so until after his untimely death some thirteen years later.

President Parks was, in many respects, a very great leader. I never have known any other man who had equal power to develop ethical standards among young women and to inspire them with ideals of service. He worked untiringly for them and always held their unquestioned loyalty. He had earned and gained the respect of legislators all over the state and the confidence of parents.

In later years, I had many delightful visits with Dr. Parks at national education gatherings and at my home in Philadelphia, in Cleveland, and in Montclair, New Jersey. He never failed to give me strong endorsements to his friends and always entertained the hope that I should some day return to

the South. He often indicated his desire to have me succeed
him as President at Milledgeville. He invited me to come
down from New York University to make a consultant
survey of his institution early in January 1927. I had agreed
to do so, but before the date arrived he was suddenly killed,
in December 1926, on the streets of Tampa by a careless
auto driver. The board, early in the spring of 1927, gave me
its unanimous call to return to Georgia as his successor. My
wife was seriously ill at the time. She earnestly desired that
I should not take on administrative service again and so
I finally declined the call.

I have never ceased to recall my two years of service in
Milledgeville as supremely happy years. The city has an atmosphere of old-time Southern courtesy and hospitality
peculiarly its own. Its people always give to the second Mrs.
Suhrie and to me a royal welcome when we return; and my
former students, scattered all over the South, never fail to
remind me of the good times we all had together in "dear
old Milledgeville" in the long ago. I have met scores of them
all over the South, and in other sections as well, when I
have addressed teachers associations and educational conferences. Many of them have held very responsible positions of
leadership in state, city, and county school systems, and in
university schools of education and teachers' colleges. Nothing could so completely gratify my heart's desire as a reunion on the campus of the college in Milledgeville of all
my former students in that college. The college began its
existence the year I began teaching, and we could celebrate
both anniversaries together.

President Jasper L. Beeson and his gracious wife lived in
the mansion for a decade after President Parks' death and
during Dr. Beeson's presidency. Dr. Beeson always gave me
a warm welcome at the mansion and a royal presentation in
the college auditorium.

President Guy H. Wells and his delightful family moved

into the mansion after the retirement of the Beesons. During his administration—for nearly twenty years—I was invited to the campus about once a year and was always royally entertained at the mansion and given a very gracious hearing in the college auditorium by a thousand or more charming Georgia girls.

The beautiful city of Milledgeville with its broad paved boulevards, its stately elms, its magnificent college buildings and church edifices, its park, its historic cemetery, its restored capitol building and its seven thousand dogwoods, is a dream among all the cities of its size in America; and the friendships I formed there will warm my heart so long as life lasts.

Back on Native Soil

I was at home at once on the campus of the big Pennsylvania State Normal School at West Chester, near Philadelphia, Pennsylvania. President George M. Philips, personally helped me to find, for rental, a fine old residence in the center of this beautiful city of century-old brick- and stone-dwelling houses.

I had once before been invited to join the faculty of this institution. That was when I was a fellow in education at the University of Pennsylvania. I had many friends on the faculty and was treated by them as a comrade from the beginning.

Dr. Samuel C. Schmucker, the dean of the faculty, if not by title, surely by years of service and by prestige as a schoolman, invited me to become a member of his X Club. This club had in its membership a dozen schoolmen, physicians, ministers, and lawyers. I greatly enjoyed the fellowship of this group of very distinguished men. I was probably the youngest of all. For years after I left the city, I continued to hold membership in the club and to journey each month to West Chester to attend its meetings. Each member rode his hobby once each year in the presence of the group and stood for the most searching cross-questioning by the group on what he had said.

My classes in the normal school were excessively large. I met six sections daily. Half of them numbered ninety or above. My schedule, in terms of number of hours taught daily, was double what it ought to have been, and when measured by student hours was three or four times as high as it ought to have been.

There were five recitation hours each morning; I taught the first two and the last two of these. There were two recitation hours in the afternoon, and I taught both of these.

President Philips was especially glad to have so many students enroll in my elective sections in rural sociology. And he was doubly glad that I could hold their attention and interest. I played medicine ball for three-quarters of an hour each afternoon to keep myself physically fit. I attended a lecture by Dr. E. L. Thorndike of Teachers College, Columbia University, each week in Philadelphia.

At the Christmas Holiday season, I attended a meeting of the Pennsylvania State Teachers Association at Harrisburg. I was chosen to serve as president of the Pennsylvania State Normal School Teachers Association. The membership was not more than a dozen. The following year, when the association met in Scranton, there were three hundred members in attendance and seventy-five of these attended an evening banquet. I had invited Dr. Nathan C. Schaeffer, State Superintendent of Public Instruction, to be the principal speaker. Nearly all of the state normal school principals were present as guests. One of my problems was to get these men seated without placing any who were rivals (or worse still, bitter enemies) in uncomfortable proximity. When I had completed this task, I told the guest speaker I thought he might well give us a discourse on "brotherly love." He laughed heartily in agreement. Notwithstanding some obviously unpleasant antagonisms among the presidents, we had a very pleasant evening together. Our session the next day was attended by about three hundred normal-school teachers and interest in their problems grew from year to year thereafter until about 1919, when the State Bureau of Teacher-Education and Certification began conducting annually an official three-day session attended by all of the several hundred teachers in the fourteen state normal schools.

I extended my acquaintance very rapidly among the schoolmen of Pennsylvania, New Jersey, Delaware, and Maryland; and the invitations that came to me for lectures at city and county teachers institutes were numerous and insistent.

I attended the Cincinnati meetings in February, 1915, of the National Council of State Normal School Principals, and the National Council of Education as well as those of the Department of Superintendence of the National Education Association. I heard, on the program of this latter group a notable debate on "Military Training in Our Public High Schools and Colleges" in which debate Dr. Nathan C. Schaeffer, State Superintendent of Public Instruction, in Pennsylvania, and Dr. John H. Finley, State Commissioner of Education, in New York, were pitted against each other.

My attendance at this meeting greatly extended my personal acquaintance among the national leaders in our teacher-preparing colleges and in our state and city school systems. I was no longer a provincial; I could always be proud of the part my president, Dr. George M. Philips, played in all such meetings. He was a stalwart. He had served as executive secretary of the Pennsylvania State School Code Commission which had written and secured enactment by the Pennsylvania State Legislature of the most comprehensive and best organized state school code in existence at that time. To put this measure into effective operation, required the repeal of twenty-three hundred and five state school laws previously enacted. This gigantic task was chiefly the work of the commission's executive secretary. He was a hero among the public school forces of the state he had served so well for a whole generation. To be on his faculty was to bask a bit in the limelight. It was a truly great privilege to be intimately associated with him. His friends among the schoolpeople of his state were legion. Everywhere he went, at a state convention, he was given a quiet ovation. I never have known any other public servant who so fully enjoyed the privilege of helping the masses of the people to enter into their birthright of educational opportunity. How he did enjoy helping any one of the graduates of his school to a well-earned promotion in the public-school service and how they loved him for his fatherly interest in them!

After I severed my connection with his faculty, Dr. Philips frequently invited me to return to the Normal School to address the students and teachers. Before I took up my work some years later as head of the School of Education in Cleveland, Ohio, I had a long conference with him. The wise counsel he gave me on that occasion proved to be invaluable to me when the political storms broke over my head in subsequent years.

Said he on one occasion (and I have never forgotten it): "Dr. Suhrie, we need never fear the consequences of any injustice another may do to us; but we must always be fearful lest we do some injustice to another. In public office one must serve all with complete fidelity."

He was very kind to my little five-year-old daughter. When he was above sixty, he liked to play that he was her "big beau" and send her, now and then, a nice little gift and with it a "love note." She always revered his memory. He once said to me in a whisper: "When the politicians are attempting to wreck my program and me, it helps me to recall that your dear little girl still loves me. It's a wonderful thing to have a little sweetheart of her age."

Dr. Philips was my guest at a quiet luncheon in the

basement of the Statler Hotel in Cleveland, Ohio, just two weeks before he was stricken on his way home from the big annual banquet of his alumni society in Philadelphia. We talked over all my perplexing problems and there were many of them. In the calm and quiet of his sunset years, nothing worried him. His serenity reassured me in my determination to go forward with my program as he had done with his through so many years of fierce political badgering. The memory of this man, of the battles he had won for the children of his state and of the sweet spirit in which he met all opposition has been reassuring to me in all my administrative service in the more than thirty years since his passing. He truly was—in the language of the Good Book—"the servant of many."

Dr. Philips was a reader and a thinker. Throughout his long life, he had gathered up autographed copies of the great books of his generation. The Philips Memorial Library on the campus of the college contains this remarkable collection.

West Chester Teachers College has become one of the first-ranking centers of the State's musical culture. How precious are the memories of the many occasions when I journeyed from New York to the college to be the guest of President and Mrs. Swope, to speak in the morning to the faculty and students of the college in the Philips Memorial Auditorium and to attend Professor Hausknecht's evening program of Christmas carols with a chorus of five hundred voices. These were never-to-be-forgotten occasions. Once I tarried at the president's office after the program to greet some friends. In came the college janitor, tears streaming down his cheeks. Said he: "Any one who can't appreciate music like that jest ain't livin' right!" He expressed my sentiments perfectly. Oh, that the spirit of such occasions could continue throughout the year in our hearts and homes and communities. What a paradise on earth we should have!

5

COLLEGE
ADMINISTRATION

Bᴇᴛᴡᴇᴇɴ ᴛʜᴇ ᴀɢᴇꜱ of forty-one and fifty, I gave my best services in two well-known educational institutions as follows:

1. To administration and teaching, for two and a half years, in the historic University of Pennsylvania, an institution of rather conservative type and aristocratic traditions, state-subsidized but not state-controlled. I served as director of apprentice teaching and built up co-operative relationships with the public schools of Philadelphia and suburbs; also as assistant professor of rural education.

2. To the administration, for six and a half years of:

a) The Cleveland Normal School, a municipal institution governed by the Cleveland Board of Education and its agent, the city superintendent of schools. This was an agency for the pre-service education and training of teachers at the junior-college level for the city-school system; and

b) The Cleveland School of Education, an agency for the in-service and advanced academic and professional education of teachers and principals in the Cleveland and suburban-school systems. This was (in 1918) a paper institution without corporate entity. It represented nothing more substantial than a loose working agreement between the Cleveland Normal School and the Western Reserve University by the terms of which the principal of the normal school assumed the title of Dean and operated a group of extension courses during the academic year and in the summer session. I decided to accept Superintendent Spaulding's challenge to make it, in due time if possible, a top-notch degree-granting senior teachers college with appropriate offerings at the master's level.

Setting Up Apprenticeship Teaching in Philadelphia School System for the University of Pennsylvania

In 1913, the Department of Education of the University of Pennsylvania was expanded into a School of Education, one of the co-ordinate professional colleges of the historic university. Professor Frank P. Graves, the historian of education, was called from Ohio State University to become its first dean and Dr. Harlan Updegraff, of the Bureau of Education, Washington, D. C., was called to head its new department of educational administration and to organize and conduct an annual schoolmen's week conference.

In the summer of 1915, while I was guest professor in the University summer school, as I had been each year since 1911, I was offered a place on its regular staff to serve as director of apprentice teaching, director of the summer demonstration school, and assistant professor of rural education.

This new position was one of the twins arriving at my home on July 21, the other being my youngest daughter, Ruth. Big day!

I hesitated about accepting the call. I was happy in my work at West Chester, had a very important sphere of influence, and had been there only a year. It was late in the season and President Philips held out to me substantial inducements to remain. Among these was the hope and expectation, privately expressed, that, in due time, I might become his successor. It was a hard decision to make. Finally the die was cast; I accepted the call.

I commuted for a year from West Chester to the University, arriving on the campus in West Philadelphia before 8 o'clock A.M., six days each week.

My first assignment of duty after the opening of the term in the fall was to work out and secure the approval of some plan for co-operative relationships with the school system of Philadelphia. This required patience and tact, because I was not provided with a budget with which to pay any differential to those co-operating teachers in the elementary and secondary school of the city whom I should invite to serve as sponsor teachers in the training of apprentices assigned to them, with the approval of the city school authorities.

By the end of the first year, we had a good working agreement in full operation; and we had established professional relationships that were highly co-operative, and personal relationships that were friendly with teachers, and principals, and with district and associate superintendents of the city-school system.

I continued to receive many calls to lecture in the county and city teachers institutes of Pennsylvania, New Jersey, Delaware, and Maryland. These contacts not only widened my acquaintance with schoolmen, but broadened the basis of co-operation between our school of education and the public-school systems which it could best serve.

I was chosen in the spring of 1916, to serve as secretary of the Schoolmen's Week Conference, an annual spring meeting of the public-school leadership of Pennsylvania, New Jersey, Delaware, and Maryland. It became my duty to compile and edit the proceedings of this Conference. The university was spending thousands of dollars each year in publishing a suitable number of copies of these proceedings so that one might be furnished free to each of the overhead administrative and supervisory officers in the public-school systems of the four states above mentioned. This annual publication had to be prepared with meticulous care to conform to the very best standards governing such publications. I spent more than a month each year in the preparation of these proceedings. The addresses of some of my Pennsylvania Dutch friends needed much editing, not to say translation, to make them acceptable for publication.

In the summer of 1916, I compiled and edited for the American Association of Political and Social Science a volume entitled *New Possibilities in Education.*

In the fall of the same year, I was requested to organize a course in the principles of teaching for the Philadelphia League of Nursing Education with special reference to the teaching problems of the nurses in charge of instruction in the hospital-training schools of the city and its suburbs. I spent one afternoon each week visiting one or other of the nurse-training schools of the city, to observe the teaching which was being conducted therein and to organize demonstrations in teaching to be presented before our class of one hundred teachers of nursing at our weekly meeting in the old Pennsylvania hospital. This class of nurses was attended by teachers of nursing and directors of nursing schools in Philadelphia, Reading, Chester, West Chester, Wilmington, and Atlantic City. This work, with increasing interest, was carried on for more than two years and until I withdrew from the university to begin my work in the city of Cleveland. Growing out of my associations with the Philadelphia League of Nursing Education, I was invited for a number of years to appear on the annual programs of the National League of Nursing Education.

Early in the spring of 1917, in co-operation with the United States Bureau of Education, we conducted at the university a three-day conference on rural life and education. Several hundred leaders in the rural areas, county and district superintendents and supervisors, grange officers, rural pastors and other rural leaders attended. I served as co-ordinator of these programs on behalf of the university. This assignment gave me a stimulating enrichment of experience and prompted new educational interests of wide sociological import.

Late in the spring of the same year I recruited students for our summer elementary demonstration school, selected and organized a staff of expert teachers from the best public and private elementary schools of the country, and then, during the summer session, administered the program of the demonstration school. I not only performed these functions, but took full responsibility for conducting the seminar in elementary education for which the summer demonstration school served as a laboratory. The demonstration staff which I had recruited for the summer session included outstanding class-room teachers from the public-school systems of Newton, Massachusetts; Buffalo, New York; Minneapolis, Minnesota; Salt Lake City, Utah; and Cincinnati and Cleveland, Ohio.

The seminar, numbering about two hundred, was open only to students who should spend at least one hour each day in observing the teaching in the demonstration school. The topics presented in the seminar grew out of the organization, administration, and practices of the demonstration school. Each speaker was allowed thirty minutes for the presentation, in outline form, of the special points calling for elucidation and for clarification through discussion.

Thirty minutes was then devoted to the discussion of issues that had been raised by the speaker or by members of the seminar. I served as moderator. This seminar was the center of interest on the campus of the summer session for all who desired to become master artists in the conduct of elementary school classwork.

Provost (President) Edgar Fahs Smith, of the university, seemed unable to see any good reason for having a school of education until he had spent two full mornings with us in the demonstration school and in attendance at the eleven to twelve o'clock seminar. His "conversion" was complete.

Thereafter he was an ardent supporter of a professional school for the preliminary education and the continuing in-service professional education of teachers.

Four calls came to me before the close of my second year at the university to go elsewhere. President Bruce R. Payne, George Peabody College for Teachers, Nashville, Tennessee, invited me to become the successor of William K. Tate as professor and head of the department of rural education in that institution. Dean Will Grant Chambers, of the School of Education of the University of Pittsburgh invited me to a professorship in education in that institution. The President and Secretary of the State Normal School at Indiana, Penn-sylvania, assured me that if I should consent to come to the campus of that institution for a conference, I should be elected to its presidency at once. It was, at the time, the larg-est of Pennsylvania's State Normal Schools. These calls all came early in the spring of 1917.

Provost Smith of the university assured me that I should have a bright future in the university, if I would put aside all thought of leaving. Accordingly, I decided to remain, not-withstanding to do so meant the passing up of an oppor-tunity to have a salary in one of these institutions about four times what I was then receiving. I had done that once before, and so I didn't find it too difficult to do so again. Promotion it seemed to me should be conceived of as an enlarged sphere of influence and usefulness, not merely in terms of advance-ment in rank or salary. I have never regretted that decision.

In midsummer of the same year, President Sparks invited me to become the head of the Department of Education in the Pennsylvania State College. Again I decided to remain at the University of Pennsylvania.

During the latter part of the summer session of 1917 and in the absence of Dean Graves from the campus, I saw an opportunity to get an allocation of Smith Hughes funds for the training of vocational teachers in the University of Pennsylvania, if certain step could be taken promptly and certain guarantees given to the State Board of Education. I called the matter to the attention of the provost. He authorized me to make presentations in person to the State Board of Education in Harrisburg. This I did, and the University received the grant requested.

The University of Pennsylvania was not then, nor is it now, a state institution. It had, however, for many years, received annually, a substantial grant of funds in aid (as have other nonpublic institutions within the state, including Temple University, the University of Pittsburgh, and at times, a few others) from the state treasury through legislative appropriations. The provost of our university had the onerous task thrust upon him each biennium of justifying this practice before the legislature and of making request for increasing sums. The problem before him was: Should the university, which was governed by a self-perpetuating board, continue to seek appropriations from the state while continuing to operate as a private or endowed institution; or should it make a renewed and more determined effort to raise money from private sources to cover its mounting deficits?

The provost appointed an alumni committee to study the situation and to make recommendations. United States Senator George Warton Pepper, formerly Dean of the Law School of the university and a member of its board of trustees, was made chairman of this committee, which finally presented in terse language the following recommendation:

"It's time for the University of Pennsylvania to quit living in unlawful concubinage with the state legislature."

This, in effect, made the provost's task more difficult. He called me to his office one day and requested that I appear with him before the board of trustees at its next regular meeting, and explain why our university seemed so much less popular in the legislature and among citizens throughout the state than Temple University in Philadelphia, or Pennsylvania State College, or the University of Pittsburgh.

I respectfully suggested to him that he request the dean to perform this service. His reply was that the dean was not nearly so well acquainted in the state as I was and that I should, therefore, be able to make a more pointed, and impressive presentation based on the known attitude of Pennsylvania state school leaders. I reluctantly responded to the assignment. There was no doubt in my mind about my having the undivided attention of the board, which had in its membership the governor (ex officio), a senator, and half a dozen former state attorneys general. When the meeting ended, a dozen of its members came forward to commend my frankness and to tell the provost they wanted a full session with me on this topic in the near future. Provost Smith heartily congratulated me on my presentation and assured me again of his satisfaction in the decision I had made the previous summer to remain permanently at the university.

At this same meeting, the board, on the recommendation of the provost, granted release (at the close of the then current semester), to a distinguished member of the university's medical faculty who had a call to the University of California; and on the provost's recommendation the board took further action authorizing him to grant release at the middle of the academic year to any professor who might, in the meantime, receive a satisfactory call elsewhere. The reason for this unusual action was that the war was on, that the university is a men's college, and that the draft was depleting our university enrollment by hundreds each month.

Within thirty days thereafter, late in November, while enroute west to address the Nebraska State Teachers Association in Omaha, I stopped off in Cleveland, Ohio, to meet Doctor Frank E. Spaulding, Superintendent of Schools, and to consult him about the selection of teachers for our

1918 summer session at the university. I learned while in Cleveland, that the principalship of the Cleveland Normal School was soon to be vacant.

On my return to Philadelphia from Omaha, a week later, I was a bit surprised to meet Superintendent Spaulding of Cleveland on our campus in Philadelphia. He made known to me his interest in my coming to the Cleveland Normal School as principal and said that, in case I was really interested, he wanted my permission to ask Provost Smith of our university whether, if my decision should be favorable, I could be released at the middle of the year. I gave my consent and he called upon the provost by appointment that morning. The provost explained the recent action of the board, quoted above, and said that, though he hoped I would remain, he had no other alternative than to grant me my release if I should ask for it. Within the next ten days, I went up to Cleveland, on the superintendent's invitation, to look over the situation. The official invitation was extended to me while in the city, and I did not long delay my acceptance.

I had, only three months before, bought and moved into an attractive new house in Drexel Hill, a suburb of Philadelphia. I knew my family would have to continue to live in it until I could find a place in Cleveland. The war was on and there were many considerations which obviously might have made me hesitate. Provost Smith had made it clear to me that he had definite plans for the enlargement of my sphere of opportunity in the university and outside of it. On the other hand, the new position would double my salary at a time when the cost of living was mounting daily, but more important still were three other considerations:

First, the University of Pennsylvania, it seemed to me, was not likely to step courageously forward to embrace its superb opportunity. It had lost its chance a few years before to attract Professors Bagley and Coffman of the University of Illinois, Dr. Hosic of the Chicago Normal College, and other men of real distinction in their several fields; and it seemed to have no great urge to provide facilities for a modern demonstration and experimental school setup on our campus. (This latter was a matter of deep concern to me, inasmuch as Superintendent Spaulding had assured me that the whole school system of Cleveland should be a part of the laboratory setup in addition to an expanded demonstration school on the campus of the Cleveland Normal School.)

Second, Dean Jessup, of the University of Iowa, in a recent survey of the teaching staff of the Cleveland school system, had made it seem that the situation there was ripe for a great forward movement in upgrading the professional qualifications of the five thousand teachers of the fifth city.

Third, the privilege of working as an understudy to Dr. Frank E. Spaulding who was then, almost by common acclaim, the most eminent public-school superintendent in the United States was somewhat overpowering.

So I decided to accept the call. That I had been correct in my appraisal of the opportunity was soon made manifest by the receipt of letters from half a dozen different men of great prominence in the field of teacher education, representing all parts of the country, and including Dean Coffman, of the University of Minnesota, Professor Bagley, of Teachers College, assuring me that I had wisely chosen to respond to the best challenge offered any man of my training, outlook, and interest that had come during the year.

Farewell to University of Pennsylvania

By January 28, 1918, I had concluded my work of the first semester at the University of Pennsylvania and, for the first —and last—time in my life, was ready, with the full official approval of my superior officers, to transfer to a new position in the middle of an academic year. This was the hardest transfer I was ever called upon to make.

Dean Graves was a scholar of wide repute and had helped me to extend my acquaintance among his friends in ever-widening circles. He was a lovable man, and had never failed to manifest his personal good will as well as his interest in my professional growth and advancement.

Professor Yocum, my immediate superior in the department and my best mentor of graduate days, was obviously disappointed—very deeply disappointed. That was heartbreaking to me. He was a lonesome man. His students were always deeply appreciative of his fine gentility and of his towering intellect, but not many had put forth enough effort really to comprehend his superb and permanent contribution to American democracy and to the fine ethical and religious concepts upon which it had been built up.

He accompanied me to the train when I left Philadelphia for Cleveland. At the depot, he broke the silence with an altogether unexpected question: "Dr. Suhrie, why do you want to go into administration?" "I don't except as a means to an end," was the answer. He still looked puzzled.

Then I recalled to him the familiar story about John C. Calhoun. On a Saturday afternoon, his classmates at Yale, urged him to go out with them to play ball. He declined saying that he'd have to study the Constitution of the United States.

"Why, you won't need that to pass your examinations" they urged.

"No, I know I won't," said he, "but I'll surely need it when I get to the United States Senate."

He looked more puzzled than ever until I explained that I could never be the kind of professor of college administration I wanted some day to be, unless I should first have an adequate experience in the field of college administration.

After I got myself established in Cleveland, he served me well in each of four successive summer terms by giving to the whole corps of our Cleveland public-school teachers, a series of superb lectures on his "Five Forms of Conduct Control," and another on "Education for American Democracy."

When I was called, seven years after leaving Philadelphia, to establish in New York University, a department to train administrative officers and teachers for normal schools and teachers colleges, he was supremely happy. And when, some years later, he visited our big annual conference of teachers college students from all over the East in New York City, he expressed himself as profoundly impressed with what was being accomplished in unifying the teachers college forces and in democratizing the internal organization and spirit of the teachers college.

Professor Yocum never lost an opportunity to help me to achieve any professional goal I had set for myself.

The memory of Dr. Edgar Fahs Smith, Provost (President) of the University, moves me deeply. He never lost an opportunity to express his appreciation or to give me a word of encouragement. He was a profound scholar, and a genuinely dedicated servant of his university and of mankind. I like to recall how big a factor his encouragement of me was in my personal and professional development. When I took my leave of him (never to see him again), he said: "We'll not forget you; you must come back some day and continue your service to your native state and mine. I have big plans for you."

A year later, he made a supreme effort to bring me back to the state. When there came a vacancy in the office of State Superintendent of Public Instruction, on his own initiative, he recomended me to Governor Sproul for appointment to that important post. I was not really interested in state school administration and I knew I was not well prepared for it. I had made up my mind to make teacher education my life work. I had numerous letters from important school officials all over the state approving my "candidacy." This was embarrassing to me for I was not a candidate and made that fact very explicit to all my well-wishers. I did not know at the time who was sponsoring my appointment. The Governor, I was told, had been interviewed by a reporter on a Philadelphia paper to whom he was reported to have said that he was ready to invite me for an interview with a view to appointment. My position was made known to him by a friend and, in due time, he issued the call to a much abler and far more experienced authority on state school administration, Dr. Thomas E. Finnegan, of New York.

I have not forgotten Edgar Fahs Smith. I have often thought that my greatest benefactors have been those who most helped me to believe in my own future. He was one of the chiefest of these.

Tribute to a Beloved Mentor

I was a frequent visitor in Dr. Yocum's seminar and in his home between 1918, when I left the university, and 1936, when his death occurred. In the spring of 1931, when he had completed twenty-five years of notable service at the University of Pennsylvania, I suggested to Dean John H. Minnich that a tribute meeting be arranged and held in Irving Hall on the University campus during the spring Schoolmen's Week Conference. The suggestion was acted upon, and a special program set up for the spring meeting of 1932.

President Penniman presided. Professor Yocum was an honor guest on the platform. The speakers were all men in prominent positions who had completed their doctoral studies and requirements under Professor Yocum's direction, namely: Professor J. Q. A. Rohrbach, Professor of Education, University of Pittsburgh; Professor Charles E. Peters, Head of the Department of Sociology, Pennsylvania State

College; Professor John H. Minnich, Dean of the School of Education, University of Pennsylvania; and Professor Ambrose L. Suhrie, Head of the Department of Teachers College Education, in New York University.

The hall was filled with Dr. Yocum's former students and his friends in the University. Each of the addresses was definitely concerned with an elaboration of some one of Professor Yocum's more important contributions to education.

It is my privilege to reproduce here two excerpts from my own address. These statements must stand as my appraisal of Professor Yocum's professional services and as my tribute to his lovable character:

> The appearance on this program this morning of the president of the university and of four other men from four different institutions to speak on as many different topics presents in itself no unusual circumstance. The fact, however, that we who are on this platform and hundreds of you who are in this audience have come together gladly on this occasion from widely scattered sections, not merely to discuss important themes having to do with public education, but more particularly, to pay tribute by our presence to the achievements and services of that distinguished educational leader who is our honored guest, lends very real significance to this gathering. Altogether apart, therefore, from what any or all of us may say on the subjects, announced on your program, this occasion is sure to be one that will long be remembered. For it would seem impossible that we, who were here in this university at an earlier day, should sit together in this hall with our beloved preceptor for a friendly hour's visit by the fireside of memory without calling up in happy association, scores of occasions when, in the lecture hall or around the seminar table, we engaged in the friendly combat of ideas with one who was as magnanimously generous in his tolerance of conclusions, he could not accept as he was inspiringly tenacious of those convictions which he had

arrived at for himself by years of patient and scholarly toil.

If it were necessary artificially to superinduce for this morning hour, that friendly and pervasive attitude of good will toward our guest which we all desire shall be the continuing and characteristic undertone of this meeting, I should need only to recall to you one of the many occasions when, in interpreting the fine human qualities of England's greatest schoolmaster, Professor Yocum became himself, quite unconsciously, the living embodiment to us of those gentle traits of character which had made Thomas Arnold the idol of all his boys at Rugby.

Because our guest of honor has been accustomed to exalt truth above its discoverer and dynamic ideas above the men who merely entertain them, it will doubtless bring less of embarrassment to his modest soul and consequently more of satisfaction to his many former students and other personal friends here assembled, if we who speak on this program will survey the recent history of educational progress in fields related to those in which his distinctive contributions have been made rather than to celebrate his outstanding professional achievements by cataloging them and labeling them with his name.

Suffice it, for the present, to say that, in a day when piecemeal specialization threatened our program with chaos, Professor Yocum was able "to lift up his eyes to the eternal hills" and to see the far horizons as well as the details in the foreground of the landscape.

We have not come together to place ultimate evaluation upon his work which is not finished, but to congratulate him upon the importance and distinctiveness of his achievements during a twenty-five year period of service here in our alma mater and to bid him God-speed on his further journey through the fruitful and happy years which we all hope may lie ahead.

In the closing years of his life Professor Yocum made many significant studies in the field of religious education in cooperation with Dean Athern, of Boston University.

First Lesson in Public Relations in Cleveland

I arrived in Cleveland one day ahead of schedule. The news reporters for the city papers had planned, as I afterward learned, to be present in the assembly to hear my first address to faculty and students. It seems that no one in the normal school had notified them of my presence in the city till after the morning convocation had adjourned. They had a grievance. Each of them called up and asked me for a picture and an appointment for an interview at my office. I rather proudly told him that I had no photograph. (I was sure that would indicate clearly that I was a professional man and not a head-line hunter.) I arranged to give each an interview as nearly as possible at his own convenience.

The first reporter to arrive representing the morning *Cleveland Plain Dealer* was Clyde R. Miller (noted in recent years as an expert in analyzing hidden propaganda). He was accompanied by a photographer, but decided, after seeing the picture taken by him, that its representation would have little news value on the third day after my arrival.

The reporter for the evening *Cleveland Press* brought with her a young artist to make a sketch of the characteristic features of the new normal school principal. I was not aware during the interview that she was sketching me. When I saw my name as a legend under her drawing on the first page of the *Press* the next evening I was sorry that this reporter, too, hadn't found some good excuse for not printing it. A day later, I received a letter from a college classmate at Wooster inquiring about my health. He said he had seen my picture in the *Press* and could not help wondering whether I was well. I learned a lesson. I was sorry I had not had the best photographer in Philadelphia send to each paper, days in advance, the very best picture he could make of this subject.

There must have been at least five thousand graduates of the Cleveland Normal School, chiefly public-school teachers, living in the Cleveland area who knew and loved my very handsome and affable predecessor and who naturally hoped that the new principal of *alma mater* might be equally "easy on the eyes." That picture in the *Press* destroyed any hope I might have had for a warm-hearted reception by the alumni. They had seen a cartoon of me and had mistaken it for a likeness. That was my first impressive lesson in public relations.

I joined the Cleveland Chamber of Commerce at once and sought the acquaintance of men of prominence in the affairs of the city. And I began looking around for a top-notch professor of journalism to sponsor our normal-school paper. In due time, I found her in the person of Miss Clara Ewalt. Six and a half years later, when I was about to withdraw from the service in Cleveland, she presented me "a scrap book of remembrances" containing literally hundreds of clippings from our metropolitan newspapers reporting happenings of interest to the public from the activities of our Cleveland Normal School and our Cleveland School of Education. In it, too, was the record of the acclaim given our school paper when year after year it won first or second prize in the national College Press Association contest at Columbia University.

After my first painful lesson in public relations I made up my mind never again to have any part in hiding the light of our school under a bushel. Our work in all departments of the institution was given ample—and always helpful—interpretation in our metropolitan press. Miss Ewalt had taught all of us how to co-operate intelligently and effectively with representatives of the press in interpreting our institutional service to the public-school system.

Thorny Administrative Problems

I found the situation bristling with unsolved administrative problems.

My first office callers were two young women from Polish families who had failed to be graduated in the previous June class because they had not completed all the formal-course requirements. They had returned in the fall and had, so they said, picked up their deficiencies. In the meantime, it had been noised about in faculty circles, that the new school superintendent had said in a public address that henceforth the normal school would be expected to grant its diploma only to such persons as might be considered acceptable candidates for appointment to teaching positions in the elementary grades of the city-school system. The faculty members seemed divided on the issue of whether either of these young women should be granted a diploma. These girls quoted my predecessor as having promised each of them a diploma as soon as she should secure a grade in each of the uncompleted subjects of the formal curriculum. This, they said, they had done. I wrote him for an official answer as to whether such a promise had been made. His answer was circuitous and noncommittal.

In the meantime, I had several interviews with the young women and their parents. In the course of these interviews, it become increasingly clear that one of them had a very serious defect in her speech, due to a cleft palate and that neither of them could speak the English language, acceptably. They seemed to have little knowledge of correct sentence structure and their pronunciation was so distinctly foreign that no American child would be likely to understand what they were saying.

They claimed that no one of our faculty members had ever called their attention to these shortcomings and insisted that I must be prejudiced against their nationality, their religion, or something else; and they assured me that influential friends down at city hall and at school headquarters would see them through with or without my consent. The situation had some elements of humor in it. I was reminded of the mayor of a Pennsylvania German community who, when presiding at the local high-school commencement, said proudly: "Ven I endered dis hoch schule [high school] I couldn't say *norse* and I couldn't say *souse;* but in dis vonderful hoch schule de teachers soon learned me to say *bose* like a real English mann."

I referred the issue of the granting of diplomas to the faculty whose responsibility it was to make the decision. They voted, unanimously, not to grant the diplomas.

This set a precedent in our school; namely, that a diploma should mean something more fundamental than a mere record of completed courses in a formal curriculum. Our diploma was henceforth to be a certificate of competency in teaching at the novice teacher's level of performance.

I never heard from city hall, but word did come to me from reliable sources that one of the hold-over assistant superintendents at school headquarters had remarked in many places that the new normal-school principal "lacked the spirit of accommodation." Maybe he was right, for I always have found it *twice* as hard to accommodate a school politician as to accommodate the ordinary garden variety of cityhall politician. The later may be ignorant of what the public service calls for; the former has no excuse for not knowing.

The war was on and enrollment in the normal school was very low. It was less than a month until an entering class of mid-year high-school graduates should normally seek admission.

Superintendent Spaulding called me up one morning to ask what I had found the prospects to be, for a good enrollment in the spring quarter. I had to tell him that of the four candidates who had presented themselves, I thought no one was even a fair prospect. They seemed to be the left-overs, physically handicapped, mentally slow, culturally deficient. This report prompted the inquiry: didn't I think it would be well to go personally to each of our public high schools in the city and its suburbs, and to tell the members of senior classes what teaching has to offer as a field for important public service and for intense personal satisfaction? I told him I thought it would and assured him that I'd be glad to go if properly invited, but cautioned him that I did not wish to appear in the role of one attempting to pry a rose-bud open with a handspike.

In a few minutes, my telephone began to ring and I had, in due time, a pressing invitation from each of our Cleveland high schools to visit it and to address the senior class on teaching as a career. I accepted all of the invitations; and the next week, at the meeting of the schoolmasters' club, I received additional invitations to visit the suburban high schools. I accepted all of these, too.

I have a very vivid recollection of my experience on the first of these visits. It was in a big high school located in a high class residential district. I appeared on the scene at 7:30 A.M. and was taken immediately to the assembly hall. The times were out of joint. The war was on; teachers were leaving the service in droves for war work. Salaries, which for elementary teachers had been only five hundred and forty dollars when Superintendent Spaulding arrived in the city during the preceding summer, had since been raised, but even so, almost any other occupation afforded better remuneration than teaching. I can laugh now about my experience that morning—but it wasn't funny then.

The principal, a gray-bearded veteran, a Harvard graduate, who had written text books in Latin, had assembled in the auditorium all the senior girls—three or four hundred in all. He gave me a very cordial and gracious welcome at the door. He conducted me to the platform. Then, as we stood together in the presence of these charming girls he said something like this: "Dr. Suhrie, I did not invite our young men to this meeting for it has always seemed to me that public-school teaching is hardly a suitable calling for a man of ability and standing." The thought that flashed through my mind was this: "How does he expect these bright young women to classify himself and me? Does he want them to think of us as members of the third sex?"

He went on: "Girls, you are all members of our senior class. Most of you will be given diplomas at the next commencement. Many of you have high standing for you have excellent ability and you have been industrious; added to that, you have personal charm; you come of good families; your parents are college graduates; college is in your blood, and you have the money to go. So God bless you and success attend you.

"But there are a lot of you who have mediocre ability; some of you are loafers and flunkers and if you get through at all, it will be by the skin of your teeth. No college will take you. You probably haven't the money to go anyway, and so I don't know what I could better advise you to do than to go to the normal school and get ready to teach. Dr. Suhrie, the new principal of that school, is here and he will now tell you about it."

This was the first time in my life that any one had presented me to a public audience as the principal of a school for the feeble-minded. My temperature rose perceptibly. I was a guest and had to observe the amenities or I should have told the girls this story: Over in Pennsylvania, a bartender's wife, a recent immigrant, was much disturbed by the grades on her daughter's report card. I had warned her when she enrolled the child, that she might find it hard to make good grades. Day after day the mother asked me: "How ist Rosy gedden along?" My answer: "She finds everything hard." Finally, it dawned upon the mother that maybe Rosy didn't have what it takes to get on in school (for example: what we now call an I. Q.). A little while later, and after she had had some time to think the situation over, she came to me one morning and said, with the ardor and enthusiasm of the scientist who has finally worked out a formula that is sure to revolutionize industry: "Mr. Suhrie, *my Rosy ist so dum! See ist so dumb!!* I know *now* vat I do mit her; *I make a school teacher of her!!!*"

I did not dare to tell that story much as I should have liked to do so. I could not help noticing, however, how much the thinking of a Harvard graduate can resemble that of an unlettered immigrant when he is making a pronouncement on a subject about which he is grossly ignorant.

The girls gave me a good hearing. I told them of the Moravian bishop Cominsky, who declined the presidency of Harvard University because he was unwilling to give up his opportunity to serve the little children of his own country. This, he thought, was a far more important life work. I told them, also, of Froebel, Pestalozzi, and Herbart and of our own Horace Mann, Henry Barnard, and Francis Parker. I told them, too, of Suzan Blow and Patty Hill and of their marvellous service to the little children of our country. I did what I could to exalt the dignity and power of the teacher's calling. The response the girls gave me was all that could be desired, but I feared I had made few, if any converts. The times were "out of joint."

When the address was over, three young women came forward to make appointments for an interview at my office. In the interview, each one told me about the same story: that her grandparents and her parents, all the high-school teachers whom she admired, and her minister all had advised her *not* to prepare for a career in teaching. All three of these girls enrolled in the normal school at the next entrance period. All of them were young women of superb ability and of high purpose and all of them made good in teaching.

The enrollment in the fall was not good, but it was much better than it might have been had we not made an heroic effort to counteract the propagandas against teaching which were being put forth by many of the teachers in our school system in these discouraging days. A year later, we succeeded in perfecting a far more adequate and successful plan for enlisting the interest of young people in "the ministry of teaching."

I was shocked to find how inadequate was the budget authorized for the operation of the normal school and greatly troubled to learn that the extension courses and summer session had no other assured resources except the income from tuition charges. I knew, however, that Superintendent Spaulding had a much larger concept of the place of our enterprises in Wade Park, than any previous superintendent of schools in the history of the city had had and, I was confident that when the time should come, he'd find the money more adequately to meet our needs. This he surely did.

I soon discovered that there was an uncomfortable incoordination of schedules as between the extension-class meetings and the grade-teacher-group meetings. This was a source of great irritation to the many hundreds of teachers who, on at least two or three occasions during the semester, were expected to be in two different places at the same time. By the opening of the fall session, I had secured agreement that all extension classes in the school of education be given on the afternoons and evenings of Tuesday and Thursday and on Saturday mornings, and that all junior-high-school and grade-group meetings of teachers be held in the afternoons of Monday and Wednesday.

It was clear to Superintendent Spaulding and to me, that a complete reorganization of the demonstration and training school staffing had been long over due. The teachers and principals in these schools had found their places by the operation of the rule of seniority. Our ablest and best trained principals and teachers were imperatively called for in these positions. So, we discontinued the training schools, then in operation in the city, and created new ones near to the normal school, by transferring such teachers as had been satisfactory from the abandoned training schools, and by appointing new principals for these schools and recruiting full quotas of training teachers from among the better educated candidates from outside, as well as inside, of the Cleveland school system.

This inevitably caused some heartaches, but nobody was given a cut in salary and, within a few months, it was clear to all concerned that we had been governed by but one consideration, the improvement of the service.

On the second day in my office I had a visitor who, after introducing himself as the representative of a publishing house in the city, announced that he was "on the war path" and then proceeded to prove it. He claimed that the school owed his company three hundred dollars on a senior-class annual issued the previous year. I told him that if he'd show me a contract signed by my predecessor or some faculty sponsor representing him, and would bring me a receipt, signed by an officer of the college or of the student association, indicating that the proper number of books had been delivered on time, I'd see what could be done to meet the obligation.

He stormed, said I was unreasonable and must be dishonest. I reminded him that until his arrival I didn't know that any one held a claim, valid or otherwise, and that I thought his language had been unnecessarily offensive. He stormed some more. I suggested that he let me have some time to look into the matter and to confer with the manager of his company. This made him madder than ever and I thought for a time I was going to be put out of my own office by a stranger. I phoned for the janitor and the belligerent visitor retreated.

I found, on inquiry, that the books had not been delivered on time and that there had been little chance to sell them before the session adjourned. The students hadn't repudiated any moral obligation. They had not had time to collect the money. The publisher was willing to make a reasonable adjustment on the amount of the bill. The faculty sponsor of the next student committee on annuals had learned some caution and I insisted on the establishment, as soon as possible, of the policy of getting the student association to raise its annual budget before making any commitments for the expenditure of funds not yet in hand. Year after year we found it easier to raise an adequate student associate budget and to expend such funds in accordance with accepted practices. I learned, early in my experience as a teacher, that financing the student activity program affords unequaled opportunities to teach efficient group organization, intelligent co-operation and a sense of individual responsibility for group decisions and group action. Within two years after the incident above referred to, we had our funds in the student-association treasury a month before commencement and an authorized budget before the close of the school year. This budget had a twenty-per cent reserve or contingent fund and that meant that we had money on hand to meet ordinary emergencies. Provision was made for the proper authorization of expenditures under each sub-budget and for a full audit of all accounts at the end of the academic year. Many of our most thoughtful students learned through the operation of this student-association budget, how to make and operate family and personal budgets. I used to tell them that any school activity whether curricular, co-curricular or extra-curricular, that does not have educational significance in the out-of-school environment, should be abandoned as unworthy of a place in the school's program. Much of our happiness and unhappiness in life grows out of the way we handle our money. Blessed is that man who has learned early in life to meet his financial responsibility to himself, to his family, to his church, and to his community.

Within a month after I took up my work in Cleveland, I received a rather curt letter from the state school superintendent, a stranger to me, stating that, for years the Cleveland Normal School had violated certain standards agreed upon in a state conference of summer school and extension directors, and citing as examples, in point, that as many as fifteen semester hours of credit had been certified to his office for teacher certification purposes as having been completed in a six-week summer session. He said that was about double the amount authorized. He further cited the case of a Cleveland teacher who had on her transcript, from the Cleveland Normal School, a total of twenty-two semester hours of credit in one skill subject, Penmanship.

Then he directed me to scale down all such excess and unauthorized credit allowances on transcripts to be issued thereafter.

My response to his request was that I did not care to pass any adverse judgments on the official acts of my predecessors in office and that I thought I should fulfill my duty to his office by furnishing on request, either from him or from an individual former student, a faithful and accurate transcript of credits recorded in our registrar's office.

I had great satisfaction in telling him that I had already issued an official announcement that no student would be allowed to register in the forthcoming summer session for more than six-semester hours of credit nor in the extension courses of the next academic year for more than six-semester hours of credit.

I never heard again from the writer of that curt letter until several years after he had left office, when he visited our school as a guest speaker. I listened with interest to what he said to our faculty and students; "Your school enjoys an enviable reputation for its high standards of requirement and for its marvellous professional services and spirit."

During the school year of 1918-19, while Superintendent Spaulding was on leave for war work in Europe, and acting Superintendent Jones was my superior officer, we had serious budget problems. The board of education seriously considered closing our school as had been done with municipal normal schools in many other cities. In February, it was voted to give our school about one-third of its normal budget and to instruct me to maintain only a skeleton-faculty organization. Also, to cancel all plans for the next summer session. These actions were taken without consultation with me and without any official notice until the report of the board's action appeared in the city papers.

I was not too much concerned about the cut in budget for the next academic year, though it almost completely demoralized our faculty and made it wholly impossible for us to hold the interest of the several high-grade professional men whom I had hoped to add to our staff. I was confident that on Superintendent Spaulding's return in June, he would find some way to avoid dismantling our program. This, in due time, he did.

But when I learned that the summer session had been cancelled without consulting me, I requested the acting superintendent to give me a hearing before the board. A special meeting was called for the purpose. The president's attitude as he explained the board's action, was very apologetic. He said it was done "more in sorrow than in anger" and that the board dared not face the possibility of any such sizable deficit as had been incurred the previous summer. He had in mind the sum of $64,000.00 which was the figure, as I remember, which had been reported to the board. When I showed him the figure authorized by the board's official accountant, namely $444.00, the board rescinded its action but cautioned me to put on a conservative program. The acting superintendent seemed almost paralyzed by the fear that I might, under all the circumstances, fail to develop a satisfactory summer school enrollment and so he hedged by delaying the nominations of our summer-school staff for confirmation by the board.

On the Thursday preceding the opening of the summer session, he advised me to write all members of the staff that the summer session would be cancelled. I told him that in as much as he had officially authorized me to invite them, the board would surely have a pack of lawsuits on its hands if I should act upon his advice. He did not insist.

On Saturday, Superintendent Spaulding arrived in town and called me at once. I told him the situation. He instructed me to go ahead with the official opening on Monday. This I did. At noon, I reported to him that our enrollment was about two-thirds as large as during the preceding summer. He seemed as pleased as I. At four o'clock, he called me to inform me that the board had unanimously confirmed the appointment of our summer-school staff.

From that day forward, the morale throughout our whole public-school staff began to pick up. The Superintendent spent his major effort during the fall and winter in setting up and securing the approval of a higher, better co-ordinated and more equitable salary schedule. The schedule for the normal school faculty was much advanced. Annual increments of increase were higher and additional merit increments were provided for. It was possible, thereafter, to attract and hold more high-grade professional talent in our faculty and administrative staff and to have an adequate clerical staff.

Supreme Opportunity

The long-term opportunity challenged me more than the immediate problems and difficulties disturbed me.

My supreme opportunity at the time was to build up a program of courses and services in the Cleveland School of Education that would challenge the interest and enlist the support of the three thousand five hundred elementary-school teachers of the city, who were in service in the first six grades; also the upper-grade elementary-school teachers, many of whom were soon to be transferred to the new junior high-school service.

During my first month in the city, Superintendent Spaulding, on leaving his office at five o'clock in the afternoon, drove out almost daily to my office in Wade Park and picked me up for an open-air ride and a conference on the problems which confronted us in determining long-range policies related to the improvement of teaching in our entire public-school system. I presented my best suggestions for the solution of these problems. He was very keen in his analysis of my proposals. In due time, I had formulated a program for the forthcoming summer-school session. He promised his unqualified support of it before the board of education. On his invitation, I presented it to the board at a luncheon meeting in the Olmstead Hotel and received from individual board members much commendation upon it. One member insisted that I had not asked for enough money to put the program over successfully. He moved a substantial addition to the summer-school budget. This motion was unanimously adopted. My recommendations had included the authorization to invite a couple score of notable teachers from universities, colleges, and public-school systems from far and near to give practical courses and demonstrations of good teaching at all levels and in nearly all school subjects during the oncoming summer session. This recommendation, too, was unanimously approved.

On the request of the superintendent, I gave public announcement to the program of courses and the list of guest instructors from a score of American universities and notable public-school systems. These announcements were made at two meetings early in March, each attended by about two thousand teachers from the city and its suburbs. One of these meetings was held in the East Technical High School and the other in the West Technical High School on the following day. I made it crystal clear that to get the best instruction our profession could afford, no teacher need incur the considerable expense involved in going to New York or Chicago during the summer of 1918.

By April first, we had issued an attractive pamphlet announcing all details of our new and greatly expanded program for the summer session. Demonstration teaching in all grades of the elementary and secondary schools was strongly featured.

When the summer term opened, we had one thousand, two hundred and forty-six of our Cleveland public-school staff in attendance, including all except two of our approximately one hundred elementary-school principals. The enrollment during the previous summer session had been about three hundred. All teachers and principals were enrolled in one particular course, meeting in two sections of six hundred each and designed to set forth clearly the philosophy underlying the best of modern elementary-school objectives, the proper motivation of student effort, and the most effective classroom procedures and practices.

Professor William H. Kilpatrick, of Teachers College, Florence Bamberger, of Johns Hopkins University, Emile B. De Sauze, of the University of Pennsylvania, Raymond Moley, of Western Reserve University, former Superintendent William E. Chancellor, of Washington, D. C., Dr. William Betz, of the Rochester School system, and Miss Jessie Evans of the Philadelphia School System, as well as demonstration teachers of distinction from many notable public-school systems who, at the time, were serving on our staff of demonstration teachers at the elementary and junior high-school levels, participated in this general seminar course.

In the summer session, Dr. De Sauze conducted a program of foreign language study and teaching which provided courses in French and Spanish and demonstrations in teaching in each of these languages at every level at which it was being taught in the junior and senior high schools of the city.

This language institute was conducted after the first summer on the campus of Western Reserve University.

At the close of the first summer session of the new administration, it was clear that the teachers and principals of the city system would give hearty support to a comparable program of in-service and advanced professional education during the regular academic year under the auspices of the Cleveland School of Education and that they would join in an active campaign to recruit to the entering class in the Cleveland Normal School for pre-service education and training a better type of teaching prospect, and in more nearly adequate numbers.

In the fall of 1918, courses were offered in the Normal School and in the School of Education by a score of new instructors, never before participating in such a program, including Professor Charles Swain Thomas, of Harvard (English) and Professor Emile B. De Sauze, of the University of Pennsylvania (Modern Languages).

Year after year, the scope of offerings during the summer session and during the academic year was materially broadened and the number of competent experienced professors added to the staff was correspondingly increased.

At the close of Dr. Spaulding's first year of service in Cleveland, in August, 1918, he was granted leave to serve for one year on the educational staff of General Pershing's American Army in Europe. At a farewell luncheon at the school of education, he addressed the members of the board of education, the members of his headquarters staff in the Cleveland school system and the members of the faculty of the school of education. He gave strong endorsement to the new program in the school of education and made it clear that the progressive up-grading of the quality of the teaching in our public-school classrooms was largely dependent upon the active support the teachers should give the program of the school of education in its efforts to give them practical help in professional self-improvement.

Problems, Personal and Domestic

If I had realized how many personal and domestic problems I should have in making a transfer from Philadelphia to Cleveland I should certainly have hesitated about this move. Only three months earlier I had bought a beautiful new house in Drexel Hill, a new suburb of West Philadelphia, and had moved my family into it. When the time came to begin my work in Cleveland, I left my wife, and two little girls in the care of my younger sister who had been our dependable and capable homemaker since the birth of our younger daughter two and one half years earlier. Mrs. Suhrie was a semi-invalid. I secured accommodations at the university club on Euclid Avenue pending the time when I might secure suitable accommodations for my family in Cleveland Heights near the normal school. Below is given, in outline, the succession of events which made my first year in the new position an exceedingly difficult one.

The futile search of a whole month for a house; quarantined for three days for smallpox (on wrong diagnosis); tonsillitis and several days' lay-off while attending Atlantic City Convention of normal school principals to interview and check up on candidates for appointment to our summer-school faculty; some weeks of very strenuous conferences in Cleveland on the transfer and reorganization of our three training schools; spring vacation trip to Philadelphia to move my family and furniture; another severe attack of tonsillitis causing delay in moving; a short period of hospitalization (operation, hemorrhage and blood transfusion); a week of rest by physician's orders at Atlantic City; removal of family and furniture to Cleveland; a streptococcus infection and a lay-off; strenuous period of preparation for summer session;

unending problems with a demented landlord; impossibility of procuring nursing service or satisfactory domestic help (when we left Philadelphia my sister married and established her own home); during this first summer school my wife's illness was so serious that I was able to get little sleep; the strain was terrible; after the summer session's close I was able to move my family into an attractive new house with all modern comforts on down payment of five hundred dollars; then I had to go to the hospital for a serious operation; just before the opening of the fall term I suffered a two-weeks' lay-off from an acute attack of ptomaine poisoning; Armistice Day and general "flu" epidemic came on apace; we lost, in twenty-four hours, one of our most promising young teachers; board considered seriously closing our school and converting our building into an emergency hospital; for weeks a third of the members of our faculty and student body were on sick leave; Mrs. Suhrie had two periods of hospitalization during our first year in Cleveland; due to the board's serious shortage of funds, there was real danger for a time that the normal school might be closed permanently; finally voted to reduce the budget to $30,000.00 for the next year (thus maintaining a mere skeleton organization) and to cancel the next summer session. While these actions were later rescinded, it was inevitable that the institutional morale of the Cleveland Normal School should fall to a low level for many months. I was invited to the headship of the department of education at Swarthmore College, but declined, because I was unwilling to desert a ship that had struck the shoals. I knew that to do so would completely demoralize our faculty. I decided to remain at least till Superintendent Spaulding's return in June. With the ship's captain at the helm again the Cleveland school system was soon off the rocks and headed for port. The legislature authorized a higher tax levy for operating schools. The voters supported such a levy; the next year the board, on the superintendent's recommendation, adopted a better salary schedule and the morale of the school system was soon completely restored.

Western Reserve University Goes into Partnership with Cleveland Public School System

Before accepting Superintendent Spaulding's invitation to the principalship of the Cleveland Normal School, I called, by appointment, on President Charles F. Thwing, of Western Reserve University, in his office on the campus, early in December, 1917, for a short conference concerning the "affiliation" then in force between the Cleveland Normal School and Western Reserve University. I did not make any inquiries about the nature of the contractual agreement between the two institutions, because I was assured by him that the agreement was working smoothly and, that if I should come, he would regard me as one of the deans of the university and that, as a prospective annuitant of the Carnegie Foundation for the Advancement of Teaching, my name would be transferred from the University of Pennsylvania list to the Western Reserve University list by agreement already entered into between himself and Provost Smith of the University of Pennsylvania, who had highly commended me to him at a recent meeting of the Carnegie Board in New York. He gave me a cordial invitation to become the dean of the school of education. I did not ask for confirmation of my appointment by the university board, inasmuch as I understood from the president that my deanship in the university would bear an *ex officio* relationship to my basic appointment as principal of the Cleveland Normal School which appointment would, in due time, be confirmed by the Cleveland Board of Education, to which body I should look for my salary and for the budget with which to operate the normal school. I was told that the in-service or extension courses then being offered in the school of education were adequately financed by the tuitions they produced and that this was equally true of courses given by members of the normal school faculty and by members of Western Reserve University faculty. After I had been installed in office at the opening of the second semester, I found this statement to be correct.

When I began to nominate summer-school staff members to the superintendent for official appointment, I found there was trouble brewing. Every week, indeed every few days, President Thwing sent some young university instructor to me with a note indicating that he would like to have me nominate the bearer to the summer-school staff of the school of education. That clearly implied that he desired that I place such person on the payroll of the board of education. I had no authorization to do that and for two reasons, as follows: first, it had been the practice, previously, to have the university authorize any one of its faculty to offer a course in the school of education only if he were willing to take the risk that the income produced by it would be, at least, enough to cover the stipend he should receive for giving it; second, the courses needed in the summer session, of 1918, were of such a character, that they could not be successfully given by the type of young instructor the president was recommending to me for appointment.

The university instructors whom the president had sent to me for appointment naturally got the impression that I was unco-operative and I could not avoid getting an impression that the president was expecting me to provide employment during the summer-term for certain impecunious young instructors, otherwise out of employment during the summer months. The situation was an unhappy one. It had some elements of embarrassment in it, too, for Superintendent Spaulding. So he and I went together to call on the president and to ask for a more explicit agreement with the university, concerning not only the issues that had caused us embarrassment, but also concerning the credit status of courses henceforth to be given in the school of education. We desired, also, to learn the university's attitude toward the construction of official curricula in education and the granting of degrees on their completion.

We seemed to make no progress in these conferences chiefly, we assumed, because it was clear that the agreement entered into, in the summer of 1915, between him and my predecessor, was a verbal one and had never been referred to the faculty of the university or to its board of trustees for approval.

Our negotiations were suspended from August, 1918, to July, 1919, while the superintendent was on war duty in Europe, because the acting superintendent was not willing that I should press for any further meetings with the university authorities until his return.

On the superintendent's return, there seemed to be more urgent need than ever before for some practical, workable solution of our troublesome problems. So with Dr. Spaulding's approval, I went to the president's office to discuss three matters with him: first, the financial obligations of each of the parties to the contract; second, the credit status of courses which had been completed or should subsequently be completed in the Cleveland School of Education; third, whether the university was willing to set up curricula in education at the senior college and graduate levels and to grant appropriate degrees on their completion. These matters had not been settled when the "affiliation" of the school of education with the university was agreed upon, in the summer of 1915. The president, who was nearing the age of retirement, seemed never to be willing to take these issues up with the university faculty or with the university board and, we of the public-school system, were in no position to do so. My visit to his office, therefore, accomplished exactly nothing.

Superintendent Spaulding and I later went together for another appointed conference late in 1919 but we, too, accomplished exactly nothing.

When, early in the spring of 1920, it was announced that the superintendent would retire at the end of the school year (in August 1920), from the Cleveland school system to accept appointment in Yale University, I was more anxious than ever to see some suitable working agreement entered into that would effectively serve the interests of our Cleveland teachers who had, on my advice and in good faith, enrolled for and had completed courses in the Cleveland School of Education.

Superintendent Spaulding agreed with me that there was nothing to be gained and valuable time to be lost by temperizing any further in negotiations with the president of Western Reserve University; so he authorized me to go to Columbus for a personal interview with President William O. Thompson, of Ohio State University, and to invite his counsel. I went to his office in Columbus by appointment. He received me most cordially. He said it was his policy to regard the boundaries of the Ohio State University campus as coterminous with the boundaries of the State of Ohio. He said the city of Cleveland was, among all the state's municipalities, the heaviest taxpayer, and that he was disturbed to see so little service given to the teachers of Ohio's metropolis by either local or state institutions. He might, he said, send a commission up to inspect our Cleveland Normal School and to confer with the officials of the Cleveland school system if I'd approve that course. I told him that this would, I was sure, meet with the hearty approval of Superintendent Spaulding, and that I, personally, would be very happy to have such a commission come.

Shortly thereafter, on a date agreed upon in advance, a commission from the university spent several days as the guests of the officers and faculty of the school of education and the officials of the Cleveland school system. The commission included Dean McPherson, of the Graduate School, Dean Arps, of the school of education, and three additional members who were department chairmen in the Ohio State University faculty. This commission, in due time, made a report to the university school of education faculty, recommending the organic affiliation of the Cleveland Normal School with Ohio State University. This recommendation was unanimously adopted. Shortly thereafter, a committee of the general faculty of the university, after studying the recommendation, unanimously endorsed it to the university faculty which body unanimously approved it. President Thompson then presented the recommendation to the board of trustees which body unanimously approved. The president so notified me, at the same time complimenting our Cleveland Normal School and Cleveland school of education on the highly satisfactory impression they had made on the visiting commission.

The Cleveland Board of Education, on Superintendent Spaulding's recommendation, approved the proffered "affiliation" leaving details to be worked out with the university and then later presented to the board for final approval. When this action was reported in the Cleveland dailies, the fireworks began.

Western Reserve University was, at the time, promoting a campaign locally to raise endowment funds. When its friends read in the papers that Ohio State University would henceforth grant degrees to the graduates of the Cleveland School of Education they were aroused.

President Thwing telephoned Superintendent Spaulding and expressed great surprise that he had made such recommendation to the board. He seemed to remember that Western Reserve University had once upon a time agreed to grant these degrees. The superintendent replied that the president and board of trustees of Western Reserve University had never taken such action and that we had never been given any forthright assurance that they would do so.

Shortly thereafter, a meeting of the trustees of Western Reserve University was called to consider whether the university would be willing to grant appropriate degrees to the graduates of the school of education on the completion of appropriate curricula. Though Superintendent Spaulding was not a member of that board, he received a call to attend that meeting which he did. Only trustees and the school superintendent were present. Dr. Spaulding explained to the chairman and members of the board of trustees that he was not a member but was present as school superintendent on invitation. The trustees engaged in a lengthy discussion in which the superintendent took no part. When the matter came to a vote, there was a deadlock. The chairman, who favored the granting of the degrees by the local university, called upon the visiting superintendent to vote. He explained again that he was not a member of the university board of trustees but that he was willing to comply with the wishes of the president of the board and then voted affirmatively. This broke the tie and the board agreed to grant the degrees. Details remained to be worked out; the board authorized its chairman to appoint a committee of three to represent it in conference with a like committee to be appointed by the Cleveland Normal School, in working out detailed agreements to be presented later for approval by each governing board separately.

On Superintendent Spaulding's invitation, this university committee came the next morning to my office in the school of education for a conference. He was present in person. The chairman of the visiting group of three, representing the University, began his remarks by criticizing me for going to the state university to seek "affiliation." Superintendent Spaulding assured him and his associates that I had done so with his full and hearty official approval in advance, and that the reason why he had given his approval was that all our attempts to get action from Western Reserve University authorities over a period of more than two years had been in vain. He reminded the visiting committee that if its members had come to the conference with some constructive purpose, such purpose could easily be made manifest by the presentation in writing of definite proposals for an organic "affiliation," involving co-operative action. He told them that until such proposals were ready for presentation in writing, there was no need of further conference. The meeting was adjourned.

Time was running out. Shortly thereafter, Superintendent Spaulding was to hold his last official meeting with the board of education before leaving the city for Yale University, on August 15. The newly elected superintendent was out of town on his annual vacation. Before this board meeting at the school headquarters, the committee representing Western Reserve University, presented proposals of "affiliation" to Superintendent Spaulding. These had been well worked out, were definite and were clearly stated.

The superintendent, before announcing to the visiting committee what action he would recommend on their proposals, asked me two questions: first, did I think it impossible to maintain a double "affiliation," that is to say, one with Ohio State University and another with Western Reserve University? I answered that theoretically it was not impossible, but that in practice, it would be very difficult; second, would I advise him to recommend to the board that we enter finally into the "affiliation" with Western Reserve University on the basis of the committee's proposals?

I answered that I had no way of knowing what the attitude of his successor, who was not available for conference, would be, that I thought the proposals workable, but that I would not favor accepting them if, to do so, meant repudiation of the action previously taken, agreeing to proceed to work out in detail some final plan for organic affiliation with Ohio State University. He informed me that it was his judgment that if he did not recommend the completion of an "affiliation" with Western Reserve University, the Board would, in due time, rescind its previous action, opening the way for the completion of organic "affiliation" with Ohio State University. I replied that such action on the part of the board would be highly unethical, not to say reprehensible. He replied that he agreed with me, but was in no position to control, or even to influence, the future action of the board after his retirement from the school system. So I advised him to recommend the second "affiliation." He did so. This seemed to restore peace in the board. No one moved to rescind the action, authorizing the later completion of "affiliation" with Ohio State University; it seemed unlikely, however, that this proposed "affiliation" would, under all the circumstances, be completed in the immediate future.

In a conference I had with President Thompson, of Ohio State University, some weeks later, he made it clear that he was happy that we had secured action of some kind on the local scene, and that he did not hold me in the least at fault in the position I had taken. We agreed to await any further developments.

Early in September, 1920, a joint conference committee representing the Cleveland Board of Education and Western Reserve University, which had been provided for in the resolution authorizing the "affiliation," met in my office to organize for action. Its membership was as follows:

Representing the Cleveland Board of Education:
  E. M. Williams, President of the Board
  R. G. Jones, Superintendent of Schools
  Ambrose L. Suhrie, Dean (Head) of the Cleveland School
    of Education

Representing Western Reserve University
   G. W. Leutner, Dean of Adelbert College (for men)
   G. C. Robinson, Professor of Education, Mather College
     (for women)
   Sidney S. Wilson, Treasurer of the University

I moved the election of Professor Robinson as chairman of the joint conference committee. This nomination was seconded by Superintendent Jones and unanimously adopted. Dean Leutner moved my election as executive and recording secretary of the joint conference committee. This nomination was seconded by Mr. Wilson, Treasurer of the University, and unanimously approved. This staffing of the joint conference committee turned out to be a good working arrangement during the next four years, and with only minor changes in personnel, for many years thereafter.

While I served as executive secretary of the committee, there never was any friction or division whatsoever. I prepared all the recommendations which were presented to the committee for official approval. There were, during the period, forty-four regular meetings of the committee. I was free to make any recommendations for faculty appointments which Superintendent Jones would approve, and for which funds were available in the school-of-education budget. I was free to negotiate with individual Western Reserve University faculty members for the offering of courses particularly needed in our program, since the university had authorized them to take on one extra course each during the academic year in the school of education, if invited by the joint conference committee to do so, the same to be paid for out of fees resulting from such course. No outlay on the part of the university was involved. The board of education carried the full burden of expenses for administration of the school of education.

In a period of four years the executive secretary presented two hundred and seventy-three resolutions for the approval of the joint conference committee. All of these except two were, after discussion, unanimously approved. These two were withdrawn by the executive secretary, modified to meet objections, re-presented and unanimously approved. I have never in my life been privileged to work with a group of committeemen more understanding, more reasonable, or more agreeable. When I withdrew from the committee to go on my way to New York, the chairman wrote me a letter on behalf of his associates which added warmth to my file of letters of appreciation from the good and the great.

Our meetings were always luncheon meetings and did much to keep us all informed concerning the operation of the joint enterprise. They helped us to develop, through informal discussion, a remarkably fine attitude toward four other institutions in Cleveland which had something of importance and value to offer our Cleveland public-school teachers. These institutions, some of whose courses (and instructors) were, on occasion, incorporated in the offerings of the school of education, included: Western Reserve Historical Museum, Cleveland Museum of Natural History, Cleveland School of Art, and Cleveland Museum of Art. It is doubtful whether in any other American city, the total resources of all the institutions which can serve the cause of public education have ever been so fully placed at the disposal of these interests or so fully used by them.

I never could be optimistic, however, about the ultimate outcome of the "affiliation" with Western Reserve University. The central authorities of the university never in my day raised any money to sustain the budget or to expand the services of the school of education. The university allowed some of its buildings to be used during the summer sessions for the foreign language classes and demonstrations and, in return for this, the public-school system trained its prospective teachers in the Fairmount junior public high school.

A dozen years after I left the city, the municipality ceased to provide financial support to the school of education, believing it to be the responsibility of the state to educate teachers for the public schools. Western Reserve University then took over the school of education. The fortunes of Western Reserve University, too, were low at the time. Though Dean Leutner, who later became president of the university, seemed to be genuinely interested when I knew him as a member of the joint conference committee, money was not available. In recent years, the university school of education has been reduced to a department of education and I am told that today (1955), fewer than a dozen beginning teachers trained in the department enter the Cleveland school system each year.

I have always thought it a great misfortune that the provisional "affiliation" with Ohio State University could not have been confirmed by definitive contract and activated when the way was open and then, in the least possible time, fully developed. It would have been good for both universities to enter into friendly competition in the service of the teachers of the city, and this could have been a great blessing to tens of thousands of Cleveland school children. Ohio, in the years since then, has generously supported five state universities. If Ohio State University, in 1920, had been permitted to establish a local branch of the university in Cleveland or to maintain two schools of education, one in Columbus and one in Cleveland, the state's principal city, there is no doubt the state would have been generous in its support of this local service or institution. It is sad to relate that there is probably no other city of equal size in our country today which, in recent years, has made such inadequate provision *on the home scene* for the preparation of recruits to the public profession of teaching and for the continuing up-grading of its public school teaching staff through adequate provisions for advanced in-service training. The way was open in 1920, when the Ohio State University offered the Cleveland School of Education an organic "affiliation," for the allocation by the university to it of liberal financial support for all its legitimate uses in developing an adequate program to meet the needs of Ohio's principal city.

One member of the Cleveland Board of Education, conspicuously lacking in social vision, with no conception of the inadequacy of Western Reserve University's financial resources to support the program, called for and with a fanatical zeal to protect his *alma mater* from the necessity of competing with stronger forces, was able, effectively, to prevent a great forward movement in the continuing up-grading of teacher qualifications, which was one of the distinctive aims of the Spaulding administration.

> For of all sad words of tongue or pen
> The saddest are these: "It might have been!"

Consultant Survey

There were two particularly difficult problems that seemed almost unsolvable:

a) When, in the spring of 1920, the superintendent's new salary schedule established a relationship between increments of post-high school education and increments of salary, the teachers who, "across the span of the years," had taken summer-school and extension courses naturally desired to have these courses count for salary increments. They did not seem to know that the normal school, over the span of thirty years or more, had kept no orderly records, that class-credit sheets had been promiscuously placed into filing drawers, and that courses and credits had not been assembled on individual student cards.

b) Teachers did not seem to understand that many of the courses they had taken in years past could not be expected to qualify for college credit, inasmuch as they were merely review courses given by drillmasters, whose scholarship rating was much below the level of college graduation. Furthermore, the records showed that as many as fifteen semester hours of credit had been, in some cases, certified as having been completed in a six-weeks summer session.

The situation was full of friction which was not of my making. The board of education had provided us with no adequate funds to bring the records up-to-date. Moreover, there were no established standards by which one could decide what rating (as credit or non-credit) should be assigned to a given course taken "in the long ago."

Finally, in the fall of 1921 (and after the joint conference committee had gone into action), I appealed to the Cleveland Foundation, Raymond Moley, Executive Secretary, for a grant of funds to provide for a consultant survey to be made by a commission of experts from outside the city. Such a grant was promptly made available. I proposed, for the consideration of the joint conference committee the following names for such a commission: Professor William C. Bagley, of Teachers College, chairman; Dean John W. Withers, of New York University; Professor George Gailey Chambers, of the University of Pennsylvania, secretary. These selections were approved and, in due time, these men made two separate visits for consultation with many local groups (or with their representatives) in the Cleveland public-school system and in Western Reserve university. Professor Chambers, who had had a very wide experience in evaluating credits, finally wrote a formula on the accreditation or non-accreditation of courses previously completed which formula proved satisfactory and acceptable, both to the committee of consultants and to the joint conference committee of the Cleveland School of Education and Western Reserve University. This solution was finally accepted by the teachers interested as impersonal and official. In due time, all records of credits were properly assembled on the grade cards of persons to whom they severally belonged and each course so entered was rated as creditable toward a particular degree or as not creditable toward any degree. Henceforth, all causes of friction on the score of credit evaluation ceased. This was the beginning of "an era of good feeling" in the Cleveland school system.

The official report by the Consultant Survey Commission to the Cleveland Foundation was published by the university. It was a brief but comprehensive document clearly sanctioning the policies that were in operation in the Cleveland School of Education and clearly indicating that its program of service to the teachers, principals, and supervisors of the Cleveland metropolitan area was the most satisfactory, and the most complete program for up-grading teacher qualifications then in operation in any American city.

Administrative Policies and Practices

The most important of all the many worthy professional objectives of the Cleveland School of Education during my administration was to exemplify in its organization and co-operative spirit as well as in its specific classroom practices in all grades and subjects and activities, the very best the country at large had, at the time, to offer. Our organizational and administrative setup was geared to the accomplishment of these general objectives.

By 1920, the Cleveland School of Education had absorbed the Cleveland Normal School in a unified organization and thereafter there was a junior teachers college primarily to provide basic education and pre-service professional training for those who were candidates for the two-year diploma, admitting to elementary-school internships; and a senior teachers college primarily to provide advanced education and on-the-job training for teachers who were candidates for the bachelor-of-education degree or for the master-of-arts degree in education to be conferred by Western Reserve University.

Courses to be accepted for credit in the senior teachers college had to be approved by the joint conference committee of the Cleveland School of Education and Western Reserve University. They might be given by either of the "affiliated" institutions or by certain other institutions in the city (Cleveland School of Art, Cleveland Museum of Art, Cleveland Museum of Natural History, and Western Reserve Historical Museum) when course and instructor had been approved in advance by this same committee. All approved courses in the Cleveland School of Education, regardless of the institution offering them, were announced in its official bulletins.

Enrollments in the senior teachers college took place in the gymnasium of Western Reserve University, where all instructors from any of the institutions above referred to, were available for consultation and course approval. Any student enrolling for courses in two or more different institutions, paid the tuitions due for all such courses at one time and place, in the registration hall.

The educational museum (Professor William M. Gregory, Director) with tens of thousands of dollars' worth of slides, models, and educational films, was located in the school of education building. From this collection, two trucks daily delivered teaching materials (visual aids) on requisition to any public school in the city.

The Cleveland Public Library maintained its principal branch library in the school of education building. This branch library could (and did) command the total resources of the main library on the Mall, which maintained in this branch library, many special collections of books of chief interest to teachers in general and to special groups of teachers (for example, children's literature).

The same basic faculty regularly appointed by the school of education served its upper and lower biennium curricula. Special teachers and officers already on the payroll of the board of education at school headquarters, offered courses on invitation from the dean of the school of education (with the approval of the superintendent of public schools); for example, one on *The Aims and Practices of Junior High Schools* by the assistant superintendent in charge of the administration and supervision of the junior high schools of the city.

During the summer session, many specialists in the various departments of the public-school systems of many other American cities were invited to Cleveland to provide special opportunities for our local teachers. The school of education was able to set up substantial additional summer-school and extension courses offerings:

a) in an *Institute of Americanization* under the leadership of Dr. Raymond Moley, Director of the Cleveland Americanization Council.

b) in an *Institute of Public School Health Service* under the leadership of Dr. Childs, Director of the public-school health service of Cleveland, and Professor Thomas D. Wood, Director of health service, of Teachers College, Columbia University.

c) in an *Institute of Public Recreation* under Dr. Roland Haynes, Director of the Cleveland Recreation Council.

We were able to have the special programs, above referred to, underwritten by the respective co-operating associations or councils. This nearly doubled the summer-school budget and enabled us to bring to the city, year after year, such notable experts as Dr. Arnold Gazell, of Yale (child development); Dr. W. H. Burnham, of Clark (personality development); Dr. E. V. McCollum, of Hopkins (nutrition); Dr. W. R. Davis, of Harvard (industrial diseases); Robert Irwin (sight conservation); Dr. McMurtrie of Ottawa, Canada; Dr. Thomas D. Wood, of Teachers College, Columbia University (school health services); Dr. Henry Goddard, of the Ohio State Bureau of Juvenile Service (feeble-minded).

It was the policy to allow no college teacher to undertake more than fifteen hours of teaching in the junior teachers college or twelve hours in the senior teachers college (and graduate courses). If a professor's time was divided, as it generally was in the case of our best-equipped teachers, between the junior teachers college and the senior teachers college service, the load was scaled to these ratios: Salaries were increased materially from year to year, in accordance with the provisions of a "merit" schedule which did not admit of any extra class instruction in other institutions by regular staff members.

As may well be imagined, the development of an adequate and a wholly satisfactory program for the in-service and advanced professional education of teachers for a large, complex city-school system presented many difficult problems. Greater Cleveland covers a wide stretch of territory along the lake front. Rapid transit did not exist. Fortunately, the resources of the Cleveland Public Library were so adequate and its services so pre-eminently satisfactory, that we were able to gratify the wishes of public-school teachers by establishing fifteen centers of instruction distributed over the city and its suburbs with adequate library reference materials available in each center and a library service geared to the needs of the particular courses offered in it. These centers of instruction were in branch libraries and in public schools. It is doubtless true that, in no other place in the country, could one make a better claim for the thesis that the boundaries of the campus of the college were coterminous with the boundaries of its service area.

Our campus elementary demonstration school of twenty classroom groups (kindergarten to sixth grade inclusive), served the junior teachers college during the academic year and the senior teachers college during the summer session and also on Saturdays during the academic year.

All courses that called for demonstration were given on the campus on Saturday mornings; also, a wide variety of highly specialized services; such as, courses for (1) teachers of the physically handicapped, (2) teachers of sight-saving classes (3) teachers of feeble-minded children.

The campus-demonstration school was in operation from Tuesday morning to Saturday noon during the academic year and from nine to noon. When as many as a thousand teachers in service were enrolled in Saturday morning classes, it served admirably as a demonstration center and especially for demonstrations on the effective use of visual aids. Our museum of instructional materials (visual aids) was in the same building.

The total laboratory-school equipment for the junior teachers college consisted of:

a) an elementary demonstration school of twenty classroom groups (kindergarten to sixth grade inclusive) on the campus of the school of education.

b) three elementary training schools (kindergarten to eighth grade inclusive), each located within walking distances of the school of education.

c) one junior high demonstration school in operation during the summer session, and one junior high training school in operation during the academic year, both located near the campus.

d) five "cadet centers" at each of which (under one roof or in several buildings not far apart), twenty or thirty graduates of the junior teachers college were inducted into responsible classroom teaching under the direction of a supervisor of "cadets" or interns. There was one (sometimes two) such centers in each of the supervisory districts in the elementary-school system of the city.

e) five curriculum study centers. These were typical elementary schools in each of which intensive study of some aspect of the elementary-school curriculum was undertaken in a series of controlled experiments, under the direction of the principal, and with the help of experts from the school of education and the public-school-headquarters staff.

The senior-college courses in methodology were given at the school of education building on Saturday mornings where a full quota of elementary-school classes and classrooms were available for demonstration purposes, and where teachers could visit the educational museum to find suitable visual aids for the effective conduct of particular projects in teaching.

Selective admission (and progressive elimination of the unpromising), was a fixed policy in the administration of the junior teachers college.

In due time, our joint faculty-student committee on recruitment worked out an effective plan for securing the active and willing co-operation of all our high schools in arousing the interest of high-school graduates in preparation for teaching as a career. The several alumnae groups from the twenty-one public, private and church-related secondary schools of the city and its suburbs who were enrolled in our junior teachers college, each extended an invitation to its principal to spend a certain day on the campus as the special guest of his alumnae. These visitors were guests on the platform at an all-college assembly early in the day. After an address of welcome by the president of the student association, each was introduced to the audience by one of his alumnae. All of the other members of his alumnae groups joined in giving him a heart-warming ovation. A short symposium program was then conducted by student officers to inform the guests of the specific purposes of the institution and of its attractive features.

All the principals were entertained at luncheon by the officers of the student association. The table hostess of each was one of his own alumnae. A short speaking program was put on in compliment to the guests. Then, each was conducted to a particular classroom where he had an hour's private conference with the alumnae from his own high school. Finally, the principals were brought to my office for a final conference with the officers of the college and members of the admissions committee. We acquainted them with our admission procedures and invited them to help us interpret, sympathetically to their students, the service of our Junior Teachers College and the opportunity which teaching affords to men and women of certain talents and attitudes toward public service. One of the principals made an eloquent plea for help. He said he very earnestly desired that we send to a morning assembly at his high school, the full team of speakers who had interpreted teaching as a career and our college as a training ground for it in the morning assembly period. All the other principals made a similar request. I told them this would require all the members of that team of officers to be absent from our campus each morning for a month. I told them we couldn't spare them—that each one of them, as a student officer, was more or less indispensable to us in the operation of the college. I made a proposal that seemed to please all of them—that we send back to each high school on a given morning (which we finally agreed upon), all the alumnae of his school and have them put on a symposium program at the assembly hour. These speakers were effective and many of them truly inspiring. They made it clear that teaching is for those who are deeply dedicated to the service of childhood and youth, who are willing to be students of books and of human nature all their lives and who find joy in it, a deeply satisfying occupation.

We worked out a plan for reporting periodically, to each of these principals how well (or how badly), each of his alumnae had done in intelligence and performance tests and in classroom performance. It was interesting to note the growing enthusiasm of some of these principals for sending to our college a fair share of upper-quartile students.

It was the policy of the administration of the school of education to organize and conduct, under the direction of the best professional talent available, any course for which there seemed to be a special need in the further improvement of the administrative, supervisory, or teaching service in the Cleveland school system. It was clear by 1923 that, with our rapidly expanding junior- and senior-high school program, we should be giving special training at the graduate level to a selected group of young men who were promising prospects for appointment to the principalships of these schools. I organized, and personally conducted, such a course for a group of men in the city-school system who had been designated for such training by the superintendent and his deputy, in charge of the administration of high schools. The course was conducted on a seminar basis, though we often invited specialists from the school-headquarters staff to make special presentations. Most of the junior- and senior-high school principals appointed during the next ten years were selected from this group.

Distinctive Emphases in Instructional Program

A good bright boy once made this significant distinction: "A professor," said he, "is one who professes, but a teacher is one who really can teach." Some people think this distinction has considerable validity.

There has been a centuries-long search for men and women who "really can teach." Enrolling in a teachers college will not help to make a young man or young woman a teacher in the best sense of that term, unless the institution has on its staff, at least a few really competent teachers, that is, persons who "really can teach." And to find such persons in adequate numbers has always been difficult, not to say, at times, impossible. Good teaching can't take place without good thinking. Theory and practice are definitely related. A good theory of teaching is the rational explanation of successful performance in teaching; and excellent performance is all-but-the-perfect embodiment and exemplification of sound theory. Coherent rational thinking is involved in the development of sound theory and in successful teaching performance. The late Professor Bode used to say: "Unfortunately, even a teacher must have some kind of an I. Q."

When I hear a man say: "That is an excellent theory, but it won't work," I know he's talking gibberish or obsolete pedagogy, or some strange tongue, that he's setting up a dualism between theory and practice. "What, therefore, God hath joined together, let not man put asunder."

The demonstration school is the indispensable laboratory of any good professional school for teachers. The successful demonstration teacher, the artist teacher, is the person who can break down the dualism which has, for centuries, separated theory from practice. The men whose theories have survived the ravages of time, are the men who have embodied those theories in successful teaching performance or have inspired others to do so.

Many a man of wide repute in education is, in reality, little more than a "phrase maker" unless he "really can (and does) teach," successfully.

I am reminded of a story that is told of the late Dr. Gunsaulus of Chicago. The day he entered upon his duties as president of Armour Institute he went to his office early, opened up his roll-top desk, and sat down to do some good thinking and planning before the crowd should be upon him, before the endless procession of callers should begin.

He had scarcely been seated, when someone began pounding violently on his office door. He arose and opened the door. Before him stood a stranger, a nervous little man who looked as though he hadn't eaten a meal in many days nor slept for weeks.

The stranger began: "You are Dr. Gunsaulus. Well, here is a perpetual-motion machine which I have invented and I want you to explain why it won't run." Purveyors of abstract unapplied methodology have always been inventors of perpetual-motion machines which, in too many cases, cannot be made to run.

The teachers of our children and adolescents want working answers to such questions as these: How can I get Johnnie to define for himself a purpose in his school life? How can I help him to find the problems in his home life and in his school life which he needs to solve for himself now? How can I help him to work more intelligently, more effectively, and more faithfully on solving these problems?

Most teachers are "from Missouri." They want to be shown how other and more successful teachers help Johnnie to educate himself by working intelligently and energetically alone and with others. The observation of good teaching, and the thoughtful analytical examination of every step in the process, provides the most effective solution of the probem of methodology.

Teachers don't want to be *told* by a professor, who is not himself a good teacher, how to teach under ideal conditions: they want to be *shown* how the garden variety of teachers can do a good job of teaching, under conditions which are not always ideal.

When I took up my work in Cleveland late in January, 1918, with a deep-set purpose to help its several thousand teachers significantly and promptly to up-grade the quality of their classroom performance, I knew in my heart that all my efforts would surely be in vain, unless I could set up a program that would introduce them every day during the summer term, and every Saturday morning during the school year, to some inspiring teaching performances by really great and inspiring teachers, teachers who could think clearly, perform skillfully, and then cheerfully and, with open minds, submit their classroom performances to objective appraisal by really well-trained conference leaders and the group who had witnessed the demonstration.

In due time, we had an admirable setup for rehabilitation service. A single illustration will suffice. There were about seventy-five teachers of German in the junior- and senior-high schools of the city who were suddenly thrown out of employment as teachers of German by the action of the board of education in voting to abandon German as a subject of instruction in the schools of the city. Two results were at once apparent: first, that the board was under moral obligation to give these seventy-five teachers employment teaching some other subject (or subjects) for which they had had some preparation; second, that the several thousand children whose German classes had been abandoned, desired an opportunity to study French (principally) or some other modern language. It was at once made manifest that most of the teachers of German had been, earlier in life, quite as well prepared to teach French as to teach German, but not having done so, they were now "rusty" in this subject.

We set up demonstration classes in the teaching of French under the direction of a truly great master of the art of teaching French to American children. There was nothing routine, formalistic, or dull about the performance of Dr. Emile B. De Sauze, internationally known in language-teaching circles. The ex-teachers of German, promptly enrolled in numbers in his classes where *re-learning French and ob-*

serving the skillful teaching of French to high-school young-
sters proceeded hand in hand and challenged their interest
and their best efforts. During the academic year, Dr. De
Sauze supervised their classroom teaching of French.

In a year, many of the former teachers of German were
teaching French better than they had ever taught German.
Every week they had seen a master-artist teacher conduct
class work inspiringly. They didn't learn "methods" *apart
from* use. They learned methods *in* use.

A great English teacher in our demonstration school was
complimented by one of his observers on his performance
in the demonstration school. He thanked her and then asked
her to give him some constructive criticism for his improvement. Her response was: "Oh, Professor, won't you give us
a course next year in *Methods of Teaching English?*"

Said he: "Why, madam, my *method* of teaching English
is *the way* I teach English. You have just complimented me
on it." She had been accustomed to keeping "methods" in
cold storage, apart from use. She hadn't yet caught the idea
that method, rightly conceived, is *the way* and *the life* of
teaching and that the most effective way of learning to teach,
is to see much good teaching that is so dynamic and effective
that it *commands* or *compels* pupil attention, pupil co-operation, pupil participation. There can be nothing more inspiring than to see a truly great teacher *in action*. The best
of what is called "method" is always caught rather than
taught. It is contagious; it has an afterglow that compels intelligent adaptation, not blind imitation.

Of course, every good performance in teaching will bear
analysis, and that is why every demonstration in a laboratory
school for teachers may well be analyzed and made the subject of group discussion, so that its strong points may be
made explicit and may be consciously and intelligently imi-
tated. It must always be remembered that a class demonstration is a spotlight performance. That is why, in the

elementary grades, it is best that the demonstration be given by the grade teacher regularly in charge of the class. There is, then, less likely to be any "exhibition" teaching. In all good demonstration teaching the children, not the teacher, become the center of interest to the observers, what they do, how they do it, *and why?* What is their conscious purpose as individuals and as a group—and how did they arrive at such purpose? What part did the teacher play as an inspirer or as a conscious director? Good teaching will always bear analysis and a class demonstration that has not been analyzed is as likely to do harm as to do good. Its strengths and its weaknesses need to be explicitly pointed out in an objective and impersonal analysis of the total performance, in the setting in which it occurs.

Because I have chosen to emphasize in this record, a feature of our total program that was distinctive; namely: the demonstration of good teaching, the reader may easily assume that we had little interest in sound scholarship; not so. Year after year, we did all we could, within the limits of our financial resources, to enlarge the range and scope of solid content courses but without any subsidy from the University we were, of course, unable to do this as fast or as fully as we desired.

The range and scope of the demonstration program in the elementary-school department of the Cleveland School of Education on any typical day during the summer session, or on a typical Saturday morning during the school year, is illustrated by the sample program printed on page 255.

At the junior-teachers-college level, the future teachers were daily inspired by the distinctive character of the demonstration school program and spirit. In the affiliated training schools a marvellous spirit of co-operation between sponsor teachers and apprentices, prevailed. One day, I went down the corridor of the Bolton Training School and was saluted by a fourth-grade boy named Antonio. He pointed to a young woman-apprentice teacher at the other end of the long corridor and said proudly: "She's going to make a good teacher."

"Why do you think so, Antonio?" I asked.

"Oh, we're all helping her!" was his reply.

Most junior-teachers-college classes were so conducted that any student might be called on at any time to take over and lead the group conference.

To every one of the policy-forming committees of the faculty, the student senate assigned a number of students. In these joint student-faculty committees a division of votes was never taken. An issue was discussed "until," as the ministers in New England used to say, "reason and the will of God prevailed," that is, until there was substantial unanimity in the joint membership of the whole group.

The student association organized a many-sided program of extra curricular activities and services. Its senate was the most responsive, the most co-operative and the most responsible group of student officers I have ever known. As an illustration: When the American Association of School Administrators and the American Association of Teachers Colleges met on one occasion in Cleveland it was agreed that all members of our junior-teachers-college faculty should absent themselves from our campus on a certain day to attend one or other of the more than thirty conventions in session in our city, and to permit the student officers to operate the junior teachers college for a full day without any direction or help from their elders.

On that day, several hundred visitors were on the campus. They had come in response to an invitation that had been extended to them through the public press by the student officers. The president of our student association served as president of the junior teachers college, the vice-president served as dean, the secretary served as hostess to visitors, and each of the classes of that day was under the leadership of one of its own members. There were one hundred responsible student leaders in charge of as many class sections.

Miss Patty Hill, of Teachers College, Columbia University, was guest speaker at the chapel hour on the invitation of the student president. The visitors requested a meeting with the student officers in the auditorium at the close of the afternoon session. Such a meeting was held, and numerous questions were asked by visitors, in an attempt to find out what was to account for the remarkable initiative, versatility, sense of responsibility, and co-operative spirit they had seen manifested throughout the day in all departments of the institution. The student president presided and was assisted by a panel of student officers.

On a subsequent occasion, the entire faculty of the junior teachers college, together with the principals and teachers of the associated demonstration and training-school teachers, went for a day's visit to the Detroit Teachers College and its laboratory schools, leaving it to the students of our junior teachers college to staff our demonstration school, and all three of our training schools and to conduct these schools as well as the college classes, wholly under college-student leadership. The total number of classrooms they staffed that day numbered at least one hundred and thirty.

On the Monday evening after our return from Detroit, all who had been on that trip, assembled on call at the school of education, to gather into one sheaf, the benefits derived, and to listen to reports on what had happened in our absence from the demonstration school, the three training schools and the junior-teachers-college classes, all of which had been completely staffed by college students. Miss Ida M. Deighton, the most experienced and the ablest of the training-school principals was the first to claim the floor. She read a report that had been left on her office desk by the young college senior who had served as principal of the elementary school of thirty-two classrooms in the principal's absence. When she had concluded, she addressed the chair and said: "Dr. Suhrie, I had been a principal of schools in this city for twenty years before I could have written such a report."

This was a kind of slogan in our junior teachers college: "Always thank the students in advance for what you hope they'll do and then they'll not dare to disappoint you." This is in line with the dominant philosophy of Thomas Arnold's boys at Rugby. Herbert Quick, his biographer, records the fact that, when any Rugby boy was tempted to dissimulate or prevaricate or tell a downright lie, he was sure to end the argument with himself by saying, "It would be a shame to lie to the Master, for he'd believe you."

Year after year, when commencement came around and I handed out diplomas again and again, I said to myself: "Well, here is a student officer who has been so lovable as a working companion in this big happy school family and, whose influence and services have been so indispensable, that I shall miss her more when fall comes and she is gone than I could possibly miss the support of almost any individual member of the teaching staff."

Somehow, when fall came, there was always some one of equally fine spirit and ability to take her place. The spirit of a really great school is immortal. It never dies; inspired students, great teachers and human administrators constitute the leaven that each year re-leavens the influx of new students and new teachers. The influence of any truly great leader, whether in the principal's office, at the teacher's desk, or in the ranks of the student body, remains long after he has withdrawn from the institution.

It was the definite purpose of the administration of the school of education:

a). to appoint to the staff of the demonstration school, only persons who had achieved notable success as classroom teachers.

b). to make available to such teachers, the consultant

services of all faculty members in the school of education.

c). to create a team spirit in the whole staff of the demonstration school which would make the school a unified working organization, which would grip the interest and sustained attention of all children enrolled therein.

d). to make the demonstration school and each of the training schools, cadet-center schools, and curriculum-study schools promotion centers, for every growing teacher and principal serving therein.

I was always glad to release any teacher from any of these schools to accept a well-earned promotion elsewhere in our Cleveland school system, or outside of it. I was proud on one occasion to have Dr. Otis W. Caldwell, Principal of the Lincoln School of Teachers College, in New York, invite two of our demonstration-school teachers to join his staff at greatly increased salaries.

In many instances our most appreciated demonstration teachers, whose classrooms were crowded with observers on Saturday mornings and during summer sessions, were so happy over the enlarged sphere of influence in the whole city-school system which such responses of interest in their work, indicated that they were unwilling to accept transfer even when such transfers should involve advancement in rank and/or salary. Their professional spirit seemed to rise above any and all consideration of personal advantage.

I have often thought that about the best assurance a young teacher can give her boys and girls that she really cares for them, is to learn their names with the least possible delay. I used to set up a challenge for our students at the opening convocation of freshmen in the college-assembly hall. I undertook to motivate their efforts in this way:

"Young women, our committee has granted you provisional admittance to this college. You have taken certain intelligence and performance tests and I hope you have made a good showing. But your standing in this school is still pro-

Cleveland School of Education of Western Reserve University
Summer Session

DAILY PROGRAM OF DEMONSTRATION CLASSES
in Elementary Demonstration School
for Tuesday, July 29th, 1924

Period	Grade	Place	Topic and Demonstration	Teacher
9:00	Kng.	101	Self-directed activity	Pierce
	1B	102	Reading: Sentence building and silent reading	Benedict
	1A	103	Reading; unit developed in connection with opening exercises; rhythm	De Witz
	2B	106	Reading: Indian stories	Scott
	2A	110	Reading and writing, U. S. money	Rochefort
	3B-A	105	Finish early Cleveland project (setting up stage)	Lawrence
	5B-A	205	How our country was kept together (the Civil War)	Bucks
10:00	Kng.	101	Manual arts: blocks, number	Pierce
	2B	106	Use of scroll saw in connection with Indian projects	Carey
	2A	110	Spelling development: games and devices	McGovern
	4B-A	204	Spelling	Feiten
	6B-A	201	English: playwriting as a project	Lally
	1B	102	Manual arts: blocks; (open to Miss Trace's Class)	Benedict
	1A	103	Language: a group of poems: play at the seashore	De Witz
	3B-A	105	A visit to Cleveland today by an Indian, by La Salle, by Moses Cleaveland and by Lorenz Carter	Bucks
	4B-A	204	Folk dancing: the whim	Whiteworth
	5B-A	205	English: modern poetry	Stewart
	6B-A	201	Arithmetic: the making of graphs	Brett

Except when otherwise stated, the privileges of observation of demonstration classes and exercises listed above are open only to students regularly enrolled in one or more credit courses offered by the school of education.

Observers are permitted to *enter* classrooms or *leave* classrooms *during the intermission* between periods *only*, and are requested not to enter classrooms when marked closed. While demonstrations are in progress, observers are expected to maintain *complete silence*. All are expected to remain for the conference which follows the demonstration. Before the demonstration lesson begins, a professor will be designated to serve as leader of the conference which follows the lesson.

bationary. The most important hurdle is still before you. You must convince me that you are a good prospect for the teaching profession. I'll tell you now how it can be done. If you are smart enough to teach me your name within the next few days, and to do it so effectively and impressively, that I can never forget it, I shall consider you a good prospect. If I don't learn your name I shall, I think, rightly, assume that you haven't done a very good job in teaching, for I am surely anxious to learn the name of each and every one of you in the least possible time, and I assume you are all anxious to learn at once, the name of each of the other members of this class."

They all took up the challenge with obvious joy. I remember one occasion when, on arriving in my office after the adjournment of this first convocation, I found to my surprise and delight, that a score of freshman students were assembled there to give me their help. They had arranged themselves in a circle. They opened the circle to let me in. Then the leader said:

"Dr. Suhrie, we're here to teach you our names. I'll ask each of these girls in turn to introduce herself. Then we'll give you a chance to prove that you can name all of them in turn. We hope you'll make a good score and if you miss the name of any girl, we'll assume that she hasn't made herself very interesting or that she has failed to give you any adequate line-up of associations."

I took up the assignment and made a perfect score. The members of the group were obviously surprised. Then I suggested that two or three of the girls, in turn, be asked to do the same thing. They all made excellent scores, none of them perfect.

Then the chairman requested the girls to shift places in the circle. They did. Then she asked me to take the test again. I did so and made a perfect score. She then called upon a girl who had not yet taken the test. She had had three reviews and came through with a perfect score.

Throughout the week, informal groups of a half dozen or a dozen in the corridor or elsewhere, gave me the same kind of try-outs. I always insisted that they ask one or more of their own group to take the test, also. It was amazing how much fun we had, how many students really mastered the names of *all* their classmates in an incredibly short period of time. The challenge I gave the girls on the first day of the term, proved to be a wonderfully effective means to the early integration and socialization of the whole group.

One of our joint faculty-student committees worked up what they called *The Prospective Teacher's Personal Fitness Index*. It set up many of the important objectives in personal (or personality) development. That index is here reproduced.

THE PROSPECTIVE TEACHER'S PERSONAL FITNESS INDEX

Every prospective teacher should earnestly strive to achieve personal fitness by acquiring a fair degree of mastery of each of the following six trinities of personal virtues.

1. *Sympathy, fellow feeling, co-operative spirit*

Is kind and respectful to pupils, classmates, instructors; does not interrupt others; does not hurt others' feelings; does not gossip; treats all with same respect regardless of social position or wealth; is tactful, unselfish; is not jealous of those who are more popular or "successful"; gets along well with others; takes an interest in and does full share in group activities; will perform if necessary a comparatively unimportant part in class activity or group program as willingly as if it were the leading part; takes turn, in the milk line, in registrar's office, and in other such situations; contributes all that can be expected to the life of the school.

2. *Trustworthiness, honesty, sincerity*

Conscientiously performs work of each day's classes and does not depend on general knowledge of the subject nor upon help of others in securing assignments and making reports; does not "bluff" or pretend; can be depended upon to meet obligations; e.g., voting at elections, attending social functions, and performing committee work; does a fair share of any piece of group or co-operative work; does not shift the blame for a mistake or fault upon another or upon some event; works as conscientiously in the absence of the instructor or training teacher as in his presence; will sever relationship with an acquaintance or friend rather than be disloyal to the right; will be loyal to the teaching profession, school, and school system.

3. *Leadership, initiative, originality*

Has individuality, personality; is a person whom you will remember; is not passive but active in work of class, section, club; does not "let George do it"; is one who finds things to do; is able to organize or carry through a club project, assembly program, or other activity; makes good use of leisure time; in "recitations" is a student who contributes rather than one who is "called on"; when given a piece of work to do has "ideas" about how to do it.

4. *Self-control, moral courage, strength of character*

Has control of temper, tongue, impulses; can persevere in a difficult task until it is properly completed; is not daunted by failure; is not unduly influenced by the fashion or whim of the moment in dress or conduct; can avoid the bizarre in "make-up," dress, and appearance; will stand for what seems to be right even when it is not popular to do so.

5. *Open mindedness, fairness, judgment*

Is not over-critical; opinions are not determined by the impulse or conversation of the moment; does not accept, without question, the opinion of another; waits to hear both sides before deciding a question; is tolerant of other religions and races; is a good loser; does not grade fellow students on the basis of mere personal likes and dislikes; is cautious in drawing conclusions, especially about people; will inspire a feeling of fairness and justice in all decisions and acts.

6. *Faith, optimism, enthusiasm*

Is cheerful; sees the bright side; has "pep"; does not take the joy out of life and work; is enthusiastic over own work, as well as over the good work of others; is not lifeless; has a sense of humor; does everything as though it was a pleasure; in the presence of this person one thinks of the "good that men do" rather than of the things that "are out of joint."

The students in each class section were invited to score each other periodically on each of the six trinities of personal achievements or virtues indicated in this index. It was amazing to students and faculty members alike, to see the character development that resulted from having each student's classmates give her a rating on her social and ethical performance.

One girl came to me, and said: "Dr. Suhrie, do you think I should rate in the lowest quartile of my class section on *forthrightness?*" I advised her to ask her best friend in the class for her judgment. Her best friend said to her what no teacher would have dared to say (even if he were sure it was true):

"Why, Jennie, if you don't know that you're the biggest bluffer in our class it's time you learn it, for all the rest of us have long known it." That is about what her score was intended to convey to her in a completely impersonal manner. She came to my office to thank me for the advice I had given her and to tell me that she intended thenceforth, deliberately, to seek the approval of her classmates and to ask their constructive criticism and help to that end.

Off-Campus Professional Services

The extra-curricular activities of a successful teachers college executive are likely to be chiefly extra-mural. There are two good reasons why it was necessary for me to concern myself, actively, from the beginning of my service in the Cleveland School of Education with problems of public relations: first, it was imperative that I should learn first-hand, and as quickly as possible, of the educational programs and practices in the teachers colleges in other places, far and near; and, second, unless I should interpret widely and successfully, the interesting innovations in our Cleveland program for the in-service and advanced education of our city public school teachers, I could not hope to attract to our city and to our college faculty, the expert leaders which the successful operation of our program would require.

At the close of my third year as head of the Cleveland School of Education, I was invited to participate in the February, 1921, program of the National Council of Normal School Presidents in Chicago. President Livingston Lord, of the Eastern Illinois Normal School at Charleston, presided at this meeting. My topic had to do with the problem of developing more friendly and more co-operative relationships between faculty members and students on the campuses of our teacher-preparing institutions.

Though our historians of education freely admit that our state normal schools were, from the beginning, the most democratic of all our educational institutions, the organization and administration of these schools, at the close of World War I and after we had made the world "safe for democracy," still bore some of the earmarks of authoritarianism. I made a very earnest plea for a kind of fellowship among teachers and students which was not common at the time in our teacher-preparing institutions. As the official head of one of these institutions, I was in a position to give and did give a lively description of some of the policies and practices of this institution. My address was well received. As president of the Municipal Teachers College Association the same year, I prepared the program and presided over the sessions of the association in Chicago, a little later in the same week. We had an audience at each session of about four hundred. Before these meetings were over, I had invitations to visit and to lecture in a score of the big summer schools of the West. The nature of my administrative responsibilities in the big summer session of the Cleveland School of Education made it impossible to accept these invitations for the on-coming summer session.

At the Easter vacation season of 1921, I went west for a week of engagements in the Kearney, Nebraska, State Normal School. In my audience of students that week, were several young men who have since become notable leaders in the teacher-education program of our country: Dr. Herbert D. Welte, President for a quarter of a century of the Teachers College of Connecticut at New Britain, former Dean Noyer of the Ball State Teachers College in Indiana, and President Freylund, of the Stout Institute in Wisconsin.

In the summer of 1922, I was able, after the opening of our summer session in Cleveland, to get away for my first transcontinental trip, filling lecture engagements and providing consultation services on teachers' college problems. I accepted appointments in twenty-eight of the summer schools in the West; in Nebraska, Minnesota, the Dakotas, Montana, Washington, California, Nevada, Utah, and Colorado. In eighteen of these twenty-eight institutions, the authorities voluntarily gave me honoraria in excess of the amount for which I had asked. This, I take it, was not because the service was notably superior to what had been expected, but primarily because I was willing to give, and did give, many extra lectures and to conduct many extra conferences in addition to the daily auditorium addresses, and faculty conferences originally requested and regularly scheduled.

One of the notable experiences I had on this long trip from Cleveland to San Jose, California, and back again, was my first meeting with a very affable and high-spirited young man who has since risen to prominence on the national scene. Never shall I forget the very pleasant acquaintance I began at Peru, Nebraska, with the young principal of the campus-high school, Samuel M. Brownell. He sat in the front row at all my daily lectures in the auditorium, and in all my special appearances before classes in education. His extra-curricular activities that summer were courting the dean's charming daughter and taking long evening walks with me on the banks of the Missouri River. We talked at length about his plans to become a school administrator and about some suitable place to get graduate training in preparation for such service. I advised him strongly, to go to Yale University and to work with my former big chief, Dr. Frank E. Spaulding. In due time, he did so, completing his doctorate in education there, and, a dozen years later, after successful experience as a public-school superintendent, returning to become Dr. Spaulding's successor as Professor of School Administration in his alma mater. In the meantime, he had married the dean's daughter and with her, raised a notably promising family of four children.

I'm sure young Brownell did not dream, when first I met him, that he should someday be United States Commissioner of Education, but I was sure, even then, that he was on his way to some such high destiny.

One little incident which occurred at Peru, during my stay of a week there, has been recalled to my mind a thousand times since. My first day on the campus was the Fourth of July. The president and the faculty, with their families, had a picnic dinner in the park. I was a guest. After the "barbecue," the President called upon me to speak to the faculty seated in the bleachers in the ball park. The sun was scorching hot. The dinner had been substantial. To gain and hold the attention of my audience was, under these circumstances, a real challenge. After I had gotten under way, I gave a vivid description of a modern "activity" school in action. The Peru State Normal School was not then being operated on the activity pattern and the dean, a very kindly man, unconsciously took on the look of a man "from Missouri." He, quite obviously, had some questions in his mind as to whether his guest and visitor might not be leading his faculty to the brink of the river. So he took the floor and asked me pointedly: "What, then, is a good school, anyhow?" I understood he desired to have me give him a definition. I had been giving illustrations. I wasn't too sure I could give him a satisfactory definition, so while I was looking heavenward for the inspiration which seemed slow in coming, I did what the students in our classes ordinarily do, when we ask questions for the answers to which they have made no serious preparation. I began talking, hoping the right idea might arrive before the close of the paragraph.

Thorndike says we think only in self-defense. I was obviously on the defensive, and I had to think; so this is what I said: "A good school is a place where young people—of any age—come together to educate themselves, and each other, with the effective help of inspiring teachers."

This statement, turned out when my mind was at white heat, has been quoted all over the country ever since, and with more obvious approval than almost anything else I have ever said before an audience of American teachers.

By 1922, my work in Cleveland was so well organized and I had so many capable associates, that I was able to get away often during the year to respond to the calls, which came in increasing numbers, for addresses before state and national groups of teachers, principals, superintendents, and administrators and, also, before teachers-college and university-school-of-education faculties.

In the fall of 1923, I was given the principal evening assignment before a national group of teachers college presidents, who had come together at the Terre Haute, Indiana, State Normal College, to celebrate the one-hundredth anniversary of the establishment of the first American normal school at Concord Corners, Vermont, by Samuel Reed Hall, in 1823. My topic was "The Teachers College as a Professional School."

In this address, I stressed selective admission and the progressive elimination of all who do not give satisfactory promise of becoming successful teachers. I defined the character of the special laboratory-school equipment necessary in the operation of a professional school for teachers. I made provision for internship training. I described the character and defined the purpose of the educational museum necessary to provide, adequately, for the up-to-date teaching materials needed to make classroom instruction vivid and dynamic. I gave a clear and vivid description of the general education, the professional equipment, and the personal character of acceptable staff members in a professional school for teachers. I may, I think not inappropriately, quote several of the concluding paragraphs of this address, as indicating the distinctively professional character and the genuinely democratic spirit of a good college for teachers:

The dominant note in all educational theory in America for the past twenty-five years has been democracy. Democracy, if it means anything at all, means a mode of organization, a group life in which there is voluntary or compulsory surrender of every individual right which conflicts with the common welfare and a reservation to the individual of every right which does not conflict with the common welfare or the public good. The first conception suggests co-operation and unity and therefore strength and safety. The second suggests variation and selection and therefore improvement in the realm of ideas and consequently of behavior. There can be neither unity, strength, nor safety among men who have not learned to co-operate. On the other hand, there can be no progress in a society where complete conformity in all the details of individual conduct is required and enforced by external authority.

If democracy is to be our most generally accepted social philosophy, then all who teach must get by precept and by example, a clear conception of what it is, and of what it is not, in order that they may help to bring about such changes in our educational system as will make it a dynamic force for human betterment.

We have been overemphasizing freedom and have said too little about compensating service. The fundamental conception of democracy is service for the common good in return for the protections of government. The best teachers colleges are so organized and so administered, as effectively to teach young people, both by precept and by example, to discriminate between those personal liberties which can be exercised without menace to the common good and those which cannot and to govern their conduct accordingly. In this school, all forms of official restraint are rapidly disappearing and external compulsion of any kind is becoming increasingly unnecessary and, therefore, unpopular.

The old conception of the pupil-teacher relationship was something like this: "I am your teacher; you are my pupil. I spend my time laboriously inventing tasks for your discipline. You spend your time with equal diligence in trying to avoid these tasks, and if you don't succeed in making an escape, that is, if by some form of external compulsion, I can force you to do what you don't want to do, I shall feel compelled to give you a diploma and then, of course, you'll be educated."

The new conception is different. The teacher is one who has the power to create a social atmosphere that is surcharged with the spirit of mutual helpfulness. She is neither a task setter nor a timekeeper. She is a comrade and in her presence, individual effort and group co-operation are easy and natural. Education is then a privilege and the young teacher is aflame with zeal to bring its benefits to children everywhere.

It was now clear that, from the date of this address in Terre Haute, Indiana, I had been accepted as an authentic voice in the councils of the leaders of the American teachers-college movement that was sweeping the United States between World War I and World War II.

From December, 1923, forward, and even before I went to New York University the next fall to open a new department for the preparation of teachers-college officers and staff members, I had more calls for addresses and for consultation services in teachers colleges and in university schools of education than I could possibly accept, and they came from all parts of the country.

It was significant that, within a period of eight years after that address was printed and widely circulated early in 1924, I was called to state conferences of normal-school faculties in eighteen different states. During these years, I appeared often on the programs of the American Association of Teachers Colleges which, in 1922, superseded the old Council of Normal School Presidents.

I was called upon in the spring of 1923, to present the Cleveland plan for the in-service education of teachers to the Schoolmen's Week Conference at the University of Pennsylvania. I described the sweep of the movement which enlisted each year four thousand of the six thousand teachers of the metropolitan area of Cleveland in classes and activities given afternoons, evenings, Saturdays, and summer terms, and told of the emphasis, in season and out of season, on the demonstration of good teaching at all grade levels and in a wide variety of subjects. It was clear from the response which this presentation received, that the leaders in the states represented in this conference; namely: Pennsylvania, New Jersey, Delaware, and Maryland, earnestly desired to have similar provision made in their teacher-training colleges, so that all teachers be given an opportunity to *see* more good teaching demonstrations and to participate in the discussion of the purpose and significance of innovations in both educational aims and teaching procedures.

The wide dissemination of authentic information concerning the points of emphasis in our program for the professional up-grading of the teaching staff of the city of Cleveland, in due time, attracted national attention, bringing to the school, each year, a large number of superintendents, principals, and teachers from all over the nation and from foreign countries, the latter having been encouraged to see the program in operation by such agencies as Teachers College, Columbia University, and the International Institute of Education in New York.

For a period of eight years before coming to Cleveland, I had been engaged with a competent collaborator, Robert Philip Koehler, in research on the selection and gradation of words for the elementary-school spelling list and on the learning difficulties peculiar to individual words on such lists. I had made a contract with the John C. Winston Publishing Company, of Philadelphia, to prepare a series of spelling texts and an accompanying manual for teachers. The excessive demands upon me in my first two years in Cleveland, postponed the completion of this undertaking. At the close of the summer session in 1920, I went into a retreat at Green Springs, Ohio, and in ten days of intensive work, completed the project (including a manual of four hundred and twenty pages for teachers, setting forth the considerations which should govern the selection of words to be included in each of the grade lists, tersely stating the principles of spelling instruction and giving specific treatment to the learning difficulties peculiar to each hard word in the total list of four thousand words).

My collaborator, a former graduate student in my classes at the University of Pennsylvania, was the most meticulous research worker I have ever known. He spent several years in doing basic research for this book series. What real enjoyment I had in "fighting out" with him all the major policies which governed the preparation of these publications.

This book series (the "Spell-to-Write Spelling Books") was widely adopted. Our publisher shipped six carloads of these books at one time into one midwestern state. These books continued on the market for many years. My royalties were substantial. One of these royalty checks arrived in time to enable me to complete payment, in cash, for the new home we bought in the beautiful residential city of Montclair when we moved East in the summer of 1924.

Farewell to Cleveland

When I presented my resignation to Superintendent R. G. Jones early in the spring of 1924, after six and a half years of service to the Cleveland school system, he offered me substantial inducements to remain (advance in salary, greater freedom to accept calls for lecture-consultation service and to write text books), but my mind had, for some time, been set upon returning to university teaching. The right opportunity had finally come, and I was ready to embrace it. I told him my decision was final.

The superintendent then requested me to name my successor. It did not seem to me that I should assume that responsibility. I did, however, suggest the names of three persons of national reputation and of suitable training and experience, all of whom, I advised him, he might well consider as eligible. He selected one of these, Dr. Charles W. Hunt, of the University of Pittsburgh, who gave the institution excellent leadership for nine years and who, for a period of approximately thirty years, beginning while in Cleveland, has been, until his recent retirement, the distinguished executive secretary of the American Association of Teachers Colleges and of its successor, the American Association of Colleges for Teacher Education.

My program, during the remaining spring and summer months, was crowded with extra calls. Many elementary principals desired that I make one more visit to their schools. Many high schools asked for one more chapel talk. All these occasions were very happy ones.

The superintendent asked me to summarize for his headquarters staff the substantial progress in humanizing the teaching and counseling services I had observed in our schools, during my association with them. The elementary-school principals' association made my going an occasion for the expression of their good will. This group had made Mrs. Suhrie and me guests at a lakeside luncheon during every summer season since we had come to the city and we made its members, guests at a banquet given the faculty and senior class each spring at the school of education. This last one was an especially memorable occasion. The president of the senior class presided and the president of the principals' association responded to her address in compliment to the future employers of the memebrs of her class. They were both very complimentary to each other and very kind to me.

We had, a little while before, worked up, together, an impressive banquet program in celebration of the semicentennial of the Cleveland Normal School. Mrs. Suhrie and I were guests of the alumni association, at its annual banquet in the gymnasium of Western Reserve University at the close of our last year in the city. On that occasion, Professor Harry N. Irwin, the director of our Senior Teachers College and Graduate Courses, my intimate associate and friend of many years, presented to me, on behalf of the Faculty of the School of Education, a Life Membership in the National Education Association and a beautiful and expensive traveling bag. This was an occasion I can never forget. Nine hundred friends were present.

Twenty-one years later, when I returned as a guest speaker at a tribute dinner given in honor of Dean Irwin, President Hunt's successor, on the occasion of his retirement, I was able to exhibit to many of my friends that same traveling bag and to announce that it had accompanied me through all of our forty-eight states and thirty-five foreign countries. On that notable occasion, I was privileged to present to the retiring dean, a treasured volume in which I had written the following inscription:

My dear Harry, I have known you for more than two-score years; and no fleeting shadow has ever come across the shining pathway of the friendship you so generously gave me in the first year of our acquaintance at Wooster College.

I have seen you fight many a good fight courageously; I have seen you hold steadfastly to our boyhood faith in the essential nobility of men and in the goodness of God; I have seen you maintain your personal and professional integrity unfalteringly to the end of a long and distinguished career in educational service.

And so let it here be "written in the book" that, across the span of more than half a century since I began my teaching career, I have known no more intelligent and skillful leader of young people, no more trustworthy and sincere friend in the deep vicissitudes of life.

May this little book, entitled: *The Magic Realm of the Arts* and written by a mutual friend, the late Henry Turner Bailey, remind you, unendingly, of our personal and professional associations with him and with each other, in this beautiful and inspiring Wade Park setting in the precious days that are gone.

And now that you have earned the right to loiter at leisure along the sunset trail—unhurried by the call of duty

and unworried by the relentless demands of public office—
it is my fervent prayer that the evening time of your well-
spent life may be as full of contentment and of peace as its
active—and often anxious—working days and hours have
been full of kindliness and of helpful service.

Superintendent Jones accepted an invitation to visit the
school of education on a Saturday morning near the close of
the year to address a capacity audience of Cleveland teachers
in the school auditorium. He made this an occasion to pay
high tribute to the organization and spirit of our school and
to the high professional quality of our faculty. He praised
the accomplishments of the college during his administration.

Tribute to a Great Public School Superintendent

My memory of my personal and professional relations
with Superintendent Frank E. Spaulding, who invited me to
Cleveland and who withdrew from Cleveland four years before I did, is a very satisfying one. He invited me to go with
him to Yale. I was glad he did not press the invitation for, on
reflection, I was sure that our joint efforts in the program of
up-grading the professional services of the Cleveland teaching staff would bear little permanent fruit unless I should remain to further develop and more fully to stabilize the program we had inaugurated.

I shall always remember my Big Chief as the most alert
and constructive school superintendent I have ever been
privileged to know. He was a just judge of the worth of his
associates in the big city-school system. He was an arch encourager of effort and a generous rewarder of achievement.
He inspired deep and abiding professional loyalties. He demonstrated to his supervisors and principals, how to deal justly
with their teachers. He was singularly free from sham and
showmanship. He was a professional schoolman of the
highest integrity. It was a real privilege to work with him;
none of his associates ever worked *for* him; they always

worked *with* him and *for* a great Cause. He was the *embodiment* of that Cause.

In all our personal relations, he treated me with great consideration in the vicissitudes of life. He was no stranger to compassion.

In 1936, sixteen years after Dr. Spaulding had withdrawn from the school superintendency of Cleveland to accept the Sterling Professorship of Educational Administration in the Graduate School of Yale University, I had the honor to be one of a group of twenty-one men (former colleagues, colleagues, and his doctor of philosophy graduates), invited to write a chapter each for a volume to be entitled *Educational Progress and School Administration* and to be issued by the Yale University Press as a "tribute to Frank E. Spaulding" on the occasion of his retirement from educational service. In the preface of this notable publication, Professor Clyde M. Hill, his successor and the compiler and editor of the volume, says:

"The best evidence of his worthiness to be thus honored by his former associates is to be found in the last chapter of this book." This chapter includes scores of pungent paragraphs, collected as excerpts from Dr. Spaulding's own official pronouncements while serving as a city school superintendent in one or other of the five American cities in which he held that high and honorable office. His conception of the power and responsibility of this office may best be gained from his own statement: "No other type of educational position in America compares even remotely with the city and large town superintendency. By contrast, the power of the university presidency, public or private, seems insignificant; its responsibility, vague and indefinite."

And here is his appraisal of the importance of the truly educated and deeply dedicated classroom teacher: "The intelligent teacher, full of contagious enthusiasm, of energy, of hope, of courage, of love for children and for his profession, of self sacrificing spirit, of devotion to selfless ideals, is more potent than all other educational factors combined."

It is not difficult to understand why his associates in five important cities have idolized this great leader. The memory of my very intimate association with him, for two short years, is as precious as any of the memories I have of highly intellectual and deeply dedicated professional leadership and service.

"Here was a man! When comes there such another?"

He and his lovely life companion are living in a quiet apartment in the Casa de Manana, La Jolla, California, "down by the sea." It is surely worth such a trip across the continent as Mrs. Suhrie and I take about once each year to see them.

Dr. Spaulding is still writing and publishing notable professional books at eighty-eight and, from the quality of his writing, I can think of no reason why he should not go on indefinitely.

My "blessings on thee, little man!"

6

UNIVERSITY TEACHING

W HEN I accepted the call to New York University down on Washington Square in New York City, I was fifty years of age. I was mature enough in experience and in judgment to choose my big chiefs, Chancellor Brown and Dean Withers, with extraordinary care and discretion; each of them generously gave me the greatest possible freedom and the best possible counsel, co-operation, and official support to the end of my service with him.

I, there, undertook the organization of a new department to provide courses for the advanced professional education of administrative officers and teachers in normal schools and teachers college. The call to this position gave me, I verily believe, as wide an opportunity for service and as great freedom in adapting means to ends as any American university professor has ever enjoyed.

By previous agreement, I was free to spend as much as two days each week in visiting tax-supported state and municipal normal schools and teachers colleges, to familiarize myself with their pressing problems of organization, administration, staffing, curriculum, improvement of instruction, demonstration and apprentice teaching, the supervision of interns and the like.

I was free to organize and did organize the teacher-preparing forces of the East, the better to co-ordinate and unify their state programs of pre-service and in-service education of teachers, to up-grade certification standards and requirements, and to democratize the organization and the spirit of faculty-student relationships on the campuses of teacher-preparing institutions.

The call soon came to me for lecture and consultation service in teachers colleges and university schools of education and in state associations of their staff members; also to help in defining the purpose and functions of student associations in teacher preparing colleges.

Teaching the Teachers of Teachers

When Dean John W. Withers, of the School of Education, of New York University, had concluded his second visit to the Cleveland School of Education as a member of the Consultant Survey Commission in the spring of 1922, he expressed to me the hope that I might, in the near future, join him as a member of the staff of the University and organize and preside over a new department of Teachers-College and Normal-School Education. He said he earnestly desired that I have an opportunity to teach presidents, deans and staff members in other American teachers colleges to adopt and to promote the reforms in teachers education which had made the School of Education in Cleveland, as he believed, a center of interest among all leaders in teacher education in all parts of the country. In each of my subsequent meetings with him during the next two years he repeated the invitation.

Dean George F. Arps, of the School of Education, of Ohio State University, after participating in a three-day inspection of our school by a special committee of the University, expressed a similar interest in the possibility of my coming to Ohio State University at Columbus.

I knew the time was drawing near when I should have to make some final decision in the matter. I had engaged in administration for a period of years as a means to an end. My plan was to return to university teaching in due time and I thought the time had come. I told Dean Withers frankly that I was afraid to become a university professor because of the danger that doing so might remove me from the arena where professional problems are real and must be solved to an academic retreat where problems are likely to be hypothetical and purely academic and do not urgently call for solutions. I told him that I had a haunting fear that, in two or three years, I should find myself stranded on a dream island, cut off from the mainland of reality, and then have to be content the remainder of my life with verbal solutions to hypothetical problems. He insisted that he really desired to have me join his staff and that if I would indicate what it would take to interest me he'd make a real endeavor to meet my conditions. It was clear to both of us that salary would be no primary consideration for the University's salary scale for professors, I knew, was much below what I was then receiving, to say nothing of the raise I would be (and later was) offered if I should decide to decline the call to New York.

Early in the spring of 1924, I went to New York on the Dean's invitation for an extended conference with him on the matter. I told him that unless I could spend at least two days each week in visiting normal schools, teachers colleges and university schools of education, in actually coming to grips as a visiting consultant with the problems of these institutions, I could not hope to do as much for the cause of teacher education in the new position as by going on with my work in Cleveland. He said that he would be glad to set up for me a schedule that would make this possible. He assured me that he wanted me to have the widest possible freedom in developing a new department according to my own convictions as to how it should be done and, that I should not be held on the campus when my best judgment should prompt me to be in the field. I had a conference also with Chancellor Brown in which he assured me of his earnest desire that I come. I believed then, as I still do, that these two men, as official superiors, really desired to give me as complete freedom of action as any man could hope to enjoy in any American university. Because I never, for a moment, doubted their complete sincerity, I decided to cast my lot with them. I found them able to keep faith superbly through all the years of my service with them.

Ohio State University would doubtless have given me a better salary. Dean Arps rated teaching as a function above administration and called several men to his staff as professors at $10,000 each per year when his own salary as Dean was only $6,000.

I finally made up my mind that, with all the limitations of New York University in equipment and financial resources, it would, for a number of reasons, afford me the best possible opportunity to make, if I were able to do so anywhere, a really unique place for myself in the American teachers college movement. Time and events proved that my judgment had been correct. The opportunity surely did come and I embraced it with enthusiasm and zeal.

In July, I bought a house in Montclair, New Jersey, and at the conclusion of the summer session in Cleveland in middle August, I moved my family East and began at once developing plans for my work in New York University when the fall term should open, early in October, 1924.

During the month of September, I visited a score of normal schools and teachers colleges in New England and the Middle Atlantic States. I organized my university courses, in as far as possible, to include the consideration of all the problems I had found in the institutions visited.

At the time I joined the university faculty, Dean Withers said there were one hundred thousand teachers, principals and superintendents of schools living and working within commuting distance of Washington Square. That number must have materially increased within a few years thereafter, as the term "commuting distance" came in each successive year to mean more and more miles.

In a course I offered at 11 A.M. to 1 P.M. on Saturdays entitled: *Personnel Problems of the Public School Staff* to which all types of staff members at every level of experience and service—instructional, supervisory and administrative—were admitted, I had a large class each year almost from the beginning and up to the outbreak of World War II. Between 1925 and 1940, we had an enrollment each year of commuters from eight (and sometimes nine) states including representatives from such cities as Washington, Baltimore, Dover, Wilmington, Chester, Philadelphia, Harrisburg, Pittsburgh, Scranton, Trenton, Camden, Newark, Elmira, Poughkeepsie, Albany, Syracuse, New Haven, Hartford, New Britain, Springfield, Worcester, Providence and points between. I used to call this class my "little League of Nations." Any important happening in school circles from Washington to Upper New England and west to Ohio was sure to be reported and, if important, discussed in this class.

My other basic courses were all less general and were intended expressly for teachers-college officers and for professors in teacher-preparing institutions. A few years after the opening of the department, when we began offering courses in residence, not only during the academic year and the summer session; but, also in an intersession and when extension courses were given in certain Teachers College centers in New York, Pennsylvania, New Jersey, Massachusetts and Connecticut, we had graduate students enrolled in the department from all parts of the United States and from many foreign countries. Sometimes, in a single course as in the intersession, we had enrollments from almost every state in the Union.

As the demands justified it, we added staff members as follows: in 1925, Miss Anne Rochefort of the Cleveland School of Education; in 1930, Professor Alonzo F. Myers, the Director of Teacher Education and Certification in the Connecticut State Office of Education and in the same year Professor Ned. H. Dearborn, the Director of Teacher Education and Certification, New York State Office of Education; and in 1934, Professor George H. Black, former President of the State Teachers College, Ellensburg, Washington, and for summer sessions, President Roscoe L. West of the State Teachers College at Trenton.

Our specialized courses in the department were on the aims, organization and administration of teachers colleges, on their curricula, on the work of the demonstration and training schools and, in a special graduate seminar, on the improvement of the curricula offered in our own School of Education. To this special seminar representative advanced students from each of the twenty-four departments of the School of Education were admitted on the recommendation of their respective chairmen.

The work of the demonstration and training school departments of teachers colleges throughout the East was, in due time, much improved through the courses offered by Miss Anne Rochefort, a specialist in this field with much practical experience in this branch of the service.

Professors Ned H. Dearborn and Alonzo F. Myers, each of whom had been a state director of teacher education and certification, gave the state teachers colleges a pronounced impetus to give up all wasteful duplication and unseemly competition and to unite themselves into well-co-ordinated state systems of teacher education. Professor Dearborn organized the National Association of State Directors of Teacher Certification.

As department chairman, I endeavored to keep intimately in touch with all the teacher preparing institutions of the East, state supported, private and church related, by weekly visits to one or more of them throughout the academic year, and to those in other sections by visits as occasion afforded the opportunity, and more systematically, during the month of June when the big summer schools of the West and South were insistently calling for lectures and for consultation services.

Between 1930, and the time when the second World War began to disrupt our program, there were generally about a dozen, sometimes more, graduate students each year who completed requirements for the Ph. D. degree or the Ed. D. degree with thesis in the field of teacher education; and there were three or four times as many others who completed the master's degree requirements with majors or minors in this field.

In the course of time, some of the state normal schools and state teachers colleges within striking distance had staffs, thirty, forty, or even fifty per cent of whose members had studied in our department for longer or shorter periods; there were teachers colleges as far away as the Mississippi, a dozen of whose staff members had been students in the department, and there were also many representative teachers college faculty members from the Pacific Coast as well as individual students from Latin America, South Africa, China, India, and other foreign countries, far and near.

The term-paper and the thesis sponsoring load of the department was, from the beginning, a very heavy burden upon all the members of the staff. I have a deep-seated conviction that the counseling-service of the graduate professor at its best is of far greater value to his students than his classroom teaching ever can be. I made it a matter of policy to be available to my students for short conferences on term-paper studies as nearly as possible at their own convenience and for more extended conferences on their theses and documents by appointment and at some length. Because of the high percentage of commuting students, this policy made it necessary that my services should be available in the late afternoons, and evenings and on Saturdays. My service load on Saturdays was inordinately heavy. It ran generally about as follows:

8 to 9 A.M., consultation at my office

9 to 11 A.M., seminar

11 to 1 P.M., seminar

1 to 3 P.M., consultation at my office.

The number of part-time students holding responsible positions in teachers colleges and public-school systems who commuted from one hundred to two hundred miles for week-end study in my classes made it almost imperative that I hold myself available for conference on Friday evenings and on Saturday at eight in the morning and again in the early afternoon. On many occasions it was wholly impossible to take time out for lunch without delaying the caravan of automobiles back to South Jersey, Eastern Pennsylvania, Connecticut, Massachusetts, or Delaware.

Many of the ablest candidates for advanced degrees had not had adequate preparation in English in their under-graduate days and this made it doubly important that their theses and documents be scrutinized with something more than ordinary care. It was well worth the effort to labor diligently with and for these men and women, for scores of them later rose to places of distinction in the United States Office of Education, in state offices of education, and in teachers colleges and university schools of education.

Two years before I retired, the department of teachers college education and the department of arts college education, were combined into a department of higher education. I served for one year as co-chairman of this new department and then at the beginning of my last year of service Dr. Alonzo F. Myers, whom I had brought to the university a dozen years earlier, was, with my hearty approval, made chairman.

Drafted for Collateral Administrative Service at New York University

One of the outstanding characteristics of the School of Education of New York University during Dean Withers' entire term of service from 1921 to his retirement in 1938, seventeen years later, was its continuing and rapid increase in numbers, even during the depression years. There were one hundred forty-one enrollees (most of them part-time students) in the old School of Pedagogy when he arrived on the campus; and when he retired there were twelve thousand students in the new School of Education, its successor. When I came to the University in the fall of 1924, there were one thousand more students in the School of Education than there had been a year earlier.

The University was so short on classroom space for the increasing number of students and on office space for the corresponding increase in faculty members that the situation would have seemed hopeless by 1925 had not Dean Withers, assistant dean Milton E. Loomis "the chancellor of the exchequer," and secretary Ralph E. Pickett, been resourceful enough to think up some unusual measures to meet the emergency. They organized a School of Education Realty Corporation with a million-dollar capital (subscribed by board members, professors, and students), took title to a half dozen different office buildings and hotels located on the block immediately adjacent to the university's Main building, leased the same to the University for a period of years at a rental sufficient to pay the interest on the stock purchased and then finally, as soon as the University was able to take its assets over for cash, liquidated the corporation. In the meantime, the new twelve-story school-of-education building was built on one-fourth of this block, office and classroom space was made available in other buildings acquired and temporary quarters for the University book store, cafeteria, etc. were made immediately available. This was a service of far-reaching importance to the whole University.

I had come to the University to teach, not to formulate administrative policy or to engage in administrative service, but the call for such service was insistent. After a year on the campus, the Dean asked me to assume the chairmanship of a special committee to whom he had assigned the task of formulating and recommending a pattern of general and detailed organization for the School of Education. On my advice, he doubled the size of the committee so as to include every discordant element known to exist in the faculty. I was determined that if there were fundamental differences among us as to how the faculty should be organized to perform its policy-making and administrative functions, these differences should be ironed out before any recommendations should be presented to the Dean and faculty for consideration and adoption.

For two months, our committee labored, in season and out of season, to bring the members of our group into complete agreement upon some satisfactory pattern of organization, knowing that if we could avoid majority and minority reports we should be on our way to an early and possibly a unanimous adoption of the committee's recommendations.

The recommendations finally made and unanimously adopted created the basic organization of the School of Education which continued in force to the end of Dean Withers' administration and beyond. This basic organization provided for eight policy-recommending committees, and a general committee (or senate), to which the recommendations of each of these eight standing committees should be presented for adoption (with or without amendment), for tabling, or for reference back to the committee of origin (with or without instructions). This general committee, or senate, included in its membership, the dean, the two assistant deans, the chairman of each of the eight standing committees and as many as three additional members of the faculty appointed by the Dean at his own discretion.

The administration of the statutes of the University and the policies of the School of Education were to be attended to by the Dean with authority to delegate by definite assignment such of these duties as he might wish to the assistant Dean of Instruction or to the assistant Dean of Finance.

The Dean appointed, without delay, two assistant deans and assigned to each certain definite administrative responsibilities.

I was appointed chairman of the committee on curricular adjustment and revision. I served in this capacity to the end of Dean Withers' administration. The labors of this committee in setting up functional and therefore flexible undergraduate curricula and patterns of graduate advisement were prodigious. I once wrote a short article for the *Educational Service Magazine,** indicating how very complex these problems were and giving our (always tentative) solutions for them. From the graduate seminar, devoted to the study of curricular adjustments and revisions in the School of Education of New York University, which I conducted, came recommendations for the setting up of six advisory divisions—each under a director—to provide counseling services to graduate students preparing for educational service at one or other of six levels of educational services as follows: I. General Public Schools Administrative and Supervisory Service, II. Teachers-College and University School of Education Service, III. Arts College and Junior College Service, IV. Secondary School Service, V. Elementary School Service, VI. Miscellaneous and Special School Services.

There was an advisory set-up for graduate students pursuing their studies in any one of these six divisions. The fixed requirements in graduate study in any one of the advisory divisions were negligible.

---

* See *Courses and Curricula Offered in University Schools of Education* in October, 1929, issue.

We conceived it to be the function of the division of teachers-college service to help the graduate student engaged in, or preparing to enter upon, such service to find the graduate courses in any two or more of our twenty-four departments which would best equip him to perform efficiently in some important teachers-college assignment.

For example, here is a candidate for the doctor's degree who desires to prepare to be a professor of English in a teachers college. Under our advisory set-up, he was directed to consult his general adviser (the head of the department of teachers-college education) in the selection of courses intended to give him an understanding of the teachers college as a professional school: of its aims, its organization, its administration, its curriculum, its counseling and placement services, its committee and extra-curricular services, and its laboratory school facilities and programs. He was directed to consult his special adviser (the head of the department of English) in the selection of courses in English content and method. English was to be his specialty in his college teaching and in his services as a departmental supervisor in the affiliated laboratory schools.

This pattern of faculty counseling service presupposed complete understanding and intelligent co-operation between the student's general adviser and his special adviser. Such understanding, needless to say, did not always exist and such co-operation was not always given. It was not intended to limit the student's choice of courses to two departments. We had a few department chairmen who were extreme departmentalists. They seemed willing to place the individual graduate student in bondage to a single department that is, to hold him in a sort of academic peonage.

It has been my observation that the advisory services of many graduate professors are generally less efficient than their instructional services. This, it seems to me, is due to two personal limitations: (1) their experience in the field of service for which the student desires to prepare is limited; (2) they suffer from an apron-string conception of the function of a counselor.

Inasmuch as it was one of the principal functions of the department of teachers-college education to teach the effective organization and administration of teachers colleges and university schools of education, it was natural that the Dean should call upon the head of this department to help develop administrative patterns and procedures for handling the registration of eight thousand, ten thousand, or twelve thousand students in three afternoons and one morning at the opening of each semester (or for handling five thousand students on one day at the opening of the summer session). It was a prodigious undertaking to work out and co-ordinate plans for such registration, but our committee and its chairman finally completed this task.

Inasmuch as the assistant dean of instruction to whom the implementation and administration of these plans had been originally assigned, did not care to undertake the task, the Dean prevailed upon me to carry that burden, also. I, therefore, spent the vacation month of September for a number of years in perfecting anew each year, the operation of the registration machinery and in drilling several hundred guides and monitors to function efficiently in routing students to advisers, counselors, curriculum directors, department heads and officers of the faculty and to the bursar's temporary office on the first floor of the Main building.

In due time, our advisement machinery was made to operate so smoothly that many registrars and deans from institutions of all sizes and from far and near came to observe our registration in progress from the balcony of our several gymnasium floors and on the first-floor halls where students formed in twelve lines to pay tuitions and to receive class cards.

As chairman of the committee which had set up and secured approval of all undergraduate curricula and on patterns for the advisement of graduate students, I prepared the advisement pamphlets issued each year by the School of Education.

I compiled and edited each year all material for the School of Education catalog except that which had to do with administrative policies and financial arrangements. Our governing purpose was to make the catalog not only a good manual of administration for the officers and faculty, but a source of much help to the individual student in securing the advisement he might desire and need.

The burden of these collateral administrative services I carried for nine formative years and up until my first and only sabbatical in the second half of the academic year of 1932-33. Much of the "bone labor" involved in this administrative service provided very practical and profitable experience for my best graduate students. Many teachers-college presidents gave our department credit for having trained certain of their staff members to effect substantial reforms in the operation of the registration machinery on their home campuses. This I have always thought a significant service, for I well remember that, as a graduate student in the summer session of a certain big mid-western university years before, I stood in line from Monday morning until Wednesday afternoon to get the *wrong* official answer from a very distinguished dean. I'm sure that if that hadn't happened to me personally, I should never have been willing to give up so many vacation days to "oiling up" the registration machinery at New York University.

In all my courses in teachers-college organization and administration, I sought to provide in our own big complex institution, the opportunity for many graduate students to discover administrative problems that needed study and then to give them an opportunity to analyze such problems and make reports in my seminars on their progress in finding working solutions for them. We endeavored to keep the graduate students of college administration alert to the unsolved problems in administrative service in their own institutions as well as to help them to discover the unsolved administrative problems of our School of Education in which, as students, they might be expected to have the consumer's viewpoint and interest. All our courses in *Current Problems in Teachers College Education* were conducted for the very specific purpose of alerting our graduate students to the fact that no problems of organization, administration, curriculum, or instruction remain solved, that all such problems call for new and better solutions each year, that college administration is a dynamic not a static function.

The service of our Committee on Curricular Adjustment and Revision was much less efficient than it might have been, had department heads been less inclined to proliferate courses. President Bruce R. Payne, of George Peabody College for Teachers, used to say: "When I find a professor who can give *one* really good course, I thank God for that, and then let him ring as many changes on it as he may wish to." Then he added significantly: "I think it is a mistake, however, for a serious minded graduate student to take more than one course with any professor unless he feels the need of an inordinate amount of review."

President Leroy Burton, of the University of Michigan, used to request the presiding officer, before introducing him to a large audience of teachers, to announce a change of topic for his lecture on the ground that "I do not want this audience or any other audience to get the notion that I am limited to any one topic for this lecture." Almost everywhere in our graduate schools and departments there is much wasteful duplication in courses, much repetition of the same material in each of two or three different courses. And some times there is much unseemly competition for the right to invade instructional areas already assigned and fully occupied.

During the latter years of my tenure at the University I served as a representative of the School of Education faculty in the University Senate. I participated in the confirmation of Dr. John H. Finley, Editor of the *New York Times*, as Director of the University's Hall of Fame. Also, in the confirmation of a group of electors whom he nominated to choose those "heroes of the republic" who should be honored by having their busts placed in the Hall of Fame in the arcades of the Gould Library of New York University, up in the Bronx. And in the war days, I had the privilege of voting approval of a certain "self-denying ordinance" recommended by the financial officers of the university, cutting $8,000 from the coverage of the group-insurance policy of each university professor. It wasn't easy to vote away a part of the security we had counted on for our old age, but the University's finances were in trouble; many of our students were in fox holes; and there seemed to be no alternative. I always try to do cheerfully whatever circumstances compel me to do.

Organization and Direction of Eastern-States Association

When the normal school department of the National Education Association went out of existence by combining with the American Association of Teachers Colleges at its Cleveland meeting in 1922, making the latter the over-all national organization to promote the further development of the teacher-education movement in the United States, a re-assessment of the usefulness of all the normal school organizations then in existence had been made and a study of the need for new organizations (if any) was in order. At this Cleveland meeting of the Association, a special committee on re-organization recommended that in each of the regional areas of the United States (New England, the Middle Atlantic States, the Old South, etc.) an affiliate be organized to provide sections and programs for faculty members of teachers colleges as distinct from administrative officers in such institutions. It was thought the latter group of officers might continue to be best served in annual meetings of the national parent organization (the A.A.T.C.). A normal school or teachers college president from each of the areas above referred to was assigned to organize the regional affiliate in his own area. President J. A. Pitman, of Salem, Massachusetts, was the only one of the total list thus appointed who proceeded at once to set up a regional affiliate of the parent national association in the area assigned to him; namely, New England.

Two years later when I arrived in New York (1924), I made up my mind at once that such a regional affiliate was much needed in the Middle-Atlantic States. After ascertaining that the man appointed to organize it was not interested in doing so, I proceeded, in the spring of 1926, to gather in a goodly group of normal-school and training-school-staff members at the Hotel Pennsylvania for the organization of such a regional affiliate. I found the officers of the A.A.T.C. had lost interest in the organization of these affiliates. I, personally, was deeply impressed with the desirability of them, so I proceeded to set up an independent organization and invited to this organization meeting also representatives from student associations of normal schools and teachers colleges within striking distance of New York City. In conference with them, I set up and later publicized a program to provide also for their special interests. By the spring of 1927, it was clear that many faculty members and student delegates in most of the normal schools of the eastern states desired to attend these meetings and that they regarded New York City as the logical place for annual meetings that could appropriately include all teacher-training institutions in the territory from Washington up to the northern point of Maine and as far west as Ohio.

The second meeting of our regional association late in

April of that year, was attended by about four hundred faculty members and two hundred students from the several normal schools all over the East and chiefly, of course, from the metropolitan area. It was, in due time, apparent that both presidents and faculty members had more concern to help promote student interests than they had in programs for either administrators or instructional staff members.

I had taken the lead during the first two years in sponsoring the regional association and in developing and publicizing its programs. There were no funds available for promotional expenses, and so I had to persuade the authorities of New York University to provide free clerical services and funds for printing, and postage. I, personally, bore all expenses of travel to the institutions concerned. At the close of the second meeting, I arranged to compile and edit the proceedings of the Association for each of the first two meetings. These volumes appeared under the title *Problems in Teacher Training* and were sold for one dollar apiece to defray the cost of printing. Each succeeding annual issue had a higher serial number.

A constitution and by-laws was adopted at the second meeting. I was elected President; Professor William C. Bagley, of Teachers College, was elected Vice-President; Lester K. Ade, later principal of New Haven State Normal School, was elected Secretary. The title, *Eastern-States Association of Professional Schools for Teachers,* was a cumbersome one, but since this organization would have in its membership, in due time, the one hundred university schools of education, teachers colleges, normal schools and training schools for teachers in the District of Columbia and the eleven states north of Virginia and east of Ohio, there seemed to be no better title available.

I served the Association as President for seven years (1926-1932 inclusive) and each year visited at least sixty of the institutions which held membership. *During my last year*

*in office, I succeeded in bringing into active membership
every institution that was eligible and in visiting every one
of them. There were exactly one hundred.*

Except one year, when the Self-Government Committee
Inc., of New York, Richard Welling, Chairman, furnished
traveling expenses, I, personally, bore all traveling expenses
in making these visits. New York University continued to
subsidize the Association by paying the expense of stationery
and postage, and by providing adequate clerical help during
the first eleven years (while I served as President for seven
years and while my college associate and successor, Alonzo
F. Myers, served as President for four years).

For a period of thirteen years, the Association continued
to issue its annual volume of proceedings, under the title of
Problems in Teacher Training. These volumes were widely
circulated in teachers colleges and university schools of education all over the country. That they were considered a
valuable contribution to the literature of teacher education
in the United States was evidenced by the insistent call for
them, long after the several editions had been exhausted.

When I had completed my last year of service as President and had issued the seventh volume of *Problems in
Teacher Training*, Professor William C. Bagley, of Teachers
College, Vice-President of the Association (and dean of
teacher education in the United States) wrote me the following gracious note:

My dear Dr. Suhrie: You deserve to be highly complimented on and warmly commended for the consistently
high professional quality of the seven volumes of proceedings (*Problems in Teacher Training*) you have compiled
and edited while you served the Association as its organizer
and chief executive officer. It is clear that in organizing
these annual programs, and in securing the active cooperation of scores of workers in the ranks of the faculties and
student bodies, and in the masterly conducting of these pro-

grams, as well as in compiling and editing these volumes, you have exhibited a genius for developing latent talent in our profession and that in defining the purposes of our institutions and in creating unity of purpose among them you have each year put a far greater amount of bone labor into the enterprise than would have been necessary to issue annually a substantial volume of your own authorship on *Problems in Teacher Training.*

Our profession owes you a heavy debt of gratitude.

May I add that your inviting student participation in the Association and your masterful development of student leadership in the home institutions which hold membership in the Association has demonstrated that you possess real genius for the leadership of young people.

The student addresses given in these early meetings were printed in the volumes of proceedings. Through the personal generosity of Mr. Richard Welling, of the Self-Government Committee Inc., New York, we were able to send the fourth volume to the ranking student officer of each of four hundred American colleges outside of our own membership here in the East. The fan letters which came to our office from student leaders in far-away places were heart-warming as was the evidence that our annual volume was being read from cover to cover and from coast to coast by many officers and faculty members of normal schools, teachers colleges and university schools of education.

After the close of the term of our third president, Dr. Arthur Van Den Berg, of New Paltz, New York, and at the end of the thirteenth annual meeting of the Association, the annual volume of proceedings was no longer issued. The Association began issuing in its stead the *Teacher-Education Journal,* a quarterly, as its house organ.

Inasmuch as this was my recommendation, it was perhaps natural that the President of the Association, Dr. Ernest Townsend of Newark, New Jersey, should request me to organize and edit the *Journal*. I accepted the call and served as Editor from June, 1939, to June, 1942. The third number of the first volume (December, 1939), was a one-hundred-twelve-page issue, celebrating the hundredth anniversary of the opening of the first American public normal school at Lexington, Massachusetts. A large edition, containing a write-up of the beginnings of the normal-school movement in each of the distinctive regional areas of the United States was included in this special number and a copy sent to the library of each teacher-preparing institution in the United States. This special issue was much commended. To pay the extra cost of this enlarged issue, I had to advance $250 which was refunded later by the Association. The cover page of this centennial number contained a beautiful picture of the "Cathedral of Learning" of the University of Pittsburgh. In that issue was included an article entitled: "Buildings Can Also Teach." Each issue of the *Journal* reproduced on its front-cover page, an attractive air view of some one of our representative Eastern state teachers-college campuses.

The first issue of the *Journal* which appeared under the editorship of Professor F. E. Borgenson, of New York University, my successor, in September, 1942, was made a tribute number in my honor. Some of its features, including the banquet at the Hotel Commodore in New York at which I was presented a leather bound, hand-lettered *Book of Remembrance* are included therein. The Association printed several hundred extra copies of this issue and sent them to me with its compliments. This gracious courtesy I have much appreciated.

Unfortunately the *Journal* was one of the casualties of World War II. Happily, the National Education Association has since resumed the publication of a journal of teacher-education under a similar title, namely *Journal of Teacher-Education*. In the first issue of this new *Journal* complementary reference is made to the very influential Journal our Association had published for five years (1939-1944).

After the first dozen annual meetings of the Eastern-States Association of Professional Schools for Teachers, the emphasis in its programs shifted almost completely to student interests; so it became necessary to organize each year a dozen to a score of separate panel discussion groups on as many different topics representing the wide diversity of problems in co-operative living which were then arising on the campuses of our colleges. With an attendance, for many years, of as many as two thousand students annually, it was necessary to have in each panel group as many as one hundred to two hundred students with panel participants from a score of widely scattered institutions. I, personally, helped organize these panel programs for a period of years after I left office as President of the Association in 1932, and thereafter, this important service was rendered in turn by such able Presidents as Dr. Lester K. Ade, and his successor, Dr. F. E. Engelman, of New Haven, Dr. Herbert D. Welte, of New Britain, Dr. John G. Flowers, of Lock Haven, and Dr. Forrest Irwin, of Jersey City. In recent years Dr. Patterson, of the department of education, of Lock Haven State Teachers College, and others, have given yeoman service to this enterprise, and faculty members have been in great demand as consultants in the several panel groups on each annual student program.

Attendance since the war has been limited to about eight hundred students because accommodations for a larger number can no longer be provided in the conference halls of any hotel in New York City.

One of the best features of this Association is that the student delegates from each institution organize themselves to put on an effective symposium in the home college as soon as possible after each annual meeting, summarizing for the whole student body the benefits derived from attendance and listing the reforms and improvements which may be made in the local college concerned in each case by the adoption or adaptation of policies and practices in operation elsewhere and recommended for wider use.

Friday evening, the student-faculty banquet in the grand ballroom of the Hotel Pennsylvania or the Commodore Hotel has always been a soul-stirring event. A picture of one of these banquets (1942) appears in this volume, as does also a picture of most of the young people who had accepted engagements on the student programs ten years earlier (1932).

The most popular banquet speakers in the metropolitan area always seemed pleased to accept invitations to address our student-faculty banquets. Among those to honor our young people by addressing them were: Walter Damrosch, Mrs. Edwin Markham, Wilson MacDonald, William C. Bagley, Albert B. Meredith, Edwin W. Adams, Daniel A. Polling, Cameron Beck, Samuel C. Schmucker, Lorado Taft, Herman H. Horne, Albert B. Cohoe, and William O'Shea. Many of these addresses were broadcast over the air from the banquet table.

The number of banqueters, after the third year, was usually about twelve to fifteen hundred and, by 1942, it had increased to seventeen or eighteen hundred.

At the banquet table with the officers of the Association, about twenty distinguished guests were seated. These included state commissioners of education, university, and liberal-arts college presidents, editors, city-school superintendents and retiring teachers college presidents. Solos, quartettes, a capella choirs were special features of every banquet program.

The theme of the last banquet at which I served as toastmaster in 1932, was *The Quest for the More Abundant Life* (through Music, Damrosch; Art, Taft; Poetry, MacDon-

Student Delegate Speakers from One Hundred Teachers Colleges Appearing on the Program of the Eastern-States Association of Professional Schools for Teachers, Hotel Pennsylvania, Spring of 1932.

Front Line from left: Dr. Myers, Dr. Winship, Dr. Suhrie, Mr. Welling, Mr. McDonald.

Tribute Banquet Eastern-States Association of Professional Schools for Teachers, Hotel Commodore, New York, March 27, 1942.

ald; Science, Schmucker; Philosophy, Horne; and Religion, Cohoe).

The banquet programs usually presented tributes to distinguished retiring presidents of member institutions by representative students.

I recall vividly that in 1931 after I had gotten the student program set up so that it could be administered thereafter by student leaders, I was invited to the platform at the Saturday morning general session as a guest of honor. At the conclusion of the program, the student chairman called upon me to dismiss the meeting with a final message to the "home folk" in the member institutions. I had been almost overcome with the sweep of the power of student leadership as manifested in the meetings that morning. I commended the speakers and praised their group achievements. The chairman had no sooner dropped the gavel than two hundred or more students surged up to the platform to say a kindly word of appreciation to the student officers or to me. Among them was a tall, handsome young man (Joseph E. Burk), who at the time was a graduate student of mine at New York University. He had been dean of men in the North Texas State Teachers College at Denton before coming to New York. He clasped my hand as only a Texan can and almost wrenched my arm from the shoulder socket. He looked at me through tear-dimmed eyes and said:

"Dr. Suhrie, how in the world did you ever get those young people from a hundred different institutions scattered all over the East—strangers to each other and strangers to you—to come together and, speaking in the prophet voices of a new day, put on a program like this one? It was an artist's mosaic of co-operation and good will."

By that time, I was looking at him through the mists too: "It's easy," was my reply. "All I need to do is to thank them in advance for what I hope they'll do, and then they don't dare to disappoint me."

Many educational and other associations are dead but just won't lie down. This association is alive. It was created to meet a need and it has waxed strong in leadership and influence because it has met that need in a marvellous way. No professional movement I have ever been privileged to initiate, or to be identified with, has given me so much continuing satisfaction as this one. I have twice been the guest of honor at the banquet table since I retired from service to it in 1942, and on each of these occasions I have been delighted with the abundant evidences I have seen of the continuing vitality and increasing power of this Association.

I here publicly confess that I have real pride in being remembered as the founder of the Eastern-States Association of Professional Schools for Teachers and as its first president for a period of seven years.

And I acknowledge my profound obligation to Mrs. James A. Adair (nee Mildred Wells), my secretary for fourteen years at New York University, for a prodigious amount of constructive planning as well as for the voluminous correspondence she conducted in promoting the annual meetings of the Association over a period of years; as also for helping me and my successor, Dr. Alonzo F. Myers, for eleven years in preparing copy for the annual volumes of proceedings of the Association (*Problems in Teacher Training*, Volumes I to XI inclusive). I have never in all my life known any other secretary who was willing to give—and did give so freely—of her superb talents, "beyond the demands of duty," to the promotion and service of a great cause.

Flying Professor in Field Service

The demands made upon a university professor for services which are apart from his strictly professional duties on the campus may be, and sometimes are, many, varied, and important. And such services, when performed efficiently and without neglecting his duties on the campus, may greatly enhance his prestige as a public servant and increase the range of his experience and the effectiveness of his campus service in teaching and counselling.

The department which I organized in New York University was the third of its kind in the country. Dr. Carter Alexander at George Peabody College for Teachers and Dr. William C. Bagley at Teachers College, Columbia University, preceded me in opening up graduate courses specifically designed to promote the improvement of the services of teachers colleges. The few professors who offered such courses in the twenties were distinctly in the limelight and were in heavy demand for lectures at teachers associations and for consultation services in state offices of education and on the campuses of state and municipal normal schools, teachers colleges and university-schools of education.

My acquaintance in all parts of the country was already very large when I went to New York University. The calls for off-campus services were immediate, numerous, and insistent.

The effectiveness of my service as a professor on the campus was conditioned by my acquiring adequate and dependable information concerning state, regional, and national policies and practices in teacher preparation. Giving lectures as a guest speaker on any college campus and participating in faculty conferences thereon, almost always opens the door for a real insight into the work of the institution concerned such as can seldom be gotten from the publications of the institution or from magazine articles about its innovations and desirable practices.

So I accepted a reasonable number of the calls that came, taking care to distribute them among all the distinctive regional areas of the country and all types of teacher-preparing colleges, state, municipal, church-related and privately endowed, also among the national, regional and state associations of the teacher-training forces of the country.

I soon came to regard the nation as my "parish" and to consider it the duty and the privilege of "the pastor" to call as frequently as possible upon his "flock."

By dropping off, when possible, in one or more of the teachers colleges on my way to national, regional, or state meetings of my professional guild, I soon came to have a lot of reliable information concerning the policies and practices of particular individual institutions and to have a hold upon the interest of their officers and leading faculty members.

By the time I had been at New York University ten years, I had completed a personal visit to the campus of every tax-supported institution of higher education in the United States including schools and colleges for Negroes. This did not just happen; it was a planned program in which I utilized vacation periods and a sabbatical leave to complete the enterprise begun twenty years earlier and carried on with vigor long before going to New York University.

On these visits, I was generally engaged to speak to all the students and faculty members in a general-college convocation and to the faculty in a special conference; and almost everywhere, because of my known interest in the work of student associations and extra-curricular activity programs, I was called in for consultation with these groups in a meeting of their student leaders and faculty sponsors.

I was called, too, as lecturer and consultant to the associations of teachers-college and normal-school faculties in about all of the states which held periodical convocations of such groups, some eighteen in all.

These field contacts kept me alert to needs that I should otherwise never have sensed or read about. On the testimony of my most alert graduate students on the campus at New York University, these field trips greatly added to the effectiveness of my service to them. It meant, too, that every year there came into my classes, graduate students who were eminent faculty members on leave from institutions out on the frontiers in far-away places with whom I already had a personal acquaintance and with whose professional and administrative problems I was already somewhat familiar.

The question is sometimes raised by the executive officers of graduate schools of education as to whether some of their staff members do not spend too much of their time in the field and away from their classes on the campus. Doubtless, some do. It would seem that any member of the staff, who can not be trusted to decide how best to use his time in the interest of his students and the total service for which he is responsible, is not ready for a graduate-school professorship. It should be understood that the unit of graduate research which a good graduate student may at any time profitably undertake is generally large enough to occupy all his time in intensive work for at least two weeks and it should be remembered, too, that graduate work at its best does not consist exclusively of lectures but also of periodic seminar meetings devoted to the critical analysis of reports and to setting up projects of inquiry, locating and evaluating source materials, making field trips to colleges, etc. This means that it is possible for a graduate professor so to plan his service that his absence from the campus for short periods does not disadvantage his students if they plan equally well.

I was no more than well established at New York University when I was invited to important posts in two other institutions, both in the spring of 1927. One of these calls was to the deanship of graduate instruction at George Peabody College for Teachers in Nashville. The other was a unanimous call to the presidency of the Georgia State College for Women at Milledgeville, an institution in which I had previously served as a professor. Because of my wife's long and increasingly serious illness, I finally decided that I should not again undertake major administrative service and, too, I was happy in my work at New York University and greatly pleased with my opportunity there. So I finally declined each of these calls.

During my entire residence of eighteen years at New York University, I attended the University's commencements but twice. My calls for commencement addresses in teachers colleges and universities during these years took me anywhere from Silver City, New Mexico, or Ellensburg, Washington, in the far West to Providence, Rhode Island, or Harrisonburg, Virginia, in the East, and from Southern Methodist University, Dallas, Texas, or Milledgeville, Georgia, in the South to Minot, North Dakota, or Mount Pleasant, Michigan, in the North.

I appeared frequently on the program of the American Association of Teachers Colleges to report at its annual February meetings on studies I had made with the co-operation of presidents of teachers colleges in all parts of the country.

I visited the member institutions of the Eastern-States Association of Professional Schools for Teachers—one hundred of them—scattered all over the northeastern states and the District of Columbia for addresses to students and for conferences with faculty and student organizations.

I spent the six-week period between the closing of my class work in late May and the opening of the summer term (after July 4th), in a wide swing through the big summer schools of the South, the Southwest, the Mid-West, and the Great Lakes region. This was my schedule for many years. I spoke and conducted conferences in state teachers associations during the fall and spring seasons for many years.

None of these field trips during the academic year kept me away from the campus for more than a few days at a time. It was possible to go by plane in the late afternoon or at night to Kansas City, Dallas, Nashville, Atlanta, Omaha, New Orleans, Chicago, Minneapolis, Milwaukee, Denver, Portland or Bangor, give an address or two in a state association and be back in my office in the morning of the second day. On one occasion, I spoke in the state teachers college at Cape Girardeau, Missouri in the morning, at the southern sectional meeting of the Illinois State Education Association at Carbondale in the afternoon, and in the State Teachers Association of Tennessee at Nashville, in the evening of the same day.

During my first and only sabbatical leave, I was in every state in the Union in eleven months, spoke to state teachers associations, to the teachers in a score of our large cities in all parts of the country and in all the tax-supported university schools of education, teachers colleges and normal schools which I had not previously visited as well as in many I had previously visited. I also spoke in scores of high schools. The aggregate number of teachers in service, college students preparing to teach, and adolescents in high schools whom I addressed that year was probably approximately two hundred thousand.

When I left New York on my longest sabbatical trip, after a hurried visit to friends who were patients in New York City hospitals, I said good-by to my elder daughter Eloise at the Pennsylvania depot. She was, at the time, a graduate student in New York University. She said, "Father, you look tired. You should spend the winter relaxing under a palm tree in Florida." I told her the story of the New England mother of twelve who remarked that "A vacation is a good time to ache in a new spot."

The next morning, I spoke to two thousand young women in Winthrop Normal College in South Carolina. In the afternoon, I spoke to the faculty; at night, I went to Atlanta. I spoke the next morning in Oglethorpe University, at noon I put on a broadcast from the University, and at four o'clock in the afternoon, addressed the eighteen hundred teachers of Atlanta in the big Baptist Tabernacle. The next morning, I spoke in the Georgia Military College at

Milledgeville, and at the eleven-o'clock-hour, in the auditorium of the State College for Women. On the platform were seated several score of my old neighbors who made my return the occasion for a Roman holiday to give me a surprise. Then followed a luncheon at the president's mansion, where I was the guest of seven former students who were teachers in the demonstration school at the college, following which President Wells of Collegeboro drove me down for an address to the students and faculty of the State Teachers College there. Another faculty reception and we were off that evening for Americus, Georgia, where I was to speak the next day.

That night, I wrote my daughter in New York the thrilling story of the first three days out. She wired back: "Stay in the South, Daddy, and this trip will be the making of you yet."

I made a hurried trip to my old haunts in Florida, spoke in Stetson University, in the State University at Gainesville, and the State College for Women at Tallahassee; in the State Association and all the teachers colleges of Alabama and Mississippi, and visited Martha Berry College for the first time. Then up the tier of states on the east bank of the Mississippi River to the mid-winter meeting of the American Association of School Administrators at Minneapolis, and down the tier of states on its west bank. I spent two weeks in the colleges and big city school systems of Texas, flew from Brownsville to Mexico City, where I was the guest for five days of the Ministry of Education. Then, on to Arizona, New Mexico, and California where I spent three weeks visiting and lecturing in colleges, meeting at the end of the first week with the college presidents and deans at the Huntington Estate in Pasadena, a week later with secondary-school principals at San Jose State College and a week later still with the superintendents of schools at the state capital.

Then, I went up to Oregon, Washington, Idaho, and Montana; through Utah, Colorado, and Wyoming into the Black Hills; finally completing a visit to the very last of all tax-supported colleges in the United States at Bemidji, Minnesota, where I spanned the Mississippi River, with one foot on its right bank and the other on its left, just below the spillway from Lake Itasca. As I stood there with my back almost literally against the Canadian border I saw "in my mind's eye" my beloved South, the land of my adoption, the historic East and the heroic West and thanked God in my heart for my birthright as an American citizen. I re-dedicated myself to the cause of the children and youth in all our schools and colleges in each of our forty-eight friendly states.

I came on down through the teachers colleges of Wisconsin and Michigan to Cleveland where my friend and successor, Dr. Charles W. Hunt, had invited me to be the special guest of the Cleveland School of Education and of its Alumni Society after an absence of nine years. Those were two glorious, never-to-be-forgotten days.

Then, I flew on to New York for a surprise visit with my daughter, Eloise, and a farewell visit with my beloved chancellor, Elmer Ellsworth Brown, whom I knew should retire from office before my return from another long trip into the West that would take me to North Dakota, Texas, and points between, before the opening of our summer school in New York. I had sent him my logbook at the close of each month and my projected itinerary for the next succeeding month. Always he sent me a card of appreciation written in longhand, the last of which I still treasure: "I have read your logbook for May. *It can't be done*. I also received your proposed itinerary for June. *It can't be done*. May God preserve you for one more impossible month." On the day of his retirement, July 1st, he went to the hospital for a serious operation. On my return a few days later, I called to see him. He called up the memory of a letter which the faculty of the School of Education had written him some time before on the occasion of his wife's death. I did not tell him that I had, at the request of the Dean, framed up that letter. Here is a copy of it:

To Elmer Ellsworth Brown, Chancellor

You have been a good friend to all of us; to some of us through many years.

We have observed with unbounded admiration the gracious life you have lived among us while carrying the burdens of high office; we have observed with something more than unbounded admiration the transcendent faith which has somehow enabled you with cheerful spirit to fortify anew each day the uncomplaining courage of your devoted wife through long illness and infinite suffering.

In your bereavement, we hope that this renewed assurance of our deep sympathy, of our profound regard and of our abiding affection may help to fortify your courage anew each day through all the good years that lie ahead.

Your Devoted Friends and Comrades,
The Faculty of The School of Education,
of New York University

His dear wife had been an invalid for fifty years and in spite of the incessant demands of high office he was always by her side when she most needed him. I shall always revere the memory of his true nobility.

I served as consultant to the Teacher Education Study of the American Council on Education at the Southern Illinois State University at Carbondale for one year.

While at the University, I found time, with the assistance of Mrs. Myrtle Garrison Gee, of Montclair, to compile and edit the *Story World* series of supplementary readers published by the World Book Company of Yonkers. These books contained newly written stories not duplicated in any other series. They had excellent initial sales, but came on the market only a little while before the Great Depression, when school boards for a time almost ceased buying supplementary reading materials of any kind.

In the summer of 1934, after a spirited intersession at Washington Square, with a large, lively class representing all parts of the nation, I left New York on July 3 on the Holland-American liner Volendam, accompanied by my daughter, Ruth, with a bevy of her college chums for twelve weeks in Europe. We stepped lively through twenty-one countries, visiting castles, museums, art galleries, and places of historic interest, viewing lofty mountains and placid lakes, attending the Passion Play at Oberammergau and the Shakespeare Carnival at Stratford-on-Avon, meeting interesting people from the rim of the Mediterranean to the shores of the Baltic and coming home, finally, with a genuine appreciation of the peoples we had met and their cultures and with real gratitude to God that our ancestors had chosen to make us citizens of the United States.

Yes, my extra-curricular activities while at the University were among the most enjoyable and enriching experiences of my life; played a significant part in giving me some breadth of national and international interest in education, and thus making it possible for me to bring to my classes some corresponding enrichment of service.

Among my most pleasant memories of my extra-curricular activities at New York University were a number of occasions when I was called upon to serve as toastmaster at some important educational banquet. On one of these occasions, I presided at the farewell tribute dinner given by the Alumni Society and faculty of the Jamaica Teacher Training College to its retiring President, Dr. A. C. MacLachlan, in the grand ballroom of the Hotel Pennsylvania, where Governor Miller, a former student of the guest of honor, was the chief speaker.

On a half dozen occasions, I helped to organize the program and then to serve as toastmaster at the New York University School of Education banquets held at the midwinter meetings of the American Association of School Administrators—in Chicago, Cleveland, Washington, Atlantic City, and New Orleans. These banquets were usually attended by from three hundred to six hundred guests and were always notable occasions.

And finally, at the request of Dean John W. Withers, I presided at the banquet held in the Astor Hotel in New York on the evening of the dedication of our new twelve-story School of Education building at Washington Square on March 1, 1931. The annual convention of the American Association of School Administrators in Atlantic City had just adjourned and the guests at our banquet tables numbered seven hundred fifty of the most eminent men and women in American education at all levels of the service and from literally every state in the union.

Our committee consisting of Dr. Ned H. Dearbon, Chairman, Dr. Robert E. Speer, and myself had arranged this banquet program as a surprise tribute to Dean John W. Withers whose portrait, painted by Robert A. Kissock, head of the Art Department in the School of Education, was presented by the toastmaster to the University on behalf of the Faculty and accepted by Dr. George Alexander, Vice-President of the University Council.

The Honorable John H. Finley, Associate Editor of the *New York Times,* was the principal guest speaker. He lifted the little town of Ben Lomond, West Virginia, the Dean's birthplace, out of its obscurity and placed it in bold letters on the map of the world. Dr. John W. Cooper, United States Commissioner of Education, and Governor Myers, of Ohio, one of the Dean's former students, also spoke. The Dean's best beloved teacher of childhood days, Mrs. Ella McConnell, was present at his side as the special guest of the occasion; she had come on from Elyria, Ohio, at eighty to do honor to her boy Johnnie; she proved herself, as all who were present will remember, the star performer.

This was a never-to-be-forgotten occasion.

My memories of my field services while at New York University are as happy and satisfying as are those of my associations with my big-hearted big chiefs, my friendly and co-operative fellow professors and my always appreciative students.

Farewell to Eastern-States Association, to *Teacher-Education Journal*, and to New York University

At a public banquet at the Hotel Commodore in New York City on March 27, 1942, the officers of the Eastern-States Association, which I had organized and served for eighteen years, presented me with a leather-bound, hand-lettered *Book of Remembrance* which I shall always treasure and which I shall, in Shakespeare's language, "bequeath to my children's children as a rich legacy." Here is the inscription it contains:

To Dr. Ambrose Leo Suhrie, whose inspired direction of the Eastern-States Association of Professional Schools for Teachers has won the respect and affection of all who have worked with him, we present this testimonial volume.

May these letters and pictures serve, during the years to come, as a continuous reminder of our esteem for a vigorous leader, a wise counsellor, and a beloved friend.*

Officers of Eastern-States Association
of Professional Schools for Teachers

This tribute volume was presented to me by Roscoe L. West, President, Trenton State Teachers College; President, American Association of Teachers Colleges; and Past Presi-

---

* During the hard days of a long and serious illness which followed two years after my retirement from New York University, this book, with the very pleasant associations it recalled, helped me to see many reasons why I should struggle to get well and to carry on. It had healing in its pages in those difficult days.

dent, Eastern-States Association of Professional Schools for Teachers, with the following comment:

It has been well said that "an institution is the lengthened shadow of one man." If this statement was ever true of any institution or any organization, it is true of the Eastern-States Association of Professional Schools for Teachers. When Professor Ambrose L. Suhrie came to New York University about eighteen years ago, he had a vision of the kind of work which could be done in these Eastern states by such a professional organization as this one. He started from nothing and by means of his own vision and enthusiasm secured the coöperation of people interested in teacher education in this area. From that very humble beginning has developed the Association which we have today, which, over these years, has influenced thousands of people.

The greatest contribution, it seems to me, which Dr. Suhrie has made to this Association was the insistence from the very first that students must be included. I know of no other similar organization which has developed a program involving, as this one has done, administrative staffs, faculties, *and* students. Through this development we have all been impressed with the desirability of coöperative action and of understanding the part which students must play in their own education.

Professor Suhrie has made many other contributions to teacher education in various parts of the country, in the South, at the University of Pennsylvania, in the Cleveland School of Education, and at New York University. I suppose that no other man in the United States has visited as many institutions educating teachers as he has visited. One could make a long list of the contributions which he has made. I am sure, however, that he would rather be remembered by us as the founder of this Association than by any other accomplishment.

Back of every great organization there must be an idea. The United States of America existed in the minds of such

men as Samuel Adams, Benjamin Franklin, and Thomas
Jefferson before it became a reality in actual operation.
You may recall that Thomas Jefferson was more interested to be remembered by the ideas which he had sponsored than by the offices which he had held. Although he
had been Secretary of State, Ambassador to France, Vice-
President of the United States and President of the United
States, on his own epitaph he never mentioned any of
these offices but wrote these words: "Author of the Dec-
laration of American Independence, the Statute of Virginia for religious freedom, and Father of the University
of Virginia."

In carrying forward his idea Dr. Suhrie has always
acted with perseverance, with friendliness, and above all,
with constant faith in the young people of our colleges.
He has taught us to work together for the achievement of
forward-looking programs in these institutions. He has
demonstrated in his own life the friendly, coöperative
spirit of adventure which is so characteristic of democracy
at its best. We salute him and wish him many years of
health and happiness for further service to the cause to
which he has already given so much.

Dr. Suhrie: This "Book of Remembrance" which we
herewith present to you, in the name of this Association,
was compiled by students and faculty members of the
Teachers College of Connecticut at New Britain. The title
page and table of contents were written by Dr. Herbert E.
Fowler, the book was bound by hand by Mr. Frederick J.
Roach, a student in the Industrial Arts Department of the
Teachers College of Connecticut at New Britain. He also
made the cover with the design and the lettering. The volume contains resolutions, personal tributes, and testimonial
letters from your friends and associates, the United States
Commissioner of Education, the state commissioners of
education here in the East, and presidents, deans, faculty
members, and students of the member institutions of the
Eastern-States Association. It also contains many interesting
pictures of the one hundred universities, teachers colleges,

and normal schools you have visited within the Association.

All of us who have participated in creating this token of appreciation for your untiring and inspiring leadership are proud of our associations with you and take this means of wishing you continued happiness in all the new adventures which lie ahead.

My acceptance of the gift was as follows:

Mr. Toastmaster: I am, of course, profoundly grateful to you for the altogether too partial tribute you have paid to my work and worth in commending me again to the considerate attention of this goodly company of my friends.

President West: I am likewise profoundly appreciative of the kindly words you have spoken in presenting to me this precious book of remembrance.

And to all of you in this large and representative audience who have had any part in the preparation of the content or in the making of this marvellous collection of personal tributes and picture embellishment or who have participated in the ovation you have just given me I am more grateful than I have any means of adequately indicating to you. I feel all the more strongly the tie that binds us together because I am able to remember so clearly that on nearly a score of these annually recurring banquet occasions since this Association was organized you and thousands of others who are not here tonight have joined in giving me similar manifestations of your continuing good will.

This is notably the largest banquet audience that has ever assembled under the auspices of our Association. There are State Commissioners of Education, State directors of teacher education, Presidents of teachers colleges, deans of universities and colleges, faculty members and students in numbers from the most remote parts of the service area of this Association as well as from all nearby colleges. I am deeply touched by President Welte's assurance that many of you from the far-away places have manifested a special interest in this banquet program because the officers of our

Association had deliberately planned to make this occasion a very happy affair for me and for those who are nearest and dearest to me.

I wish with all my heart that I might be able to share justly on this public occasion with all the good helpers I had during the earlier years the honors, which, tonight as on many former occasions, you have altogether too generously and too exclusively conferred upon me alone. My good friend Professor William C. Bagley lent the prestige of his international reputation to our struggling organization by serving as our first vice-president. Dr. Lester K. Ade, was the genial and efficient first recording secretary. Dr. Samuel A. Rutledge was the industrious and always coöperative first executive secretary. He sleeps tonight in the hills of his beloved East Tennessee. A score of distinguished leaders and helpers of earlier years have passed to their reward, the latest being Dr. Lida Lee Tall of Maryland. A dozen others have retired. Many of these are absent tonight. But I know they are thinking of us. Several of them have graciously remembered me here at the banquet table with telegraphic messages of personal good will. To all of the generous friends and efficient and self sacrificing helpers of the earlier days, I wish to extend my heartfelt thanks and, in particular, to a certain capable and devoted young woman, Miss Mildred Wells, now Mrs. James A. Adair, who, as my personal secretary at New York University for a period of sixteen years, was a tireless worker in the interests of this Association.

This occasion is a particularly happy one for me because it recalls so vividly the many visits I was able to make to each of your colleges, to each of the one hundred member institutions of our Association, during the seven years in which I served as president. In one single year—the last year I held office—I was able to visit all of them. And it was my rare privilege, in almost all instances, to address the entire group of faculty and students in the college assembly. These were occasions that I shall always remember with great satisfaction.

I am far from ready to retire from active service for I believe I am still capable of rendering much useful service to my country in an hour of great need.

When my time comes I shall hope to retire to my cottage home in the hills to feed my birds, to attend to my bees, to gather my flowers and to live in the sweet memories of this happy occasion and of other happy days that are gone.

My best wishes to you, one and all, "now and evermore."

Representative letters from the *Book of Remembrance:*

> Teachers College of Connecticut
> New Britain, Connecticut
> March 10, 1942

Dear Doctor Suhrie:

The letters in this *Book of Remembrance* are something more than a personal tribute to you. They have been written as *authentic appraisals*, by your contemporaries, of a great democratic movement in American Higher Education in which you played the leading role; they constitute an important part of the official record of the inception of that movement and are available for publication in your memoirs or any other publication in which the history of the professional services of the Eastern-States Association of Professional Schools for Teachers may, in due time, be appropriately and adequately written up.

> Herbert D. Welte, President
> E. S. A. P. S. T. 1941-42

> FEDERAL SECURITY AGENCY
> U. S. OFFICE OF EDUCATION
> Washington
>
> March 10, 1942

My dear Doctor Suhrie:

As the time of your retirement from a long and fruitful career in the schools of America approaches, I wish to express to you a few thoughts which occur to me with respect to that occasion. In doing so, I have been assured that I speak also for a number of the staff members of this office.

The social significance of the retirement of professional men in public life varies greatly in the case of different individuals. In your case, the event is of unusual significance for several reasons. Among these reasons are the unusual length, the broad scope, and the quality of practical helpfulness which have characterized your professional activities. Your services to American education have extended over more than half a century. You have served with unusual success as a public-school teacher, supervisor, principal, and superintendent; as a college teacher and administrative officer; and as a National leader in different educational organizations and capacities. There are educators in every State in the Union who remember your services in their schools and communities. You have never been narrowly professional in outlook, and your influence has been felt in many social and civic fields other than education. With experience in a wide variety of educational situations, your reputation is secure as an educational leader with a keen sensitivity to the problems of workers actually on the firing line; and as an authority on the methods of meeting such problems.

Retirement time for you, as for all master teachers, is a milestone rather than a finishing point in a career of usefulness. In the wider knowledge, clearer thinking, and finer feeling of your students, and in their future impress upon generations of pupils yet unborn, your professional career will continue for many years to come. You can retire from your present position, but you can never completely retire from American education.

Very sincerely yours,
J. W. Studebaker
Commissioner

SCHOOL AND SOCIETY
William C. Bagley, Editor

My dear Suhrie:

In welcoming you to the ranks of professors emeriti, it is a privilege to congratulate you upon the notable contributions that you have made to the cause of education. I could not list these even briefly in the short space of this letter, but I wish to mention with especial emphasis three that, in my judgment, have been particularly outstanding in the field that you and I have been concerned with for more than thirty years—the professional education of teachers.

Chronologically, the first of these was your development of the Cleveland School of Education. I had the good fortune to become acquainted with this institution rather intimately, as you will recall, just before it was affiliated with Western Reserve University. Under your able administration it had become one of the outstanding institutions of its kind in the United States and undoubtedly the leading professional school for teachers among those connected with large-city-school systems. It was your leadership and your skillful guidance that gave it this distinguished status.

When you were called to New York University to organize a graduate department to prepare administrators and instructors for normal schools and teachers' colleges, I rejoiced, for I was confident that no better person could have been chosen to undertake this important task. The marked success of your work at New York University has abundantly confirmed my judgment.

The third, and in my judgment the culminating achievement of your career, was represented by the organization and remarkable development of the Eastern-States Association for the Professional Education of Teachers. This was the first regional association of such institutions, and no other organization in this field, whether regional or national, today approaches it, either in the members attending its annual gatherings or in the contributions that it is making to the development of professional insight and enthusiasm. The plan that you conceived and carried out for bringing to the annual meeting not only the instructors of the member institutions but large delegations of students was, as the events have proved, no less than the work of genius.

And so, dear Suhrie, my heartiest felicitations and my sincere wishes for many happy and useful years yet to come. May I add, too, that I shall always cherish the close friendship, both professional and personal, that has been ours.

Cordially and faithfully,
William C. Bagley
Emeritus Professor of Higher Education
Teachers College, Columbia University

TEACHERS COLLEGE
COLUMBIA UNIVERSITY
New York

March 6, 1942

My dear Dr. Suhrie:

President Welte's suggestion that the Eastern-States Association of Professional Schools for Teachers recognize, at this time, your contribution to its development and to the advancement of teacher education in the United States is a happy and appropriate one.

It has been my personal good fortune to work in the field of teacher education during the last twenty-five years—formative years for the professional education of America's teachers, in which you have exercised consistent leadership—a leadership characterized by untiring effort, constructive imagination, enthusiasm for the better education of America's teachers and a firm belief in the value of universal education. You have had the vision to see needed changes and the courage to advocate them. You have also had an unshakable faith in the professional standards and sound judgments of college students preparing to be teachers.

These three characteristics have resulted in the Eastern-States Association of Professional Schools for Teachers and the Teacher-Education Journal—two professional accomplishments among your many that are ample cause for pride and satisfaction.

Another phase of your leadership that deserves much wider recognition and emulation is your ability to obtain the interested co-operation of large numbers of people and in ways that made them grow professionally as they participated. The number of persons whose educational careers you either started or accelerated by sharing your enthusiasms with them must be a source of great pleasure to you as you think over these crowded, busy years. May you enjoy many more.

Sincerely yours,
E. S. Evenden
Professor of Higher Education

NEW YORK UNIVERSITY
OFFICE OF THE CHANCELLOR
Washington Square, New York

12 March, 1942

Dear Professor Suhrie:

I count it a distinct honor to be numbered among the friends who are now tendering you a sort of *bon-voyage* package, in the form of confessions of admiration and affection.

You came to New York University ahead of me, laden with the fruits of scholarship and the benefits of wide experience as teacher and administrator. When I arrived on this scene, you had already made a great name for yourself here, and your prestige and influence have continued to grow within my observation without abatement. The length and breadth of the teacher-training fraternity of this country know you as a sympathetic friend, sound advocate, and staunch leader. I daresay no man has a more spirited following and few indeed there are who command the range of your constructive influence in public education today.

I therefore proudly salute you as a colleague and wish you long years of continued usefulness in those channels to which release from more exacting responsibility may now enable you to turn.

Cordially yours,
Harry Woodburn Chase
Chancellor

NEW YORK UNIVERSITY
SCHOOL OF EDUCATION
New York, N. Y.

March 10, 1942

My dear Dr. Suhrie:

I have known you, Dr. Suhrie, intimately for more than a quarter of a century. We became acquainted when you were head of the Cleveland School of Education and I, of the Harris Teachers College of St. Louis. From the first, I was deeply impressed with your scholarship, professional insight, and sincere devotion to the cause in which we were both deeply interested. I earnestly hoped that opportunity might be found for closer association with you in professional service to education. Fortunately, that opportunity came in 1924 when, in the reorganization of the School of Education of New York University, you accepted my invitation to organize a new Department of Normal School and Teachers' College Education; the position that you have filled so ably since that date. No one could have done a better job. Your profound insight into the problems and possibilities of teacher-education in the United States, your honest wholehearted co-operation with your associates in both the faculty and student body, and your genuine unselfish devotion to the profession of education and all intelligent and well-directed efforts to improve it regardless of where or by whom such efforts are made, have commanded the respect and admiration of all of us who have had the great privilege of long and intimate association with you.

Cordially and sincerely yours,
John W. Withers, Dean Emeritus

NEW YORK UNIVERSITY
School of Education
Washington Square, New York

March 9, 1942

Dear Dr. Suhrie:

Your approaching retirement from the active lists in the University brings vividly to mind my very first impression of you, sitting at the head of the table as chairman of the Education Committee of the New Jersey Council of Religious Education, when I was Secretary of that organization. That was before I came to the University and when you had been here only a short time.

You were interested then, as you still are, in the most significant things which are creative, progressive, enriching of individual personality, and humanizing in society. When I came to the University in January, 1929, I found you beginning the work of reconstructing the curriculum of the School of Education and establishing, in the face of tremendous difficulties, the pattern now so well established and so uniformly accepted by your colleagues in the faculty.

It is such a pleasure to be able to say, without a mental reservation, that, throughout these years of our association, I have known in you only co-operativeness in service, patience and courtesy under opposition, Christian fortitude under adversity and disaster, courage in discouragement, and bubbling good humor in almost every situation. I am glad that your approaching change in status while you are still so young and vigorous gives to me, among your many other friends, the occasion to say what we should have said earlier and more frequently: I am grateful to God for you and your qualities as a scholar, as a teacher, and as a man. Most of all I am humbly grateful for your friendship.

Very sincerely,
Samuel L. Hamilton
Professor of Education
Chairman, Department of Religious Education

STATE OF NEW JERSEY
Department of Public Instruction
Trenton
March 12, 1942

Dear Dr. Suhrie:

To you has been given the opportunity to provide a type of leadership unlike that given by any other person in this department of higher education. To visit and study every tax-supported teacher training institution in the United States (more than three hundred of them) as you have done represents an exploration of the field never before accomplished and stands as one of your significant contributions in the education of teachers.

We of New Jersey have been grateful for your generous help in many phases of our program of teacher education. It was not so long ago that during one commencement season we were honored by your attendance at every teachers college commencement (six of them) held in the State.

You have made so many contributions to the development of the education of teachers that it is impossible to include in a letter any adequate appraisal of them. Long will the results of your leadership be felt throughout the length and breadth of the land.

I hope that we may continue to have your counsel and advice. We count it a blessed privilege to have worked with you in these times.

Very sincerely yours,
Charles H. Elliott
Commissioner of Education

AUGUSTA, MAINE

March 20, 1942

My dear Dr. Suhrie:

You have a long and enviable record in the field of teacher education in this country, a record which is bound to make its impress felt for many years to come.

Your activity in founding and sponsoring the Eastern-States Association of Professional Schools for Teachers is an enduring contribution in the field of American education. This valuable organization has served to weld the teacher-training institutions of the eastern states into a cohesive, comprehensive unit for the purpose of considering crucial problems in teacher education. The Association will, in the years ahead, continue to function and exert its influence in this important field.

I recall with pleasure your frequent visits to Maine, and I remember vividly the occasions when, with the co-operation of the State Department you performed the almost superhuman feat of making a complete visit to all of the seven teacher-training institutions in Maine (including the university) in a single week; incidentally this was before the days of travel by air, and in order to make the visits, it was necessary to cover one thousand miles by automobile outside of school hours.

I know you well enough to know that in retirement you will continue to be actively, usefully and pleasantly employed. Such a vital personality as yours cannot remain dormant. It will continue to be active as long as health and life lasts.

My best wishes are yours in the years ahead with the hope that they may be richly filled with enduring happiness and satisfaction.

Yours very sincerely,
Bertram E. Packard
(Retired) Commissioner of
Education, State of Maine

THE COMMONWEALTH OF MASSACHUSETTS
Department of Education
State Teachers College at Fitchburg

March 20, 1942

Dear Dr. Suhrie:

You are personally responsible for the most hopeful expression of democratic philosophy in the history of college education in the United States. The convincing evidence of the value of live-student participation in the formulation of administrative policies and programs as demonstrated in the eastern-states teachers' colleges will undoubtedly influence other institutions to utilize more fully the latent resources of their students.

Charles M. Herlihy
President

UNIVERSITY OF NEWARK
Newark, New Jersey

March 9, 1942

Dear Dr. Suhrie:

It is difficult, indeed, for one who has known you as long and as intimately as I have, to express to you adequately my feeling of indebtedness for your many personal and professional services through the decades of our almost uninterrupted association.

It has been my good fortune professionally to be one of your contemporaries. You have lived and worked through an era of development in the professional preparation of teachers which quite probably will not be matched in achievement by any similar era in the next quarter century. The contributors to the achievements of that era have been many. They have been alert, energetic, clear-thinking men, devoted to progress in a spirit of unselfish service in a truly great educational program in behalf of the youth of this country. In this group, the name of Ambrose L. Suhrie stands out conspicuously as one of those endowed with creative genius and the will to high achievement.

May we hope that you will find the opportunity and the free time to review and reinterpret your philosophy of education and publish it for the benefit of the generations that lie ahead.

With assurances of high regard, I am

Sincerely yours,
George H. Black
President

TEACHERS COLLEGE OF CONNECTICUT
New Britain, Connecticut

March 13, 1942

Dear Dr. Suhrie:

So close have you been to this institution and to each of its instructors that I feel as though your retirement from active service is that of an intimate friend. This respectful intimacy is the result of your living your philosophy with us even as you would have us live it with our students and among ourselves.

Personally, I believe the beginning of democratic living at this institution is entirely due to your many visits, your many vivid pictures of your philosophy in action in other teacher-training institutions, to your unfailing guidance in our various student-faculty committees, and to your generous encouragement and inspiration during our first staggering steps.

Officially you may be retired but the real you, exemplified in your philosophy, can never be retired. Everywhere and in all worthy activities of this college you are present. And what is true here is true in hundreds of other teacher-training institutions. Even though you are retired, yet, in reality, you are not retired, for in hundreds of young and older lives you will live on and on and on.

From one of the old school who was hard to convince the whole way.

Sincerely and cordially yours,
Charles Edgar Pratt
Associate Professor of Biology

The *Teacher-Education Journal,* which I organized in 1939 as the house organ of the Eastern-States Association, I continued to edit for three years (my last issue, March, 1942). My successor, Professor F. C. Borgeson, issued the June 1942 *Journal* as a tribute number in my honor. He included the following dedication by the President of the Association and a score of carefully selected quotations (some of them extended ones) from my publications.

TRIBUTE TO AMBROSE LEO SUHRIE

To DR. AMBROSE LEO SUHRIE, founder and first president of the Eastern-States Association of Professional Schools for Teachers and first editor of this *Journal,* an inspired leader of young people everywhere, an ardent friend of teacher education, and a wise counsellor who has earned the respect and confidence of those with whom he has worked all through the years, we affectionately dedicate this number of *Teacher-Education Journal.* He has faithfully directed our Association since its inception in 1926 and, for his inspiration and coöperation, we are most thankful.

We recall with pleasure his visits to our member-institutions and the words of wisdom and cheer he left with us. We remember his advice and counsel which appear in the early yearbooks of our Association. We believe that his philosophy of student-faculty cooperative government and his realistic approach to educational problems in bringing together student and faculty delegates at the spring conferences have been important contributions to American education. We feel that these conferences have been the most successful demonstrations of democracy at work that we have witnessed among educational groups, and we predict that these contributions will stand forever as a monument to his vision and courage.

In these dark days of war and catastrophe, no man knows what the future holds. The outlook does not appear promising for the moment nor does it seem evident that permanent values can be readily identified. But if there are any such values in this world, one of them is an abounding faith in mankind. There is inspiration in the thought that what our good friend, Dr. Ambrose Leo Suhrie, has founded, no man can destroy. His has been a labor of love, inspired by a fundamental belief in teachers and in young people. We shall be eternally grateful to him for keeping that faith.

Herbert D. Welte, President
Eastern-States Association of
Professional Schools for Teachers

And there came at last a time for me to say good-by (1) to my office, which had been the scene of much happy fellowship in learning, (2) to my apartment, where I enjoyed for fourteen years about all the creature comforts that are really significant and much good fellowship with my daughters and our friends, (3) to my associates in learning and in living, the members of the faculty and student body with whom I had the happiest of all possible professional and human relationships, (4) to my daughter and her husband for whom I felt the deepest affection.

This wasn't exactly easy; nor was it too hard.

Will Rogers used to say, "You can always tell a New Yorker, for he's sure to be on a dead run for a hole in the ground." After burrowing around day and night in subway tunnels for eighteen years I must have looked like a scared rabbit most of the time. The tempo of New York was ungodly. And I was glad to get away from it; to beat a retreat for the tall timbers in the Blue Ridge Mountains of my beloved Southland. I had, for years, longed to live in the open spaces and to see the far horizons.

On the day when my work came to a close I taught my university classes in the morning, had luncheon with the Chancellor, spent the afternoon in farewell conferences with faculty members and students, was a guest for dinner in the newly established home of my daughter and her husband and then at 10 P.M. was accompanied by them to the Pennsylvania depot where they bade me farewell and I entrained for "Dear ol' Dixie."

Tribute to Dean Emeritus John W. Withers of New York University

Dean Emeritus John W. Withers who had brought me to New York had made his exit from office and from the city some years ahead of me. It was my privilege to make a presentation on behalf of our School of Education faculty to him on the occasion of the faculty banquet given in his honor at the Astor Hotel on Saturday, May 14, 1938, in anticipation of his retirement on September 1, of that year.

I wish to record here a deep sense of gratitude to him for bringing me to the University, and for opening up to me superb opportunities for happiness in service.

He was a man of vision and power and exalted purpose. He was always sure to understand without explanation, to commend with sincerity and to help lift the personal burdens of the members of his official family. I can say of him as of Chancellor Elmer Ellsworth Brown:

I revere the memory of his true nobility.

He served New York University nobly for seventeen years as Dean; he has since served the institution nobly for seventeen years as Dean Emeritus.

With his gracious wife, Margaret, he lives in a beautiful mansion, "under the palm trees," on the Gulf Coast at

Bradenton, Florida, where Mrs. Suhrie and I have a glorious visit with them each year. Such people should live forever —and they usually do, if not in the flesh, then in the loving memories of the multitudes to whom their lives have been a benediction.

7

RETIREMENT
AND RETREADMENT

W<small>HEN</small> I retired from New York University, and before I had time to "re-tread" for the unfinished portion of life's journey, I received a letter from our then United States Commissioner of Education, Doctor John W. Studebaker, in which he said in part:

"Retirement time for you as for every other master teacher is a milestone rather than a finishing point in a career of helpfulness."

It had never occurred to me that I should (or could) suddenly give up the professional interests of a life time. I had thought of retirement as a kind of readjustment to be made intelligently and purposefully; not as a sudden break with reality. I thought of it as an opportunity to shift from my shoulders, a part of the load that had grown too heavy to be carried in comfort and to take on some new interests more appropriate to my years, to the state of my health, to my place of abode, to the nature of my social obligations, and to my personal inclinations.

I was almost, but not quite, broken in health from the strain of my wife's long and serious illness and from the super-service load I had carried in the university during my entire tenure of eighteen years. Obviously, my first duty was to take active measures for bringing about complete physical rehabilitation with the least possible delay. Hydrotherapy and a complete reconstruction of my eating habits brought me, in due time, to a state of health and vitality which I had not known for many years. Since then, I have developed with each succeeding year, a heightened enthusiasm for my work, for my recreation, and for life in general.

An opportunity came to serve the cause of Negro education for a few years under the patronage of the General Education Board of New York; and then to become resident educational consultant at Southern Missionary College, Collegedale, Tennessee, where I have my home in a very happy setting in the hills among as good neighbors as any man could wish for.

Period of Readjustment

All my life I've been teaching my classes in school and college and university that education is, in part, a process of adjustment and of continuing readjustment. I have never conceived of retirement, so called, as a sudden and violent breaking away from one's life interests. I have thought of it as an orderly process of readjustment.

When I gave up my work as a professor at New York University, I received scores of letters—some of them from lifelong friends—saying in substance: "Now, for the first time in your life, you're free to do what you have always wanted to do." These letters, written in the kindliest spirit, seemed to imply that I'd been in slavery. They revealed a total misconception of my outlook on life.

As a matter of fact I have, all my life, done about what I wanted to do; it has been a part of my lifelong philosophy that if one doesn't teach himself to enjoy his daily work he is not likely ever to enjoy life. The normal life of most normal individuals consists chiefly of work. My lifework has never involved bondage; I have always been a free man in the very best sense of the term. Retirement conferred upon me no essentially new freedoms. I didn't need them. I had always chosen the work that most appealed to me; I continued to do so. I had always chosen the locale of my home; I continued to do so. I had always chosen my friends; I continued to do so. I had always had all the real necessities of life; I continued to have. Because all my life I had been making friends, I felt the need of making new friends in the new setting. Because I had spent my early life in the country and loved rural life and pastoral settings, I chose to make my home again in the hills. Because a mild climate is generally more congenial to people of advancing years than a rigorous one, I chose to come south. I had lost my heart to the Old South when I first took up residence down here, in 1905. During all the years since I left, I have been in the South every year and in most years in all parts of the South, so coming back, was coming home.

Five years before I "retired," I had made arrangements to "re-tread." I was not well and so, I progressively adjusted from the city grime and noise to the pure air of the countryside and the tranquillity of a woodland home. Because I have always loved to garden and to raise berries and grapes and other fruits, I anticipated my retirement by five years and selected a beauty spot in the hills of western North Carolina where a little terracing would give me fine gardens, vineyards, fruit orchards, berry vines, and rows of flowering shrubs, and where I might have the view of mountains on the far horizon and of placid lakes in the foreground, and the odor of pine woods, and the songs of birds. There I built a beautiful New England colonial cottage. The investment was a modest one.

During long years of labor and frugal living, I had been unable to build up any substantial backlog of investments. Had I retired a few years earlier, the university doubtless would have treated me with the same generosity as others who left the service at that time—would have given me an annual retiring allowance of $4000. When I retired, we were in the throes of World War II and the university was in very straitened financial circumstances. So my retiring allowance, built up jointly by the university's and my personal contributions, amounted to less than $1500 per year.

In 1915, when I entered upon service at the University of Pennsylvania, my name was placed upon the role of prospective Carnegie pensioners on a non-contributory basis. When I went to Cleveland, I was promised by the president of Western Reserve University that it would be transferred from the University of Pennsylvania list to the Western Reserve University list. By some oversight this was not done and I did not learn of the omission until some years later when, because of the change of the Foundation's Charter by the New York State Legislature, it was impossible for me to have my name restored to the list of eligibles. So when I retired, I failed to get the annuity of $1500 per year which, except for the omission referred to above, I was morally and legally entitled to and would now be getting.

My expenses, in the meantime, due in part to the serious and continued illness of my wife and to my own need of medical and surgical attention, continued to be high. All these factors kept me alerted to the desirability—nay, the actual necessity—of continuing to produce income. This was, in all probability, a blessing in disguise for the reason which follows: When it was announced early in the spring of 1942, that I should soon retire from New York University, friends far and near conspired to get up banquets and parties and tribute meetings and to say farewells with flowers —chiefly orchids. All this, which was planned and executed with the kindliest of motives and which was deeply appreciated by me, inevitably resulted in my coming to realize that a lot of people were aware that I was getting well along on the sunset trail, that a break was about to come in my service, and that maybe I wouldn't be around much longer.

It required several years' time to live this feeling down. Then, with the return to better health, I regained my old outlook on life, a new joy in living, and a new zeal for my increasingly interesting work. I have firmly resolved never to be old again.

Visiting Professor in Atlanta University

As early as 1908, I began to visit Negro schools and colleges and, by 1910, I was asked for counsel on the service programs of several of the colleges in this group.

While at New York University for a period of eighteen years, I came back to the South every year to meet lecture engagements and to render educational-consultant services in Southern universities and colleges. During these field trips, I gradually increased the number of my visits to Negro colleges. I was always received with such graciousness and courtesy that it gave me very real pleasure, knowing as I did of their straitened financial circumstances, to halve my honoraria when filling engagements in these institutions.

By 1933, I had visited (and in most cases lectured in) all the tax supported Negro colleges in the United States, North and South; and before leaving New York University, I had lectured in at least half of all our Negro colleges and universities. While in the university, I had in my graduate courses, a number of notable leaders of the Negro group who were college presidents or outstanding professors. For some years, before leaving the university, I made up my mind that, if circumstances should be favorable, I'd devote much of my strength during the remainder of my active life to the service of this people. The opportunity came without any particular effort on my part.

Dr. Leslie P. Hill, President of the State Teachers College at Cheyney, Pennsylvania, a student in my graduate courses at New York University, requested Dr. Jackson Davis, of the General Education Board in New York to set aside funds for my service to the cause of Negro education in the South, during the academic year 1942-43. President Rufus E. Clement, of Atlanta University, invited me to come to his institution as a visiting professor for the year. I conferred with my friend, Dr. Otis W. Caldwell, who, on his retirement from Lincoln School of Teachers College in New York, had served one year in that capacity at Atlanta University. His experience confirmed my judgment that this would afford me a strategic opportunity to extend my service in the general improvement of Negro education on all levels, elementary, secondary and collegiate. The grant by the General Education Board was made; it included a travel fund which would make it possible for me to visit other Negro colleges on call as my program might permit.

I went to Atlanta, in the fall of 1942, a month in advance of the opening of Atlanta University, and, with the permission of Superintendent Willis A. Sutton, of the Atlanta public-school system, I made a short visit during this month to each Negro elementary and secondary school in the city and its suburbs and into practically all of the individual classrooms in these schools. I gained in this series of contacts, a clear picture of the physical and social setting in which Negro teachers and Negro children were doing their work in a typical Southern city.

When President Clement approved the list of courses I suggested it might be wise to offer and made up my schedule, he generously made provision that I might teach my classes on Thursday, Friday, and Saturday. This made it easily possible, by careful planning, to visit Negro colleges and universities as far away as Florida, Texas, Virginia, and Missouri. Before the end of the year, I had increased the number of Negro colleges which I had personally visited from fifty to seventy-two. I may add that, since then I have extended the list to include all of the approximately one hundred Negro institutions of higher learning in the United States, except three in Texas. These, I plan to visit during the current year.

My classwork with Atlanta Negro teachers and principals and with teachers and principals who commuted from other communities of the state was very enjoyable. One of my courses which had an enrollment of eleven during the first semester, increased its enrollment to fifty-three during the second semester.

I remained in Atlanta University during the summer session to participate in the workshop which was under the general direction of Dr. Ambrose Elder who, in the fall of that year, became head of the department of education in the university.

President Clement, at the close of the year officially commended me for my service to the university and voluntarily participated in making the plans which resulted in my being invited to become educational consultant to the Co-operative Negro College Study during the next academic year. Again, my salary and traveling expenses while engaged in this special service were covered by a grant to the Study by the General Education Board of New York.

I appreciated the opportunity during the year spent in Atlanta University to familiarize myself with the organic arrangement by which four undergraduate Negro colleges, namely: Morehouse College (men), Spellman College (women), Morris Brown College (co-educational), and Clark College (co-educational), have been brought together on adjacent campuses, where their separate faculties and student groups may enjoy a common bond of academic fellowship and may profit by their proximity to each other and to the graduate school courses and activities and the library and laboratory facilities of Atlanta University.

I considered it a real privilege to have professional fellowship with the outstanding leadership of these affiliated colleges (especially President Mays, of Morehouse), and to get acquainted with the many distinguished Negro leaders in education at every level of service, elementary, secondary, and collegiate, who came to the university during the year to lecture or to participate in conferences. My presence on the campus of the leading Negro graduate school in the South gave me a splendid opportunity to get acquainted with the corps of Jeannes supervisors in Negro elementary schools, with the directors of great foundations for the promotion of Negro education, and with the splendid men who direct Negro education from the state offices of education in the South.

I may add that I greatly enjoyed my official and personal relations with Dr. Jackson Davis, of the General Education Board in New York, and President Rufus E. Clement, of Atlanta University. They left nothing undone to make my experience as a visiting professor at the university both a profitable and a happy one.

And can I ever forget any one of the score of occasions when some one of the chapel audiences in the colleges visited during the year, sang for my special benefit, one or other of the following soul-stirring spirituals:

"Were You There When They Crucified My Lord?".
"I'd Like to Be a Christian in My Heart,"
"Deep River," or
"Standing in the Need of Prayer?"

How marvellous are these "Africo-American contributions to American culture" as my friend, the late James Weldon Johnson, of Fisk University, used to call them!

Consultant to Co-operative Negro College Study

In the spring of 1943, the General Education Board of New York made a grant of funds to the Co-operative Negro College Study, President H. Councill Trenholm, of the Montgomery State Teachers College, Chairman, to provide me a comfortable salary as consultant to the Study and a travel allowance to cover my living and transportation expenses while in the field, making periodic visits to Negro colleges, during the academic year of 1943-44. The Study Commission which had been in existence for some years, agreed that I should confine my consultant and counseling services to ten Negro colleges as follows:

Alabama:	State Teachers College, Montgomery
	Alabama Agricultural and Mechanical College, Normal
Florida:	Florida Agricultural and Mechanical College for Negroes, Tallahassee
Kentucky:	Kentucky State College, Frankfort
Louisiana:	Southern University and Agricultural and Mechanical College, Baton Rouge
Mississippi:	Jackson College, Jackson
North Carolina:	Fayetteville State Teachers College, Fayetteville
	Winston-Salem State Teachers College, Winston-Salem
South Carolina:	State Colored Normal, Industrial, Agricultural and Mechanical College, Orangeburg
Virginia:	Hampton Institute, Hampton

The presidents of these institutions were called together by Chairman Trenholm for a meeting at Montgomery in middle August, to determine the nature and scope of the services I should be asked to undertake and to set up a timetable for my visits to the several institutions.

It was agreed that I should plan to spend three weeks in each of the ten colleges on a rotation schedule, which would bring me to each college once in every ten weeks of term-time.

The first of the three visits to each college included in the Study, as planned, should be to help the college faculty to determine which problem or problems it should undertake to study co-operatively during the year. I went before the faculty of each of the ten institutions, at my first scheduled meeting with the group, to furnish a list of problems which the presidents had thought might be profitably studied. I interpreted the importance of each and indicated, in part, how the study of it might be pursued.

It was my idea that the college faculty might, under the leadership of the president or the dean, resolve itself into a committee of the whole and study intensively and comprehensively, a single important problem; or the college faculty might divide itself into two or three groups, under competent leadership, and each group might attempt to make a comprehensive study of some one problem. I presented a list of a dozen problems which it seemed might prove to be of college-wide interest, such as:

a) How can the faculty and students of our college most effectively improve the English usage on our campus, inside and outside of college classes?

b) How can we set up, and effectively operate, a program of health education and health service on our college campus?

c) How can we set up and maintain a dynamic program of student activities, providing vital experience in leadership and followership to all our college students?

It is interesting to note that some faculties voted to study but one problem and to attempt to enlist the interest of both faculty and students in a single enterprise; that others voted to undertake the study of two different problems concurrently; and that still others voted to undertake the study of three different problems, concurrently, under competent leadership in each case.

It is still more interesting to note that each of the ten college faculties voted almost unanimously to place its exclusive or its principal emphasis on the study of problem number one, listed above.

It was voted, almost unanimously, in some of the college faculties that any study undertaken should include students as well as faculty members in its working team or teams.

I spent the first week's visiting-period in each college, helping to get its purpose in any study to be undertaken clearly defined and to insure, in as far as possible, good teamwork on it in my absence. It was gratifying to see how effectively some of the study groups were able, from the beginning, to motivate their studies.

During the first ten weeks, I completed my rounds and had effected a functioning organization of the committee (or committees) which should undertake to conduct a study (or studies). In one large college, which I am just now thinking of, the first independent meeting of the faculty which followed my first visit brought together the whole faculty and an almost equal number of representative (and some volunteer) students, to study the problem of English usage and to insure complete co-operation of both groups in this study. At this meeting it was agreed:

1. That every student would be encouraged to keep a hip-pocket notebook in which he should record:

   a) The new vocabulary terms which should arise from day to day in his studies, in his campus conversation, and in chapel talks by students, faculty members, and visitors.

   b) A list of words, correctly spelled, which had been marked as misspelled in his term papers, examinations, and outlines.

   c) A list of words which faculty members and students had found him mispronouncing (in class and outside of class).

   d) A list of ungrammatical sentences which some friend or friends had heard him use in class or elsewhere, on or off the campus; such as, "Every one of us have their own faults."

2. That ample drill be provided by students for the correction of these mistakes; and, on occasion, by the instructor in any class in which it might be an economical use of time to do so.

3. That students be publicly commended by teachers for evidences of improvements in overcoming vocabulary inadequacies, and mistakes in spelling, pronunciation, and sentence structure.

4. That a "word secretary" be elected in each class section to present to the class, in a two-minute period at the close of each session:

    a) Mistakes by students (or teachers) that call for correction.

    b) Evidences of progress by the group and/or by individuals, in overcoming certain specific habits of incorrect usage.

On my second round of visits to each college campus, I saw clear evidence that its faculty and students had taken hold in dead earnest to get a working solution to the problem or problems it had undertaken to solve. It was most gratifying to see scores of well-kept hip-pocket notebooks, to hear students drilling each other on corrections and, especially to hear the "word" secretaries give their summaries at the conclusion of class periods.

Unfortunately, I was taken desperately ill in New Orleans when I was less than half through with my second round of visits to the colleges included in the Study. I was unable to take up my work again till late in the spring and, then, soon found I had to abandon it again. The year and the grant had expired without our being able to bring into form, for printing, the results of any of our studies.

I have, however, seen many evidences, as I have visited some of these colleges in recent years, that the co-operative studies launched in 1943 have since accomplished much in making faculty members and students, alike, conscious of certain problems on the campus that imperatively call for systematic and long-continued-group study. This was especially true of efforts to make a frontal attack upon the problem of improving English usage.

The material I distributed in some of the schools was quite evidently studied with great intensity. For example: I had distributed a score of statements by eminent men emphasizing the reason why all freshmen should consider the course, or courses, in English Communications the most important of all academic interests on the campus. Here are some of these statements:

WHY STUDY THE ART OF SPEAKING AND WRITING?

Language is the greatest invention of the human race; it is one of the most precious of all our cultural heritages.

Have you ever thought of the mighty power of words and "fine phrases" to breed love or hate in the home, in the school, in the community, in the nation, in the world? Words and "fine phrases" can bring peace or war, Dante's *Paradiseo* or his *Inferno*.

"The chief requisite of language is that it be pure and kind and true, the outward grace of an inward spirit." —Ellen G. White.

If you would know the real importance of learning to write and speak with clarity, effectiveness, and some measure of artistry, read what follows:

"The most useful instrument any teacher can acquire for all kinds of academic purposes is correct and effective English." —William C. Bagley.

"I recognize but one mental acquisition as an essential part of the education of a lady or a gentleman; namely, an accurate and refined use of the mother tongue." —Charles W. Eliot.

"The greatest of our language faults is to be conscious of none." —Thomas Carlyle.

"When I have something to write, I write it as well as I can and then I keep on re-writing it until it offends me no more." —Henry James.

"One can learn immediately from any speaker, how much he has lived by the poverty or the splendor of his language." —Ralph Waldo Emerson.

"Let me at least be clear; then if I am wrong I can be corrected." —William C. Bagley.

"Colorful language is effective language because it commands attention." —Ambrose L. Suhrie.

"The flowering moments of the mind drop half their petals in our speech." —Oliver W. Holmes.

"No man can give a truly spiritual interpretation to any of our great literary classics unless he has a cultivated voice." —Hiram W. Corson.

"Eloquence, like swimming, is an art which all men might learn, though so few do." —Ralph Waldo Emerson.

"Without a trained voice, no leader in public worship, can so vocalize the great literature of the Bible as effectively to suggest its spiritual power." —Byron W. King.

"The poet is the interpreter of the beauty of the universe. The speech of God is a foreign language to the great masses of the world; the poet stands in the Courtroom of Time and translates the words into understandable phrases." —Wilson McDonald.

"Men and women of refinement and culture are no more offended by B. O. than by B. E. (bad English)." —Ambrose L. Suhrie.

"Blessed is the man who, having nothing to say, abstains from giving us wordy evidence of the fact." —George Eliot.

"His words, like so many nimble servitors, trip about him at command." —John Milton.

"Talking is one of the fine arts . . . and its fluent harmonies may be spoiled by the intrusion of a single harsh note." —Oliver Wendell Holmes.

"Only the men and women who are acquainted with the great literary masterpieces of all languages in all ages are prepared for world citizenship." —William Peterfield Trent.

Why is it so difficult for the most earnest of our students to make progress in overcoming their faulty language habits, their outstanding grammatical mistakes, their vulgarisms, their illiteracies, their misuse of words, etc? The answer to this complex question is not a simple one.

1. Language is the comprehensive term we use for the most complex set of habits civilized man has ever been called upon to acquire.

2. In the highly impressionable years of early childhood, habits of any kind—good or bad—are easily acquired and quickly become somewhat "fixed" or "set."

3. The language habits of the average individual, once deeply grooved, are harder for him to break than any of his other habits, unless it be his eating habits.

Shakespeare says: "If to do were as easy as to know what were good to do, chapels had been churches and poor men's cottages princes' palaces."

In conclusion I must add that the zeal and enthusiasm of the college presidents, deans, and faculty members generally for these studies and the co-operative spirit in which all—faculty and students—responded to my efforts, will always be a very inspiring memory. Of course, I found it a very delightful experience to work with Dr. Fred McQuistion, of the General Education Board of New York and President H. Councill Trenholm, of the State Teachers College, Montgomery, Alabama, who were officially in charge of the Study. However inadequately we may have achieved the declared purposes of this co-operative enerprise, my part in it gave me a profound appreciation of the progress our Negro colleges have been making in spite of all the handicaps under which they have had, until recently, to operate. Teaching turns out to be a highly preferred occupation for Negroes of high character and intelligence, who have been able to make the unreasonable sacrifices, which, until recently, have been involved in completing a college education. Employment in other occupations of comparable social and economic status are not generally open to even the best-educated Negroes in the South. And so, in states which have had, for even a little while, public-school-salary schedules which provide equal wage scales for White and Negro teachers of equal education and experience, it is found that the average amount of post-high school education of the Negro group is higher—in many places considerably higher—than in the White group. The schools and colleges for Negroes in the South are able to command the services of a very high percentage of the ablest members of the race. To anyone who knows the situation first hand and intimately, it is surprising how many very high class, intellectually alert, and able leaders there are among the administrative, supervisory, and teaching staffs of our southern Negro schools and colleges.

In Dry Dock for Repairs

Had I not, early in life, acquired the notion that this human body of mine is a machine that could not be either abused or neglected except at my own peril, I might have been "laid away" long ago. I learned, at a very early age, to regard sickness as a symptom of disease and to take active measures at once to remove all causes for continuing physical deterioration. It seems appropriate that I should, here, list the danger signals I have had all along the way, and the responses I made to these signals.

In Part One, I told briefly the story of my childhood illnesses and accidents. At that period of life, I was not in good health but, before reaching manhood, I had gained vigorous health.

While in Florida, between 1905-1910, where sanitary conditions were bad before the Rockefeller Sanitary Commission had gone to work on clearing up mosquito-breeding places, I contracted a very severe case of malaria. I cleared it up within two years while a Fellow at the University of Pennsylvania. Immediately after my arrival in Georgia, in the fall of 1912, I had a re-inoculation. The next June, I spent in the hospital in Clifton Springs, New York, and cleared it up again. A specialist at the University of Pennsylvania told me shortly afterward, that the disease had left me with liver and spleen, four times normal size. He gave me the discomforting assurance that these organs could never again be reduced to normal size. I was not willing to accept this verdict. I went to the physical-education department for corrective exercises—exercises that would knead the torpid organs and increase the flow of blood to and through them. By systematic corrective-gymnasium work several times daily—temperately at first, and for short intervals, and then more vigorously and for longer periods—I was able, in twelve months, to demonstrate to the physician, that he had not been a good prophet. What he said couldn't be done, had been done.

Once, while I was living in Philadelphia, a surgeon snipped my tonsils, laying the foundation for a much more serious operation years later. This second operation was performed without delay as soon as the need for it became apparent.

While in Cleveland, I went to a dentist to have three infected teeth removed. While I "slept," this inexperienced "dental blacksmith" knocked the bottom out of my right antrum cavity while in hot pursuit of the well-anchored roots of my teeth. If I hadn't gone to a first-class surgeon by midnight of that day, I shouldn't be here to tell the story. He found the wound just ready for gangrene. By careful daily irrigation, for three months, the wound was ready to heal. My father lost his life at sixty-eight by neglecting the wound resulting from the removal of an infected tooth. I had learned a lesson and so I employed expert medical service *at once*.

At the age of sixty, a kidney infection, the aftermath of a severe attack of the flu, threatened trouble, but prompt attention to it at the New York Post Graduate Hospital, by means of a new therapy, promptly disposed of that infection.

At the close of a very strenuous summer season in New York University, at the age of sixty-three, I was taken very seriously ill while working on my little farm in western North Carolina. I was rushed to the Mountain Sanitarium and Hospital at Fletcher, North Carolina. This is a Seventh-day Adventist medical institution and as such, places great stress on the therapeutic value of hydrotherapy. I had been under such prolonged strain through many years over my wife's long and serious illness and was so generally run down that I was alarmed over this sudden, acute illness. I feared my working days might be over, but in less than a month, Dr. John F. Brownsberger, my competent and faithful physician, took me to the train in Asheville, and sent me on my way back to New York to take up my fall work again at the university.

Four years later, I went back again to the Sanitarium at Fletcher as a patient for the month of May, to clear up the after effects of a severe attack of the flu, contracted while in attendance in Atlantic City upon the meetings of the American Association of School Administrators and the American Association of Teachers Colleges. The daily hydrotherapy treatments soon put me on my feet again for my teaching in the June intersession at the university.

During the four years intervening between these two periods of hospitalization at Fletcher, I spent my vacations at Thanksgiving, Christmas, Easter and in August, down on my farm in North Carolina, taking daily hydrotherapy treatments at the sanitarium which was not far away.

There is a Seventh-day Adventist secondary school at Fletcher. The adolescent boys and girls do all the chores about the sanitarium and hospital, and, in out-of-class hours, work on the farm and in the gardens and fruit orchards. I became acquainted with these youngsters. They daily ministered to my necessities. Their mode of life made a profound impression on me—no drinking, no smoking, no swearing, no midnight carousing at roadhouses, no wild driving on public highways; they were always courteous, helpful, friendly, resilient, jovial, and co-operative in the highest degree. Their religious ideals and their knowledge of the Scriptures were amazing. Daily, I heard them singing beautiful hymns as they went about their work serving trays and cleaning rooms and corridors. Sometimes a group of them would come to my room and ask whether I'd like to join them in evening worship. I wasn't able to go with them so I invited them into my room. The services they conducted were most impressive and touched me deeply. I have always been able, profoundly, to respect the convictions of any person who is as obviously sincere as were these young people.

During my vacation periods down at the sanitarium, I was invited again and again by Madame Jasperson, the principal, to speak to these young people in the school chapel. They always gave me a wonderful reception.

Early in my last year at New York University, 1941-42, I had the good fortune to be introduced to a celebrated German specialist, Dr. Max Gerson, who, so it was said, had prepared the menus for the German army during World War I, but who, because of his race, was in disfavor with Hitler and so moved to the United States and became a substitute professor of nutrition in the Columbia University Medical School. He examined the tissues in the interior of my mouth for a period of fifteen minutes, then threw his spatula down and gave me the verdict:

"*You are starving to death!*"

"No," said I, "I am a hearty eater."

"Yes, I know," said he, "but you're a restaurant eater: the

evidence is unmistakable! The restaurant feeds the sink and gives you the husks."

"What am I to do about it, Doctor?" I asked.

"The remedy," answered he, "is home cooking!"

I explained that my home had been, for years, a place in which to sleep but not a place in which to eat, that my wife was an invalid in a sanitarium, that my daughter had been away at school and college, that she was teaching out on the Island and came home only on week-ends and that I had never learned to cook.

Said he, "I can teach you in five minutes."

Then he pulled out a pad and quickly made a list of the utensils which I should need. I had all of them but one—a potato baker.

He proceeded to list for me, the foods I should avoid and those I should have:

"No meat. Meats are too acid for men over fifty. You must have ample protein foods, but you can get them in more acceptable form.

"One big Idaho baked potato every noon.

"Plenty of pot cheese (made from skimmed milk).

"Plenty of leaf vegetables.

"Plenty of fresh butter.

"Plenty of fresh fruit.

"Plenty of fresh tomatoes.

"Raw or steamed carrots and other root vegetables: onions, beats, etc.

"Almonds, pecans, and other nuts in moderation.

"Soy beans, lima beans, lentils, and garbanzos.

"Properly cooked, but not toasted, peanuts.

"A quart of yogurt, daily.

"Citrus fruit, daily."

I followed directions religiously. Some of my colleagues were good enough to come to my apartment, on occasion, to sample my cooking.

Within that academic year, I made substantial gains on my way back to health. I learned, after I had moved South, that Dr. Gerson had been called into consultation by government committees on the problems of food values and on the causes of malnutrition and that he had accomplished astounding reforms in the eating habits and general improvement in health of many of his colleagues at Columbia University.

When I left New York University in mid-summer, 1942, though I had made much improvement, I was not yet well; and, fearing I might again need hospitalization, I looked up the Seventh-day Adventist medical institutions in the South. Fortunately, there was one in Atlanta under excellent management. During my year at Atlanta University, I had hydrotherapy treatments every week at this sanitarium and spent a month at the Christmas season as a patient therein.

While there, I studied the *Ministry of Healing* by Ellen G. White,* the textbook of Seventh-day Adventist therapy. I was profoundly impressed with the fact that, though written a generation earlier, it was in complete harmony with what Dr. Gerson had told me about foods; for example, said he: "The Idaho potato grows in the Snake River Valley on volcanic-ash soil which contains, in abundance, every mineral which is found in the human body. If you will take a big Idaho potato, scrub it clean, bake it slowly, cut it wide open, fill it with butter and then eat it 'hair, hide, and all' you'll have an almost complete and perfect meal."

While on a field trip out from Atlanta on the Co-operative Negro College Study in the late fall of 1943, I was taken desperately ill on the campus of Dillard University, in New Orleans. As soon as I could safely do so (or before), I made my way back to the Atlanta Sanitarium. I was there prepared for a serious operation late in December at St. Joseph's Hospital in Atlanta. After the operation, I went back to the Atlanta Sanitarium for a period of convalescence. The hy-

* Pacific Press Publishing Association, Mountain View, California.

drotherapy treatments were continued, daily, for six months.

In the fall of 1944, I moved to the campus of Madison College and Sanitarium near Nashville, and made my home with very dear friends, Mr. and Mrs. Edwin Besalski for a year. While there, I continued to get hydrotherapy treatments, worked in the garden, trimmed shrubbery, and felled dead trees. I reverted to and enjoyed about all the farm experiences of my adolescent days. I did a lot of face-lifting on the campus of the college and on the grounds of the sanitarium. I spent hours each day in the out-of-doors, slept long hours, and ate the best of all foods.

While at the Atlanta Sanitarium and, later, while spending the summer in the North Carolina hills at Fletcher, and the fall with the Besalskis at Madison College, I continued to read the official blueprint of the educational program of the Seventh-day Adventist secondary schools and colleges and about the very remarkable world-wide medical-and-health service of this denomination. These, and many other features of the dynamic program of this religious group, impressed me so much that I finally found myself seeking its fellowship and ready to undertake an active part in its world-wide educational program.

Resident Educational Consultant at Southern Missionary College

In 1938, when I delivered the commencement address at the Martha Berry College, Miss Berry said to me: "Dr. Suhrie, if you will come to the Berry Schools and serve as our consultant and counsellor when you are through with your work in New York University, our boys will build you a nice comfortable cottage on our campus grounds; you will not need to invest a penny. We shall provide for you a residence so long as you live." She had, in the meantime, died and I suppose, because of my substandard health at the time, that invitation was not repeated by her successor.

After I had made a good comeback in health, I determined to attach myself, when the right opening should come, to some small college having a work-study program. It was natural that I should consider the possibility of finding the right setting in one of the dozen Seventh-day Adventist colleges which are scattered from Massachusetts to California and from Texas to Michigan. I greatly preferred to locate in the Old South. So I went, first, to visit Southern Missionary College at Collegedale, Tennessee. President Wright was absent. Dean Walther invited me to speak at a special evening convocation of faculty and students in the college chapel. I spoke on a favorite theme, "Making and Keeping Our Schools Democratic in Organization and Spirit." The response the young people gave me was wonderful; and the meeting was no sooner adjourned than a dozen, or it may have been a score, of college students came to the front of the hall to great me. One charming young woman (Margaret Tucker) spoke first: "Dr. Suhrie, why don't you move over?"

"Over where?" I asked.

"Over to Collegedale, of course; we need you on this faculty. Please come."

"I haven't been officially invited," said I.

Then a young freshman (Melvin Hickman) spoke up: "Well, I'll make it official right here and now!"

I thanked him; we all had a good laugh, bade each other good night, and went our several ways.

Two days later, I received at my home on the grounds of Madison Sanitarium, a very friendly letter from President Wright of Southern Missionary College, saying he had heard of my visit and wondered why I hadn't come when he was home. I replied that I had wondered why he had left the campus just before my first visit.

He gave me an invitation to return soon. I did. He met me at the station and inquired whether I could consider coming to Collegedale on permanent appointment. I replied that I had already been invited by the students. He had heard of that, too. A few days later, and after conferring with the board, he sent me an official invitation to join the faculty of Southern Missionary College, in the fall. He issued the call, on faith, and I accepted it, on faith. Neither one of us knew the other very well, but I was sure I would enjoy working with him and I surely have from that day to this.

At my next meeting with the president, we easily agreed on the nature of the program and service I should undertake. I told him I wanted a third-of-a-service load and that a third of a salary would be O.K. My title, we agreed, should be Resident Educational Consultant.

I moved to Collegedale in September. I taught two classes. I observed and listened for a year before aggressively taking hold of any projects. I wanted to gain the confidence of the people, to get acquainted with faculty and students and with the pattern of life on the campus, before making any suggestions for change and improvement.

The college was offering, for the first time that fall, the sixteenth-year's work and graduated its first class of six at the end of my first year on the campus. President Wright can better tell my readers than I, just what I have undertaken to do for the College during the nine years since we sent out our first graduating class in May 1946, and can give an impartial appraisal of the significance of my service to the institution since then:

President Wright's Appraisal of Consultant's Services

We knew we needed Dr. Suhrie's help. We were determined to make life on our campus interesting for him. We evidently succeeded for, before the end of the year, he was ready to build his own home on the campus and settle down. We agreed that he should build his cottage where he wanted it—in the beautiful woodlands on the edge of the campus, and that he should pay for it without getting title for it, taking in lieu thereof, a rent-free lease for the remainder of his life. After he remarried in 1950, and after Mrs. Suhrie had been on the campus for a year, the rent-free lease was changed to include her in its benefits, giving Dr. and Mrs. Suhrie each a survivor's rent-free lease.

At the end of the first year the board, on my recommendation, placed Dr. Suhrie on permanent tenure. He placed his resignation on my desk at once and has reminded me at the end of each succeeding year since that I am free, on my own initiative and without giving cause, to dispense with his services. He has assured me again and again that he doesn't expect, or desire to be, kept on the list of active workers unless he is, in my judgment, performing satisfactorily. Since he has come here, he has twice been bidden elsewhere. President Anderson, of Montreat College, a new Presbyterian College in North Carolina, desired his services as head of the department of education. The Head of the Department of Education at Stetson University in Florida, where Dr. Suhrie began his college teaching fifty years ago, offered him a place on his departmental staff. Either of these two positions would have trebled his salary, but he had made his commitment here; he had put his hand to the plow and was unwilling to turn back.

The service projects Dr. Suhrie has undertaken include the following:

1. Organized and sponsored, for a period of four years, the conduct of our college student association.

2. Prepared, in due time, a pamphlet entitled *S. M. C. Student Organizations at Work*.

3. Wrote (and has twice revised) our *Handbook of Organization and Working Policies* for the administration and faculty of Southern Missionary College.

4. Visited annually and spoke in all secondary schools of Southern Union of Seventh-day Adventists.

5. Visited and lectured in all Seventh-day Adventist colleges of North America.

6. Attended and participated in several Summer Conferences of Principals of Seventh-day Adventist secondary schools of North America.

7. Attended and participated in Summer Conference of Deans and Presidents of Seventh-day Adventist colleges of North America at Boulder, Colorado.

8. Conducted a successful campaign for funds for furnishing the parlors for our College residence halls.

9. Conducted Arbor Day programs at Southern Missionary College, directing the planting of five hundred dogwood trees and azaleas.

10. Attracted gifts of special collections of books to our college library.

11. Visited and spoke in all colleges, secondary schools, and mission stations in Central American and Antillian Unions of Inter-American Division of Seventh-day Adventists.

12. Participated in solicitation of funds for a new medical clinic for Southern Missionary College.

13. Served as chairman of the special committee that recommended a site for our new college health center and our proposed hospital and sanitarium.

14. Has been and is deeply concerned to enlist the interest of men and women of means in donating a hospital and sanitarium to the college. He desires to help us to give this college, and our neighboring communities, the very best possible program of health education, health protection, and emergency-health service.

15. Reorganized the Southern Missionary College catalog, interpreting the educational significance of the work-study program, and adding greatly to the value of the publication as a manual of counsel to students.

16. Made survey of common errors in speech and writing on the campus of Southern Missionary College.

17. Prepared pamphlet on *Improvement in English Usage at Southern Missionary College.*

18. Served as executive secretary of Southern Missionary College faculty, of the Southern Missionary College Faculty Senate, and of the Committee on Improvement in English Usage.

19. Helped to make college faculty meetings first-class educational seminars.

20. Sponsored the annual spring clean-up day at Southern Missionary College.

21. Launched a reforestation project on mountain lands belonging to the college.

22. Has given many professional presentations of English classic literature before college classes and auditorium groups.

23. Has conducted drill periods for volunteer Spanish-speaking students desiring to perfect their English pronunciation.

24. Has represented our college at inauguration and commencement exercises in other colleges and universities.

25. Has made his composted garden a magnificent demonstration to all his neighbors in the valley. His fruit trees, his berries, and his vineyard are among the best in the county, and our young people learn gardening from him without any precept teaching.

26. Has aroused in the Collegedale Community, and among its home owners, a genuine interest in beautifying home grounds, woodland parks, and public highways by the planting of dogwoods, azaleas, and red-crepe myrtles. This valley promises, in due time, to be one of the real beauty spots of "sunny" Tennessee.

27. Has each year, for a period of eight years, served as Co-ordinator of Orientation-Week Programs and Activities. He prepares all the details of this program with great care so as to insure to the young people, a very happy experience while getting acquainted with each other, with their teachers, and with college life here.

28. Has taken an active interest in living conditions and community developments in our trailer colony, which came into existence on the edge of our campus almost over night, in the fall of 1946, when two hundred and fifty-six World War II veterans, or GI's, appeared upon the campus to register as college students. He organized a monthly

"Town Hall" meeting and helped the citizens of this unique community to set up a village government all their own. This enterprise accomplished much in making life more comfortable, interesting, and attractive to the men, women, and children, living in GI Town.

29. Helped, over a period of years, to condition our officers and faculty for the steady up-grading of our college program to the level of accreditation by the Southern Association of Colleges and Secondary Schools.

When Doctor Suhrie came to our campus, the college was experiencing that rather difficult metamorphosis of growing from a junior college of many years' standing to that of a senior college. The administrators and faculty were in the process of making the patterns for an arts college to serve our denominational needs here in the South. The presence of Doctor Suhrie on our campus has been a real inspiration; he has been a good guide as we have charted the course for the standards and policies of the institution. We have found that his sense of professional ethics is without a peer.

This chapter would be lacking if it did not include a personal testimony. I have come to think of Doctor Suhrie as my professional guide and personal consultant. His very presence inspires to truer values and a higher plane of endeavor. His membership on the president's council has provided guidance and counsel of the highest type. If I were to attempt to epitomize this man, who stands professionally head and shoulders above his fellows, I would summarize by saying that I consider him a thoroughly educated Christian gentleman.

Of course I am profoundly grateful to President Wright and his colleagues on the faculty of Southern Missionary College, as also, to the students who have come to, and gone from our campus, for the rare privilege I have had of working with and for them. And surely, Mrs. Suhrie and I have had the very best neighbors here that could be found anywhere. We love this little town for the charm of its setting in the hills and woodlands, but particularly, for the character of our neighbors and the warmth of the friendship they have given us.

Lecture-Consultation Service at Home and Abroad

Since settling down in Collegedale, in 1945, as resident-educational consultant to Southern Missionary College, I have always been free to absent myself from the campus from December 20 to February 15, and at other times, irregularly, if invitations should come for lectures and consultation services elsewhere. I have generally been absent from the campus for a series of such engagements during the summer season, when the demand has been insistent in the summer schools of state universities and state teachers colleges in the South, the Mid-west and the Northwest. I have also made trips to New England and the East in the autumn season, to revisit the teachers colleges in those sections and, on one occasion, to Texas to serve as consultant for a month (in October), at the new Texas Southern University, in Houston. Within a period of three years, beginning in the fall of 1949, I visited every state in the Union, in meeting lecture engagements and giving consultant services in state universities, in state teachers colleges, and in Seventh-day Adventist colleges and secondary schools. I made two such special trips covering all of New England and the East, two trips to the Northwest and up into Canada, four trips to the West Coast and the Southwest, three trips to the Lake Region and out on the Plains, and two trips to Latin America. On these foreign trips, I lectured in colleges, secondary schools and mission stations.

My special interest in the work of the Seventh-day Adventist colleges and secondary schools, may be explained by the following incident: When I was desperately ill in St. Joseph's Hospital, in Atlanta, ten years ago, following a surgical operation, the director of the Atlanta Sanitarium, whose institution had nursed me for a month in preparation for the operation, came to see me daily to make sure that I was having at least minimum care and attention at a time when trained nurses were not to be had and only office girls, who volunteered for a couple of hours daily as "practical" nurses or attendants, were available even in the best hospitals. This gracious woman, Mrs. Luella Doub, told me, one morning, that she had just finished reading the *Book of Remembrance* which the Eastern-States Association of Professional Schools for Teachers had given me and which I had left in my room in her sanitarium.

Said she: "I am now familiar with what your lifework has been. I know you have visited and lectured in tax-supported colleges and universities all over the United States. How rich your experience must have been over a period of several decades! It is now my earnest hope and prayer that you may make a good recovery and that you will then help our Seventh-day Adventist colleges in this country, a dozen of them, and our eighty secondary schools, to see their educational opportunities a little more clearly and fully, and greatly to improve their educational services."

Well, the work-study program of these institutions, the emphasis on education for healthful living, and for character-building as I had observed it at Fletcher, North Carolina, did interest me greatly. And in due time, when I had fully recovered, the call came very insistently, without promotional effort on my part, to do what Mrs. Doub had suggested.

I went merrily on my way into all the Seventh-day Adventist colleges in North America including Canada, Mexico, and Central America, into those in the islands of the West Indies, and into those in certain countries in northern South America. This was a very rich experience. I found that in Latin America, especially in Mexico, there is tremendous enthusiasm for the Adventist work-study type of secondary schools and colleges. The son of a former president of Mexico, who was a big distributor of farm machinery in Monterey, and a grower of fine citrus fruits in the immediate vicinity of our Adventist hospital and secondary school at Montemorellos, told me with enthusiasm that if enough teachers, trained to conduct the work-study type of secondary school, could be secured to staff the schools of Neuva Leon (the state in which Montemorellos is located), he was sure the school authorities would enthusiastically convert all their secondary schools to that type (like the one at Montemorellos). He is a liberal supporter of the local health center which is serving nearly two hundred patients daily, in its hospital, sanitarium and clinic. One of its unique features is the service of a Bible instructor, who assembles emergency patients out in the mountains and transports them, in his private plane, to the hospital and then, after convalescence, returns them to their homes.

It is a fixed policy of the Seventh-day Adventist church to locate its secondary schools whenever possible in the open country, on good farm lands, and to teach all adolescents to work with their own hands not only on the farm, in the dairy, in the garden, and in the laundry; but, also in the industries maintained by the school on or near its campus to provide students an opportunity to earn their own maintenance. Most of the adolescents enrolled in these schools earn a substantial portion of their total expenses for maintenance and schooling while pursuing a standard secondary-school program of "academic" studies, and getting much valuable collateral training and experience in matters distinctly "practical."

It is not necessary to explain that my own background of adolescent life on the farm, my own struggle to get an education without making any demand upon my parents for financial assistance, and my own appreciation of the educational values I had derived from learning in my adolescent days to do many kinds of useful work outdoors on the farm, prompted in me a very strong desire first, to learn to know these schools intimately by personal visitation of them and secondly, to help those responsible for their management and the teaching in them, to define their purposes a little more clearly and to adapt their programs of instruction a little more fully to their professed purposes; namely: to educate the head, the heart and the hand. Finally, I hoped I might be able to help them progressively, to up-grade the preparation of their teachers and the quality of their teaching.

During the past five years, I have made my way as a visitor (and at my own expense) into at least half a hundred of these secondary schools in all parts of our country, and in certain Latin American countries to the south of us.

Within three years after my retirement from New York University, I was twice invited by a representative of the United States Government to go as an educational consultant to several Latin American countries. I was not then in a suitable physical condition to take the health risks involved. If the call were to come now, I'd probably respond with considerable enthusiasm and primarily, because I believe these Latin American countries—all of them—are deeply interested in the work-study program of secondary and collegiate education with which I am now primarily concerned.

Life Begins at Eighty

On a certain occasion, a sharp-tongued toastmaster had completed a facetious (and intentionally uncomplimentary) introduction of the last of a panel of banquet speakers. The retort of this quiet, genial little man was: "Your toastmaster is said to be a great wit. After hearing the introductions he has given to the several banquet speakers this evening, I'm inclined to think that it is half true."

Walter Pitkin, some years ago wrote a book under the title *Life Begins at Forty*. As an octogenarian, with more active interests than ever before in my life, I'm inclined to think Professor Pitkin's book-title expresses only a half-truth.

When Justice Holmes, of the United States Supreme Court, at the age of ninety-two, was taking a morning walk with his friend, the Chief Justice, a young woman with sprightly step crossed the street in front of them. Said Holmes with spirit: "Oh, that I were seventy again!" Only a young man could have had such youthful flutterings under the fifth rib; and he was ninety-two. I'm only four score, plus.

When Mrs. Suhrie and I were covering the West Indies last December and January, by a series of rapid flights, my beloved "Prexy," Kenneth A. Wright, appointed a faculty-student committee at Southern Missionary College to take public note of my approaching eightieth-birthday anniversary (February 28).

Mrs. Elva B. Gardner, the gracious registrar of the college, was appointed chairman of this joint committee.

The committee and the community were able to keep their secret in seventeen languages. When the surprise-party program which had been arranged with meticulous care, broke over an audience filling the college auditorium, I was, it seems, the only one who had not been let in on what was coming. I was sitting in the front of the hall greatly enjoying the introductory portion of a discourse by a visiting speaker, T. E. Unruh, of Pennsylvania. His theme was, "Brotherly Love." The discourse, hardly more than well begun, came to an end rather abruptly, and from no apparent cause, except that one of my colleagues came to the lectern and took over.

It seems appropriate that Mrs. Gardner, the chairman of this tribute-program committee, rather than I, should tell my readers the story of that never-to-be-forgotten event.

Mrs. Gardner:

"The program of the evening has been planned after the pattern of the television program: *This Is Your Life* and what a life we are reviewing tonight! Our committee has requested Professor Charles E. Wittschiebe to preside at these festivities."

Professor Wittschiebe, Chairman:

"We are honoring tonight a great man—great in every dimension; a great gentleman, a great Christian, a great educator. Like all great educators, he is attracted to children, and children are drawn to him." [At this moment, Professor Suhrie received his first clear intimation that he was the honored guest. Slowly his eyes lowered from the speaker to the children seated in front of him.] "We shall ask his little friends—his neighbors and fellow Hallow'eeners, the children, to bring our guest to the platform." [The audience, quite spontaneously, began singing a certain familiar song written specifically for birthday celebrations. The guest of honor having been escorted to the platform, the chairman continued.]

"We have known Professor Suhrie for nine years as a neighbor, companion, and friend (and as a famous compost gardner), but we didn't know he had so many long-time friends among the good and the great in the far-away sections of our country and in many foreign lands, until we began setting up this tribute program.

"Professor Suhrie's friends, who have been invited by the committee to be present with him on this platform tonight and to speak on this tribute program, and those who, because they could not be here in person, have sent, at the committee's request, tape recordings of the tributes they have prepared (with photographs to identify themselves to this audience), are only a small fraction of the multitudes of former students and colleagues in the many important institutions in which his life's work has been done who would, I have no doubt, like to be present in person to warm his heart by a friendly handclasp and a word of congratulations. I shall, for brevity's sake, merely announce the names of the speakers and have each give his position in educational service, and his relationship to Professor Suhrie.

"First we shall have the tape-record messages and tributes."

Mrs. Ruth Suhrie Allaway, daughter, Port Washington, Long Island, New York:

"A happy birthday, Father, dear. We wish we could be with you to celebrate this important birthday. We are so happy to know that you are well, busy, and happy at eighty. As my children grow older, I realize as never before, what a good, and above all, patient father you have been. So happy birthday to you. Bob and Roger want to say something, too. Who knows, you may even hear David, but that will be incidental. He is two years old this week and full of talk, generally off schedule. Happy birthday!"

Robert Allaway, son-in-law, Port Washington, Long Island, New York:

"Hello, Pop; this is Robert. Happy Birthday! Congratulations on being eighty years old. I wish I could be with you tonight, but I have to do my homework. I am sure you are very happy to know you have so many friends. I hope everyone will remember his part tonight, so that in ten years, we can do it all over again when you are ninety. Twenty years from now, when you are a hundred years old, you will probably have to give the party yourself, the rest of us will all be too old. Happy birthday! Good night!"

Roger Allaway grandson, from his home on Long Island:

"Hello, Grandpa; this is Roger. I want to say happy birthday. I hope you will have a nice birthday party. I will be eighty years old in only seventy-two more years. I hope I will then have as many friends as you have. Happy Birthday!"

Dr. Samuel M. Brownell, United States Commissioner of Education, Department of Health, Education, and Welfare, Washington, D. C.:

"Happy birthday, Dr. Suhrie! And greetings to you, Mrs. Suhrie. Mrs. Brownell, the daughters, and Richard can't be present with me this evening for which they are sorry and so am I. But it is nice to come into your birthday party even if only for a few words. We all wish you many happy returns of the day.

"It would be nice for me, if you and I could transport ourselves back for a hike in the Peru hills in southeastern Nebraska, where in your encouraging way, you once made the neophyte high-school principal feel that you were interested in his ideas and in his future. Perhaps you did not fully appreciate what your friendliness meant to me. Your continuously cordial interest, during the intervening years, has extended to my various occupations and to my wife and children. Each one of us has enjoyed the occasional visits we have had with you at professional meetings and in our home. We regretted that you didn't get to Connecticut last fall. Now we look forward to seeing you when you next visit Washington.

"I still marvel and wonder how in the world you've been able to make your circle so big of those in whom you maintain a personal interest and on whom, as a result, you exert an influence of high idealism and desire to demonstrate that they are worthy of your confidence in them.

"Our affectionate best wishes to you and may we be seeing you and Mrs. Suhrie, soon. The latch string is always out for you at the Brownell house in Washington."

President Emeritus, Dr. Leslie Pinckney Hill, State Teachers College, Cheyney, Pennsylvania:

"Doctor Suhrie, your friends across the nation today, from ocean to ocean, will be wishing, as I am, that they could be with you in person, to shake your hand and feel the benediction of your friendly smile. They would congratulate you upon that providential gift of the years which you have made so fruitful, not only for yourself, but for all of us. No man alive has been more intimately or more productively associated with the education of teachers throughout the United States. Everywhere you have created, and left behind you, respect for the dignity and power of the teaching profession.

"I am especially grateful that you have never failed to visit the Negro schools, North and South, inspiring thousands of their students and leading out many of our principals and presidents to further study. I was one of these at New York University. There, your classes were always gatherings of friends seeking guidance in the challenging adventure of teaching.

"I have had the honor of being your host-president many times at the State Teachers College at Cheyney, Pennsylvania. Your presence on our campus was always a major event. You brought understanding sympathy and the ripe wisdom of wide experience. We knew that you saw, in the lack of adequate educational opportunities for one-tenth of our citizenry, a danger to the whole structure of our democratic society; and, that your voice and pen would always be bravely engaged in our behalf. No one will ever be able to estimate the value of that high service to a disadvantaged people.

"Please, Doctor Suhrie, accept for yourself and Mrs. Suhrie, heartfelt greetings from both of the Hills and prayerful best wishes for many more years of gracious creative living."

Dr. Floyd O. Rittenhouse, Dean, Emmanuel Missionary College, Berrien Springs, Michigan:

"Dr. Suhrie, this is Floyd Rittenhouse speaking to you directly from Emmanuel Missionary College at Berrien Springs,

Michigan. For a while, I had prospects of being with you at Collegedale for this significant anniversary, but as recent events have made impossible a visit at this time, I am doing the next best thing, which is to send you these few words of greeting.

"Dr. Suhrie, I hope you realize how truly important this occasion is. I hope you sense how great a blessing your life has been to all who have had the glad fortune to come under your influence. How kindly has been the Heavenly Providence which endowed you with character and wisdom but also with health and vigor so that many, like myself, who have come to know you only during the last decade, have benefited and enjoyed the full impact of your vigorous and stimulating personality. In all truth, I count your friendship and encouragement as one of the most significant developments in my own life, during recent years. There are literally hundreds who feel the same way and who, if they could, would happily add their voices at this time in a fraternal birthday wish for health and happiness to you in a very rich measure.

"Dr. Suhrie, we salute you on this day of days—your full four score! We salute you for your brilliance of mind, for your unfailing wisdom, for your everlasting good humor, and above all, for your spotless character. May the Heavenly Host look down in joy upon your wise and hoary head and your generous heart and give you peace. Nellie and my two girls join me in saying 'So long, old friend, and may God bless you and Mrs. Suhrie until we meet again.' "

Dr. Ray C. Maul, Assistant Director of Research, National Education Association, Washington, D. C.:

"Dr. Suhrie, I am Ray Maul, sitting in my office in the headquarters of the National Education Association in Washington; but in spirit, I am very much in Collegedale to do honor to the grandest man in education I have ever known.

"As you become eighty years young—and I would be mistaken if I said eighty years old—you really are at a mid-point in life; you can look back upon the full accomplishment of your highest ambition—a continuous period of service to your fellow men. As a master-teacher of teachers, you have not only influenced the lives of those thousands who have been your students, but through them, you have helped to shape the lives and attitudes of those tens of thousands who have been taught by your students. What, indeed, could be a richer reward than your own knowledge of this magnificent accomplishment?

"But at this mid-point in your life, you now look forward —forward to many more years of continued service. I still need your sage advice and counsel from time to time. Literally thousands of us will continue to look to you. We know you will not fail us. God bless you."

President Ermo H. Scott, State Teachers College, Farmington, Maine:

"A king-sized greeting, Dr. Suhrie, from the Farmington State Teachers College campus down in Maine. To join on this unusual occasion, with others of your wide-flung family, is a marked compliment which I share with Mrs. Scott, with Bonnie, who is a high-school freshman, and with our ten-year-old Robin. Would that I could express, adequately, the measure of your contribution to teacher education in our state colleges which now reflect the self-dedication which you have so highly exemplified. Would that we, who now serve these colleges, could achieve your level of service in inspiring young people with a vision and energizing their efforts toward its realization.

"This is a personal "thank you" from two to whom you opened the door. It is based upon many recollections of your initial visit to the old Castine Normal School, in 1931. That evening, when the brilliant moon path, caught by shadowy outlines of the little bay, fell upon a fatigued traveler relaxing by the flames of a simple home hearth, a newly married couple were just a bit overwhelmed by the privilege of entertaining a famous professor from a great university. Encouragement led to the 1937 inter-session class with its reunion luncheons and the friendships which still endure. The '38—'39 year of life at Waverly Place, with its midnight call to approve the twelve-word Martha Berry dedicatory statement; with the young expectant mother counting manuscript words destined for the *Journal;* and with the flu which so successfully wrecked your perfect attendance record with the Eastern-States Association. Later my privilege, as a faculty member, of assignment to some of those instructional areas out of which you had earlier gained and developed so much of your understanding wisdom to those who sat with you.

"As I look out this afternoon upon a cleansing seventeen-inch Maine snowfall, it re-enforces the knowledge that God has been good to admit us to the kinship of the hoary circle which encompasses such worthy personal and professional concerns, blending into that which you have typified; you, the master-teacher; you, who loved to teach; you, who have sought to be the million-dollar teacher; you, who have brought dignity and status to teachers through your personal concern, industry, and continual inspiration to others.

"So from us all, a happy birthday, 'Grampy.' May the next eight decades be even richer than those that have gone before; and may the members of your many foster-children continue to be multiplied."

President John D. Messick, East Carolina State College, Greenville, North Carolina:

"I have known you, Dr. Suhrie, at New York University since the early thirties; and it gives me a great deal of pleasure to participate in this, your eightieth-birthday celebration.

"You were a member of the committee that examined me, one very cold February day, in 1934, to decide whether I merited the award of the doctor-of-philosophy degree from New York University.

"When I was Dean of Elon College, you used to stop by with me, annually enroute to your mountain home at Hendersonville. During the World's Fair in New York, you gave me the use of your entire apartment, where my family and I spent several days and, of course, we appreciated that very much.

"Since my coming to East Carolina College, I have invited you, Dr. Suhrie, several times here, as a lecturer for some of the conferences held during the summer. And, of course, Mrs. Messick and I are always happy to have you as our guest. I have the highest regard for you, Doctor Suhrie, as a man, as a scholar, and as an educator who has a comprehensive knowledge of the teachers colleges of America (as well as other colleges), which is probably unsurpassed by that of any other individual. Your leadership in American education, your versatile interests and your affable personality, are all outstanding even among great people. I am happy to count you as a dear friend. And now, to you personally, Doctor Suhrie, I wish the happiest possible birthday and continued joyful living as long as life lasts. May my best wishes be impressed upon you just as in times past, because I count you as one of my very, very dear friends."

Dr. Marion Emory Shea, President, Patterson State Teachers College:

"Happy birthday, Dr. Suhrie. A very happy birthday to a great and kind and good man, a wise counselor, a real friend.

"When you took on the job as advisor for me, you little realized that you were to play so big a part in seeing me through to my doctor's degree, in advising me on changes in positions, in helping me to write articles for magazines, in encouraging me to undertake tasks I thought were beyond my capability. You were right; I could do them and I have done them! And my thanks go to the one who saw, in his student, what the student, herself, could not see.

"If you haven't recognized my voice up to this point, let me mention two or three very happy associations. A trip to Europe when you conducted a spelling bee, and your daughter Ruth won a photographic prize; rides to your sister's home in South Jersey, or to the homes of your friends in North Jersey; the day you dropped off at my home in Aberdeen, Maryland, and stayed for the night with my parents; your delight when you heard I had changed my name from Marion Emory to Mrs. J. Joseph Shea. From both of us, Dr. Suhrie, from Joe and from me, our best wishes for a long life filled with the love of family and friends, and the memories of all your wonderful days."

Elder E. E. Cossentine, Educational Secretary, General Conference of Seventh-Day Adventists, Takoma Park, Washington, D. C.

"It is a real pleasure for me, on this occasion, to express my congratulations to you, Dr. Suhrie. It is a wonderful thing for a man to be able to make the contribution which you have made to the field of education—over sixty years of successful teaching, administrating, and counseling. Through these years, you have been a man greatly respected, loved, and appreciated. Throughout the entire country, you are held in the highest respect in educational circles; and, so, today we pay tribute to you for this life of service which you have given so willingly to the youth of America. I know thousands of young people, both in this country and in many other countries, who, on this occasion, wish they could be with you to express their appreciation and their congratulations, personally. May the rich blessings of God be with you, as you carry on, bringing to all of us help, counsel, and inspiration, for the daily tasks, and encouragement and vision for the future."

The Chairman:

"Now we shall hear, in person, from a few of Dr. Suhrie's friends, some of whom have journeyed from afar and some of whom are his superior officers in the local college. They are so well known here that they need no formal introduction."

Mrs. Inez Henry, Assistant to the President of Martha Berry College, Mount Berry, Georgia:

"Dr. Suhrie, it gives me very real pleasure to be here in person to join with your friends in these festivities. I have known you for more than twenty years. I can never forget the first time you visited our campus. State-School Commissioner Dugan, one of our board members, had called from Atlanta to tell us of your coming and to bespeak for you, a good hearing. President Green, in the absence of Dr. Berry, called together our twelve hundred college and academy students. Our boys came into our beautiful chapel in mid-morning dressed in blue overalls, the girls in pink dresses. You gave us a thrilling message then, as you have done so many times since.

"Then, I recall when you and your daughter, Ruth, were guests of Dr. Berry, at the Mansion on Easter Day a year later, and when each of you spoke in chapel on the following morning.

"And I recall very vividly, the occasion in May, 1937, when you flew down from New York to attend the tribute banquet our alumni society gave Miss Berry at the conclusion of thirty-five years of service, and when you gave our college-commencement address on the following Monday morning.

"I remember, too, the many occasions when you met us in public gatherings in New York. The most notable of these was one at which you presented Miss Berry to the officers of New York University for honorary life membership in the Kappa Delta Pi Education Honor Society. She was especially appreciative of your citation on that notable occasion.

"In one of the last letters she ever dictated to you from her death bed, I well remember that she begged you to return often to the campus to give some inspiring message to her boys and girls. And this you have done.

"I bring you greetings from your host of friends on the Berry College campus, including our new president, Dr. Lambert; our resident trustee, Mr. Gordon Keown; and a thousand Berry boys and girls. This necktie was woven by the girls in our weaving room and we hope that it will be a tie that will bind you still a little closer to Berry."

Dr. Paul L. Palmer, Dean, College of Applied Arts and Sciences, University of Chattanooga:

"Dr. Ambrose L. Suhrie, Good Friends, and Neighbors: James Boswell, in his notable biography of Dr. Samuel Johnson, made this statement: 'We cannot tell the precise moment when friendship is formed. As in filling a vessel, drop by drop, there is at last a drop which makes it run over; so in a series of kindnesses, there is at last one which makes the heart run over.'

"I'm honored and proud this evening, Dr. Suhrie, in behalf of my University of Chattanooga colleagues, the entire membership of the Lookout Schoolmasters' Club, and your many associates and friends in the Tennessee College Association, to express our appreciation of the manner in which your overflowing kindnesses to us, have in a very few years ripened into enduring, stimulating, and enriching friendship.

"We marvel at how much zest you get out of life, considerably beyond the years when most people cease to do so. The American philosopher, George Santayana, once remarked, 'There is no cure for birth or death save to enjoy the interval.' Our tribute and debt to you is not only that you have enjoyed and continue to enjoy life, but even more, that you have helped most of us to more worthy and enjoyable living. I have yet to see you move into any group and not leave its members richer for your having been there.

"I am happy, therefore, on behalf of your host of friends in the Chattanooga area and Tennessee educational circles to wish you many more years of good health, rewarding friendships and God's richest blessings in helpful service among us."

Dean Richard Hammill, of Southern Missionary College:

"Dr. Suhrie, it gives me pleasure to present to you, on behalf of the officers and faculty members and student officers of our college, this beautiful and very useful brief case."

President Kenneth A. Wright, of Southern Missionary College:

(The substance of what the President said is given at length in an earlier section, in his listing and appraisal of Dr. Suhrie's services to Southern Missionary College.)

Professor Elmore J. McMurphy, of Department of Speech, Southern Missionary College then read *The Lamp Lighter* by J. C. Hyer, after the hall had been darkened and while an usher lighted lamps one by one on the outer rim of the hall:

"Once in an old New England town . . . From on a hill I could look down . . . And see the street lamps one by one . . . Light up the dark.

"When he was done . . . The old lamp-lighter changed the night . . . into a starry field of light.

"I know some folks who as they go . . . Light little lamps that gleam and glow . . . In others' lives with rays divine . . . That in the darkest nights will shine."

The Chairman:

"Now the ushers will bring in their cargo." (*They brought to the stage two bushel baskets full of letters and telegrams which had come from far and near to the committee.*)

(One of the delightful surprises of the evening was the appearance on the platform of Mrs. James A. Adair of Westfield, New Jersey, who served as Professor Suhrie's secretary at New York University for a period of fourteen years; Mrs. Luella Doub, the nurse who attended him while convalescing in the Atlanta Sanitarium; Elder Lawrence Scales, the young minister who served as the first president of the student association at Southern Missionary College which Professor Suhrie had sponsored; and President and Mrs. A. A. Jasperson, of Madison College, who were among Professor Suhrie's friends at the Sanitarium in Fletcher, North Carolina, a dozen years ago.)*

The Chairman:
"Dr. Suhrie, the audience would like to hear from you."

Dr. Ambrose L. Suhrie, Emeritus Professor of Higher Education, New York University, and Resident Educational Consultant, Southern Missionary College:
"Of course I am profoundly grateful to all my friends from far and near who have had a part in this program as, also, to the committee that prepared it and my good neighbors who make up this large and friendly audience.

"I'm reminded of a similar occasion some twenty-five years ago when some of us who were the friends of the poet, Markham, got up a similar tribute program in Carnegie Hall, New York, to make manifest our good will to that grizzly octogenarian. When his turn came to make response, he said: 'I was hoping this foolish committee would put this function off to a more appropriate time some ten or twenty years hence.'

"I'm glad you took no chances with fate by postponing this very pleasant occasion. Of course, I'm greatly honored by the busy men and women who have taken time out to make

---

* Many of the tape recordings (notably a symposium of Dr. Suhrie's former colleagues at New York University) are omitted from this record for lack of space.

tape-recorded messages and to send them here. I'm sure, too, that none of you can fully understand how it warms my heart to hear these spoken messages and to receive this public manifestation of good will here in the local community.

"When I built my woodland cottage here in Collegedale some eight years ago (and before Mrs. Judson of California became Mrs. Suhrie of Tennessee), I gave a party to the little children of this community. They have been my boon companions ever since. How it does give me a flutter under the fifth rib to hear, on every return to town from my travels afar, the happy voices of little children ringing through the woodlands: 'Dr. Suhrie is home again!' and in recent years, it has given me even more pleasure to hear that announcement preceded by a ringing welcome to Mrs. Suhrie. These children will always be welcome in our home and at our fireside. And when they grow up and want to get married, I'll be glad to have them ask my judgment as to whether I think they are old enough. How we do enjoy the confidences of the young people in our academy and college! We both treasure their friendships as among our most precious possessions.

"My heart goes out tonight in gratitude to God for the sustaining friendships He has enabled me to accumulate across the span of eighty happy years brimful of the good things of life.

"I have no disposition whatever to consider this a farewell party. I feel young in spirit. I still have plans and aspirations and hopes aplenty.

"Mrs. Suhrie and I have a comfortable cottage in the woodlands and a happy home. Our deep freeze is full of the good food we raise in our composted garden. We have a cellar full of the sweet unsweetened grape-juice from our composted vineyard. We made forty-two gallon jugs of it last year.

"In the fall, our friends from Maine send us a shipment of MacIntosh apples; from Vermont, maple syrup; from central New York, butternuts; from Oregon, filberts; from northern

California, almonds; from southern California, English walnuts; from North Carolina, sauerwood honey; from Georgia, pecans; and from Florida, citrus fruits. All through the year, messages of affectionate good will come to us from across the continent and around the world.

"We have superb friends and sweet memories. We still have much useful work to do. And so, let me address the future as Edwin Markham did in the last verse of the last poem in his book entitled, *Eighty Songs at Eighty:*

> Now I turn to the future for wine and bread:
> I have bidden the past adieu.
> I laugh and lift hands to the years ahead:
> 'Come on: I am ready for you!'

"After this delightful evening with my friends from far and near, *I am sure that Life Begins at Eighty.*"

The Chairman:

"This has been a very happy occasion not only for you, Dr. Suhrie and Mrs. Suhrie, but for all your friends who have been privileged to be here.

I think we should have a word from Mrs. Gardner, the chairman of this birthday-celebration committee."

Mrs. Gardner:

"Our thanks will be sent to all who have furnished us tape-recorded tributes. In due time, we hope to have their presentations and those of the speakers who have been here in person made available, in print.

"May I ask all who have been special guests of the committee to come to the platform, immediately after adjournment for the making of a photo.

"After the photographs have been taken, will all the platform guests and the members of my committee come over to the Suhrie cottage where Mrs. Suhrie will serve refreshments. Thank you all. Good night. Dr. Suhrie, *Life Begins at Eighty.*"

8

REFLECTIONS
AT SUNSET

My PROFESSIONAL AND SOCIAL INTERESTS have been varied and active during all of the sixty-four years in which I have been engaged in twig-bending. And I have learned some things:

I have finally found some of the answers to Herbert Spencer's question: "What knowledge is of most worth?"

I am beginning to recognize some of the values in education which promise to be enduring and permanent.

I have come to understand some of the significant differences between mere schooling and real education.

I have arrived at a clear knowledge of what is involved in building a character, as distinct from merely making a reputation.

I have come to know from experience, something of the value of reflection and meditation.

"Nothing that is human is alien to me."

I am having increasing concern as to whether the human race will be able to survive the agencies of destruction it has invented and developed to the point of great efficiency; as to whether we shall be able to avoid ultimate self-extinction through the use of alcohol, tobacco, and other narcotics; as to whether stable homes are ultimately to disappear completely; as to whether we really have enough interest in our civil liberties to protect them from complete destruction; as to whether we will give our schools adequate protection against their blatant enemies; as to whether our institutions can survive the challenge of irreligion; as to whether we can survive the disintegrating influences of the comic strip, the radio, the cinema, and television; and as to whether we shall ever get rid of the racial and national hatreds, and smaller group animosities which breed wars and prevent the development of true human brotherhood.

I am neither a sour pessimist, nor a blind optimist; I am a practical, middle-of-the-road realist.

My Profession, Past, Present, and Future

The public-school movement came on in force by mandate of law in New England and the East in the days of Jacksonian Democracy, in the eighteen hundred thirties. It spread quickly to the Mid-West and before the Civil War to the Pacific Coast. It did not reach the Old South until after the War Between the States.

The public schools, according to one of their most ardent and influential advocates, Henry Barnard, of Connecticut, were to be "free to all and good enough for all." It was much easier to make them "free to all" than to make them "good enough for all." To do the latter should require tens of thousands of properly prepared teachers. Such teachers were not to be found in numbers. What were the friends of the common school to do? Two alternatives presented themselves:

First, they might delay the opening of schools until an adequate number of properly educated and professionally trained teachers should be available. This would surely mean interminable delays.

Second, they might open schools at once, appointing as teachers, such persons as were available without primary reference to any proper and adequate qualifications for the service. This seemed the only workable choice to make under all the circumstances.

The normal-school movement of Horace Mann, James G. Carter and others soon followed, to give teachers on the job without training, an opportunity to pick up their deficiencies, by institutional study, between the short three-to-five-months public-school terms of those days.

Naturally, it required many years to make the mandates of the law effective in the rural districts of the several states. Even so, the increase in actual enrollments in the latter half of the nineteenth century took place at a more rapid pace than the increase of prepared teachers, or the increase of institutions for teacher preparation.

When the first public normal school was opened in Lexington, Massachusetts, on July 3, 1839, three candidates presented themselves for admission. Competent authorities say that the academic preparation of these candidates was about equal to that of an average sixth grader of today.

It required a half century for the state normal schools of Massachusetts to up-grade entrance requirements to the level of high school graduation. And it required seventy years, from the opening of the first state normal school to the time when each state had set up some kind of a tax-supported, publicly controlled teacher-preparing institution or institutions. It must be at once apparent, that no state normal school could achieve academic respectability until, in the area it served, high school facilities should be within reasonable reach of all homes.

The South had scarcely begun establishing public-high schools until after the turn of the nineteenth century, sixty years after the opening of the first State Normal School at Lexington, Massachusetts. Progress did not take place along an even front. It was not until a dozen years after the close of World War I that high schools were reasonably accessible "to all the adolescents of all the people," and almost nowhere in the "deep South" were high schools universally accessible to Negro adolescents until much later. In a few places, they are not yet available to the members of this group.

Generally speaking, it was not possible in the country as a whole to set a standard of secondary-school graduation for admission to normal schools and teachers colleges, until about the time when the Great Depression began. Until that standard had been attained in the service area of any teachers college, it was inevitable that pre-service teacher education should be, in that institution, on a "tricks-of-the-trade" basis.

Competent authorities have concluded that between 1839, when the first state normal school in the country was opened, and 1929, the year of the stock market crash, a period of ninety years, the standards of teacher education advanced on the average about the equivalent of one academic year in every thirteen calendar years. Strange as it may seem, during the depression years (about ten of them) the up-grading of teacher preparation was greatly accelerated. Employment as a teacher in these years—though the salaries were low—meant a certain measure of economic security. Former teachers sought re-employment. Competition became so keen, that the impression soon got abroad that there was a great surplus of teachers. There was an over-supply of certificated candidates in many, perhaps in most areas, but not an over-supply of properly educated and professionally trained teachers. There never has been nearly enough such teachers and there is not likely soon (or perhaps ever) to be.

When I retired from New York University in 1942, President George H. Black, a frequent visitor at the Cleveland School of Education and a former student of mine at New York University, wrote me as follows:

"It is an interesting fact that the period of your service for seven years in the Cleveland School of Education and for eighteen years in New York University, a total of a quarter of a century (1917-1942), corresponds exactly to the period when our profession has made its most rapid strides in up-grading the general education and professional training of the whole public-school teaching staff."

That was the period when the teachers college movement was at its height.

Dr. Ben Frazier, of the United States Office of Education, issued an official summary report in the fall of 1941, just before Pearl Harbor, saying that fourteen of our forty-eight states were no longer issuing teacher certificates to novice teachers below the level of four years of post-high school education of an acceptable sort; and that fourteen other states would soon reach that same standard. There was, at that time, one state, Rhode Island, in which the average education and training of the whole teaching force of the state was, according to the State Director of Teacher Certification, approximately the equivalent of five years of post-high school work or, for practical purposes, the equivalent of the master's degree.

A close look at the quarter century—1917-1942—brings into focus three striking facts, as follows:

First, was the emergence of the teachers college, the successor to the normal school, as a full-fledged, degree granting institution. While the public-normal school, from its origin in 1839, had pioneered the way in the preparation of elementary-school teachers, it had not achieved status:

a) as the producer of qualified high school teachers nor
b) as a center of general learning in its service area.

Both of these steps were accomplished in substantial fashion by the opening of World War II. The old N.E.A. Department of Normal School Presidents and Principals became the American Association of Teachers Colleges (1922). It was within the framework of this organization, that teacher education grew in stature, and made possible the formation of the American Association of Colleges for Teacher Education. Only as the teachers college proved itself, was it accorded full membership in the family of higher institutions of learning.

Second, after the end of World War I, the professional

status of the high-school teacher as a college graduate was achieved. In the twenties, before the onset of the Great Depression, standards of requirements for high-school teachers were advanced rapidly in all of the states. Only the teacher of the vocational subjects was permitted to enter the high-school classroom without the bachelor's degree. It was on this solid foundation that the present concept of the adequately prepared high-school teacher—five years of well ordered study—was laid. But even more impressive was the impact of this step upon the status of the elementary-school teacher.

Third, it was during the twenties and the thirties that the role of the elementary-school teacher was given professional status. Two influences stand out most prominently in bringing this about. One was the contribution of psychology to our understanding of child growth and development; the other—a quite different one—was the emergence of America as a world power, and the attendant realization that every boy and every girl must be given, at an early age, an adequate educational basis for life in a complex society. Gone forever was the simple, self-contained, uncomplicated life. The most remote place on the face of the globe and the strangest people on earth became, almost overnight, and integral part of the life of every American.

The contribution of the elementary school to the preparation of each child began to appear in a new light. No longer was "what was good enough for me" good enough for my child. The simple three R's curriculum steadily gave way to the growing realization that a new set of realities must be faced. The required background of the qualified elementary-school teacher, was henceforth to be conceived of in broader and more inclusive terms. Not only must the newly developed techniques of classroom teaching and management be mastered, but the adequate teacher must be a broadly educated person.

These dramatic changes in the American educational scene

were tragically interrupted, of course, by World War II. The American people quickly subordinated their devotion to many civic interests and constructive activities to the all-out war effort. When we emerged in 1945, many abandoned interests could be taken up again. The foundation had been soundly built in the two preceding decades, and the basic belief in free public education reasserted itself.

The task confronting educational leaders in 1945 was stupendous. More than 700,000 persons had left classroom teaching in the five-year war period. Certification standards had literally gone by the boards. In the fourteen states reported by Dr. Frazier in 1941, as having established the bachelor's degree as the standard requirement for the novice elementary school teacher, the most aggressive leadership had a platform for the renaissance which quickly followed in full force. First (and within three years) newly employed teachers were able to meet at least the bachelor's degree standard, and the four states which maintained the five-year standard began to attract a goodly number of qualified candidates.

By 1950, therefore, the high-school teachers of the nation had not only fully recovered their 1942 status, but were moving steadily forward.

Among the elementary schools, however, the state-by-state conditions varied more widely. But by the same token, the greatest progress has been achieved by them. The number of states to set the bachelor's degree as the minimum pre-service preparation requirement for the elementary-school teacher has practically doubled, being twenty-seven in 1954. In like manner, the other twenty-one states have moved forward, with every one of them progressing on a solid front.

The reorganization movement, chiefly meaning the elimination of the one-room, one-teacher, eight-grades school, has done much toward bringing an improved program of instruction to children in the wide-open areas. The number of such units has been reduced from 75,125, in 1948, to 48,735, in 1953. The total number of school districts has been reduced from 104,074 to 66,472, in the same five-year period. Not only has this movement made for better educational opportunities in the rural areas, but it has also contributed significantly toward the solution of the problem of teacher shortage. The wastage of man power, to which all America has become increasingly sensitive since 1950, has been reduced by the elimination of many school units with fewer than ten enrollees each.

By far the most dramatic and spectacular, however, has been the steady up-grading of the whole corps of elementary-school teachers—numbering 683,156 in 1953-54—in average academic attainment. In 1948-49, only 49 per cent of all elementary-school teachers in service were college graduates; in 1953-54, no less than 65.5 per cent—practically two of every three—have attained this level of preparation. Also, in 1948-49, as many as 16.8 per cent had completed less than two years of college work, whereas, in 1953-54, this number was reduced to 6.4 per cent.

Gratifying as are these evidences of the advance in general education of our whole national corps of teachers at all levels, it must be remembered that these measures are quantitative, and that the effectiveness of professional service must always be measured qualitatively.

It is significant that elementary-school teaching has, in recent years, made an increasing appeal to young men. In 1930, there was on the average in each of the five tax-supported teacher preparing institutions of Connecticut, exactly one-fifth of one man. Twenty years later, there were, in some of these institutions, as many men students as women students. By the same token, the secondary school no longer has a monopoly of men teachers. If, in the near future, the rapid growth of school enrollments at all levels is to result in a shortage of men teachers it is likely that this shortage will be as much felt at the secondary-school and college as at the elementary-school level. There are two apparent reasons: First, parity of salary, second (and far more important), an increasing number of the ablest young men have come to understand that when John Amos Comenius, the Moravian bishop, declined the presidency of Harvard University, it was because he was keen enough to see a much wider sphere of usefulness in the field of elementary education even in his own country. Women no longer have a monopoly on elementary-school service.

Members of other professions and the public generally, when I began teaching, used to characterize teaching as "the noblest of professions and the sorriest of trades." The contrast was, in those days, sharply drawn between, let us say, medicine and teaching. It was pointed out that for entrance upon the practice of medicine, the candidate required long years of expensive pre-service education and professional training, followed by an internship and that any raw recruit without education or training could be admitted to the ranks of "the teaching profession." The physician was completely and adequately prepared *before* entering upon his profession: the teacher entered upon his calling without real preparation. It is significant that many teachers who began this service twenty-five or thirty years ago with little general education and with no professional training have, during the years since then, engaged systematically in summer school and extension-course study until now, they may and often do, rate higher in their profession than the physician who was completely trained before entering upon his calling and, who has been in many instances, almost completely stagnant since.

Truly, it can be said that elementary education is "on the march," that the elementary-school teacher is at the point of winning real professional status, and that the future opportunities in public-school teaching are brighter than ever before.

What finer reward could come to those who carried the torch in the formative period of the professional education of American teachers? And what supreme satisfaction some of us have had in marching with the torchbearers!

This seems to be the right place for a word of personal testimony. Teaching, and every other aspect of the educational service, in which I have been engaged for more than three score years have been an unbroken joy to me.

About twenty years ago when I was in full vigor of mind and body I was invited to deliver the commencement address in a very large Eastern state teachers college. The state commissioner of education was on the platform to present me to a very select audience. At the conclusion of the address, I resumed my seat beside the very distinguished minister who had offered an impressive invocation. Said he with feeling: "I'm furiously jealous of you!"

"Of me?" I asked. "Please explain."

"Well," said he, "it is evident that children and adolescents and their teachers come to you, freely, for help at a time when your efforts in their behalf can count mightily. You are engaged in the glorious ministry of teaching. You can be a builder of character in the formative period of life. I, as a minister of the gospel, must spend much of my effort upon those who have made wrecks of their lives. You can spend most of your effort upon creative living; I must spend much of mine on reform work. Your work is inspiring, mine is often depressing."

In each succeeding year, I realize more fully the wealth I have accumulated in abiding friendships and in precious memories. It seems to me that the man who has not accumulated this kind of wealth along the way must be poor indeed, when his sunset years come upon him, no matter how much material wealth he may have acquired.

So I can recommend the profession of education wholeheartedly to any young man or young woman of character who has good health and fair ability, who loves children and youth, and who has the faith to believe what Jesus said when He announced the age-old truth that "it is more blessed to give than to receive." Membership in this profession has given me an opportunity to live a dedicated life that has been full, and rich and supremely satisfying.

God Save Our Country

It is not safe for anyone to describe the decay and predict the ultimate destruction of our civilization unless he is willing to be classified as a person who is very old psychologically, that is to say, a hopeless pessimist.

An aged countryman in the Southern Appalachians once said to me: "When I was a young man everybody considered me an "optimian"; but now that I'm getting on in years everybody seems to think I'm becoming a real "pessimian." It is true that, with the oncoming of the years, "our bones seem," as some one has said, "to be ripening for their ultimate repose," but it does not necessarily follow that there must be a high correlation between chronological and psychological age. The earmarks of the pessimist (the man of advanced psychological age) are plainly to be seen in the following story:

The surgeon said to his patient: "It is clear that cataracts have formed on both of your eyes and that if they are not removed, it will not be long until you will be entirely blind; so I have come to arrange with you for the time and place of the operation."

Said the patient in reply: "Doctor, if you don't mind, we won't go to that trouble. I don't think it is worth it and for four good reasons: first, this operation is going to hurt like the deuce; second, it will cost a lot of money; third, it might not be successful; and fourth, *there really is mighty little in this world worth seeing anyhow.*" I have nothing in common with this fellow.

On the other hand, a certain civic reformer of a half century ago, used to be so discouraged, not to say disgusted, with what he regarded as the unjustifiable optimism of his fellow countrymen, that he once expressed their *blind* faith by saying: "We expect God to take care of children, drunken men, and the United States of America."

Whether we are, by nature, pessimists or optimists, we can and ought to be realists always. I have been formulating certain important questions to each of which I must have a satisfactory answer if I am expected to believe:

a) that "America is the world's last best hope" and

b) that somehow "the Law of the Lord" which the Good Book declares is "perfect," can and will be suspended in its operation in order to insure the continuance of the so-called "American Way of Life."

Let me, at the risk of being called a pessimist, set forth in categorical form, some of the matters about which I can not help have some real concern:

1. Could the human race commit suicide by the misuse of atomic energy? Most competent authorities seem to think that there is little danger that the whole human race can be wiped off the face of the earth in a short-term holocaust: the human family is widely distributed geographically and millions of men, women, and children are too "far from the madding crowd's ignoble strife" to make good targets. These millions who, generally speaking, represent the backward elements in human society, might, it would seem, easily survive long after the centers of civilization had been utterly destroyed.

In our modern world, hundreds of millions of human beings are subject to the authority (and the whim) of a single dictator who is virtually free to launch at will, an atomic war that many seem to think could, at its worst, actually destroy civilization. They believe that the survivors would have little scientific knowledge or industrial know-how and, that the result would be to set the human race back many centuries. It has required vast knowledge, much human co-operation, and untold millions in capital, to develop the atom and the hydrogen bomb. It will require a vast storehouse of international good will and human brotherhood to prevent the unwise use of this gigantic force. Will all rulers exercise the necessary moral restraint to stay the holocaust?

2. Is there not real danger that the use of alcoholic beverages, tobacco, and other narcotics, "the triple man killers," at the present increasing rate of consumption, will break down the physical constitution of our people within a generation?

The goal of the liquor interests seems to be to make all Americans social drinkers. Statistics show that one out of every nine social drinkers ultimately becomes an alcoholic. The United Nations World Health Organization reports that the United States now has a larger percentage of alcoholics per 100,000 population than any other one of the ten leading nations included in its study.

The goal of the tobacco interests seems to be to make all American men and women and all adolescents habitual smokers. They have been approaching this goal. The deadly seriousness of this situation is clearly revealed by the increased and increasing percentage of cases of lung cancer among habitual smokers.

The increasing consumption of narcotic drugs and its appalling consequences are frightening to say the least.

The question which is forced upon all thoughtful Americans is: How long can our society continue to function normally under the impact of these mighty forces of destruction?

3. Is there not increasing disintegration of the American home and is this breakdown of the home not the chief cause of the shocking increase in juvenile delinquency? Are there any forces significantly at work to stay the complete disappearance of the home as we have known this historic institution? The divorce courts merely give legal status to the members of a family that has ceased (in many cases long ago) to have any social cohesion. Do we not need to have increasing

concern for the homes that are being established and for those
that are still nominally intact, but actually in the process of
dissolution, and providing little security to their members? Is
this not a field in which educational and religious institutions
might put on a much more dynamic program of constructive service? If so, are they equipped, ready, and willing to do
so?

4. Is it not clear to all thoughtful Americans, that there are
forces energetically at work in our country to destroy our
religious and civil liberties and that these agencies of destruction operate under cover rather than openly? Can they not
be clearly and openly identified? And is there not very real
danger that they will accomplish their purpose if the average
citizen is not effectively alerted to what is going on, and
aroused to concerted action with his neighbors?

5. Are our democratic institutions not in as much danger of
being undermined, and ultimately destroyed, by fascism as
by communism? In our collective resistance to communism,
are we not unwittingly placing fascism in the saddle? And are
not communism and fascism *both* mortal enemies of true
democracy?

6. Can not the forces, that are vigorously striving to destroy our system of public education be more clearly and
publicly identified and are we, as a people, ready—and able—
to resist these forces with grim determination? Some of the
enemies of the public schools are operating under names that
are completely misleading, names that are well calculated to
enlist the interest and the sympathy of the friends of public
education. Is it not clear that these enemies of public education are attempting to organize all the dissident elements in
some communities in an all-out attack upon the school system,
and to do so under the banner of some association that professes to be interested in school reform? Are not many of these
organizations wolves in sheep's clothing?

7. Is it not possible to develop, among our young people,

more creative and more wholesome recreation and entertainment than the "funnies," the radio, the cinema, and television can afford? Some of these agencies, it would seem, have great potential value, but have they not, to date, been used primarily, if not exclusively, for gain rather than to provide for wholesome recreation and to foster worth-while education?

8. Have we not, too exclusively, emphasized booklearning for the masses of children and youth and have we not failed to teach them the value and the joy that is to be found in all forms of useful manual labor? Have not the politicians, during the past quarter of a century, taught the masses of our young people to try to get something for nothing by joining some pressure group, or by voting for some demagogue? When will we begin to apply corrective education?

9. Can we ever reasonably hope to maintain stable institutions among men who have not been taught in childhood, in their homes, and in their churches, the ethical, moral, and religious concepts and precepts which our founding fathers considered basic to the maintenance of free institutions? George Washington said: "It is impossible, rightly, to govern the world without God and the Bible." Is it not possible for our homes and our churches somehow to overcome the appalling spiritual illiteracy of multitudes of our American children and youth?

10. Is not America, today, paying a staggering price, in blood and treasure all over the Orient, for the race hatreds which the ignorant elements in our society have long been fostering on our soil? Can't we ever learn what the anthropologists have long known, that the differences in achievements of the several more or less distinctive races of men, are not primarily due to differences of native ability, but rather, to differences in opportunity? Can we not get rid of the race hatreds which breed discord among neighbors and prevent the development of true human brotherhood?

These are only ten of the scores of problems that agitate

my otherwise peaceful mind in these days of testing, for the right to national survival. The solution to all of these and other related problems is, it seems to me, *more education of the right kind for all of our people.*

Every thoughtful American who is concerned that we shall bequeath to our posterity the blessings we have enjoyed as a nation for more than a century and half, must have some real concern about arresting the forces that would destroy the goodly heritage which our fathers have bequeathed to us.

I have a profound conviction, not a mere belief, that in all attempts to bring about desirable changes and improvements in the character and conduct of groups and of individuals:

a) persuasion (good teaching) is far more effective than either restraint or compulsion,

b) example is always more impressive than precept ever can be, and

c) what the citizen *is*, is a far more important factor in his influence for good or evil than anything he can say or do.

Every citizen, whatever his calling or station in life, who desires to help re-create America in the image and likeness of PERFECTION, will do well to bear in mind these three guiding principles. It will help him to see more clearly, and to understand more fully, the part education of the right kind plays in all effective social reconstruction.

Memories of Home and Family Life

In Part One, I made it clear that my childhood home and family life were more than merely satisfying, that they claimed my deepest loyalties then and furnish me today, with many rich and tender memories.

The memories I have of the home and family life I had with my first wife and the children by whom we were blest are likewise tender and abiding even though our home was at times shadowed by much suffering, prolonged sorrow, and poignant grief.

I met Rosa R. Ritchie, who in due time became my first wife, when I was twenty-one years of age and was principal of the Emporium, Pennsylvania, high school. She was then only fifteen years of age, and was a member of the junior class in the same high school. After I left town at the close of that year, our acquaintance was very casual; I saw her about once a year when I returned to Emporium to attend some educational gathering.

When she had reached the age of twenty-one and I had served five years as supervising principal of schools in the town of St. Marys, twenty-one miles away, I began an active courtship. For a period of several months, I saw her, usually, each weekend. Early in April, 1902, we were engaged to be married by September. After the up-set of my plans in June, I made up my mind to continue in college in Pittsburgh and to take her with me. Late in August, her mother was stricken with paralysis which confined her to her bed until the time of her death, nearly four years later. This illness, of necessity, modified our plans and indefinitely postponed our marriage, for Rosa's family needed her earnings as a public-school teacher and her sisters needed her assistance, in out-of-school hours, in nursing the invalid mother. These were hard years for both of us, but we were both steadfast in our love and in our determination to carry out our plans as soon as circumstances should permit. I saw her about twice each year. Our correspondence during four years was regular and continued to be a sustaining factor in all our planning. When her mother died, early in the spring of 1906, I had about completed my first year of service at Stetson University in Florida, and had made arrangements to spend the first six weeks of the summer quarter at the University of Chicago. On my way there, I spent several days in Emporium with Rosa at which time we completed plans to be married on August 15th. By that time, her father had gone to live with her eldest brother; her sisters have gone their several ways to Brooklyn and to St. Marys. Her home in Emporium had ceased to exist.

When my Chautauqua engagements had been completed in Illinois, Indiana, and Ohio, I hurried on to Olean, New York, where Rosa met me at the home of some mutual friends. The next day we were married at a private ceremony and went on to the summer chautauqua at Findley Lake, New York, where I had previously served for several years as assistant to the manager and where I had many personal friends. It was an ideal place for a two-week honeymoon. We were well launched in our married life and, after a little visiting in Corry, St. Marys, and Emporium, Pennsylvania, we went on our way to Philadelphia and New York on sight-seeing expeditions, and finally sailed from New York, in middle September, by Clyde Liner, for Jacksonville and up the St. Johns River to Beresford, Florida.

We took up housekeeping in a furnished apartment in DeLand on the campus of Stetson University. The second summer thereafter, we built and furnished a new house and moved into it early in the fall of 1908. In the meantime, a son, Lincoln, had been born to us, January 13, 1908. He died in infancy. A second child, Eloise, a daughter, was born to us on August 31, 1909, in Dr. Noble's private hospital in Atlanta, Georgia, during a brief visit we had in that city. Our third child and younger daughter, Ruth, was born in West Chester, Pennsylvania, on July 21, 1915.

Mrs. Suhrie's interests were domestic. Her greatest joy came from making nice clothes for the children and from giving them personal care.

When the last of our children, Ruth, was born, Eloise, six years her senior, put in an order for one more sister and three brothers. She said she wanted one brother to be governor of Pennsylvania, one to take father's place as professor in the state normal school at West Chester, and one to take Dr. Williams' place as pastor of our local Presbyterian Church.

None of these hopes was realized for no brothers came. She was always proud of her little sister Ruth, who fully reciprocated her good will and affection. They had a wonderful family spirit.

Eloise was a joyous traveling companion. Her last half-fare ride with me on one of my lecture trips took us to Kearney, Nebraska, where we saw old Fort Kearney and were guests for a week at a mid-continent hotel and at the college. On the way out, we visited the Marshall Field Store, in Chicago, to buy some gifts for mother and little sister. We also visited the Chicago Art Gallery and the University of Chicago. And I showed her, for the first time, the Father of Waters—the Mississippi. On the way back, via St. Louis, she took to sleepwalking on the train and, when spotted by a porter on the platform of the Pullman car at two A.M., beat a hasty retreat to her upper berth which she mounted, like the acrobatic performer she was, without the aid of a ladder.

When she reached adolescence, her mind was full of plans for a career. On one occasion, at fourteen years of age, she went, by appointment, to interview Municipal Court Judge Florence Allen, as a reporter for the Cleveland Heights high-school paper. Judge Allen received her and her companion most graciously and answered their questions, fully. She was a career woman and explored with the girls, any notions they had about choosing a calling. This experience made a powerful impression on the youngster's mind. When I came home that evening, she met me at the front door and announced joyously: "Father, it's settled, it's the *Law* for me!" For weeks, she interrogated me at mealtime almost every day about Blackstone, Coke, and John Marshall, about law schools and law professors, about the several branches of the law, etc. Then her interest seemed to be undergoing a change.

One day, my friend Henry Turner Bailey, Director of the Cleveland School of Art, called me up at my office to tell me that in twenty minutes, Lorado Taft would begin his famous lecture on the plastic arts in the Art Museum. I hurried home to pick up the family. Eloise, just home from school, begged to be excused. Said I: "But this is Lorado Taft. A lecture-demonstration by him to a bunch of high school boys and girls is worth, easily, $10,000." She gave her reluctant consent to join the Suhrie caravan to the Art Museum. At first she pretended to be indifferent and took on the appearance of one harboring a minor grievance. When we arrived, the lecturer was on the platform, clay in hand. By a few deft strokes he quickly formed the head of Marie Antoinette. The youngsters gasped in admiration at the speed of his performance. Then, with a bread knife, he chopped out a bit of clay between the nose and the lower jaw, slapped the plastic head under the chin and immediately converted Marie Antoinette into an old hag. Eloise nudged me and, with a most winsome smile, announced: "Father, I resign the law; it's the plastic arts for me! May I study with Lorado Taft?"

She changed her mind as most intelligent adolescents do many times. She had literary talents of a high order and for a time thought of a career as a writer. When she died at twenty four, she left a sheaf of manuscripts containing some excellent poetry of her own composition. She finally chose to be a physical educationist. This necessitated some radical changes in her college program when she was half-way through Swarthmore. She had long been an ardent camper and for several years a successful camp counsellor in swimming, in New Jersey and in New England. She was well on her way to real achievement in her chosen field, when her end came.

Ruth liked her kindergarten and was always pleased to have her mother and me visit it. The teacher told us that she was picking up reading without any instruction. She thought the child very precocious. Neither Ruth nor her mother was too much impressed. They had a secret they had never told the teacher; namely: Ruth's mother had taught her to read on the back of the breadboard in the kitchen before she entered kindergarten.

When she was only four or five years old, she frequently brought to our home, a number of the choicest little kindergarten girl friends I have ever known. They surely had a good time and gave us much merriment. I can still hear them arguing whether a certain little voting inclosure on a tree lawn down the street was a "voting vooth" of a "boating booth." I had to serve as umpire. I "split the difference" and everybody was satisfied with my decision.

When she was in the fourth grade, she brought her school report-card to the breakfast table and said: "Daddy, sign your John Barleycorn on the dotted line and do it quick. I must return this card today." I signed my "John Hancock" instead, and explained at the next meal my preference for the other John.

A few days later she reported that her teacher had a new scheme for limbering up her class socially. Every youngster was to be ready to tell a laughable story on call and without previous notice. For days, Ruth relayed these stories at home. They were all good and some of them side-splitting. On my return to town after a few days' absence, I invited her to bring me up-to-date on the stories I had missed. She blushed and said: "Daddy, there are none to report. You see, Jimmie Wilson told one which he had not previously rehearsed with the teacher. The teacher blushed and said there would be no more stories till further notice."

Ruth had a good sense of humor and, when she was in college, perpetrated many a joke at my expense. On one occasion, she and I were being entertained at dinner in the home of some friends. We were seated at the table and the blessing had just been said when she addressed the hostess: "Mrs.

Smith, father has a number of stories which, it would seem, *just must be told*. Don't you think we could all have a better time if you'd get these out of the way first?"

I've long had a weakness for saying to any company of my friends when the occasion seemed ripe for it: "Let me tell you a good story." On one occasion, she added quick as a flash: "Father always *recommends* his stories and *then* he tells them."

Ruth was an individual in her own right. She wasn't just some professor's daughter. When she was studying for her master's degree at New York University, she took a minor in teachers college education. Her turn came to make a report on a term paper in one of my classes. I invited her, as was my custom with students making reports, to take my place at the desk on the podium while I exchanged seats. She seated herself in my chair and then, after a studied rhetorical pause, she began: "Friends: I'd have you understand right now that my father did *not* write this paper!" The class fairly shouted. It was clear to everybody that she was willing to receive full credit for her work and altogether unwilling to receive any blame for mine.

Ruth, too, was a good traveling companion. She covered New England, the Old South, and the Middle West with me, and had been in half the states before going to college. She had a lot of admirers among the college presidents we visited and, for her sake, they showed us a lot of points of historic interest and much beautiful scenery I should otherwise have missed.

When she was offered a scholarship to Radcliffe, she inquired my wish as to whether or not she should accept it. I told her there were three choices I should never make for her; namely: I'd never choose a career for her; I'd never choose a college for her; and finally, I'd never choose a husband for her. A scholarship for four years at Radcliffe college was worth $3,200. Though not a rich man, I was unwilling to ruin her happiness—and possibly her life—for any such paltry sum. She wanted a career in art and so chose, with my hearty approval, to go to Syracuse University school of fine arts.

During the eight years she spent in academy and college, she never failed to write me an interesting and cheerful letter each week and never once, in all these years, wrote me for money. She didn't need to. After taking council with some capable mothers who had successfully reared daughters, we agreed, early in each summer, on the amount of the allowance she would need and made out sub-budgets for clothing, board and room, tuition, books, laundry, travel, entertainment, contingencies, etc. She kept her deposits in the school bank and paid all her college bills by check. She was free to spend her clothing allowance at her own pleasure and convenience. She always knew how much money she had in reserve. I surely was proud of the way she handled her finances from the age of thirteen when she entered academy, to the age of twenty-one, when she completed college. On the afternoon of her academy commencement day, she stacked, on my desk, four neat little black account-books in each of which were the complete entries of all monies received and all expenditures incurred for an academic year. On her college graduation day, she repeated on this performance. She had been away from home in school for eight years and could account to herself for every dollar spent, and never once did she crab about the periodic balancing of accounts. This I have always thought was a fine preparation for her future home life as wife and mother.

When we lived in West Chester and in Philadelphia, we had a number of short vacations together, as a family, in Atlantic City. While in Cleveland, we went for such outings to Kelly's Island out in Lake Erie, and to the beautiful beach at Silver Creek, New York. When we lived in Montclair, we went to Martha's Vineyard, Massachusetts, and to Spring

Lake and Asbury Park, New Jersey. Later, when Ruth and I were alone, we went to Virginia Beach and to the Great Smokies.

Mrs. Suhrie had spent her early childhood in Winburn, Clearfield County, Pennsylvania, in a section which had long had a very high record of cases of thyroid imbalance. She had scarcely reached young womanhood when the symptoms of this disease became apparent. From the time of the birth of our third child, she was afflicted with serious thyroid disturbance. She had the best attention that medical science could give her at the County Hospital, in West Chester, Pennsylvania, at the Lakeside Hospital, in Cleveland, Ohio, at Mountainside Hospital, in Montclair, New Jersey, at Clifton Springs Hospital and Sanitarium, in central New York and at the Baptist Hospital, in Boston, Massachusetts. She suffered from near chronic invalidism much of the period between 1915 and 1928, while we lived in Philadelphia, Cleveland, and Montclair, though there were short intervals when she seemed to be recovering.

When it finally became wholly impossible, even with day and night nurses, to give her satisfactory care in our private home in Montclair, we found, with the assistance of her pastor, Reverend Father Farrell, of Montclair, a high-class Roman Catholic retreat, in West Chester County, New York, in which it was possible to secure admission for her. During her stay there, for many weary months, I saw her almost daily. Father Farrell and my pastor, Reverend E. M. Wylie of Montclair, were good friends of each other and of our family and gave to her, to our daughters and to me, much spiritual consolation in those terrible days. Their friendship and respect for each other, and their thoughtfulness for all of us, softened our sorrow and gave us a living example, every day and every hour, of that sweet-spirited Christian brotherhood which I pray may increasingly characterize the relationships of all Christian ministers in their united service to God and to their fellow men.

After the patient had spent many months at the retreat, one of Mrs. Suhrie's sisters desired that we move her to a sanitarium near the latter's home, in western New York. In deference to her wish, we did so, but, to the day of her death twenty years later, in June 1948, the patient never again was free from suffering. Her remains were buried beside those of her parents in the hilltop cemetery in St. Marys, Pennsylvania.

Before the terrible pall of chronic illness fell upon her, Rosa was cheery, happy, and an altogether capable and loving wife and mother and always had many friends in the communities in which we lived.

When it became necessary, in the summer of 1928, to take her away to the retreat, it became more imperative than ever that I continue to produce adequate income to support the cost of her maintenance, and to provide maintenance and proper schooling for our daughters. The older one was halfway through Swarthmore College and the younger one was ready for entrance to a four-year high school.

My work called for my absence from home with frequency, and some times, for considerable periods of time. It was clear that I could not maintain a home and keep the daughters in school. So, I placed the younger one in a good Friends' boarding school in the country (the George School near Philadelphia), and the older one, in the Art Student's League, in New York City. The latter transferred her registration from Swarthmore College to New York University, and took some of her studies in a private physical-education school affiliated therewith.

I leased our Montclair home and moved into an efficiency-apartment near Washington Square, New York, and within a block and a half of my office in the university. I saw the older daughter almost daily on our university campus and often in my apartment when I was in the city. I exchanged visits with the younger one every fortnight, either by going to her school for a week-end, or by having her come home to my apartment, in New York City, for a visit with her sister and me.

Both of my daughters were very successful in their school work and always brought me great happiness in the relations they sustained to their student associates, to their teachers, and to me. Their mother's serious and long continued illness placed them under some strain, but they both did what they could at home and at school to carry on, courageously.

Eloise, the elder daughter was a brave soul. She had two serious illnesses before she was five years old. She bore much suffering, uncomplainingly. At nineteen, after a short period of nervous disorder, our dentist discovered that her four wisdom teeth were all impacted. Their removal, at once, was imperatively called for, and this was a major operation. While in college, she had an emergency appendectomy. Also, as a result of a mishap in the gymnasium, she had a second abdominal operation, following her graduation from college and while teaching at the George School.

After leaving the George School, she spent two years as hostess in one of the Schrafft's establishments in New York City, following which she completed requirements, in August 1933, for the A.M. degree in physical-and-health-education, in New York University. She secured appointment, at once, in the Central Missouri State Teachers College, at Warrensburg. In the middle of her first year there, she received a double promotion—one in rank and the other in salary.

On my sixtieth birthday (the last day of February, 1934), she wired me a warm-hearted message of filial love and devotion. I was in Cleveland at the time and had just concluded a two-day national conference (which I had organized for the American Association of School Administrators) on the supply of and demand for teachers. I had served as chairman of this conference. Everything had gone extraordinarily well and I was very happy. The president of Eloise's college, in Missouri, had just given me her personal message of love and had assured me that she had made a complete recovery from her recent illness and that she was very successful in her work.

Three days after my return to New York, I received a long distance call to come at once to Warrensburg. All planes in the East were grounded so I started by Pullman that night, shortly after receiving a telephone message giving me details of my daughter's tragic death.

In Cleveland, I caught a delayed plane and winged my way to Kansas City by midnight of the day after her death. President Hendrix, whom I had known as a dear friend since first we met at the University of Chicago in the summer of 1906, and his gracious wife, gave me shelter in their home and did much to soften the sorrow that had fallen upon me with frightful suddenness. The body was prepared for burial during the day I waited at their home. After a short funeral service, I brought the remains East for burial in the Fairmount Cemetery in Newark, New Jersey.

Ruth, my younger daughter, had, in the meantime, been brought down by auto from Syracuse University by two good friends, Dr. Lynn E. Brown, of Cortland, New York, whom I had named in my will as her guardian, and Dr. Ned H. Dearborn, my colleague at New York University, who had gone up with me to Syracuse on the night train to carry the sad news to her of her sister's death.

Friends gathered in numbers for the funeral, not only from university circles but from points at considerable distance. Telegrams of condolence poured in from across the continent. How kind and considerate and thoughtful our friends were in that terrible day of suffering and sorrow, and how reassuring were the words of comfort spoken by our beloved pastor,

Dr. E. M. Wylie of New York, who conducted the service in the little chapel of the mausoleum in Fairmount Cemetery, Newark, New Jersey.

My younger daughter, Ruth, completed the George School program of studies with credit in June, 1932, and four years later, secured the degree of bachelor of fine arts from the College of Fine Arts of Syracuse University. I served as guest speaker at her Fine Arts Commencement Breakfast. She was immediately appointed supervisor of art in the public schools of Valley Stream, New York. After five years of successful service there, during which period she commuted to my home in New York over week-ends, and spent summers with me in my apartment, and after completing the Master's degree in Fine Arts at New York University, by summer school and Saturday study she resigned her position at Valley Stream for an additional year's graduate study in the Fine Arts at Teachers College, Columbia University. Then, for a year she taught art in the high-school department of the Albany State Teachers College. She resigned that position in June, 1942, to be married to Mr. Robert J. Allaway, a commercial artist of distinction in New York City on July 2, 1942. They were married in the George Alexander chapel of the First Presbyterian Church at the foot of Fifth Avenue. My friend and colleague, Professor Samuel L. Hamilton, performed the ceremony. The wedding dinner was served to sixty guests at the Fifth Avenue hotel. I had introduced this young man to her three years earlier, had noted his steadfast devotion to her during their courting days under my roof in the twelfth story of a New York apartment house and was very happy, as I have been ever since, in their marriage. They have two promising sons: Roger, born October 10, 1945 and David, born February 24, 1951.

Would that all daughters of parents who strive to do their duty could be as industrious, as dependable, as loyal, and as devoted as my daughter Ruth has been.

As I look back upon the long succession of events in my family life, my memory is crowded with periods of superlative joy and of unspeakable anguish in quick succession.

Could anything be more joyous than the sight of my young wife, Rosa, planning the furnishings of any one or other of the four new houses in which, in turn, she presided as wife and mother; could anything bring more poignant grief than to see her waste away through what seemed like endless years of sorrow and suffering?

Could anything possibly bring to mortal man any greater and more exultant joy than I had in Eloise's sweet and loving companionship through the first six years of her life, before the shadows began to fall upon our home; could any man ever suffer more poignant grief than I did over her serious illnesses and her early and tragic passing at the threshold of her beautiful and promising young womanhood? Mark Twain, in the four-line inscription he wrote for his daughter's tombstone, expressed my prayer as we buried dear Eloise in the Fairmount Cemetery in Newark, New Jersey, on March 9, 1934:

> Soft southern sun, shine kindly here.
> Soft southern wind, blow gently here.
> Light sod above, lie light, lie light,
> Goodnight, Dear Heart! Goodnight! Goodnight!

Could anything possibly bring greater joy to the heart of any man who has had to be both father and mother to an adolescent daughter, than the loving response my dear Ruth has made to my efforts to give her a fair chance in life? Her faithfulness to duty, her unfaltering trustworthiness, and her loving kindness during the latter half of my long life, has given me ten thousand occasions to thank God for the privilege of being her father.

I could wish nothing better for my daughter and her good husband, than that their two sons may bring as much happiness to them as my two daughters have brought to Rosa and to me.

When I had reached the age of seventy-seven in health and vigor, two years after Rosa's passing, one of my colleagues who is head of the counseling service at our little college in the east Tennessee hills, and, who helps our young people quite as much with their matrimonial plans and problems as with their academic studies and their choices of careers, ventured to inquire why I did not re-establish my home. He knew I had been virtually homeless much of each year for twenty long years. He knew that my beautiful, modern, and up-to-date cottage in the nearby woodlands could never be a home unless I should find a suitable mate. He told me that his daughter, one of my dearest friends, who had taught in our college before she married and moved West, had found "just the woman" I "ought to marry." Well, there was challenge in such a call to duty. So I had him request his daughter to give me a bill of particulars concerning this lady. The young woman's description of the "eligible" one whom, I am sure, was not a "candidate," was so impressive that, on the day I received it, at the conclusion of my long journey through eleven Latin American countries in February, 1950, I deserted the trail home from Montemorellos, Mexico, to Laredo, Texas, to fly at once, directly to the San Pasqual Valley down near San Diego, California, to meet the youngest of five widows living under the same roof, the oldest one being her mother at age one hundred and one.

I (a young Lockinvar who had come out of the East), had gone to the West to steal a certain widow whose name was Mrs. Alice N. Judson. She was the youngest of a family consisting of her aged mother (one hundred and one), her two older sisters, and a sister-in-law. I thought it best, after several months of correspondence (courting is the word young people use), to present my suit to the whole family including sons and daughters-in-law, in "parlor convention" assembled. I had learned long ago, that when a "feller" gets married he doesn't marry an individual, he marries a family. My presentation of my suit must have been very eloquent for I had scarcely told half my story when one of the wise widows, who is a Shakespearean scholar, fairly shouted: "If it were done, it were well it were done quickly." (Thanks to William Shakespeare for that ready-to-hand speech.) To my delight it was so ordered by acclamation and, a week later (on August 5, 1950, to be exact), a local clergyman pronounced Ambrose L. Suhrie of Collegedale, Tennessee, and Alice Noggle Judson of Escondido, California, man and wife.

The bride had been born among the rows of tall corn in Iowa, had taught several years in the public schools of that state, had gone to California and completed her training as an R. N. at Loma Linda, had married a young widower with one six-year-old boy, had moved with him to his ranch in the San Pasqual Valley near San Diego, had "raised" him two stalwart sons, and had nursed him through a sixteen-year period of invalidism. Then, ten years after his death, and forty years after moving into the sun-kissed state of California, she headed with her new husband for sunny Tennessee.

(Incidentally: I was seventy before I had a grandchild. At seventy-seven, I acquired three more grandchildren and two great-grandchildren—all on one day. How's that for speed?)

On the way East, I showed my bride the Grand Canyon of the Colorado for the first time and she, for the first time, heard me lecture at Flagstaff State College. We arrived in Collegedale on the fifth day after the wedding, were met at the depot at 4:40 A.M. by the president of our little college and were given a reception by the community, the college, and the church, at the residence of our pastor on the evening of that day. Every good soloist and every good quartet in town were heard at that reception. Some valuable, and deeply appreciated, gifts were presented to the bride and groom. Ever since that happy occasion the community has taken the bride to its heart.

We live in Collegedale about nine months each year and travel extensively during the other three months. We go once a year to California to see Mrs. Suhrie's widowed sisters, her children, her grandchildren and her great-grandchildren. Last winter, we covered the West Indies by plane. This year, I showed her New England in all its October glory. If the royalties on this book are as good as the publisher hopes they will be, we'll probably fly around the world next year.

Glow of the Setting Sun

I'm sometimes asked to explain why most elderly people remember more clearly and can tell more precisely about the happenings of fifty, sixty, or seventy years ago than they can about the happenings of last week or yesterday.

Well, our "forgetteries," thank God, are just as important, negatively, as our memories are positively. Our minds can be, and usually are, trained to be selective. We can determine, for ourselves, what people and what events we shall remember forever, and, also, what people and events we shall remember *no more*, forever. If we recall often enough to consciousness, the pleasing characteristics of a friend, there comes a time when we can't forget that friend, for he has become "a living presence." If we refuse often enough to recall to consciousness the unpleasant characteristics of an enemy, of one who has been unkind or harsh or unforgiving or who has sought to injure us, by and by we "remember him no more forever." I long ago discovered that one can as effectively dispose of an enemy, if he is so unfortunate as to have one, by dropping him into "the pit of oblivion" as by casting him into "the lake of fire."

I have deliberately planned (and I now fondly hope), that when the physical infirmities of age come upon me, if ever they do, I may be conscious of "the living presence" of all the good friends God has ever given me and that my memory may then call up, vividly, all the pleasant experiences I have had along the shining pathway of the years.

James Barrie, rector of St. Andrews University in Scotland, author of *Little Minister* and of *Peter Pan*, once remarked: "God gave us memory that we might have roses in December." I'd like to add: "and orchids in January."

The physical world in which we live in childhood, in youth, and in adulthood may not be, sometimes cannot be, of our own choosing, but we can determine for ourselves, the nature of the thought-world in which we shall live in old age. The glow of the setting sun for any of us is but a reflection of the warmth of the friendships we have formed and of the golden memories we have accumulated. The reason why I love teaching above any other calling is that it affords so many opportunities every day and every hour, to make friends *by being a friend* and to be the recipient of "little acts of kindness and of love," because we generously give of our kindness and of our love to all who need them. It is possible, in a long life well spent, to accumulate such a multitude of generous friends and of happy memories as no man can number. I have never attempted to list the names of the men, women, and children whose friendship has enriched my life or of the memories that have been a perpetual benediction; but the number, I know, is legion.

My calling, and my position in it, have made it possible for me to meet and to form friendships with many good and great men and women of my profession. What grand and noble people they have been and are!

I have known all our United States commissioners of education from William T. Harris to the present incumbent, Samuel M. Brownell, except the latter's two immediate predecessors. Theirs are great names in the history of American education: Harris, Brown, Claxton, Tigert, Cooper, Zook, Studebaker, and Brownell. All have been able and devoted public servants. I have known most of them intimately and have had conferences often with them. I have counted Drs.

Brown, Claxton, Tigert, Cooper, and Brownell as intimate friends. Dr. Studebaker, who was in office when I retired from New York University, in 1942, wrote me:

"You have never been narrowly professional in outlook, and your influence has been felt in many social and civic fields other than education. In the wider knowledge, clearer thinking, and finer feeling of your students, and in their future, impress upon generations of pupils yet unborn, your professional career will continue for many years to come. You can retire from your present position, but you can never completely retire from American education."

How far-reaching has been the influence of these men from Henry Barnard the first one to Samuel M. Brownell, the able and affable incumbent.

I have had an intimate professional and personal acquaintance with many of the great state school commissioners of my time including Joyner, of North Carolina; Sheats, of Florida; Brittain and Parks, of Georgia; Eggleston, of Virginia; Harris, of Louisiana; Cooper, of California; Corson, of Ohio; Draper, Finley, and Graves, of New York; Schaeffer, Finnegan, Ade, and Haas, of Pennsylvania; Cook, of Maryland; Kendall, Elliott, and Bossart, of New Jersey; Bailey, of Vermont; Meredith and Engleman, of Connecticut; and the dean of all living members of that notable group of men, Payson Smith, of Maine and Massachusetts. No jailbird politician can ever dim the glory of his name in the annals of American education. I first met him on the lecture platform in my native state of Pennsylvania more than forty years ago when he was commissioner of education in his native state of Maine. Across the years since then, we have maintained an enduring friendship and have exchanged letters frequently. His latest to me says:

"I recall with intense satisfaction the occasions when you and I were together. These occasions were not alone those when we were meeting face to face, but the more numerous ones when I was sustained in my active work by your fine philosophy and your faith in me."

How I shall always cherish the memory of these good and great men!

The great city school superintendents of my time have been my friends: Spaulding, of Cleveland; Condon, of Cincinnati; Cody, of Detroit; Young and McAndrew, of Chicago; Weet, of Rochester; Davidson and Graham, of Pittsburgh; Corson, of Newark; Ballou, of Washington; Blewett and Withers, of St. Louis; Hunter, of Oakland; Dorsey, of Los Angeles; Bauer, of New Orleans; Wilson, of Topeka; Jones, of Memphis; Oberholtzer, of Houston; Fitzgerald, of New Haven; Griggs, of Mobile; Stetson, of Dayton; Camac, of Kansas City; O'Shea and Campbell, of New York; Brumbaugh and Broome, of Philadelphia; Hartwell, of Buffalo; Jones, of Albany; West and Weglein, of Baltimore; Gibson, of Savannah; Sutton, of Atlanta. My letter files show an interesting correspondence with each of them and with scores of others. How profound has been the impress of such men and women upon the whole pattern of American education! The average citizen has no adequate conception of the responsibilities they carry nor of the far reaching influence and importance of their service.

Among the great presidents of American universities and colleges I knew best were: Jordan, of Stanford; Dabney, of Cincinnati; Butler, of Columbia; McCracken, Brown, and Chase, of New York; Hibben, of Princeton; Hadley, of Yale; Harrison, Smith, and Penniman, of Pennsylvania; King, of Oberlin; Washington, Patterson, and Moton, of Tuskegee; Payne, Garrison, and Hill, of Peabody; Bond, of Lincoln; Howe, and Maroney, of Hampton; Banks, of Prairie View; Thompson, of Ohio State; Bryan, of Ohio; Vincent, and Coffman, of Minnesota; Draper, of Illinois; Jessup, of Iowa; Burton, of Michigan; Van Hise, and Frank, of Wisconsin; Alderman, of Virginia; Mitchell, of South Carolina; Lanier, of Texas Southern; Barrows, of Georgia; Murphree, Tigert, Conradi, and Campbell, of Florida; Clement, of Atlanta; Carmichael, of Vanderbilt and Alabama; Mays, of Morehouse; Rainey, of Texas; Williams, of Mississippi; McVey, and Donovan, of Kentucky. What dynamic leadership some of these men gave, and others are still giving, to the cause of higher education in America!

And I have known intimately many of the great women leaders in American education in my day: Caroline Woodruff, of Vermont; Charl Williams, of Tennessee; Eva Dykes, of Alabama; Florence Alexander, of Mississippi; Lida Lee Tall, of Maryland; Patty Hill, and Florence Stratemeyer, of New York; Martha Berry, Mildred English, and Inez Henry, of Georgia; Julia Bethune, of Florida; Ina Bolton, of Texas; Margaret Alexander, of Mississippi; Bertha Kain, Martha Downs, and Marion Emory Shea, of New Jersey, and many others less intimately. How mightily these and other great women of my generation have wrought in behalf of the best ideals and practices of American education!

I had a peculiarly intimate acquaintance with our presidents of state normal schools and state teachers colleges. For a period of twenty years—from 1922 to 1942 I knew all of them personally, and at the close of this period, had been entertained in the homes of most of them. Many of them were truly great men, when judged by what they stood for. Many of them were real pioneers in the world of thought and action, and left a powerful impact upon the educational thought and practice of their day and generation. Most of them were truly lovable characters. How marvellous was the fellowship they gave me. My memory of them, today, is clear and vivid and satisfying.

Among all the sweet and precious memories which crown my years with supreme happiness, few are equal to the clear recollection of the scores of occasions when it was my privilege to address large audiences of teachers and teachers-college students in all parts of the country, and to do what I could to exalt in their minds the dignity, the power, and the worth of their mission and their ministry to the children of America.

My visual memory of places, scenes, audiences, and people is so vivid that I find it easy to relive a day's experience twenty or thirty years ago in Monmouth, Oregon; in Silver City, New Mexico; in Minot, North Dakota; in Fort Kent, Maine; or almost anywhere in our forty-eight states or in the thirty-five foreign countries in which I have traveled. A few representative examples may serve to show how completely I can call up in memory and relive a particular experience of long ago:

I lectured one evening, twenty-five years ago, before the joint faculties of Tuskegee Institute. Major Moton, the president, introduced me. In my audience and right in front of me sat George Washington Carver. At the conclusion of my discourse, he gave me, most graciously, his personal greetings and invited me to spend the next morning with him in his laboratories. I accepted his invitation. I learned more that morning than I have ever learned anywhere else in an equal period of time in all my life. When I want a comprehensive review of science I relive the experiences of that morning in Tuskegee when I "sat at the feet of" or rather "kept trailing" one of the greatest scientists of our modern age. His explanations were as simple as if he were a kindergarten teacher. He said: "Dr. Suhrie, when I come to my laboratories in the morning to do my day's work, I first bow my head, reverently, and say, 'Dear God, here I am ready to do my day's work. Tell me what You would have me to do and I'll do it to the best of my ability.' Then I go to work, confident that He will reveal to me, on that day, here in these laboratories, some one of the great secrets of His universe. How marvellously He has revealed Himself to me, day after day, in answer to my simple prayer."

Another illustration comes to mind: During the month of March, 1933, I got off the train early one morning, in San Antonio. Superintendent Cochrane of the public-school system met me at the depot and took me to his home to meet his wife. Breakfast over, we hurried up to the new Thomas Jefferson Junior High School. He parked his car on the periphery of the broad acres of the campus of this unusual school. We went into the principal's office. The superintendent was called immediately to the long-distance telephone after he had had but a word with the young principal and before he had had an opportunity to introduce me to him. I saw the principal touch some electric buttons and soon heard the student body marching toward the auditorium. He went at once to the right wing of the auditorium stage to observe the boys and girls march to their places, in an auditorium that must have seated three thousand five hundred. The superintendent beckoned to the office clerk. She went to his side as he continued his response to the long-distance call. He told her to take me to the left wing of the auditorium stage. She did. I saw the assembly hall fill up to the last seat. I observed the young principal at the other side of the stage beckoning me to a seat on the platform where there were three chairs, one for him, one for the superintendent, and one for me. I occupied the chair he had designated; he took his place in front of his chair and we waited for a moment for the superintendent to come in and introduce me. The audience was evidently ready for action. So the principal, without further delay began: "Well, here you are [addressing the students] and here he is [pointing to me], but who he is God knows and has not been revealed to me." I jumped up and responded: "I know." I told them. They vigorously applauded my facetious self-introduction. The principal nodded to me to begin speaking. I did. After the kick-off we had had, everything was funny. I gave them a serious message, using stories to clinch my points. I never have had a better response from high-school youngsters before or since.

Finally, the time came when my three-quarter hour period was about to expire. I was way up on stilts, figuratively speaking. I knew that, if I didn't watch my step I would take a tumble and conclude my discourse with a terrible anticlimax.

Things had gone so well that I hoped to close the discourse, if possible, in a "blaze of glory." So I asked: "Do you all speak French?" They all nodded an affirmation in mock heroic fashion. They were in a mood for it. So with my right hand raised, I made a profound bow to the audience and said: "Reservoir!" Then I beat a hasty retreat to the wing of the stage. They literally shouted for joy. The music-master sounded a retreat, and in a moment the auditorium was empty and the classrooms were full. Everything that happened in that school that morning, as I visited classroom after classroom, is still vivid in my memory and I can and, on occasion do, relive all the experiences of that happy morning. I find it hard to believe anyone else has ever had a happier time visiting schools then I have had over the span of a half-century and more and in every one of our friendly states.

I can close my eyes by the fireside any evening of the week and relive a three-day visit I made last year to the schools and colleges of Tyler, Texas, the Rose City: I can recall all the details of the circumstances which prompted the teachers of the city to present me with rose settings for a complete rose garden at my home in Tennessee. This gift must have cost the teachers of the city a handsome purseful of money.

I recall with equal vividness my first visit, now thirty-two years ago, to the campus of Stanford University with its impressive array of inscriptions in the college chapel and elsewhere on the campus. I was a guest, on that occasion, at the home of Ellwood P. Cubberly and had a long conference with him on his method of working and the writing techniques by which he was able to turn out each day a prodigious amount of high grade professional writing and editorial service.

I often relive the happy day I spent as a guest of the Cleveland School of Education, nine years after I had severed my connection with that institution. The college-assembly period, Dean Hunt's kindly presentation of me, the response the faculty and students gave to my address, the luncheon, the visit to Miss Dorothy Pierce's kindergarten and to other classrooms in the demonstration school, and finally the alumni banquet.

I love to recall the experiences of a half-day I spent on the campus of Winthrop Normal College in Rock Hill, South Carolina, in the fall of 1935. I flew down from New York to give the convocation address to nine hundred freshmen at the opening of orientation week. All the girls seemed desperately homesick. The chins of half of them were quivering. It was a very real challenge. I just had to get these girls to laugh and to laugh heartily, or I should surely lose not only the battle but the whole campaign against homesickness in South Carolina.

In due time—and it didn't take long—they surrendered in battalions. The convocation hour closed in a blaze of glory. Then, we all went to lunch in a dining room that seated one thousand seven hundred. After lunch, it was noised about the campus that I was soon to be taken to the airport at Charlotte, North Carolina, for my return flight to New York. Nine hundred freshmen reinforced by several hundred upper-class girls crowded around the car in which I was seated. For a time it looked as though I was about to be swamped by southern hospitality. Hundreds of the lonesome, homesick girls I had seen in the morning had quite obviously decided to take on college spirit in big doses and to forget about going home to see mother. The epidemic of homesickness, it seemed, had been completely cured. That hurry-down visit to the heart of "Dear ol' Dixie" and hurry up to get back to my own registration in New York is one of the bright spots in my memory of field visits in the land of my adoption.

Some five years ago while in attendance at the February meeting of the American Association of Teachers College and the American Association of School Administrators in Atlantic City, I met the Chancellor of the Montana State University System. I had known him for thirty years. I had not seen him for some time. He had just returned from Germany. We had many things to talk about. We went into a lecture hall on the Boardwalk that seated about five hundred. In came a capacity audience. Then the panel consisting of five distinguished American educators came to the platform. It was time to open the program. Dr. Ray C. Maul stepped up to the lectern.

My seat mate, the chancellor, nudged me and said: "This program ought to be good for two of my former students at the University of Minnesota are on the panel."

Said I in response: "I know it will be good for three of my former students at New York University, including the chairman, are on the panel."

When I stroll down the Boardwalk on any bright morning of convention week, I am almost sure to be accosted by a half dozen different fine looking young gentlemen of forty to fifty, each of whom seems to take pleasure in giving me the high salute in his own way and then recalling to my mind some fine occasion in the long ago when, so he says, I put him on the high road to success as a school executive in an hour's conference at some state or regional convention of educators. I know he gives me too much credit, but why argue with a fellow who is trying to make you happy?

I like to call up in memory, the setting and the concomitant circumstances which prompted some disillusioned college adolescent in serious difficulty to come to me and invite me to become his (or her) "counsellor, guide and friend." And I like better still to recall that my acceptance of that invitation, with all its attendant responsibilities, has, in scores of instances back over the years, resulted in an enduring friendship.

My superlative joy in all my visits to schools and colleges has been the occasions when I dropped in for a few minutes with the little children in their several classrooms, on the campuses of teachers colleges all over America. A school principal in New Britain, Miss Annie C. Murnane, whose office and classrooms I had visited annually or oftener for a dozen years, and whose teachers were all former students of mine, wrote me a letter of appreciation just before she retired, inviting me to continue to come to visit her teachers and children. Said she in conclusion: "The teachers and children will always receive you joyfully."

And how my memory loves to dwell on the names of Berkey, Vaughan, Stauffer, King, Compton, Hulley, Parks, Philips, Yocum, Graves, Smith, Spaulding, Withers, Brown, Clement, and Wright. I shall always remember all of my Big Chiefs as gentlemen and as good friends.

Madame Chiang Kai-Shek says: "We live in the present, we dream of the future, but we learn eternal truths from the past."

My past is so real to me that I can quickly convert it into the present that I may distill its wisdom for use here and now. I have time to ponder and reflect upon the great truths of the Book of Books. How infinitely precious to me are its poetry, its wisdom literature, its promises! And I have time to assimilate, at leisure, and to enjoy the great books of all time, with the most responsive reading companion I have ever known, my wife Alice. I am living in such quiet contentment and serenity as only a few among the millions are privileged to enjoy.

Every memory I have of the happy fruitful experiences of the past is increasingly in a glow. I am living a richer, fuller life in the things of the spirit than ever before in my long life. The fireplace in my cottage home in Collegedale sparkles in the autumn evenings, but I like best to sit by the fireside of memory which is *always* aglow.

And, day after day as the evening shadows fall and I bow reverently before my Maker, I thank Him from the bottom of my heart that I have been privileged to be a teacher of teachers; nay more, a teacher of thousands of the teachers of teachers all over America and around the world. I close this record with genuine pride in their magnificent achievements.